Core Curriculum
For Home Health Care Nursing

1995 Edition

Edited by

Kathy J. Morgan, RNC, BSN, MPH

Sandra L. McClain, RNC, BSN

Homecare Education Specialists
Johnson City, Tennessee

AN ASPEN PUBLICATION®
Aspen Publishers, Inc.
Gaithersburg, Maryland
1995

Library of Congress Cataloging-in-Publication Data

Core curriculum for home health care nursing / edited by Kathy J.
　　　　　Morgan, Sandra L. McClain.—1995 ed.
　　　　　　　　　　　　p.　cm.
　　　Includes bibliographical references and index.
　　　　　　　　　　ISBN 0-8342-0725-7
　1. Home nursing.　I. Morgan, Kathy J.　II. McClain, Sandra L.
　[DNLM: 1. Home Care Services—outlines.　WY 18 c79663 1995]
　　　　　　　　　　　RT120.H65C67　1995
　　　　　　　　　　　　　710.73—dc20
　　　　　　　　　　　　　DNLM/DLC
　　　　　　　　　　　for Library of Congress
　　　　　　　　　　　　　95-15105
　　　　　　　　　　　　　　CIP

Copyright © 1995 by Aspen Publishers, Inc.
All rights reserved.

Aspen Publishers, Inc., grants permission for photocopying for limited personal or internal use. This consent does not extend to other kinds of copying, such as copying for general distribution, for advertising or promotional purposes, for creating new collective works, or for resale. For information, address Aspen Publishers, Inc., Permissions Department, 200 Orchard Ridge Drive, Suite 200, Gaithersburg, Maryland 20878.

The authors have made every effort to ensure the accuracy of the information herein. However, appropriate information sources should be consulted, especially for new or unfamiliar drugs or procedures. It is the responsibility of every practitioner to evaluate the appropriateness of a particular opinion in the context of actual clinical situations and with due consideration to new developments. Authors, editors, and the publisher cannot be held responsible for any typographical or other errors found in this book.

Editorial Resources: Ruth Bloom

Library of Congress Catalog Card Number: 95-15105
ISBN: 0-8342-0725-7

Printed in the United States of America

2　3　4　5

Dedication

Elizabeth (Liz) A. Guba, PhD
April 6, 1957–October 31, 1994

This book is dedicated to Liz Guba, who died—suddenly, unexpectedly—in the crash of American Eagle flight #4184.

Those who knew Liz—her family, her peers, her friends—go about their days, trying to make sense and meaning of her tragic and untimely death.

In reflection, all who had the revered honor and delight of knowing and working with Liz realize what an astounding impact she had on people and on the home care industry.

With quintessential professionalism, Liz dedicated her consulting career to assisting organizations in designing processes extremely well in order to accomplish her ultimate goal: the highest quality of care for all home care patients.

As a skilled educator, Liz benevolently embraced home care nurses, devoting countless hours to teaching us about home pharmacy services: clinical drug monitoring, the differences in laminar flow hoods and biologic safety cabinets, and the importance of collaboration and teamwork between pharmacists and nurses.

As an esteemed writer, Liz was consecrated to this project: revision of the *Core Curriculum*. In her death, as even in her life, Liz constantly inspired us onward, never allowing us to falter from our chartered course. But as a person—a friend, a daughter, a sister, an aunt—Liz taught us her greatest lessons:

> to instill quality . . . into everything we do in life's fleeting moments;
> to laugh . . . unconditionally, unquestionably; and, most importantly,
> to play . . . with child-eyed wonderment.

We shall surely miss you, Dr. Guba!

Kathy J. Morgan
Sandra L. McClain

Table of Contents

Contributors xi
Preface xv
Acknowledgments xvii

Part I   Introduction 1

1   History of Home Health Care Nursing 3
      Sandra L. McClain

2   Role of the Registered Nurse in Home Care 7
      Kathy J. Morgan and Sandra L. McClain

3   Role of the Nurse As Patient Advocate 13
      Ann H. Cary

4   Role of the Nurse As Patient Educator 20
      Marjorie B. Kraus

Part II   Care Coordination with the Home Care Team 29

5   Role of Physical Therapy in Home Care 31
      Sheryl Campbell

6   Role of Occupational Therapy in Home Care 39
      Elaine Ainsworth

7   Role of Speech-Language Pathology Services
      in Home Care 45
      Harriet Simpson Steele

8   Role of Social Work in Home Care 54
    Kathy J. Morgan
9   Role of Homemaker/Home Health Aide in Home Care 57
    Ruth Rebecca Apple and Susan M. Truscott
10 Durable Medical Equipment 66
    Jacqueline Birmingham and Craig Jeffries

**Part III Nursing Management of the Patient with
          Cardiovascular Disease 85**

11 Coronary Artery Disease/Angina Pectoris 87
    Debra Finley-Cottone and Brenda Stefanik Bartock
12 Myocardial Infarction 95
    Debra Finley-Cottone and Brenda Stefanik Bartock
13 Congestive Heart Failure 101
    Annette C. Strickland
14 Hypertension 105
    Sandra L. McClain and Kathy J. Morgan
15 Cardiomyopathy 109
    Debra Finley-Cottone and Brenda Stefanik Bartock
16 Valvular Heart Disease 116
    Debra Finley-Cottone and Brenda Stefanik Bartock
17 Pacemakers 122
    Debra Finley-Cottone and Brenda Stefanik Bartock
18 Invasive Interventions 127
    Debra Finley-Cottone and Brenda Stefanik Bartock
19 Cardiac Transplantation 133
    Debra Finley-Cottone
20 Cardiac Rehabilitation and Support 138
    Debra Finley-Cottone and Brenda Stefanik Bartock

**Part IV Nursing Management of the Patient with
          Respiratory Disease 147**

21 Asthma/Bronchitis 149
    Jeannette F. Levy

22	Chronic Obstructive Pulmonary Disease 155
	Rebecca C. Clark
23	Pneumonia 161
	Mary Tracy Parsons
24	Pulmonary Edema 166
	Antoinette Laguzza
25	Pulmonary Embolus 170
	Mary Tracy Parsons
26	Pleural Effusion 174
	Antoinette Laguzza
27	Tuberculosis 177
	Elizabeth A. Guba and Kathy J. Morgan
28	Cystic Fibrosis 188
	Kathleen Cummings
29	Mechanical Ventilation at Home 200
	Merry Mosier Foyt

Part V Nursing Management of the Patient with Neurologic/Mental Disorders 207

30	Cerebrovascular Accident 209
	Linda Rickabaugh
31	Seizure Disorder 213
	Susan C. Nolt
32	Multiple Sclerosis 221
	Susan C. Nolt
33	Muscular Dystrophy 228
	Sharron Smitherman-González
34	Parkinson's Disease 233
	Keltie Baker Kerney
35	Amyotrophic Lateral Sclerosis 243
	Tecla K. Webber
36	Alzheimer's Disease 247
	Elizabeth B. Runyon and Patricia A. Wernert
37	Mental Illness 252
	Elizabeth B. Runyon

Part VI Nursing Management of Other Patient Disorders 257

38 Diabetes Mellitus 259
    James A. Fain
39 Hyperthyroidism 270
    Keltie Baker Kerney
40 Hypothyroidism 278
    Keltie Baker Kerney
41 Arthritis 284
    Kevin L. Ross
42 Ostomies 289
    Kathleen Calitri Brown
43 Cancer 302
    Constance R. Ziegfeld and Monica Fulton
44 Acquired Immunodeficiency Syndrome 318
    Jeannee Parker Martin
45 The Terminally Ill Patient 331
    Brenda E. Clarkson

Part VII Nursing Management of the Perinatal Patient 337

46 Perinatal Home Care 339
    Roberta Kempfer-Kline

Part VIII Nursing Management of the Patient Requiring Nutritional Intervention and/or Enteral/Parenteral Therapy 355

47 Nutritional Problems 357
    Joyce K. Keithley
48 Enteral/Parenteral Therapy 369
    Fran Free and Kathryn Hennessy

Part IX Professional Considerations 389

49 Ethical Considerations for the Home Health Nurse 391
    Ann H. Cary

| 50 | Legal Principles and Home Care Nursing 399
Carol L. Schaffer |
| 51 | Continuous Quality Improvement in Home Care 409
Nancy L. Bohnet |
| 52 | Home Care Standards: Joint Commission on Accreditation of
Healthcare Organizations 413
Maryanne L. Popovich |

Index 419

Contributors

Elaine Ainsworth, MS, OTR/L
Elaine Ainsworth and Associates
Manheim, Pennsylvania

Ruth Rebecca Apple, RNC, BSN
Home Care Nurse Surveyor
Joint Commission on Accreditation of
  Healthcare Organizations
Oakbrook Terrace, Illinois

Brenda Stefanik Bartock, BSN
Cardiopulmonary Clinical Specialist
Visiting Nurse Service of Rochester and
  Monroe County, Inc.
Rochester, New York

Jacqueline Birmingham, RN, MS, A-CCC
Director, Continuity of Care
Chartwell Home Therapies
Suffield, Connecticut

Nancy L. Bohnet, RN, MN, FAAN
President/CEO
Adjunct Faculty, University of Pittsburgh
  Graduate School of Nursing
Home Health Services Foundation
Butler, Pennsylvania

Kathleen Calitri Brown, RN, MN, CETN
Enterostomal Therapy Nurse
Coordinator, The Emory Clinic and
  Egleston Children's Hospital at Emory
Atlanta, Georgia

Sheryl Campbell, RN
QA/Therapy Supervisor
Home Care—East Ohio Regional Hospital
Martins Ferry, Ohio

Ann H. Cary, PhD, MPH, RN, A-CCC
Professor and Associate Dean
School of Nursing
Louisiana State University
  Medical Center
New Orleans, Louisiana

Rebecca C. Clark, RN, CS, MSN
Assistant Professor, Department of
  Nursing
College of Health Sciences
Roanoke, Virginia

Brenda E. Clarkson, RN, DN, CRNH
Administrator, National Hospice
  Organization
Central Hospice Care
Arlington, Virginia

Kathleen Cummings, RN, BSN, PHN
Vice President, Clinical Services
Kansas City Hospice
Home Care Nurse Surveyor
Joint Commission on Accreditation of
  Healthcare Organizations
Kansas City, Missouri

James A. Fain, PhD, RN, FAAN
Editor, *The Diabetes Educator*
Associate Professor/Coordinator, PhD
  Program in Nursing
Graduate School of Nursing
University of Massachusetts Medical
  Center
Worcester, Massachusetts

Debra Finley-Cottone, MS
Manager Cardiopulmonary Program
Visiting Nurse Service of Rochester and
  Monroe County, Inc.
Rochester, New York

Merry Mosier Foyt, RN, MS
Assistant Professor and Coordinator
Creighton University School of Nursing
Omaha, Nebraska

Fran Free, RN, CRNI
Director Clinical Operations/QI
Option Care Inc.
Bannockburn, Illinois

Monica Fulton, RN, BSN, MBA
Nurse Manager
Johns Hopkins Hospital
Baltimore, Maryland

Elizabeth A. Guba, PhD
Formerly, Home Care Pharmacy Surveyor
Joint Commission on Accreditation of
  Healthcare Organizations
Independent Consultant
Indianapolis, Indiana

Kathryn Hennessy, RN, MS, CNSN
Manager, Nursing Service
Clintec Nutrition Company
Deerfield, Illinois

Craig Jeffries, Esq.
Home Care Coalition
Hida Home Care
Active Member, Virginia Bar, District of
  Columbia Bar, and National Health
  Lawyers Association
Alexandria, Virginia

Joyce K. Keithley, DNSc, FAAN
Practitioner-Teacher
Department of Operating Room and
  Surgical Nursing
Professor
Rush University College of Nursing
Rush-Presbyterian-St. Luke's Medical
  Center
Chicago, Illinois

Roberta Kempfer-Kline, RN, MSN
Perinatal Home Care Specialist
Community Visiting Nurse Services
Phoenixville, Pennsylvania

**Keltie Baker Kerney, RN, BSN, MPH,
A-CCC**
President, Tennessee Hospital Association
  Home Care Alliance
Director, Holston Valley Hospital and
  Medical Center Home Health/Hospice/
  IV Therapy/DME
Holston Valley Hospital and Medical
  Center
Kingsport, Tennessee

Marjorie B. Kraus, MSN
Head Nurse/Hospital Based Home Care
Veterans Administration Medical Center
New Orleans, Louisiana

Antoinette Laguzza, BSN, MS
Assistant Professor
Coordinator, Accelerated Nursing
  Curriculum
Creighton University School of Nursing
Omaha, Nebraska

Jeannette F. Levy, MSN
Assistant Professor/Coordinator
Creighton University School of Nursing
Omaha, Nebraska

Jeannee Parker Martin, RN, MPH
Vice President
The Corridor Group, Inc.
San Francisco, California

Contributors xiii

Sandra L. McClain, RNC, BSN
Partner, Homecare Education Specialists
Associate, Health Care Data,
 Incorporated
Johnson City, Tennessee

Kathy J. Morgan, RNC, BSN, MPH
Home Care Nurse Surveyor
Joint Commission on Accreditation of
 Healthcare Organizations
Partner, Homecare Education Specialists
Partner, Health Care Data, Incorporated
Johnson City, Tennessee

Susan C. Nolt, RN, BS, MBA
Coordinator of Field Management
 Development
First American Home Care
Lancaster, Pennsylvania

Mary Tracy Parsons, RN, MSN
Assistant Professor/Coordinator
Creighton University School of Nursing
Omaha, Nebraska

Maryanne L. Popovich, BSN, MPH
Director
Joint Commission on Accreditation of
 Healthcare Organizations
Home Care Accreditation Services
Oakbrook Terrace, Illinois

Linda Rickabaugh, RN, MSN
Associate Professor
Director, Nursing Education
College of Health Sciences
Roanoke, Virginia

Kevin L. Ross, RN, BSN
Home Care Nurse Surveyor
Joint Commission on Accreditation of
 Healthcare Organizations
K. L. Ross and Associates/Healthcare
 Consultants
Denton, Texas

Elizabeth B. Runyon, MSN
Assistant Vice President Home Health
Visiting Nurse Association of Louisville
Louisville, Kentucky

Carol L. Schaffer, RN, MSN, JD
President and CEO
Cleveland Clinic Foundation Health Care
 Ventures, Inc.
Cleveland, Ohio

Sharron Smitherman-González, BSN
Home Care Nurse Surveyor
Joint Commission on Accreditation of
 Healthcare Organizations
Oakbrook Terrace, Illinois

Harriet Simpson Steele, MS, CCC, SLP
Speech and Language Pathologist
Private Practice
Camp Hill, Pennsylvania

Annette C. Strickland, MSN
Assistant Professor
Department of Health Education
College of Health Sciences
Roanoke, Virginia

Susan M. Truscott, RN, BSN
Primary Instructor, NATP
Upper Valley Medical Centers—Stouder
 Campus
Troy, Ohio

Tecla K. Webber, BSN
Director, Saint Francis Home Health
Saint Francis Hospital
Tulsa, Oklahoma

Patricia A. Wernert, MBA
Director of Community Relations
Visiting Nurse Association of Louisville
Louisville, Kentucky

Constance R. Ziegfeld, RN, MS
Assistant Director of Nursing
Johns Hopkins Oncology Center
Baltimore, Maryland

Preface

And so we come full circle! From our early roots in the 1800s in United States health care, home health care nursing has continued its march into the 1990s and beyond. As the home care industry continues to be the fastest growing United States industry, home health care nurses continue to explore and develop new avenues for the provision of quality home care services.

The American Nurses' Association has awarded home health care nurses the highest professional nursing honor: recognition as a highly specialized professional nursing practice worthy of a national certification distinction.

This book was conceived as a method of review for taking a national certification examination. We searched for and could not find a single source document that was all-inclusive for home health care nurses. We needed a reference that was user-friendly and well organized, yet comprehensive.

We endeavored to develop a volume that could be used by home health care agencies as an orientation tool and reference manual for agency staff. Consideration was given to developing a textbook that would be a comprehensive resource for schools of nursing with home health care curricula.

Leading home health care experts and organizations nationwide were instrumental in contributing time and knowledge to this unique publication. Professional nurses are provided information on the essence of home health care nursing practice: care planning and coordination, education, counseling, health promotion, assessment, monitoring, evaluation, patient advocacy, continuity of care, and technical care provision. We hope this book assists you in your efforts to achieve the ultimate home health care nursing goal: delivery of the highest-quality patient care.

Acknowledgments

A book of this scope could not have been developed without the commitment of time, knowledge, and expertise from leading industry experts and organizations. We express our deepest appreciation to the contributing authors for producing such quality chapters.

We express our special thanks to our families and friends who consistently offered their love and moral support to ensure continuous renewal of our enthusiasm for this project.

Part I

Introduction

1

History of Home Health Care Nursing

Sandra L. McClain

A. 1700s
   1. The Boston Dispensary home care program was instituted (1796).
      a. Physicians had treated wealthy people at home, while poor or homeless people went to hospitals.
      b. The Boston Dispensary home care program attempted to decrease welfare stigmas attached to hospital care by treating all sick people at home.
B. 1800s
   1. Late 1800s: Home nursing services were organized and administered by lay persons.
   2. The Women's Branch of the New York City Mission provided the first graduate nurses in home nursing services (1877).
   3. Visiting nurse associations (VNAs) evolved.
      a. Buffalo, New York, established a voluntary agency to provide home nursing care (1885).
      b. Philadelphia and Boston established VNAs (1886).
   4. Henry Street Settlement House was established in New York (1893).
      a. It was established by Lillian Wald, founder of public health nursing.
      b. It provided not only for care of the sick in the home care setting but for preventive care.
   5. Los Angeles County Health Department instituted a home care progam (1898).
      a. Graduate nurses were hired to make home visits.
      b. This was the first governmental health department to offer such services.

C. 1900s
  1. Metropolitan Life Insurance Company offered home care benefits to its policyholders (1909).
  2. The American Red Cross introduced new services (1912).
     a. Visiting nurse program: Nurses in rural areas provided not only services to sick patients at home, but services for well-baby care and school nursing.
     b. County health departments developed similar programs, with nurses hired to provide home health care nursing.
  3. Frontier nursing services were established in rural Kentucky (early 1900s).
     a. Care was provided to rural areas.
     b. Nurses traveled on horseback.
  4. Metropolitan Life Insurance Company continued its home care benefits (1928).
     a. The original program grew rapidly.
     b. It was affiliated with 953 organizations nationwide.
     c. It employed 592 nurses for home nursing services.
  5. World War II: VNAs grew rapidly as physicians stopped their home visits.
  6. University of Syracuse offered a home care program for discharged hospital patients (1941).
  7. National Organization of Public Health Nursing convened to discuss rendering public health nursing (1946).
  8. Montefiore Hospital Home Care Program was established in New York (1947).
     a. It was founded by Dr. E. M. Bluestone.
     b. It was a hospital-based home care program, a "hospital without walls."
     c. Services were not limited to elderly or poor patients.
  9. American Journal of Public Health published reports on other hospital home care projects in New York City, Boston, Richmond, and Washington, D.C. (1953).
  10. Chronic Disease Program of the United States Public Health Service was established (1958).
     a. It defined four elements for a home care program.
        (1) Administration
        (2) Personnel
        (3) Community resources
        (4) Evaluation

b. Coordination of care had major emphasis.
11. Community Health Services Facility Grant was established (1961).
    a. It provided project grants for developing outside-of-hospital health care services.
    b. Services included nursing, physical and occupational therapy, homemaker services, social services, and nutritional services.
12. Medicare was enacted (1965).
    a. Medicare influenced expansion of home health care benefits.
    b. Medicare required agencies to furnish a minimum of nursing service plus one additional service (physical therapy, occupational therapy, speech therapy, social services, or home health aide).
13. Medicaid was enacted (1970). It mandated home care benefits.
14. Diagnosis-related groups (DRGs) were introduced (early 1980s).
    a. DRGs limited Medicare reimbursement for acute hospitalization.
    b. DRGs increased hospital-based home care programs.
15. United States Department of Health and Human Services published in 1990 *Healthy People 2000: National Health Promotions and Disease Prevention Objectives* (established goals for health prevention/promotion for the citizens of the United States by the year 2000 A.D.).
16. ANA published in 1991 *Nursing's Agenda for Health Care Reform* (emphasized expanded role of nurse practitioners and clinical nurse specialists).

D. National certification for home health care nurses
   1. Standards of Home Health Nursing Practice were established (1986).
      a. Standards were developed by the American Nurses' Association (ANA).
      b. Standards distinguished a path for home health care nurses as a specialty group.
   2. A proposal was made to ANA to develop national certification (1989).
   3. ANA issued its *Statement on the Scope of Home Health Nursing Practice* (1992).
      a. A task force was convened by ANA in 1991 to develop the *Scope* statement.
      b. The *Scope* statement defined
         (1) Beliefs

(2) Definitions and distinguishing characteristics
(3) Generalist role: Prepared at the baccalaureate level; provides technical and instrumental care for the patient, family, and/or caregiver; role in quality improvement is data collection.
(4) Specialist role: Prepared at the graduate level; manages and evaluates patient care delivery; designs, monitors, and evaluates the continuous quality improvement process.
(5) Ethical considerations
4. The first certification examination was given in 1993.

STUDY QUESTIONS AND EXERCISES

1. Discuss the evolution of VNAs.
2. Who was the founder of public health nursing? Discuss her project.
3. What is the significance of the Montefiore program?
4. Which federally mandated legislation has had the greatest impact on growth of the home care industry?
5. What impact did DRGs have on home care?
6. Review the ANA documents *Standards of Home Health Nursing Practice* and *A Statement on the Scope of Home Health Nursing Practice*. Define the role of the home care registered nurse.

BIBLIOGRAPHY

American Nurses' Association. 1992. *A statement on the scope of home health nursing practice.* Washington, D.C.

American Nurses' Association. 1991. *Nursing's agenda for health care reform.* Washington, D.C., no. PR-3.

Humphrey, C.J. 1988. The home as a setting for care: Clarifying the boundaries of practice. *Nursing Clinics of North America* 23, no. 2:306.

Martinson, I.M., and A.G. Widmer, eds. 1989. The continuum of care. In *Home health care nursing*. Philadelphia: W.B. Saunders Co.

Spiegel, A.D. 1983. Beginning of homecare: A brief history. In *Home healthcare: Home birthing to hospice care.* Owings Mills, Md.: National Health Publishing.

United States Department of Health and Human Services. 1990. *Healthy people 2000: National health promotion and disease prevention objectives.* Washington, D.C.: United States Government Printing Office. DHHS no. PHS91-50213.

2

Role of the Registered Nurse in Home Care

Kathy J. Morgan and Sandra L. McClain

A. Case/Care Management
   1. Assurance of patients' rights and responsibilities
   2. Initial and ongoing assessment of patients' health and psychosocial and emotional needs, including:
      a. History
      b. Health assessment of all body systems
      c. Home environment, including safety assessment of bathroom; environmental, electrical, fire, and equipment; hazardous waste disposal; and medication use, with appropriate teaching to patients and staff
      d. Infection control procedures with appropriate teaching
      e. Patient's/caregiver's learning requirements
      f. Financial status
      g. Support systems
      h. Patient's response (e.g., to therapies, treatments, medication, instruction)
      i. Nutritional assessment for patients at moderate or high risk for nutritional interventions (may include patients on specialized diets or enteral or parental therapy, or with other disease states)
      j. Functional assessment: walking/mobility, vision, confusion/memory loss, communication, bowel and/or bladder problems, activities of daily living, instrumental activities of daily living, and dental function
      k. Education
      l. Equipment
      m. Medication use

n. Laboratory tests: obtaining and monitoring results
o. Discharge planning
p. Identification and reporting of possible victims of abuse or neglect
   (1) Four types of abuse
       (a) Physical: pain and/or injury inflicted
       (b) Psychologic: mental stress and anguish
       (c) Financial: exploitation of resources
       (d) Sexual: unwilling participation in sex
   (2) Two types of neglect
       (a) Passive: unintentional effort to inflict harm
       (b) Active: intentional refusal to fulfill obligations as a caregiver that may result in physical and/or emotional distress
   (3) Possible contributing factors within family structure
       (a) Financial problems
       (b) Substance abuse
       (c) Patient dependence on caregivers who may not be capable of providing care
       (d) Psychiatric problems
       (e) History of family violence
       (f) Other family members requiring care (i.e., babies, children, teenagers, etc.)
       (g) Patient isolation from all but caregivers
       (h) Additional factors for children: prematurity; hyperactivity; congenital defects and/or developmental disabilities; unwanted/unplanned pregnancies; etc.
   (4) Signs/symptoms of elderly abuse/neglect: unexplained or questionable injuries or fractures; fear; withdrawal; weight loss; crying; bruises with varying degrees of color
   (5) Signs/symptoms of child abuse/neglect: inadequate/dangerous sleeping facilities; inadequate clothing; unexplained injuries or fractures; weight loss/failure to thrive; bruises with varying degrees of color; retinal hemorrhages
3. Development of the plan of care: multidisciplinary approach
   a. Identification of patient's problems and needs
   b. Establishment of goals
   c. Intervention provision
   d. Review, revision, and evaluation of the plan of care and goals

4. Care coordination of all services included in the plan of care with utilization of care conferences with team members to facilitate communication and coordination of care/services. Team members might include:
   a. Patient/family/caregiver
   b. Physician
   c. Discharge planner
   d. Other RNs
   e. Licensed practical nurses/licensed vocational nurses
   f. Physical therapist/physical therapy assistant
   g. Occupational therapist/occupational therapy assistant
   h. Speech-language pathologist
   i. Social worker/social worker assistant
   j. Homemaker/home health aide
   k. Home medical equipment provider (may include respiratory therapist)
   l. Pharmacist (may include retail pharmacist and/or pharmacy services/infusion therapy company when enteral/parenteral therapy is provided and/or in conjunction with all drug compounding, dispensing, and/or administration to the home care patient)
   m. Laboratory services
   n. Nutritionist/dietitian
   o. Private-duty services
   p. Hospice care
   q. Community resources
   r. Volunteers
5. Provision of continuity of care 24 hours per day, 7 days per week
6. Appropriate referrals, transfers, and/or discharges
7. Provision of preventive, treatment, and maintenance services
8. Nursing management of patients' needs and disease processes
9. Patient advocacy
10. Patient education
11. Supervision of environmental and personal care/support services
12. Supervision of other caregivers, formal and informal

B. Role within organization
   1. Program coordination and management
   2. Consideration of legal implications and ethical issues/dilemmas
   3. Infection control: surveillance, identification, reporting, preven-

tion, control of infections in both patients and staff; policy/procedure development and implementation (in accordance with current Centers for Disease Control and Occupational Safety and Health Administration guidelines) with patient and staff instructions
    a. Aseptic procedures
    b. Transmitted diseases
    c. Isolation precautions
    d. Personal hygiene
    e. Staff health
    f. Equipment cleaning and maintenance
    g. Supply handling, transport, and storage
4. Quality improvement
5. Risk management: identification, reporting, prevention, and control of safety and security hazards in both patients and staff
6. Research
    a. Generalist nurse: data collection
    b. Specialist nurse: identifies and designs research projects; interprets and evaluates data; institutes changes
7. Policy/procedure development, revision, and implementation
8. In-service education, orientation, and staff development

C. Nursing process in home care
  1. Patient assessment, initial and ongoing
  2. Diagnosis, initial (to develop the plan of care) and ongoing
  3. Planning, with involvement of patient and caregiver
  4. Intervention: care provision according to the plan of care
  5. Evaluation of the plan of care, including assessment of goals and modifications as indicated

D. Medicare conditions of participation
  1. Components of a skilled reimbursable visit: The RN must perform one of the following services every visit:
    a. Teaching of the patient/caregiver to carry out appropriate treatments or services (e.g., medication administration, diet instruction, intravenous therapy administration). Teaching must be for an acute or new treatment or instruction.
    b. Patient assessment (e.g., assessment of response to a new medication, assessment for signs/symptoms of congestive heart failure). Assessment must be for an acute process or for the likelihood of changes in the patient's condition.

c. Direct care services (e.g., Foley catheter change, intravenous fluid administration, sterile dressing change). These services must require the professional skills, knowledge, ability, and judgment of the RN.
2. Medicare does not reimburse for skilled nursing (RN) visits for general health maintenance, preventive care, or visits for meeting the patient's emotional or socioeconomic needs. These services can be provided in conjunction with visits for the above three covered services.
3. Patients receiving Medicare-certified visits:
    a. Must be essentially homebound
    b. Must be under the care of a physician, who authorizes services in writing
    c. Must need a skilled service (nursing, physical therapy, or speech-language pathology services) on an intermittent basis; services must be reasonable and necessary related to the patient's diagnosis; service must be of a complexity that it can be performed safely and/or effectively only by or under the supervision of a registered nurse.
    d. Skilled nursing services must be accepted standards of practice and considered specific and effective treatment(s) for the patient's condition.
    e. There must be an expectation, based on an assessment by the physician, that the patient will improve in a reasonable, predictable time.
    f. If patient is eligible for a skilled service, patient may also receive occupational therapy, medical social worker, and/or home health aide services, if physician ordered.

STUDY QUESTIONS AND EXERCISES

1. What team members should be included in the care of an elderly patient with a fractured hip?
2. What are the home safety factors that the RN should assess?
3. What are the elements in the development of the plan of care?
4. What are some infection control considerations related to patient care/services provided?

BIBLIOGRAPHY

Bernstein, L.H. December 1992. A public health approach to functional assessment. *Caring* 12:32-38.

Humphrey, C.J. 1988. The home as a setting for care: Clarifying the boundaries of practice. *Nursing Clinics of North America* 23, no. 2:305-314.

Jackson, J.E., and M. Neighbors. 1990. *Home care client assessment handbook*. Gaithersburg, Md.: Aspen Publishers, Inc.

Joint Commission on Accreditation of Healthcare Organizations. 1994. *The 1995 Joint Commission accreditation manual for home care*. Oakbrook Terrace, Ill.

Kim, M.J. 1989. Nursing diagnosis in home health nursing. In *Home health care nursing*, eds. I.M. Martinson and A. Widmer, 58-66. Philadelphia: W.B. Saunders Co.

Pillemer, K., and B. Hudson. 1993. A model abuse and prevention program for nursing assistants. *The Gerontologist* 1:128-131.

Spiegel, A.D. 1983. *Home healthcare: Home birthing to hospice care*. Owings Mills, Md.: National Health Publishing, 159-235.

Tonore, M.F. December 1992. The nutrition screening initiative. *Caring* 12:40-48.

3

Role of the Nurse As Patient Advocate

Ann H. Cary

A. Definitions
   1. Advocacy: engagement in activities for the purpose of protecting the rights of others while supporting the patient's responsibility for self-determination
   2. Paternalism: a liberty-limiting principle invoked to override people's actions or wishes for their best interests or their own good
   3. Patient Self-Determination Act: a component of the Omnibus Budget Reconciliation Act of 1990, which states that all individuals receiving medical care must be given written information about their rights under state law to make decisions about their medical care
   4. Advance medical directives: statements (written or oral) made by patients that indicate their treatment choices and/or the appointment of named, other person(s) who are chosen to make medical decisions for the patient
   5. Living will: statements by the patient about the medical treatments permitted and/or refused in the event the patient is unable to make decisions and is terminally ill
   6. Durable power of attorney: an appointed proxy, usually a relative or friend, to make medical decisions on a patient's behalf if the patient can no longer make decisions
B. Advocacy
   1. Models or views of how nurses may understand the advocacy role
      a. Rights protection model: The nurse defends the patient against infringement of rights. The nurse has the responsibility to inform the patient of his or her rights, make sure the rights and the process for exercising these rights are understood, and serves as the one to whom infringements are reported.

b. Value-based decision model: The nurse provides information and makes sure the patient obtains all the information needed to make a decision consistent with the patient's values, beliefs, desires, and life plan. Essential actions for the nurse include informing and supporting a patient's decision; patient values are explored and clarified so that congruence between choices and values are understood.
c. Respect for persons model: The nurse understands and acts on the basic human values of the patient by protecting the patient's dignity, privacy, and self-determined choices. If a patient is no longer self-determining, the nurse acts to promote a patient's wishes as defined when the patient was self-determining or as defined by his or her appointed surrogate. The nurse is accountable to the patient, society, and the profession for how the dignity and acknowledgment of human values are preserved.
d. Patient advocate model: The nurse is the health care team member responsible for promoting patient autonomy, self-actualization, and patient uniqueness. This model supports the moral authority of the nurse to make decisions for and with the patient and to help the patient achieve the best possible care. The moral imperative for the nurse derives from the continuous caring relationship with the patient as well as the time spent with the patient through which an insightful relationship develops.
e. Institutional advocate model: The nurse is the keeper of the organizational policies, procedures, and goals. Nursing actions are executed and professional relationships are interpreted through the filter of the institutional values and goals. The nurse's values are derived from the ethical standards of the institution as found in its mission, policy, and procedures.
f. Physician advocate model: The nurse is the advocate for the execution of physician expectations and subordinates patient loyalty to physician authority.
2. Four-step advocacy process
 a. Self-exploring: the nurse's self-exploration to identify own values and beliefs in order to be able to understand a patient's values
 b. Informing: an open communication activity between the nurse and the patient resulting in information exchange and comprehensive understanding

(1) Amplifying: enlarging the understanding of issues and content, which will include objective, factual data as well as subjective values and opinions
(2) Clarifying: striving to understand the meanings and consequences in a common way; resolving misunderstandings and confusion
(3) Verifying: confirming accuracy of information and reality testing
(4) Validating: returning repeatedly to any of the three activities above to ensure that the patient is truly informed
  c. Supporting: upholding a patient's right to make and act upon a choice; assisting the patient to communicate successfully with and work through the patient's supporters, dissenters, and obstructers
  d. Affirming: validating with the patient that the choices are consistent with the patient's values and goals; recognizing that patient needs may fluctuate with dynamic resources and encouraging re-evaluation and rededication to promote self-determination
3. Nurse advocacy actions: a parallel to the nursing process
  a. Assessment/diagnosis
    (1) Information is exchanged.
    (2) Data are gathered.
    (3) Values are clarified.
    (4) Clinical judgments are generated.
  b. Outcome identification: Nurse and patient identify expected outcomes described as measurable goals.
  c. Planning
    (1) Alternatives and consequences for possible actions are generated.
    (2) Actions are given priority.
  d. Implementation
    (1) Decisions are made by patient/surrogates.
    (2) Support, assurance, and reassurance are offered.
  e. Evaluation
    (1) Patient actions, goals, and outcomes are discussed.
    (2) Patient actions are reformulated based on feedback, consequences, and goal attainment.
4. Conflicts experienced in advocacy role
  a. Patient values and needs conflict with nurse values and desires.

b. Patient values and needs conflict with other providers' values, needs, and desires.
c. Patient values and needs conflict with the institution's values and needs.
d. Patient values and needs conflict with society's values and capabilities.
e. Patient values and needs conflict with significant others' values, needs, desires, and capabilities.
f. Patient values and needs are not understood by caregivers, providers, and/or significant others.
g. Multiple parties' values and desires for the patient conflict with each other.
C. Consumer protection interests: the nurse as consumer advocate
 1. Autonomy: right of the patient to be self-determining in choosing and refusing care; duty of the nurse to respect the patient's right to be free from coercion and manipulation and to respect the patient's interpretation of benefits and burdens while receiving care
 2. Nonmaleficence: right of the patient not to be harmed and duty of the nurse to do no harm
 3. Beneficence: right of the patient to expect the nurse to take actions to secure the patient's welfare and the duty of the nurse to advocate for the patient's welfare and assist the patient in achievement
 4. Justice: right of the nurse to assist the patient to expect fair and just treatment; duty of the nurse to treat the patient without prejudice and discrimination
D. Nurse patient advocacy situations
 1. Patient refuses services.
 2. Patient chooses premature discharge.
 3. Patient is unable to pay for or purchase services.
 4. Patient's waiting time for access to service exceeds need for service.
 5. Patient/agency is reimbursed for partial services.
 6. Patient becomes incompetent.
 7. Patient is intermittently competent.
 8. Caregivers neglect or abuse the patient or the treatment plan.
 9. Physician orders do not meet the welfare of the patient.
 10. Agency chooses early discharge of the patient.
 11. Nurse colleague or other health professional provider is incompetent, negligent, or provides fraudulent care.

12. Home setting is unsafe for patient care.
13. Community service does not exist to meet patient's needs.
14. Patient is discharged from institution to home care against patient choice.
15. Patient is discharged from institution to home care without adequate preparation.
16. Patient's activities must be limited to avoid self-inflicted injury.
17. Patient lives in a high-risk area.

STUDY QUESTIONS AND EXERCISES

1. Discuss two models of advocacy that are closest to your values. Give two examples of the nursing actions you implemented that reflect your view of advocacy.
2. At what point in the nursing process should questions to the patient about the advanced medical directive be made? Does your agency have a form? If not, construct one and share it with your supervisors and colleagues for comments.
3. Define the process of nursing advocacy. What nursing actions are essential to implement the advocacy role effectively?
4. Read three case studies in which the nurse acted as a patient advocate. Identify the conflict type and the nursing actions you would use to demonstrate advocacy for the patient. List any consequences for you in implementing the advocacy role.

BIBLIOGRAPHY

American Nurses' Association. 1985. *Code for nurses with interpretive statements.* Washington, D.C.

American Nurses' Association. 1986. *Standards of community health nursing practice.* Washington, D.C.

American Nurses' Association. 1986. *Standards of home health nursing practice.* Washington, D.C.

American Nurses' Association. 1991. *Standards of clinical nursing practice.* Washington, D.C.

American Nurses' Association. 1992. *Nursing and the Patient Self-Determination Act.* Washington, D.C.

American Nurses' Association. 1992. *A statement on the scope of home health nursing practice.* Washington, D.C.

Andersen, S.L. 1990. Patient advocacy and whistleblowing in nursing: Help for the helpers. *Nursing Forum* 25, no. 3:5-13.

Banja, J.D. 1992. *The nurse as patient advocate: Implications for nurse education programs.* Atlanta: Southern Council on Collegiate Education for Nursing.

Barton, A.J. 1991. Advocacy: Nursing's role in supporting the patient's right to refuse treatment. *Plastic Surgical Nursing* 11, no. 2:76-77.

Beauchamp, T.L., and J.F. Childress. 1989. *Principles of biomedical ethics.* New York: Oxford University Press.

Cary, A.H. 1992. Promoting continuity of care: Advocacy, discharge planning and case management. In *Community health nursing,* eds. M. Stanhope and J. Lancaster. St. Louis: Mosby-Year Book, Inc.

Clarke, M. 1989. Patient/client advocate. *Journal of Advanced Nursing* 14, no. 7:513-514.

Corcoran, S. 1988. Toward operationalizing an advocacy role: Helping another person to decide. *Journal of Professional Nursing* 4, no. 4:242-248.

Fedor, M.A. 1991. AIDS: Advocacy and activism. *Nursing and Health Care* 12, no. 6:289.

Fowler, M.D.M., and J. Levine-Ariff. 1987. *Ethics at the bedside.* Philadelphia: J.B. Lippincott Co.

Fry, S.T. 1992. Ethics in community health nursing practice. In *Community health nursing,* eds. M. Stanhope and J. Lancaster. St. Louis: Mosby-Year Book, Inc.

Gadow, S. 1980. Existential advocacy: Philosophical foundation of nursing. In *Nursing: Images and ideals,* eds. S.F. Spicker and S. Gadow. New York: Springer Publishing.

Gadow, S. 1989. Clinical subjectivity: Advocacy with silent patients. *Nursing Clinics of North America* 24, no. 2:535-541.

Gillam, T. 1991. Risk-taking: A nurse's duty. *Nursing Standard* 5, no. 39:52-53.

Glittenberg, J.E. 1990. A summing up: The message of health for all. *Journal of Professional Nursing* 6, no. 6:320.

High, D.M. 1989. Truth telling, confidentiality and the dying patient: New dilemmas for the nurse. *Nursing Forum* 24, no. 1:5-10.

Hutchinson, S.A. 1990. Responsible subversion: A study of rule-bending among nurses. *Scholarly Inquiry for Nursing Practice* 4, no. 1:3-17.

Kohnke, M.F. 1982. *Advocacy: Risk and reality.* St. Louis: Mosby-Year Book, Inc.

Marshall, M. 1991. Advocacy within the multidisciplinary team. *Nursing Standard* 6, no. 10:28-31.

Murphy, C.P. 1983. Models of the nurse patient-relationship. In *Ethical problems in the nurse-patient relationship,* eds. C. P. Murphy and H. Hunter. Boston: Allyn and Bacon.

Murphy, C.P. 1984. The changing role of nurses in making ethical decisions. *Law, Medicine, and Health Care* 12:173-184.

National League for Nursing. 1990. *Ethics in nursing: An anthology.* New York.

Payton, O.D., and C. E. Nelson. 1991. Patient's rights. *Clinical Management* 11, no. 5:11-12.

Porter, S. 1988. Siding with the system: Patient advocacy, benign paternalism. *Nursing Times* 84, no. 41:30-31.

Salladay, S.A., and M.M. McDonnell. 1989. Spiritual care, ethical choices and patient advocacy. *Nursing Clinics of North America* 24, no. 2:543-549.

Schaefer, S. 1989. Patient advocacy: An ethical dilemma? *Focus on Critical Care* 16, no. 3:191-192.

Stewart-Amidei, C. 1989. Patient advocacy: A simple nursing action? *Journal of Neuroscience Nursing* 21, no. 5:271-272.

Winslow, G.R. 1984. From loyalty to advocacy. *Hastings Center Report* 14:32-40.

4

Role of the Nurse As Patient Educator

Marjorie B. Kraus

A. Factors bringing patient education into prominence
   1. 1980: Omnibus Reconciliation Act: liberalized use of home health care by removing the 3-day acute care stay requirement and the limit on number of allowed visits
   2. 1983: Medicare prospective payment system: resulted in sending patients home faster, but with unmet teaching/learning needs
   3. Nurses' involvement in patient education: mandated by nurse practice acts in most states. It is included in professional statements by the American Nurses' Association (ANA); outlined in standards set by the Joint Commission on Accreditation of Healthcare Organizations; and incorporated into the American Hospital Association's *Patient's Bill of Rights.* Nurses' involvement in patient education was recently included as a nursing function in ANA's *Statement on the Scope of Home Health Nursing Practice.*
   4. The federal budget deficit, cost containment, and diagnosis-related groups (DRGs): resulted in shorter lengths of hospital stays and sicker patients at home who need education
   5. Deinstitutionalization of patients
   6. Changed nature of disease
      a. Increasing numbers of chronically ill and elderly patients have increased life expectancies secondary to advances in medical technology. Their complex medical and nursing needs include patient education.
      b. Home care is the setting for acute care follow-up, including high-technology interventions, disease prevention, and care of the chronically ill.
   7. Changes in consumer philosophy

a. Self-care and wellness are emphasized, rather than the disease-oriented medical model.
   b. Consumerism and patients' rights issues are accentuated.
   c. Patients choose home care over hospital care.
   d. Holism replaces the medical disease model.
  8. Delivery system and role changes
   a. Current nursing practice is moving away from the traditional physician hierarchical approach to a progressive team approach, with the patient as its focus.
   b. Patient education is viewed as primary intervention.
   c. The national shortage of nurses demands that nurses demonstrate the benefits and cost-effectiveness of patient education.
   d. Patient education is the target of a great deal of nursing research activity.
   e. Nurses now are able to perform procedures at home that previously were limited to in-hospital settings. Procedures warrant educational intervention for patients and caregivers.
B. Definition of patient education
  1. Patient education versus patient teaching: process versus content. *Patient teaching* is the limiting term and refers to only one component of the overall process.
  2. Patient education: giving information that the nurse believes is best for the patient to learn. Education for self-care focuses on the learner's perceived need.
C. Major health care goals of patient education
  1. Eight domains affected by patient education: individual and family development, rehabilitation, informed consent, compliance or adherence, coping, health care systems use, self-care, and wellness
  2. Patient education to promote health, prevent illness, and cope with illness
D. Family theory
  1. This theory is defined as a method of understanding the effect of family members on one another during their ongoing interactions.
  2. The family system must be assessed and taught as a unit if the patient is to succeed.
  3. Teaching one isolated family member can sometimes negate all teaching efforts.
  4. Patients who have the support of family members will achieve better self-care outcomes.

5. Families report that their ability to manage complex health care situations has improved after education.
6. Better acceptance of family members' illnesses, their altered lifestyles, and roles occur after teaching.

E. Models for patient education
1. Health belief model: Attitude and what the patient believes about himself or herself and the illness often predict degree of compliance.
2. Chatterton's model: This model examines the decision-making process the patient experiences as a health care consumer.
3. Nursing process: The process includes components of assessment, planning, implementation, and evaluation.
4. PRECEDE (predisposing, reinforcing, and enabling causes in educational diagnosis and evaluation) model: Health and health behavior are determined by multiple factors; educational efforts to affect them must be multidimensional. The model operationalizes learning theory by incorporating cognitive, behaviorist, and humanistic theories to deliver patient education.

F. Model step 1: assessment
1. Information gathering
   a. Assessment of the motivation of the learner and the family (readiness)
      (1) Assess what the patient wants to know first, what is already known, and what he or she needs to know.
      (2) Assess the learner's demographics, self-concept, role in the family, attitudes about health, learning style, skill level, language/reading comprehension, and limitations; all may contribute as facilitators or barriers to learning and teaching. Incorporate cultural assessment and negotiation into the process.
      (3) Locus of control: the way in which a person perceives his or her ability to control life; it has a major impact on willingness to learn. Note past history of compliance behavior.
   b. Assessment of learning needs and priorities: Learning needs and priorities can originate from a variety of sources that are health related, safety oriented, recreation directed, occupation oriented, or environmentally oriented.
      (1) Maslow's hierarchy of needs: helps order learning needs; basic-order needs (food, water, oxygen) must be met before higher-order needs can be met.

  c. Assessment of the nurse educator: Examine current levels of knowledge and skill, and any deficits in those areas; attitudes about teaching, learning, and compliance; and questions of congruence of beliefs.
  d. Assessment of agency: Assess imposed limitations of staffing, funding, physician and administrative support, time, predetermined protocols, and standards of care.
 2. Data interpretation: Form conclusions about the data collected. The educational diagnosis is presented as a summary statement about the patient and his or her learning and is the basis for following steps in the process.
G. Model step 2: negotiating learning goals/objectives
 1. Goals serve as a guide for developing content, implementing teaching, and evaluating outcomes.
 2. Goals ensure that learning intervention will be tailored to the situation and to the patient's needs.
 3. Goals act as a reinforcer and motivator.
 4. Goals specify mutually desired behavior change (attitude, skill, knowledge) and define roles of both teacher and learner.
 5. Well-written goals and objectives have the following characteristics:
  a. Are valid, observable, and measurable
  b. Are developed collaboratively and agreed upon by teacher and learner(s)
  c. Are based on data obtained in the assessment process
  d. Are learner-oriented and attempt to integrate learned facts into everyday life
  e. Contain elements of performance, conditions, and criteria
  f. Serve as guides
  g. Have practical usage in care plans, teaching checklists, and contracting
 6. Objectives are divided into three categories.
  a. Cognitive domain: knowledge based
  b. Affective domain: values/feelings
  c. Psychomotor: motor skills
H. Model step 3: teaching plan and intervention
 1. Theories of learning: based on philosophical beliefs about the nature of man
 2. Developmental theory: developmental growth and emotional tasks for different age groups. Age-related considerations:

      a. Learning in children depends on level of growth, development, and cognition; ability to learn changes rapidly (short attention spans; need play and active participation, praise, support, parenteral support).
      b. Learning in adolescents should consider abstract thinking, peer pressure, body image, need for individuality, involvement in goal-setting. Parenteral attendance may not be needed.
      c. Adults learn best when they see a need and an immediate use for what is to be learned. Consider respect, level of education, culture, religion, participation in goal-setting and sharing responsibilities. Value life experiences.
      d. Older people must be permitted independence in learning about their health care. Consider physiologic changes, vision, hearing, color perception, short sessions.
3. Role of memory in learning: Cognitive processes are involved; look for ways to increase retention and recall.
4. The teaching plan
      a. State learning goals and objectives.
      b. Outline the content to be taught.
      c. Specify the format for teaching (individualized, small group, large group, self-help groups or combinations). Although individual teaching is the more common intervention, group teaching is as effective as individual teaching.
      d. Describe teaching methodologies and materials: lecture, discussion, demonstration, return demonstration, role playing, programmed instruction, tests, media use, application of computer-assisted learning.
      e. Utilize a "learning contract" with patient-approved objectives as goal-met indicators.
5. Intervention in the home
      a. The home care nurse sees the family over time and develops a trusting relationship.
      b. Assessment in the home provides a more complete picture of routines, roles, social support network, and socioeconomic status.
      c. The home care nurse can ensure that patient values and goals are taken into account in decision making.
      d. Education in the home is easier and more comfortable because the patient is buttressed by familiar objects and family members.

        e. Teaching families allows the nurse to utilize the home environment as a teaching asset.
   I. Model step 4: evaluation of patient education
      1. Evaluation is a process that involves measuring behavior and interpreting results in terms of a standard of desired behavior.
      2. Follow-up assessments are conducted continuously as nursing interventions are carried out.
      3. Evaluation is carried out in the following steps:
         a. Measure the learner's behavioral change; to what extent have the learner's objectives been met?
         b. Analyze barriers and facilitators involved in the teaching/learning process (reasonable objectives; completeness of assessment; appropriate methodology for learned, suitable media; quality of interaction; format; content; time; cost).
         c. Summarize and document findings.
         d. Give constructive feedback to the patient; solicit feedback about the nurse's performance.
         e. Revise succeeding programs to reinforce learning; design new strategies to teach behaviors that were not initially accomplished.
      4. Behavioral change can be measured in several ways.
         a. Cognitive and psychomotor domains
            (1) Direct observation (rating scales, checklists, anecdotes, critical incidents); self-monitoring
            (2) Physiologic measures
            (3) Self-report (oral, written, questionnaire); records
         b. Affective domain: observation, self-report
      5. Documented learning has several benefits.
         a. Justifies time and cost in relation to effectiveness
         b. Provides communication of what works and what does not work
         c. Documents the problem-solving process and can be translated into quality assurance data
         d. Highlights future research questions
   J. Trends in patient education
      1. Further proliferation of home care services is expected.
      2. The segue from dependency to medically supervised and nurse-assisted self-care will continue.
      3. Patient education has several implications.
         a. Providers of home care will need specialized educational

preparation; need for theory and an opportunity to apply it in a supervised setting are essential.
   b. Evaluation of the patient education delivery system specific to the home setting is necessary; model development, standardization of the language of education, and delineation of roles must be included.
   c. Self-care, as a philosophic concept, is not yet operational. Issues needing clarification include screening standards to determine noncandidates; tools for self-care need to be tested; a defined legal base must be addressed; roles of mutual aid groups must be considered.
   d. Acknowledgment of influence of the family as a unit will increase; there will be continued opportunity to define the family unit, discern its role in achieving educational outcomes, and determine workable family-driven interventions.
   e. Technology provides growth in media use at home; computers link television and telephones to educational resources.
   f. Need for educational research in the home setting continues; research is essential for documentation of outcomes and cost-effectiveness. Tool development continues.
   g. Universality of patient education will emerge; all nurses in all settings will be recognized as patient educators.

STUDY QUESTIONS AND EXERCISES

1. How is the teaching of children and adolescents different from the teaching of adults? What special considerations should be made in teaching elders?
2. Discuss factors that have positive effects on compliance and cooperation.
3. What are some of the sources of patient education resources for home care?
4. What are some of the common mistakes made when attempting patient education in the home setting?
5. Choose an educational model and apply it to the home care setting. Integrate family and community systems theory within the model framework.

6. Discuss the advantages of the learning contract in home care. How does the home setting facilitate the contracting process?

BIBLIOGRAPHY

American Nurses' Association. 1992. *A statement on the scope of home health nursing practice.* Washington, D.C.

Armstrong, M.L. 1989. Orchestrating the process of patient education. *Nursing Clinics of North America* 24, no. 3:597-604.

Becker, M.H. 1974. The health belief model and sick role behavior. In *The health belief model and personal health behavior,* ed. M.H. Becker. Thorofare, N.J.: Charles B. Slack.

Bigge, M.L. 1976. *Learning theories for teachers.* New York: Harper & Row.

Cary, A.H. 1988. Preparation for professional practice: What do we need? *Nursing Clinics of North America* 23, no. 2:341-351.

Green, L.W., et al. 1980. *Health education planning: A diagnostic approach.* Palo Alto, Calif.: Mayfield Publishing Co.

Handy, C.M. 1988. Home care of patients with technically complex nursing needs: High technology home care. *Nursing Clinics of North America* 23, no. 2:315-328.

Hochbaum, G.M. July 1980. Patient counseling vs. patient teaching. *Topics in Clinical Nursing* 2:1-7.

Humphrey, C.J. 1988. The home as a setting for care: Clarifying the boundaries of practice. *Nursing Clinics of North America* 23, no. 2:305-314.

Hussey, L.C., and K. Gilliland. 1989. Compliance, low literacy, and locus of control. *Nursing Clinics of North America* 24, no. 3:605-610.

Jarvis, L.L. 1981. Health education in community health nursing. In *Community health nursing: Keeping the public healthy,* ed. L.L. Jarvis. Philadelphia: F.A. Davis Co.

Johnson, E.A., and J.E. Johnson. 1989. Teaching the home care client. *Nursing Clinics of North America* 24, no. 3:687-693.

Kick, E. 1989. Patient teaching for elders. *Nursing Clinics of North America* 24, no. 3:681-686.

Martinson, I.M. 1989. Afterword: A view for the future in home health nursing. In *Home health care nursing,* eds. I.M. Martinson and A.G. Widmer. Philadelphia: W.B. Saunders Co.

Narrow, B.W. 1979. *Patient teaching in nursing.* New York: John Wiley & Sons.

Oberst, M.T. 1989. Perspectives on research in patient teaching. *Nursing Clinics of North America* 24, no. 3:621-627.

Orem, D.E. 1971. *Nursing: Concepts of practice.* New York: McGraw-Hill Book Co.

Rakel, B.A. 1992. Interventions related to patient teaching. *Nursing Clinics of North America* 27, no. 2:397-423.

Rankin, S.H., and K.L. Duffy. 1983. *Patient education: Issues, principles, and guidelines.* Philadelphia: J.B. Lippincott Co.

Redman, B.K. 1988. *The process of patient education.* St. Louis: Mosby-Year Book, Inc.

Shannon, M. 1989. Skills in family teaching. In *Home health care nursing,* eds. I.M. Martinson and A.G. Widmer, 237-246. Philadelphia: W.B. Saunders.

Sharf, B. 1988. Teaching patients to speak up: Past and future trends. *Patient Education Counseling* 11:95-108.

Smith, C.E. 1989. Overview of patient education. *Nursing Clinics of North America* 24, no. 3:583-587.

Speers, A.T. 1989. Patient education: Theory and practice, *Journal of Nursing Staff Development* May/June:121-126.

Tripp-Reimer, T., and L.A. Afifi. 1989. Cross-cultural perspectives on patient teaching. *Nursing Clinics of North America* 24, no. 3:613-618.

Widmer, A.G., and I.M. Martinson. 1989. The continuum of care! Partners in acute and chronic care. In *Home health care nursing,* eds. I.M. Martinson and A.G. Widmer, 3-12. Philadelphia: W.B. Saunders Co.

Part II

Care Coordination with the Home Care Team

5
Role of Physical Therapy in Home Care

Sheryl Campbell

A. Description
   1. Physical therapy is the treatment provided to assist in rehabilitation and restoration of normal function following an illness or injury; treatment may involve the use of physical agents and methods (e.g., massage, manipulation, therapeutic exercise, cold, heat, hydrotherapy, electrical stimulation, and light).
   2. A physical therapist (PT) is an individual who is licensed as a physical therapist by the state in which he or she is practicing.
   3. A physical therapy assistant (PTA) is an individual who is licensed as a physical therapy assistant, if applicable, by the state in which he or she is practicing.
B. Education and training for the PT
   1. Graduated from a physical therapy curriculum approved by:
      a. The American Physical Therapy Association, or
      b. The Committee on Allied Health Education and Accreditation of the American Medical Association, or
      c. The Council on Medical Education of the American Medical Association and the American Physical Therapy Association
   2. Prior to January 1, 1966:
      a. Admitted to membership by the American Physical Therapy Association, or
      b. Admitted to registration by the American Registry of Physical Therapists, or
      c. Graduated from a physical therapy curriculum in a 4-year college or university approved by a state department of education; or

3. Has 2 years of appropriate experience as a PT, and has achieved a satisfactory grade on a proficiency examination conducted, approved, or sponsored by the United States Public Health Service, except that these determinations of proficiency do not apply to persons initially licensed by a state or seeking qualifications as a PT after December 31, 1977; or
4. Licensed or registered prior to January 1, 1966, and prior to January 1, 1970, had 15 years of full-time experience in the treatment of illness or injury through the practice of physical therapy in which services were rendered under the order and direction of attending and referring doctors of medicine or osteopathy

C. Education and training for PTA
   1. Graduated from a 2-year college-level program approved by the American Physical Therapy Association; or
   2. Has 2 years of appropriate experience as a PTA, and has achieved a satisfactory grade on a proficiency examination conducted, approved, or sponsored by the United States Public Health Service, except that these determinations of proficiency do not apply to persons initially licensed by a State or seeking initial qualifications as a PTA after December 31, 1977.

D. Eligibility for admission to PT services
   1. Patient must be homebound.
   2. Service must be under a plan of care established by a physician.
   3. Service must be reasonable and necessary to the patient's diagnosis or to restore function affected by illness or injury.
      a. Therapy must be within accepted standards of medical practice and must be considered specific and effective treatment for the patient's condition.
      b. There must be an expectation, based on the assessment by the physician of rehabilitation potential, that the patient will improve in a reasonable/predictable time or services are needed to establish a safe/effective maintenance program.
   4. Service must be of a complexity that it can be performed safely and/or effectively only by or under the supervision of a qualified PT.

E. PT as a member of the home health team
   1. Care planning is a multidisciplinary approach, with the PT being one of the team members; together (with the input from all disciplines) the plan of care is developed.

2. Communication (with different disciplines, physician, and patient/family) is essential for effective care planning and management.
3. Participation in case conferences:
   a. Enables each discipline to discuss specific roles in the plan of care
   b. Collaboration in goal setting
   c. Revision of the plan of care
   d. Problem solving
   e. Discharge planning
4. The PT will be the patient case manager when physical therapy is the only skilled discipline required.
   a. The PT must have a higher level of clinical judgment.
   b. The PT must look at the patient's total functioning ability, not just physical function and mobility.
   c. The PT may supervise the home health aide; a supervisory visit is required every 2 weeks.
5. The PT provides in-service as needed.

F. Activities are provided by the PT to patients of all ages for a multitude of different illness and injuries.
   1. Assessment and evaluation
      a. Must be provided by a qualified PT
      b. Includes functional limitations, patient condition, safety measures, treatment plan, and rehabilitation potential
      c. Home environment: evaluated to identify hazards or structural problems and make recommendations to improve safety to increase functional independence
      d. Initial evaluation: a billable visit even if it is determined that physical therapy is not needed
   2. Therapeutic exercises: must be performed by or under the supervision of a qualified PT for the safety of the patient and effectiveness of the treatment due to the type of exercise or the condition of the patient
   3. Gait training: given if the patient's ability to walk has been impaired by a neurologic, muscular, or skeletal condition or illness
      a. Gait training is considered reasonable and necessary if it can be expected to improve the patient's ability to ambulate.
      b. It includes selection and instruction of assistive devices (e.g., crutches, walker, cane, orthotic appliances, etc.).

c. If the patient's ability to walk has been impaired by a condition other than those mentioned above, gait training may be reasonable and necessary to restore lost function.
4. Transfer training: evaluating/instructing patient and caregiver in safe transfer to/from bed, bath, toilet, chair, etc., utilizing proper body mechanics and equipment (e.g., sliding board, Hoyer lift, bath bench, wheelchair, etc.)
5. Range of motion (ROM)
    a. Only a qualified PT may perform ROM tests.
    b. ROM exercise is considered skilled if the exercises are part of an active treatment for a specific disease, illness, or injury to restore a specific loss of function.
    c. If special medical conditions exist, the service of a skilled PT may be necessary (e.g., when the patient is subject to pathologic fracture).
6. Maintenance therapy is given by a qualified PT
    a. When the repetitive therapy that is needed to maintain function requires the use of a complex and/or sophisticated procedure;
    b. When the expertise of a qualified PT is required to treat the illness or injury safely and effectively;
    c. When the expertise of a qualified PT is necessary for the establishment and implementation of a maintenance program in order that physician treatment goals are achieved.
7. Ultrasound, shortwave, and microwave diathermy treatment: Because of the complexity of these treatments, they must be performed by or under the supervision of the qualified PT.
8. Hot packs, infrared treatments, paraffin baths, and whirlpool baths
    a. Treatments usually do not require the skill of a qualified PT.
    b. In certain cases the expertise of the qualified PT may be required to administer these treatments (i.e., circulatory deficiencies, areas of desensitization, open wounds, fractures, etc.).
9. Cardiopulmonary physical therapy
    a. Designed for patients with acute or severe cardiopulmonary diseases
    b. May comprise breathing exercise, postural drainage, energy conservation techniques, and cardiopulmonary conditioning

10. Prosthetic training: stump conditioning, ROM, muscle strengthening, and gait training (with or without prostheses or assistive devices)
11. Fabrication of temporary devices: tamperer prostheses, braces, splints
12. Restorative therapy
    a. Must be reasonable and necessary to the patient's condition
    b. Must be a reasonable potential that the patient will improve in a reasonable time
13. Teaching/education: teaching patient and/or caregiver the necessary techniques, exercises, and precautions that are reasonable and necessary for the illness or injury

G. PT documentation
    1. Initial evaluation: must include all necessary data to formulate the plan of care
        a. Diagnosis
            (1) Primary diagnosis: illness or injury most responsible for the need of treatment
            (2) Secondary diagnosis: other significant illness or injury that may affect treatment.
        b. Present history
            (1) Events that led to the present condition
            (2) Includes hospitalizations, treatments, and previous therapy
        c. Past medical history: significant conditions that may affect therapy
        d. Mental status
        e. Functional limitations: Therapy may be needed for
            (1) Deficits of ROM testing and muscle testing; specify
            (2) Sensory functions
            (3) Bed mobility
            (4) Transfers
            (5) Locomotion: specify distances, weight-bearing status, and use of assistive devices
            (6) Activities of daily living (ADL): If assistance is needed, is family willing and able or is assistance of a home health aide needed?
        f. Home environment
            (1) Identify hazards or structural problems in order to make

recommendations to improve safety and functional independence.
      (2) Identify family support and willingness to provide care.
  g. Equipment: what patient has, utilizes, and will require
  h. Homebound status: why the patient is homebound
  i. Vital signs: blood pressure, pulse, respiration (optional)
  j. Rehabilitation potential
      (1) Patient's condition to improve
      (2) Family's ability to provide the care
  k. Goals: short- and long-term goals; must be realistic
  l. Treatment plan
      (1) Interventions to achieve goals
      (2) Specific physical therapy activities
      (3) Frequency and duration of activities

2. Clinical note: documentation of contact with the patient
   a. Correlates with the evaluation
   b. Needed for every visit or patient contact
   c. Must be dated and signed with title
   d. Skilled activity provided
   e. Use of equipment or supplies
   f. Progress of the patient
   g. Patient response to treatment
   h. Patient/family comprehension of instructions
   i. Any other significant findings or significant comments by patient or family

3. Supervisory visits and case conferences
   a. Supervisory visit (PTA and home health aide): may be included in the clinical note or on a separate form
   b. Case conference
      (1) May be included in the clinical note or on a separate form
      (2) To show coordination of care, document all communication with the physician and team members

4. Discharge evaluation
   a. Summary of therapy provided with progress achieved
   b. Goals that were or were not accomplished
   c. Reason for discharge
   d. Instructions given on discharge

H. Activities of the PTA
   1. May provide therapy only under the supervision of a PT
   2. May provide services only within the scope of instructions developed by the qualified PT
   3. Activities the PTA can perform
      a. Noncomplex ROM and therapeutic exercise; application of heat, light, cold, and water therapy; ultrasound; and electrical modalities
      b. Bed mobility, transfers, and ambulation to improve functional mobility
      c. Report patient's progress and response to treatment to the PT
      d. Document concise accurate clinical notes for each session, following all PT documentation guidelines
      e. Confer with the PT and members of the health care team for the purpose of care coordination and planning
   4. Activities the PTA cannot perform
      a. Evaluating
      b. Teaching
      c. Supervising
      d. Testing
      e. Establishing a care plan or making changes
I. Supervision of the PTA
   1. The PT must review the plan of care with the PTA.
   2. The PT must provide specific instructions for treatment for the PTA.
   3. The PT must be available by phone for consultation while the PTA is providing therapy.
   4. Supervisory visits of the PTA:
      a. Medicare guidelines do not specify the frequency of supervisory visits for the PTA.
      b. It is recommended that a supervisory visit be made monthly.
      c. The PT must document the supervisory visit
         (1) Make a functional assessment.
         (2) Review the activities with the PTA.
         (3) Revise the plan of care as needed.
         (4) Evaluate the effectiveness and interaction of the PTA with the patient and the caregiver.
      d. A supervisory visit is not a billable visit.

STUDY QUESTIONS AND EXERCISES

1. Describe physical therapy and the activities that the PT may provide in the home.
2. Describe the documentation that is necessary by the PT and why.
3. What is the role of the PT as a member of the home health team?

BIBLIOGRAPHY

Carr, M.N. April 1994. Physical therapy in home care: Yesterday, today, and tomorrow. *Caring* 13:4.

Harrison, P., and A.E. Huebner. 1991. Physical therapy. In *The home care and documentation guide*. Gaithersburg, Md.: Aspen Publishers, Inc.

Health Care Finance Administration. 1988. *Medicare home health agency manual 11*. Washington, D.C.: United States Government Printing Office.

Joint Commission on Accreditation of Healthcare Organizations. 1994. *The 1995 Joint Commission accreditation manual for home care*. Oakbrook Terrace, Ill.

Stuart-Sidall, S. 1986. *Home health care nursing: Administrative and clinical perspectives*. Gaithersburg, Md.: Aspen Publishers, Inc.

6
Role of Occupational Therapy in Home Care

Elaine Ainsworth

A. Description
 1. The word *occupation* refers to the individual's goal-directed use of time, energy, interest, and attention.
 2. The occupational therapist (OT) usually receives referrals to treat individuals whose abilities to perform tasks of living are impaired by developmental disabilities, normal aging, injury, or illness.
B. Education and training requirements for the registered OT (OTR): The OT must have been graduated from an accredited educational program.
 1. Accrediting agencies for occupational therapy entry-level programs are the American Occupational Therapy Association and the Committee on Allied Health Education and Accreditation of the American Medical Association.
 2. The professional-level OT must meet education program requirements of the parent institution for awarding of degrees and must earn a bachelor's degree, a postbaccalaureate certificate, an entry-level master's degree, or combined baccalaureate and master's degrees.
 3. The OTR must complete academic and clinical preparations and take a national certification examination under the direction of the American Occupational Therapy Certification Board.
 4. Most states also require the OT to fulfill requirements to obtain a state license before he or she can practice; however, the OT is often eligible for a temporary license, working under the supervision of a licensed therapist, until he or she passes the certification examination.

C. Education and training requirements for the certified occupational therapy assistant (COTA)
    1. The COTA must have attained an associate degree from a 2-year accredited program.
    2. The COTA must pass a national examination for certification.
D. Utilization of aide-level staff
    1. There are no established standards for training.
    2. Home health aides may participate in the follow-through of the OTR's recommendations.
    3. Treatment is not billable as an occupational therapy session.
E. Examples of OT patients: Focus on developing the patient's maximal potential in skill areas needed to fulfill roles in life.
    1. The pediatric patient: primary caregiver(s) of great advantage
        a. Recent surgery for fracture: Treatment emphasis might focus on
            (1) Improving or maintaining range of motion (ROM)
            (2) Developing temporary compensatory techniques for self-care skills
            (3) Educating the caregiver in techniques for handling until mobility is improved
    2. The cerebral palsy patient: might exhibit visual problems or deficits in motor function, cognitive process, perceptual motor integration, or self-care skills development. The treatment plan could include
        a. Vision training
        b. Spasticity-reduction techniques
        c. Reflex-integrating techniques
        d. Splinting
        e. Positioning training for the caregiver
        f. Adaptive equipment recommendations
        g. Cognitive development tasks
        h. Perceptual motor activities
        i. Environmental adaptation recommendations
    3. The young adult head trauma patient: might exhibit motor, sensory, visual, or cognitive deficits, or maladaptive behavior patterns. The treatment plan would depend on focus, whether the patient can recover completely or must learn to adjust and cope with a diminished level of skill competency. The treatment plan could include

a. Routine daily living tasks of self-feeding, personal hygiene, and dressing
b. Appropriate social interactions
c. Handling of home management responsibilities
d. Following schedules
e. Handling of finances
F. Basis for role of the OT in home care
 1. The OT's background/areas of expertise
 2. Needs of the patient; funding source
 3. Philosophy and team approach of the agency
 4. Availability of the OT and related time constraints
G. Occupational therapy referral guidelines
 1. The OT is trained to work with all age groups, diverse physical and emotional problems, and varying degrees of acute and chronic impairments.
 2. The best guideline in determining whether an occupational therapy referral would be beneficial is an assessment of the patient's problems and deficits areas.
 3. Basing referral on the presenting primary diagnosis can be misleading and may not clarify the degree of dysfunction.
 4. Occupational therapy referral may be appropriate even if the patient has received occupational therapy in a hospital setting and/or a rehabilitation center.
    a. The patient may benefit from further self-care and homemaking training.
    b. The patient may be unable to manage effectively and safely in the reality of the home architectural environment and with different daily demands and expectations.
H. Problem/deficit areas addressed by the OT and typical treatment interventions
 1. Problem: decreased motor function
    a. Bed mobility activities
    b. Caregiver education in positioning techniques
    c. ROM exercises/activities
    d. Strengthening exercises/activities
    e. Gross motor coordination activities
    f. Fine motor coordination activities
    g. Self-care training using compensatory techniques or adaptive equipment

h. Work simplification/energy conservation training
   i. Environmental adaptations
   j. Splinting
 2. Problem: decreased tactile sensation
   a. Safety training
   b. Adaptive self-care equipment
   c. Sensory re-education
 3. Problem: decreased vision
   a. Low-vision training
   b. Adaptive equipment recommendations
   c. Safety training
   d. Patient education about community resources
 4. Problem: decreased perceptual motor skills
   a. Safety training
   b. Perceptual motor retraining
   c. Daily living skills retraining
   d. Environment adaptation recommendations
 5. Problem: decreased cognitive skills
   a. Safety training
   b. Daily living skills retraining
   c. Cognitive activities focusing on sequencing, decision making, problem solving, memory retention, and judgment; paper and pencil tasks, work-related tasks, self-care activities, homemaking or leisure activities
I. The OT as part of the team
 1. During the first visit with the patient, the OT will complete an initial evaluation.
   a. The patient's assets/limitations are determined.
   b. Problems are identified for the plan of care.
   c. Goals are established.
   d. Treatment interventions are recommended.
   e. Frequency and duration of treatment are determined.
 2. Ideally, formalization of the plan of care is the result of communication between disciplines involved through team conferences or telephone contacts.
 3. Communication between the disciplines greatly enhances the patient's quality of care.
   a. Self-care skills can be compromised with a lower-extremity fracture on limited weight-bearing status. The OT and the

physical therapist should coordinate treatment care plans to upgrade activities as the condition improves and physician restrictions change.
   b. With an insulin-dependent diabetic patient with neuropathy affecting fine motor coordination and ability to self-administer insulin, the OT and the nurse must work closely together to determine the best approach to compensate for these problems.
   c. The OT and the speech therapist must work closely together to reinforce treatment programs, as many daily tasks require the ability to communicate effectively.
   d. The OT benefits from communication with the social worker, who has increased knowledge of the impact of family on financial status, social interactions, and expectations of the patient.
4. The OT can provide valuable insights into the patient's functional skills.
5. Often the most significant people to include in the planning process are the patient and the primary caregiver.
6. The most successful treatment sessions are those that incorporate goals and activities mutually determined by the patient and the therapist.

STUDY QUESTIONS AND EXERCISES

1. Describe the types of patients appropriate for occupational therapy services.
2. What interventions would the OT utilize for a patient with decreased cognitive skills?
3. Develop a joint plan of care for the OT and the nurse for an elderly patient with acute exacerbation of arthritis with multiple joint deformities.

BIBLIOGRAPHY

American Occupational Therapy Association. 1987. *Guidelines for occupational therapy in home health*. Rockville, Md.

American Occupational Therapy Association. 1991. Essentials and guidelines for an accredited program for the occupational therapist. *American Journal of Occupational Therapy* 45:1077–1084.

Kelly, P., and M. Steinhauer. 1991. Strategies for increasing referrals for occupational therapy in home health care. *American Journal of Occupational Therapy* 45:656–658.

Menosky, J. 1990. Occupational therapy services for the homebound psychiatric patient. *Journal of Home Health Care Practice* May:57–67.

7
Role of Speech-Language Pathology Services in Home Care

Harriet Simpson Steele

A. Description: The speech-language pathologist (SLP) is a specialist in human communication; also called a speech clinician.
B. Education and training
   1. Master's or doctoral degree in speech and language pathology
   2. Clinical fellowship year
   3. Certification by the American Speech, Language and Hearing Association (ASHA), and/or
   4. State licensure in speech/language pathology
C. Professional role of the SLP in home care
   1. Conducts speech and/or language evaluations.
   2. Develops/recommends appropriate treatment programs.
   3. Schedules/provides treatment.
   4. Refers to other health professionals.
   5. Participates in patient care team meetings.
   6. Instructs and counsels family/significant other, nurses, and other home care team members.
   7. Recommends prosthetic and alternate devices for communication, including
      a. Palatal lift for velarpharyngeal incompetency
      b. Artificial larynx for laryngectomy
      c. Picture boards or electronic equipment
   8. Refers to other community sources.
   9. Conducts hearing screening to determine whether hearing loss exists.
   10. Provides aural rehabilitation after hearing evaluation by an audiologist.

a. Speech reading to supplement hearing with increased use of visual information
b. Auditory training to maximize benefits of sound amplified by a hearing aid
11. Develops and establishes a maintenance program that includes training caregivers when further significant improvement from treatment is unlikely.
12. Participates in discharge planning.
    a. Describes plan in the initial care plan.
    b. Keeps the case manager advised as discharge approaches.
13. Documents appropriately.
    a. Provides initial evaluation with diagnosis and recommendations.
    b. Provides a treatment (care) plan with long-term and short-term goals.
    c. Makes daily clinical notes for each treatment.
    d. Provides a progress summary at 30- or 60-day intervals.
    e. Provides a discharge summary with recommendations when treatment is terminated.
14. Supervises students and professional colleagues.
15. Provides in-service to home care staff.
16. Serves on professional advisory boards.
17. Develops a plan for and implements ongoing quality improvement; conducts research.
18. Develops and participates in prevention programs.
    a. Identifies children at risk for delayed language development.
    b. Provides alerting devices for hearing, visually, or vocally impaired patients.
19. Provides public education; markets services.
20. Defends appropriateness of service delivery when questions involving reimbursement arise.

D. Service delivery terminology
1. Referrals: patients with known or suspected disorders of speech and/or language and/or swallowing
2. Assessment: includes formal tests and informal measures to achieve the following:
    a. Gather objective data and subjective information.
    b. Determine whether a problem exists.
    c. Describe the nature and severity of a problem.

d. Establish a diagnosis.
   e. Estimate rehabilitation potential.
   f. Make recommendations for treatment, including frequency and duration of treatment.
   g. Establish long-term and short-term goals.
   h. State plans for discharge.
3. Treatment: intervention based on an established treatment plan
   a. Revise the plan according to regular reassessment findings.
   b. Discharge the patient when goals are reached or when the patient reaches maximal potential improvement.
4. Family involvement: Involve people in the patient's home to maximize treatment effectiveness.
   a. Help with homework practice.
   b. Learn to use special equipment with the patient.
   c. Understand and follow diet preparation needs and feeding instructions.
5. Record keeping: Provide timely and appropriate documentation (according to agency's policies and procedures); it should be concise and easily understood by other professionals and third-party payers.
6. Supportive personnel: Home health aides scheduled to provide personal care services for a patient at home may be instructed by the SLP to do the following:
   a. Assist the patient in using newly learned speech and language skills.
   b. Utilize established maintenance program skills.
   c. Carry out specific feeding instructions.
7. Cultural/linguistic distinctions: Patients with different language or cultural features may have unique communication behavior.
   a. Dialects are not treated as disorders.
   b. Diagnostic and treatment materials and strategies are adapted to accommodate these differences.
8. Interdisciplinary management: Work with other professionals to
   a. Coordinate services, goals, and plans.
   b. Ensure that appropriate services are provided along with continuity of care.
9. Quality improvement: Evaluate and monitor on an ongoing basis the quality and appropriateness of speech and language services provided.

    a. When problems are identified, action plans are developed to resolve them.
    b. Follow-up evaluations are done to demonstrate problem resolution.
  10. Safety: When presented with health and/or environmental risks, follow safety precautions.
  11. Reimbursement: Each third-party payer has specific regulations. The SLP must become familiar with each so that services meet requirements for payment. When needed, the SLP will provide additional information to ensure third-party coverage.
E. Speech terminology
  1. Speech: the motoric competency for articulation required to talk clearly and fluently; a secondary function. Eating is a primary function that uses the same structures and articulators to consume food and beverage.
    a. Articulation: movement required of lips, teeth, jaw, tongue, soft palate, and larynx to talk clearly
    b. Voice: sound production utilizing breath stream, vocal cord vibration, and resonating chambers of the pharynx and oral and nasal cavities
    c. Prosody: the rate, rhythm, and intonation of speech
  2. Language: the meaningful combination of sounds into words and sentences to communicate
  3. Swallowing (ingestion): the transit of a substance from the mouth (oral) via the throat (pharyngeal) and esophagus (esophageal) to the stomach. The process has three stages.
    a. Oral stage: anticipation and readiness to receive food; preparation (chewing and bolus formation)
    b. Pharyngeal stage
      (1) Transit of intact bolus over base of the tongue
      (2) Elevation and tilting of the larynx to protect airway from aspiration
      (3) Rapid passage of bolus through the pharynx into the esophagus
    c. Esophageal stage: bolus movement to the stomach with peristalsis
  4. Cognitive language functions: the higher-level brain functions of orientation, attention, memory, perception, auditory processing, reasoning and problem solving, and pragmatic and executive functions

F. Patient disorders treated by the SLP
  1. Speech articulation disorders
     a. Dysarthria: reduced speech clarity due to muscle weakness or paralysis resulting in altered or absent speech sounds, voice, or prosody
        (1) Major causes: Parkinson's disease, cerebrovascular accident (CVA), bulbar palsy, pseudobulbar palsy, dystonia, chorea, amyotrophic lateral sclerosis, cerebellar lesions, Bell's palsy, trauma, tumors, surgery, and multiple sclerosis
        (2) Treatment goal: intelligible speech for effective communication
        (3) Treatment methods: auditorially and visually presented sounds, words, and sentences to practice in conscious, exaggerated manner to increase accuracy. Self-monitoring is trained to promote ongoing improvement.
        (4) Equipment needed
            (a) Tape recorder to record, evaluate progress, and promote self-awareness of speech performance and self-monitoring
            (b) Augmentative devices (e.g., letter boards or electronic devices) for the severely impaired to supplement or substitute for oral speech
     b. Apraxia: difficulty in voluntarily initiating a movement in the absence of weakness or paralysis; may be oral, verbal, or limb apraxia. The patient may not open mouth or raise an arm on request, but when food is placed in front of the patient, he or she picks it up and eats it.
        (1) Major causes: CVA and head trauma
        (2) Treatment goal: to regain voluntary control of speech movements
        (3) Treatment modalities: auditory, tactile, and visual cues with and without a mirror to reprogram articulatory accuracy with sounds, syllables, and words. Facilitation with speech melody and rhythm practice is often helpful.
        (4) Equipment: tape recorder, mirror, diagrams of word production, printed graphemes, words, etc. Temporarily, topic, word, or alphabet boards are used to communicate with the family.
  2. Language disorders
     a. Aphasia: difficulty understanding or expressing ideas. Sever-

ity ranges from mild to total or global. Aphasia may involve receptive functions of listening and reading or expressive functions of talking and writing.
(1) Major cause: acquired brain injury as in CVA, trauma, or brain tumor
(2) Treatment goal: maximally effective language for effective communication of daily needs at home and in the community
(3) Treatment modalities: multisensory language stimulation beginning with the best functioning modality. Strengthen auditory comprehension, then build expressive skills orally or through picture/word board pointing or gestures.
(4) Equipment: tape recorder and alternate communication devices
  b. Delayed language in children
(1) Major causes: hearing loss, lack of stimulation or need to talk, brain injury, mental retardation, emotional disturbance, cleft palate, or multiple causes
(2) Treatment goals: elimination of causes and effective habilitation of language
(3) Treatment modalities: multidimensional approach to remove cause, to provide appropriate stimulation in environment, and to work with parents or caregivers
3. Dysphagia (swallowing disorder): difficulty managing food in the mouth (biting, chewing, forming or moving a bolus) and/or safely initiating a swallow for transit through the pharynx to the esophagus and the stomach. Dysphagia may involve liquids or solids; it is due to muscle weakness, incoordination, or tissue/structural changes caused by disease, surgery, or trauma.
  a. Major causes: neurologic damage, cancer, trauma, surgery
  b. Treatment goal: safe oral intake adequate for nutritional needs
  c. Treatment methods
(1) Evaluate at bedside to assess muscle function and competency with liquid, puréed, and solid food.
(2) Perform a videofluoroscopic swallow study to rule out aspiration.
(3) Adjust diet consistency.
(4) Teach the patient and the family safe feeding position, bolus size, and rate.

(5) Teach the patient compensatory movements.
(6) Provide ongoing assessment.
   d. Modalities: multisensory
   e. Equipment: feeding utensils, pillows, and foam wedges
4. Rhythm: stuttering, cluttering, dysrhythmia; differences in rate, with additional movements accompanying expression that draws attention and detracts from the content of a message. Stuttering is disturbing to the speaker and frequently causes him or her to avoid speaking situations or to become anxious when anticipating them.
   a. Major causes: brain injury; emotional, neurologic, or biochemical disorders; unknown
   b. Treatment goal: easier, more controlled, and fluent oral expression along with improved attitude and emotional response to nonfluent expression
   c. Treatment methods
      (1) Teach breath stream and voicing control.
      (2) Replace old habits with new behaviors.
      (3) Build a positive image regarding speech and self.
      (4) Eliminate inappropriate behaviors.
5. Voice disorders: characterized by errors in vocal cord vibration, resonance (too much or too little nasality), loudness, pitch, or quality
   a. Major causes: cleft palate, cancer, vocal abuse, neurologic disease, brain injury, trauma, faulty learning
   b. Treatment goal: effective voice for personal and professional use
   c. Treatment methods
      (1) Eliminate the cause.
      (2) Teach compensatory techniques.
      (3) Teach good vocal hygiene.
      (4) Provide prostheses and teach use of the following:
         (a) Artificial larynx for patient with laryngectomy/nontalking tracheotomy
         (b) Palatal lift for hypernasality with velarpharyngeal inadequacy or incompetency
   d. Modalities: auditory, visual, and tactile
   e. Equipment: visual and auditory representation of vocal production; tactile sensation through manual manipulation
6. Cognitive disorganization: a breakdown in higher cognitive language function. Cognitive disorganization must be differentiated from the language of confusion in dementia.

a. Major cause: head trauma
   b. Treatment goal: Increase the individual's capacity to process and use incoming information to allow increased functioning in everyday life.
   c. Treatment methods: hierarchically introduced tasks beginning at level of patient functioning and rising to highest reasonable level
   d. Modalities: multisensory
   e. Equipment: varies with individual's age, status, and interests
G. Care planning
   1. Develop a treatment plan based on assessment.
      a. Habilitate children with disabilities.
      b. Rehabilitate patients with lost abilities.
   2. Establish SLP services that are
      a. Consistent with the nature and severity of the illness, injury, or condition;
      b. Provided at reasonable frequency;
      c. Estimated for a reasonable duration;
      d. Considered in accepted standards of medical practice to be specific and effective treatment for the patient's condition;
      e. Expected to result in significant improvement within a reasonable, predictable time;
      f. Recommended to establish a safe and effective maintenance program.
   3. Make short-term goals meaningful steps toward achieving clearly stated long-term goals.
   4. Adjust treatment tasks with ongoing reassessment using objective data and functional performance observation.
   5. Record performance in goal-directed tasks in clinical notes.
   6. Summarize progress with new short-term goals.
   7. Discharge the patient when he or she reaches the goal or when reasonable progress ceases and a maintenance program is established.
H. Coordination of care by the SLP
   1. Report any undesirable health or safety factors immediately to the patient's nurse or case manager.
   2. Document the patient's functional performance level regularly in progress notes for other professionals to utilize.
   3. Leave notes in a speech-language pathologist folder at the patient's home for patient, family members, caregivers, and allied

health professionals to read. The notes should include current information regarding communication level, use of particular equipment, feeding precautions, food allowed, and home practice materials.
4. Instruct the patient's caregiver with each change in the patient's progress. Observe the caregiver following feeding instructions, using augmentative equipment, facilitating language, etc.
5. Talk with other allied health professionals. Seek assistance regarding positioning or movement limitations and share functional status information when possible.

STUDY QUESTIONS AND EXERCISES

1. What is the main difference between dysarthria and apraxia?
2. What are the four main areas the SLP treats?
3. Differentiate between speech and language.
4. Why do we say that speech is a secondary function?
5. Describe two kinds of language disorders.
6. Describe two ways the SLP assists in coordination of care.
7. Your patient status post CVA answers "yes" to all of your questions when you know the answer is "no" to some of the questions. Give three possible reasons for this behavior. What would help you determine the main cause for this?
8. Your home health caseload includes patients with diagnoses of Parkinson's disease, CVA, and traumatic brain injury. List the speech, language, or swallowing disorders each might have.

BIBLIOGRAPHY

American Speech, Language, and Hearing Association. 1984. *Health insurance manual for speech-language pathologists and audiologists.* Rockville, Md.
Guidelines for the employment and utilization of supportive personnel in audiology and speech-language pathology. 1981. *ASHA* 23:164–169.
Health Care Finance Administration. May 1989. *Medicare hospital manual 10.* Washington, D.C.: U.S. Department of Health and Human Services.
Position statement: The delivery of speech-language-hearing services in home care. 1988. *ASHA* 30.

8
Role of Social Work in Home Care

Kathy J. Morgan

A. Social worker
   1. The social worker must have a master's degree from a school of social work.
   2. The social worker must have 1 year of social work experience in a health care setting.
B. Social work assistant
   1. The social work assistant must work under the supervision of a qualified social worker.
   2. The social work assistant must have a baccalaureate degree in social work, sociology, psychology, or a related field.
   3. The social work assistant must have 1 year of experience as a social worker in a health care setting.
C. Home care services of the social worker
   1. Provide services according to a plan of treatment/plan of care.
   2. Assess social and emotional factors related to the patient's illness, need for and adjustment to care, and response to treatment.
   3. Assess relationship of the patient's nursing and other medical requirements to the patient's individual home environment, situation, any financial resources, and available community resources.
   4. Ensure community resource planning and acquisition.
   5. Provide counseling services, including home and family/caregiver evaluation; assess need for long-term care, and arrange for placement.
   6. Provide short-term therapy for management of terminal illness.
   7. Help resolve problems for high-risk patients.
D. Patients needing social worker interventions
   1. Patients who are abused/neglected

2. Patients with a high suicide potential
3. Patients with inadequate resources: food, medical supplies, medicines, or inadequate or unstable family/caregivers
4. Patients needing long-term placement
5. Patients whose home environment is unsafe or inadequate
6. Patients who are unwilling/unable to follow a plan of treatment because of
   a. Physical problems: loss of independence, altered physical image (e.g., amputation), incontinence, pain, sensory deprivation/loss, eating/sleeping problems, or reduction or loss of physical function
   b. Emotional and cognitive problems: depression, guilt, fear, anxiety, anger, poor motivation, dependence, denial, combativeness, confusion, or impaired memory/judgment
7. Patients who engage in substance abuse
8. Patients who need community resources acquisition
9. Patients who live alone

E. Social worker interventions
   1. Conducts initial assessment, establishes plan of care, and conducts follow-up visits.
   2. Coordinates plan of care with other home health team members.
   3. Provides interventions through patient/caregiver education and counseling.
   4. Participates in care conferences and discharge planning.
   5. Identifies and coordinates relevant community and financial resources for each patient.
   6. Assists the physician and other home health team members in understanding the significant emotional and social factors related to each patient's individual health problems.
   7. Provides patient advocacy services.

STUDY QUESTIONS AND EXERCISES

1. Describe the types of home health care patients who might benefit from social worker intervention.
2. What are the services provided by the social worker in home health care?

BIBLIOGRAPHY

Baer, N., et al. 1984. Home health services social work treatment protocol. *Home Healthcare Nurse* July/August:43-49.

Blanchard, L., et al. April 1991. *Guidelines and documentation requirements for social workers in home health care.* Silver Spring, Md.: Association of Social Workers.

Spiegel, A. 1983. *Home healthcare: Home birthing to hospice care.* Owings Mills, Md.: National Health Publishing.

Thobaben, M. 1988. Nurse/social worker home care. *Home Healthcare Nurse* January/February:37-39.

9

Role of Homemaker/Home Health Aide in Home Care

Ruth Rebecca Apple and Susan M. Truscott

A. Personnel qualifications of the home health aide (HHA)
   1. Medicare conditions of participation
      a. The HHA must complete successfully a training and competency evaluation program or must pass successfully a competency evaluation program.
         (1) If the HHA has not been employed as an HHA in the previous 24 months, he or she must again complete successfully a training and competency evaluation program and/or a competency evaluation program prior to providing care/services as an HHA.
   2. Joint Commission on Accreditation of Healthcare Organizations (Joint Commission) conditions of participation
      a. The HHA must be able to demonstrate competency in skills required to provide care/services; the HHA must have knowledge of subjects taught in training.
   3. Individual organizations' conditions of participation
      a. The HHA must adhere to all applicable laws and regulations.
      b. Conditions are defined in job descriptions and personnel policies and procedures.
B. Supervision of the HHA
   1. Medicare conditions of participation
      a. A registered nurse (RN) must make a visit to the patient's home at least every 2 weeks, if the patient is receiving skilled services, to assess the patient's health status and the rapport of the patient and the HHA and to determine whether goals are being met.

b. If physical therapy, occupational therapy, or speech-language pathology services are provided, the therapist may make the supervisory visit in place of the RN.
   c. Documentation of the supervisory visit should be included in the home care record.
   d. For the patient receiving HHA services only, an RN must make a supervisory visit at least every 60 days while the HHA is providing home care.
   e. A qualified supervisor must be available during all hours of operation.
  2. Joint Commission standards
   a. All Medicare-certified organizations must meet requirements of the conditions of participation.
   b. A qualified health care professional regularly must assess the patient's health status and rapport of the patient and the HHA, and must determine whether goals are being met. An on-site visit to the patient's residence while the HHA is providing care must be done every 6 months, or more frequently if required by agency policy or by federal or state rules or regulations.
   c. A qualified supervisor must be available during all hours care or services are being provided.
  3. State requirements
   a. Each state may have regulations that are more stringent than those of Medicare or the Joint Commission. The HHA must follow these regulations also.
  4. Home health organization requirements
   a. The HHA must conform to all applicable home health organization policies and procedures regarding supervision.
C. Orientation program
  1. Joint Commission
   a. Each homemaker/HHA must participate in an orientation program appropriate to the level of care to be provided and the job classification prior to being assigned to patient care/services.
   b. The following subjects should be included in an orientation program:
      (1) Organization/agency policies and procedures
      (2) Care/services policies and procedures
      (3) Infection control

(4) Basic home safety, including safe and appropriate use of equipment
(5) Community resources
(6) Confidentiality
(7) Personal safety
   c. Evidence of participation in/attendance to an orientation program must be documented.
D. Training and competency evaluation regulations for a Medicare-certified home care organization
  1. History
    a. The Omnibus Budget Reconciliation Act (OBRA) of 1987 was signed in December 1987; it required that home care organizations evaluate competency of HHAs before July 1, 1989, and complete a training and competency evaluation program before August 1, 1990.
    b. Because of delays in meeting deadlines for publishing the minimum standards, competency evaluation requirements were changed to become effective on February 14, 1990, and training and competency evaluation requirements were changed to become effective on August 14, 1990.
    c. The rule applies to all home care staff who provide "hands-on" care/services for a certified home care organization and/or hospice, regardless of the title of the staffer or the reimbursement source; it also applies to persons working under contract (or other arrangement) to the organization.
    d. After August 14, 1990, home care organizations were permitted to employ only HHAs who had been trained and/or tested.
  2. Training program requirements
    a. Organizational requirements
      (1) A home care organization may not conduct training and competency evaluation programs or competency evaluation programs if it has had a conditional deficiency within the previous 24 months (correction of a conditional deficiency does not remove the restriction).
      (2) If a training and competency evaluation program is in process and the organization is found to have a conditional deficiency during a survey, the agency may complete the current program but may not start another training and

competency evaluation program until the 24-month period is up.
(3) Training and competency evaluation programs may be provided by home care organizations or non–home care organizations.
b. Instructor requirements
(1) The training and competency evaluation program must be conducted under the general supervision of an RN with 2 years of nursing experience with at least 1 year of home care experience, and 6 months experience in supervising HHAs.
(2) An RN must oversee and plan the training and competency evaluation program.
c. Competency evaluation program
(1) Evaluation must be completed successfully by each HHA and does not require prior training if the organization thinks the HHA can pass without training.
(2) A 24-month time limit is placed on the test if the HHA does not work at all.
(3) An RN must verify, by signing the task sheet, the successful completion of each task the HHA performs.
(4) Tasks that must be demonstrated include, minimally, measurement of temperature, pulse, and respiration; basic personal care skills; and ambulation and transfers.
(5) Other areas to be evaluated must include, at a minimum, nutrition and fluid intake; food preparation; range of motion; positioning; emergencies and emergency procedures; infection control; safety measures; basic elements of body functions and changes to report; observation and documentation of patient status and care/services furnished; and psychosocial needs, including patient rights.
(6) Performance evaluations that demonstrate skills competency and include the 12 subject areas must be done at least every 12 months and may be included in the employee's annual evaluation.
(7) The HHA may not perform any task until he or she satisfactorily demonstrates competency in performing that particular task.
(8) If more than one category is not completed satisfactorily, the HHA will not be considered to have completed the

competency evaluation successfully and may not work without direct supervision until the evaluation is completed successfully.
   (9) The home care organization must have documented evidence that regulations for competency evaluation have been met, including the following:
       (a) Content/description of the training and competency evaluation program and the competency evaluation program
       (b) Qualifications of the instructor
       (c) A skills demonstration record that describes the tasks and tells which skills were taught at the patient's bedside and which were taught in the laboratory setting
d. Training and competency evaluation program
   (1) The program must contain at least 75 hours of training in which at least 16 hours of training is laboratory/clinical training.
   (2) Thirteen subject areas must be included.
       (a) Communication
       (b) Nutrition, meal preparation, and fluid intake
       (c) Range of motion and positioning
       (d) Ambulation and transfers
       (e) Physical, psychosocial, and developmental needs of the patient, including patient rights
       (f) Infection control
       (g) Maintenance of a clean, safe, and healthy environment
       (h) Observation, documentation, and reporting of the patient's status and the care/services provided
       (i) Measurement of temperature, pulse, and respiration
       (j) Basic elements of body functions and changes to be reported
       (k) Emergencies and emergency procedures
       (l) Personal care procedures
       (m) Any other tasks required by the home care organization that the HHA would be required to perform
   (3) At least 16 hours of classroom training must be provided before the supervised practical training begins.
   (4) Documentation of tasks taught must designate whether the task was taught in a laboratory setting or at the patient's bedside; return demonstrations may be done on a manne-

quin in a laboratory setting, but tasks must be performed for a patient during the competency evaluation.
     (5) A national program has not been established by the Health Care Finance Administration to approve training and competency evaluation programs.
  E. Training and competency evaluation standards for the Joint Commission
    1. For Medicare-certified agencies, the home care organization must abide by state and federal regulations also.
    2. Areas of training to be completed successfully by all personal care and support services staff include those areas discussed under Medicare regulations.
  F. In-service requirements for Medicare-certified agencies
    1. Twelve hours of in-service training must be provided per calendar year.
    2. In-services may be done during supervisory visits if new information is offered or a new task is taught at this time.
    3. In-service training may be offered by any organization.
  G. Qualifying criteria for HHA services—Medicare-certified
    1. Criteria for visits mandate one or more of following:
       a. The visit must provide hands-on personal care.
       b. The visit must provide services that are needed to maintain the patient's health or to facilitate treatment of the patient's illness or injury.
    2. The patient must meet qualifying criteria:
       a. Must be homebound.
       b. Must be under a physician's plan of care.
       c. Must need skilled nursing care on an intermittent basis, or physical therapy, speech-language pathologist, or continued occupational therapy.
          (1) The patient is physically or mentally unable to perform services for self.
          (2) No caregiver is available who is able and willing to furnish the services needed.
          (3) When skilled nursing services are provided, both HHA and skilled nursing visits/hours are combined to determine part-time or intermittent services.
    3. The physician must order HHA services and specify the types of services to be furnished and the frequency of services required by the patient.

H. Tasks that can be done by an HHA
 1. Personal care services are provided that are ordinarily performed by nurse's aides in hospitals.
    a. Bathing; dressing; grooming; caring for hair, nails, and oral hygiene; changing bed linens of an incontinent patient; shaving; applying deodorant; caring for skin with lotions and/or powder; caring for feet and ears
    b. Feeding, assistance with elimination (including enemas, unless the skill of a licensed nurse is required by the patient's condition; routine catheter care; and routine colostomy care), assistance with ambulation, changing position in bed, assistance with transfers
    c. Simple dressing changes that do not require the skills of a licensed nurse
    d. Assistance with medications that ordinarily are self-administered and that do not require the skills of a licensed nurse to be provided safely and effectively
    e. Assistance with activities that are directly supportive of skilled therapy services but do not require the skills of a therapist to be safely and effectively performed.(e.g., routine maintenance exercises and repetitive speech therapy)
    f. Routine care of prosthetic and orthotic devices
 2. Incidental/household services may be performed during the visit only if the purpose of the visit is to perform a health service.
    a. Light housekeeping: change of bed linens, light cleaning of immediate area, meal preparation, and kitchen cleanup after meal preparation
    b. Personal laundry essential to the patient's health care
    c. Grocery shopping only for essentials
    d. Errands
    e. Trash removal

I. Role differentiation and responsibilities
 1. Many terms are used to describe paraprofessionals who work in the patient's home (e.g., HHA, homemaker, chore worker attendants, aides, personal care workers, companions, and others).
    a. Role is determined by the task done, not the title used.
       (1) Supportive services: homemaker/companion
          (a) Duties: performance of simple procedures as an extension of therapy services, personal care, ambulation and exercise, household services needed to provide health

care at home, assistance with medications that ordinarily are self-administered, reporting changes in the patient's condition and needs, and completing appropriate records
    b. Each state has its own standards with various definitions of roles and responsibilities.
J. Specialty areas
  1. Hospice and/or care of the terminally ill patient: Provide safe, effective, direct patient care to increase level of comfort of the patient.
    a. The HHA will need specialized training in care of the terminally ill patient.
    b. Training will emphasize psychosocial needs of the dying patient.
    c. The HHA will provide all personal care services and household care needed with special emphasis on making the patient as comfortable as possible.
  2. Waiver state-funded: special programs/funding to provide household care not provided under Medicare and needed to maintain the patient in the home
    a. Light housecleaning
    b. Meal preparation
    c. Errands/shopping
  3. Pediatric: mother's helper/nanny-type care of infant/child in the home setting to assist parents in adjusting to new birth or illness of a child.
    a. The HHA will need specialized training in infant/child growth and development.
    b. The HHA will need training in parent/child relationships.

STUDY QUESTIONS AND EXERCISES

1. The conditions of participation mandate certain qualifications for the instructor of the training and competency evaluation program. What are these qualifications?
2. Name the tasks that must be demonstrated by the HHA during the training and competency evaluation program or the competency evaluation program.

3. List the subject areas that are to be evaluated in addition to the tasks.
4. Explain the in-service requirements for the HHA per year.
5. List two specifics that must be included in a physician's order for HHA service for Medicare-certified agencies.
6. What special training will be needed for hospice care and/or care of the terminally ill patient or the pediatric home care patient?

BIBLIOGRAPHY

Federal Register. August 8, 1989. 54, no. 151.

Federal Register. August 14, 1989. 54, no. 155:3367–3373.

Federal Register. July 18, 1991. 56, no. 138:32973–32975.

Health Care Finance Administration. 1989. *Medicare home health agency manual 11* (04-89): Rev. 222, Retrieval Title: P11R222. Washington, D.C.: U.S. Government Printing Office.

Joint Commission on Accreditation of Healthcare Organizations. 1994. *The 1995 Joint Commission accreditation manual for home care II.* Oakbrook Terrace, Ill.

10

Durable Medical Equipment

Jacqueline Birmingham and Craig Jeffries

A. Definition: Durable medical equipment (DME) is any device that is durable in nature, meaning it is not disposable; is medical in nature, meaning it would not normally be used by a person without a medical condition; and plays a significant role in the provision of the medical plan of care for the patient. If a piece of equipment does not meet those three definitions the equipment will be considered to be a convenience item and will not normally be covered by Medicare or other third-party payers. For example, a shower chair for a hemiplegic patient is durable and plays a role in the provision of care for the patient, but it is normally used by persons without a medical condition. This item is then referred to as a convenience item and is not covered by Medicare. DME used in the home has definite similarities to equipment used in a hospital or nursing facility, but usually is lighter in weight, simpler to use and more esthetic in nature. DME is a significant element of a total home nursing care plan. Without DME the care of the patient would be very difficult, if not impossible. It is important for the nurse in the home to be aware of the following points regarding DME:
   1. Types of equipment
   2. Equipment features and general uses
   3. Care planning related to integrating the equipment into the plan of care
   4. Safety considerations and troubleshooting
   5. Infection control (universal precautions are always utilized)
   6. Documentation (unless otherwise stated, should include components below)
      a. Documentation of medical necessity is done when DME is first ordered and then every 60 days thereafter.

b. The physician is responsible for completing the certificate of medical necessity; however, the nurse observes the patient's functional status in the home and documents changes in function.
c. When completing a report for the patient's physician, include the fact that the patient is using DME, for how long it is anticipated that the patient will continue to need the DME, and other pertinent information that will be useful in determining the ongoing needs of the patient.
   7. Reimbursement considerations: Third-party payers usually follow the guidelines established by Medicare, but each case should be considered on its own merit.
B. Types of and management of DME: Since there are various models of the same types of equipment and there are variations in equipment usage, always follow the manufacturers' instructions and all equipment warnings when using medical devices. If instructions are not available or there are any problems with the equipment, contact the DME dealer for assistance. Part of the expectation of a DME company is that home care personnel are specially trained in the care and use of a specific type of equipment and that someone is available for assistance.
   1. Wheelchairs (WCs): Styles and types can be standard, motorized, or customized and come in various sizes; they also have features that make them useful for specific patient conditions. The best way to obtain a WC for a patient in the home is to call a reputable DME company and describe the needs of the patient; examples of information: height, weight, and girth measurements of the patient; and potential uses of the WC. Obtain measurements of all doorways through which the WC must pass, and give this information to the dealer.
      a. Equipment features and general uses: outside width depends on the style of armrests; removable armrests make the WC narrower, and fixed armrests make it wider.
         (1) WC size: To measure a patient for width, seat the patient on a platform or chair and measure the distance from one hip to the other, and add 2 inches; the distance should be as narrow as possible but wide enough to insert a hand between the patient's hips and the sides of the WC. Standard widths of a chair are:

- (a) Slim: inside width 14 inches, outside width 20½ inches
- (b) Narrow: inside width 14 to 16 inches, outside width 22 to 24 inches
- (c) Standard: inside width 18 inches, outside width 24 to 24½ inches
- (d) Wide: inside width 20 to 24 inches, outside width 28 to 32 inches
- (e) Custom: if a patient is too large to fit in a wide chair, contact the DME company for advice. A special chair may be required.

(2) WC models
- (a) Standard: most common adult WC; features a seat and back with fixed arms
- (b) Low-seat hemichair: similar to a standard WC, but the seat is lower, allowing feet to touch floor. The patient can then use the feet to steer or propel the WC. Called hemichair since it can be used by hemiplegic patients.
- (c) Reclining: features the ability to recline; usually used with elevating legrests
- (d) Power: special WC designed for the patient with functional deficits that prevent independent locomotion of the WC
- (e) Pediatric reclining: especially suited to caring for children with body casts or other medical problems that require a reclining position

(3) WC accessories
- (a) Armrests: can be fixed, removable, standard, or deskarm models
- (b) Legrests: standard with footplates, or elevating with footplates
- (c) Heel loops: devices attached to the footplate that prevent the patient's foot from slipping off the footplate
- (d) Brake extensions: make it easier for the patient to engage/release the brake
- (e) Seat cushions: recommended for the patient who will be using the WC for extended periods of time; cushion height should be taken into consideration
- (f) WC tray: convenience item for the patient who will be using the WC for eating or other activities

b. Care planning
   (1) Skin care: A patient using a WC for long periods of time should have skin care as a primary nursing intervention. Inspect the skin of the coccyx, heels, and elbows frequently. If the patient has paresthesia of an arm or a leg, take care that the affected part is positioned to prevent pressure from parts of the WC and that the extremity is not in danger of being caught in the spokes of the wheel.
   (2) Transfer technique: must be safe for the patient and the person assisting in transfer. Give instructions on standing transfer, sitting transfer, or sliding-board transfer. Use of appropriate technique will prevent falls and is important in protecting the patient's skin from abrasions.
   (3) Progressive ambulation: If the patient is using a WC temporarily, devise and follow a plan for increased ambulation. The patient can easily lose muscle strength through extended use of a WC.
c. Safety considerations and troubleshooting
   (1) Practice safe transfer techniques.
   (2) Brake: Make sure the brake is on at all times when the WC is not being used to move the patient.
   (3) Physical therapy consultation should be ordered for the patient who needs to use a WC for prolonged periods of time or who needs to negotiate curbs in the course of the day.
   (4) WC: Inspect the WC periodically for integrity of the wheel assembly, security of the arms, and condition of the brake.
   (5) If the patient needs to be supported mechanically to prevent sliding out of the WC, plan a safe method for support. Commercial restraints are available for home use. Instruction on use of restraints is critical and should be based on the manufacturer's guidelines. Use of appropriate restraints is important to prevent accidental injury to the patient.
   (6) If the WC seems to be off balance or there is a loose part, do not attempt to fix it with standard tools; call the DME dealer and request that a repair person evaluate the WC. If it appears that the problem may cause injury to the patient, request a replacement until the WC can be repaired.

d. Infection control
   (1) Clean the WC regularly.
   (2) If the patient has episodes of incontinence, use protective padding to protect the seat and allow for ease in cleaning and drying the patient.
   (3) If the patient has a draining wound, clean the WC with an antiseptic wash.
e. Documentation: as stated in A.6.
f. Reimbursement considerations
   (1) Medicare has strict guidelines for reimbursement for a WC and accessories. Generally, a WC is covered if the patient's condition is such that without use of the WC the patient would be confined to bed.
   (2) Medicare does not pay for two types of locomotion devices (i.e., a WC and a walker).
   (3) A power-operated WC is covered if the patient's condition is such that a WC is medically necessary and the patient is unable to operate a manual WC.
2. Walkers, crutches, and canes: A walker is the locomotion device of choice when the patient has need for support because of a balance problem or a lack of strength problem; it can also be beneficial if the patient must ambulate to a location such as a bathroom sink and then stand to carry out a task. Crutches are used by the patient with a partial or total weight-bearing problem involving one leg. A cane is used to provide balance for the patient at risk for falls.
   a. Equipment features and general uses
      (1) Walkers: come as standard, folding, or rolling; with arm platforms; or with a combination of each feature
         (a) Rolling walker: generally used when the patient must ambulate on a carpeted surface or is too weak to pick up and move the walker
         (b) Arm platform accessory for a walker or crutch: used when injury to an arm prevents use of the arm
      (2) Crutches: some extend to under the arm and some have the base of support at the forearm
      (3) Canes: one-point, three-point, or four-point styles; selection depends on the degree of assistance needed for balance
   b. Care planning

(1) Adjust the height of the assistive device to the patient. Balance and comfort of the patient are maximal when the height of the device is about the same height as the head of the femur.
(2) Schedule activities of the patient using an assistive device so that the patient can conserve energy and still accomplish all tasks.
(3) Prepare and have readily available a method to call for emergency assistance in the event of a fall.
  c. Safety considerations and troubleshooting
(1) Measure the height of the walker, crutch, or cane so that the patient can use the device safely and with maximal benefit.
(2) Check rubber tips on the devices for cleanliness and to ensure that the tread will prevent slipping.
(3) Help the patient with ambulatory limitations to make the environment safe to minimize the chance of falls. Remove all area rugs, unnecessary furniture, and extension cords. Clean up spilled liquids immediately.
(4) Instruct the patient in how to go up and down steps using an assistive device recommended by a physical therapist.
  d. Infection control: Keep all devices clean.
  e. Documentation
(1) Since these devices are usually purchased, documentation of medical necessity is done at time of purchase.
(2) Documentation of the patient's dependence on an assistive device is one way to validate homebound status required by Medicare.
  f. Reimbursement considerations: Medicare does not cover more than one assistive device.
3. Hospital beds: A hospital bed is used for the patient who will be spending most of the day in bed, whose position needs to be changed regularly, who needs to be in a sitting position to eat, who needs to change positions frequently for pain control, who needs relief of shortness of breath, or who has other functional deficits that would make staying in a standard bed difficult.
  a. Types of hospital beds
(1) Manual
(2) Semielectric
(3) Fully electric

(4) Special beds such as "low-loss air beds" or "bead beds": used for patients with wounds that require the least amount of pressure to heal
  b. Equipment features and general uses
    (1) A manual bed is adjusted by cranks at the foot of the bed. A semielectric bed is adjusted by changing the position of the head and foot sections while the height of the bed is controlled by a manual crank. A fully electric bed allows for all positions and the height of bed to be controlled and adjusted electrically.
    (2) Accessories
      (a) Bedrails: an essential safety aid to keep the patient from falling out of bed. Bedrails can also be used by the patient for hand supports and positioning.
      (b) Mattresses: normally supplied with rented hospital beds. Several choices of mattresses or mattress overlays are available for the patient at risk for skin breakdown.
      (c) Bed boards: placed between mattress and support frame of bed; used for extra support. A bed board on an adjustable hospital bed must be hinged so the board can bend with the mattress.
      (d) Pillows: generally supplied by the patient; needed for comfort and positioning. At least four pillows should be available for a patient confined to bed who will need repositioning. The use of folded towels or blankets may result in unnecessary skin pressure caused by the folds or the density of the material itself.
  c. Care planning
    (1) Reposition frequently a patient confined to bed for long periods of time. As early as possible, provide caregivers with instruction in how to reposition.
    (2) If the patient has a functional deficit of an arm or a leg, a physical therapy consultation may be needed for bed mobility instructions and for bed-to-chair, or bed-to-standing transfers.
    (3) Restraints for a patient in bed must be used carefully and after a full assessment of the patient's need for restraints. Educate the family/caregiver on use of restraints before the restraints are used; bedrails should be considered a form of restraint.

(4) Therapeutic beds are designed to be used by patients with high risk of skin breakdown or who have wounds needing special care. If it is determined that the patient is at great risk, investigate the use of a therapeutic bed.
d. Safety considerations and troubleshooting
   (1) Provide instruction in electrical safety when an electric bed is in use.
   (2) Make sure that an emergency call method is within reach of a patient confined to bed.
   (3) Notify the local fire department and the police department about any patient confined to bed.
   (4) If an electric bed fails to operate because of an electrical malfunction, use an emergency hand crank to adjust the bed. Never attempt to fix the electric motor of the bed; unplug the bed from the electrical source and call the DME company immediately.
   (5) If the bed has an adjustable height for convenience of the caregiver, the bed should always be in lowest position when the patient is unattended.
   (6) Bedrails should be in the up position whenever the patient is unattended; however, confused patients may try to get out of bed and be harmed by the side rails.
e. Infection control
   (1) Protect the mattress from moisture and make sure that it is cleaned regularly with a disinfectant solution.
   (2) Clean all surfaces of the bed regularly. Unplug an electric bed before cleaning, to prevent electrical shock.
f. Documentation: as stated in A.6.
g. Reimbursement considerations
   (1) Medicare usually covers a hospital bed if the patient is confined to bed for long periods of time. There are specific types of regulations regarding which type of bed will be covered. Medicare does not cover a semielectric bed for convenience of the caregiver; the patient must be able to use the controls independently.
   (2) Formula for rent-versus-purchase option for expensive DME that may be used for long periods of time: If total rental costs of a piece of equipment will exceed cost of the equipment, a purchase may be negotiated. Encourage the patient to discuss the option with the DME company. A

certificate of medical necessity completed by the physician is important in this decision.
4. Commodes and bathroom aids: A commode is a device that serves as a portable toilet; if it is used at the bedside it is considered to be a piece of medical equipment. Bathroom aids consist of a variety of equipment used in the bathroom and allow the patient more independence and safety.
   a. Equipment features and general uses
      (1) Commode styles: stationary, drop-arm, transport, chair, and styles that can be used alone or placed over a standard toilet; style selected will depend on needs of the patient
      (2) Bathtub bench styles: tub seats, tub seats with backs, tub transfer benches, and mechanically assisted models for the patient who has difficulty standing
      (3) Safety rails: available for attachment to a wall or to the side of the bathtub
      (4) Toilet safety equipment: raised toilet seats, toilet safety rails, or over-the-toilet commodes
   b. Care planning
      (1) Select safety devices carefully for a patient with functional limitations. If the patient is dependent on a device for balance, the device should be properly installed both from a mechanical perspective and from a positioning perspective. Consultation with an occupational therapist or a physical therapist is important for the patient who needs assistive devices because of an injury or neurologic problem.
   c. Safety considerations and troubleshooting
      (1) Consider the amount of equipment ordered for a patient's room. Multiple pieces of equipment may make the room cluttered and increase the chance that the patient will trip.
   d. Infection control
      (1) Empty commodes on a regular basis.
      (2) Clean all surfaces of commodes and bathroom aids regularly with a disinfectant solution.
   e. Documentation: as stated in A.6.
   f. Reimbursement considerations
      (1) Most bathroom aid equipment is not covered by Medicare; it is considered a convenience item used for a nonmedical purpose.

(2) Commodes are covered by Medicare if the patient is confined to bed or room.
5. Trapeze and patient lifters: An overhead trapeze can be either attached to the bed or freestanding. A patient lifter is a mechanical device designed to lift/move the patient with little physical effort.
   a. Equipment features and general uses
      (1) An overhead trapeze is useful for the patient who must change positions frequently and has lower extremity weakness; it allows the patient to move independently and helps prevent sheering trauma to the patient's skin. The trapeze also serves as an assistive device for the caregiver, since the patient can participate in bed mobility more easily.
      (2) A patient lifter is usually used for transfer of the patient from bed to chair; it utilizes a sling placed under the patient and a hydraulic lifting mechanism that is activated by a crank or a pumping handle. The patient is lifted up out of bed; the lifter can then be moved and positioned over a chair, the hydraulic mechanism released, and the patient gently lowered into the chair.
   b. Care planning
      (1) Education on use of the patient lifter is critical for safety of both patient and caregiver; manufacturer's instructions should be used for details on how to attach the sling to the apparatus and how to move the lifter once the patient is lifted.
      (2) Education on placement of the sling also is important for safety in transfer and protection of the patient's skin.
   c. Safety considerations and troubleshooting
      (1) Check the integrity of the lifting mechanism and the trapeze before use.
      (2) Prepare the surface to which patient is to be moved before the sling is placed.
      (3) Keep floors dry and as clutter-free as possible.
      (4) Adjust the height of the trapeze bar so that the patient can reach it with ease.
      (5) Check a floor-standing trapeze to be sure that the floor-stabilizing legs are positioned under the trapeze extension bar.
   d. Infection control

(1) Clean all surfaces regularly with a disinfectant solution.
(2) Protect the sling used for the patient lifter if the patient is incontinent; clean it regularly.
  e. Documentation: Use of assistive devices for patient transfer is one way to document ongoing needs of the patient.
  f. Reimbursement considerations
    (1) Trapeze bars are usually covered by Medicare if the patient is confined to bed and needs it to sit up because of a respiratory condition, to change body position for other medical reasons, or to get into and out of bed.
    (2) Patient lifters are covered if it is determined that periodic transfer into and out of bed is necessary to effect improvement or to prevent further deterioration of the patient's condition.
6. Respiratory care equipment
  a. Types of equipment
    (1) Oxygen systems: Because of the variety, the nurse is urged to become familiar with the specific type of oxygen system used.
    (2) Ventilators: Home models are less complicated than those used in a hospital, since the patient is usually medically stable and ventilatory needs are identified.
    (3) Suction machines: used when patient needs assistance with clearing the airway
    (4) Apnea monitors: for patients at risk for episodes of apnea that require immediate intervention
  b. Equipment features and general uses
    (1) Oxygen is usually delivered through a plastic tube attached to an oxygen source.
      (a) Oxygen concentrator: a device that removes dust particles and nitrogen from room air and then concentrates and stores the remaining oxygen
      (b) Liquid oxygen canisters: store oxygen at very cold temperatures in a thermos-like container
      (c) Oxygen cylinders: store oxygen under pressure
    (2) Type of oxygen delivery is decided after needs of the patient are assessed and amount of oxygen needed is established.

Durable Medical Equipment 77

(3) Portable oxygen devices: used for patients who must travel from one place to another and cannot tolerate being without oxygen for duration of the trip
(4) Ventilators: variety of devices considered to be ventilatory assistive devices. Distinction must be made between needs of the ventilator-dependent patient and the self-ventilating patient.
  (a) Full ventilator-type devices provide the patient with breathing assistance and oxygen (e.g., a device connected to the patient's tracheostomy tube for extended periods of time).
  (b) Assistive devices provide oxygen and humidity under external pressure (e.g., a machine that provides continuous positive airway pressure [CPAP machine]).
(5) Suction machines: all work on the same principle. Differences in machines usually are limited to power source, either electrical or battery operated, and the turn-on switch.
(6) Apnea monitors: variety of models but essentially operate on principle that alarms will sound if the patient's respiratory and pulse rates drop below rates set on the machine. The apnea monitor is connected to the patient by electrode-type devices or bands attached around chest; some models have printouts so trends in breathing patterns can be monitored. Audible alarms sound when the respiratory rate drops below the setting.

c. Care planning
  (1) The patient needing oxygen can become independent in self-care.
  (2) The DME company plays a vital role in managing care needs of patients with respiratory problems and should be called upon during planning of care for these patients.
  (3) Adults responsible for caring for a patient on an apnea monitor must be aware that the monitor is a safety device and should not be the sole method for monitoring the patient.

d. Safety considerations
  (1) Make sure that a backup source of ventilation or oxygen is always available. A rebreather bag or a second ventilator,

depending on the policy of the DME company, should be available.
(2) Notify the local fire department and the police department.
(3) Investigate emergency warning services through the 911 system.
(4) If a suction machine is not used regularly, check it to be sure that it is in working condition by inserting the suction catheter into a glass of water. Turning on the machine to hear the motor does not necessarily indicate that connections are secure and that there is suction.
(5) Never turn off alarms on a ventilator or an apnea-monitoring device because of danger of forgetting to turn them back on.
(6) Stress the dangers of smoking by patient or family members or guests when any device using oxygen is in use.

e. Infection control
(1) Cleaning of equipment and changing of tubing at prescribed intervals are vital. A warm, moist, oxygen-enhanced environment is conducive to bacterial growth and a dangerous source of infection.
(2) Care must be taken to clean all equipment. Do not reuse one-time-use equipment or allow equipment to lie around uncovered.
(3) Because of risk of airborne infections, barrier masks may be needed.
(4) Exercise caution in use of some chemical disinfectants because of potential for dangerous, even toxic, interactions between disinfectants and equipment.
(5) Proper storage of cleaned, reusable equipment is important.

f. Documentation: as stated in A.6. and as follows:
(1) Document the need for oxygen by blood gas analysis (usually monitored and documented by the DME company).
(2) Follow the protocol established for documenting settings, patient's response, or other clinical data. Document collaboration with the DME staff regarding the patient's condition.

g. Reimbursement considerations
(1) Oxygen: Medicare usually covers oxygen if deemed medically necessary on a continuous basis.

(2) Coverage of ventilators: Medicare covers cost for treatment of neuromuscular diseases, thoracic restrictive diseases, and chronic respiratory failure consequent to chronic obstructive pulmonary disease.
(3) Suction machines: Medicare covers cost if machines are deemed to be medically necessary.
7. Blood glucose monitoring machines: used by patients with diabetes mellitus or those receiving total parenteral nutrition
   a. Equipment features and general uses
      (1) Most machines run on batteries and use test strips designed for each device.
      (2) A sharp puncture device may be required to obtain blood sample, usually from end of finger. Some newer devices do not require puncture of the skin. Check the various models available to obtain one with features best suited for the patient.
      (3) The test usually takes 2 to 3 minutes.
   b. Care planning
      (1) Instruct the patient to record all readings and to report abnormal test results to the physician immediately.
      (2) If accuracy of the test is a concern, the nurse should perform test or observe the patient's technique on a regular basis.
      (3) Remember that blood glucose monitoring is only one clinical means for adjusting insulin requirements of the patient; clinical signs/symptoms and dietary intake also should be monitored.
   c. Safety considerations
      (1) Store the device and stylets in a safe place.
      (2) If there is clinical indication that blood sugar is high and the reading on the device is low, the patient may need to have a clinical laboratory blood test.
      (3) Blood glucose monitors need to be calibrated for accuracy on a regular basis.
   d. Infection control
      (1) Discard sharps used to puncture the skin in a sharps container.
      (2) Discard all tissues contaminated with blood in a closed container.

e. Documentation
   (1) Recording of blood glucose results, changes in insulin dosage, and any clinical symptoms should be reviewed regularly with the patient and information communicated to the physician.
   (2) Capability of the patient or family member in use of the device should be documented.
f. Reimbursement considerations
   (1) Medicare covers the device if the patient is an unstable diabetic and can use the device alone or with help of family or friends.

8. Pressure aids
   a. Types of equipment
      (1) Pressure aids: available for beds, WCs, standard chairs, and as specially cushioned products for heels, feet, and elbows
      (2) Also other products: footboards, foot cradles, and cervical pillows
   b. Equipment features and general uses
      (1) Pressure-relieving mattresses: sheepskin, synthetic sheepskin, convoluted foam (egg crate), gel, water flotation, and alternating air flotation. Selection of the product depends on severity of skin breakdown or risk for skin breakdown.
      (2) Pressure-relieving WC cushions: come in a variety of styles/thicknesses, including t-foam cushion, gel flotation cushion, rubber-air tube cushion (Roho), or simple foam cushion
      (3) Heel and elbow protectors: strap-on and slip-on models
      (4) Footboards: used to hold bed linen off patient's feet, thus preventing pressure from weight of linen rubbing on the feet; also allow patient to rest feet against board to help prevent footdrop
      (5) Foot cradle: keeps bed linen from resting on patient's feet; usually used when the patient needs to have feet elevated or when area to be protected is near the knee
   c. Care planning
      (1) Regardless of number or items or quality of pressure-relieving equipment provided for the patient, the single most important element of care planning is frequent moving and repositioning of the patient.

Durable Medical Equipment 81

   (2) Frequent skin inspection and skin care are necessary. Heel and elbow protectors should be removed and reapplied so that skin care can be provided and adequate inspection of the skin can be done.
   (3) Pressure-relieving mattresses work best when the amount of padding between mattress and patient is limited. Incontinence pads and other waterproof padding should be limited to an amount needed to prevent soiling of the mattress.
  d. Safety considerations
   (1) Alternating-air-pressure mattresses are connected to an electrical outlet and should be cared for in the same way as any other electrical device.
   (2) Pins or other sharp objects should be kept away from pressure-relieving mattresses that use fluid or air.
  e. Infection control
   (1) Clean all pressure-relieving products regularly.
   (2) If a disinfectant solution is used, rinse the device thoroughly to prevent skin irritation.
   (3) A grossly soiled egg crate mattress may need to be replaced.
  f. Documentation
   (1) Documentation of medical necessity is usually done at time of purchase.
   (2) Documentation of skin condition and the fact that a pressure-relieving device is being used should be included in the medical record.
  g. Reimbursement considerations
   (1) Medicare will cover pressure-relieving products if the risk for decubitus ulcers or the existence of a decubitus ulcer is documented; there must be a relevant diagnosis (e.g., paraplegia, decubitus ulcer, or other risk factor).
   (2) Usually only one purchase of a pressure-relieving item is covered, so it is important to purchase the appropriate mattress or cushion on the first order.
9. Special equipment: various types of specialized equipment that formerly were available only in a hospital; equipment such as sequential compression devices, continuous passive motion devices, and hyperbaric chamber devices are now available. The types of DME devices that will become available in the future are unknown; however, in order to incorporate new technology into

home care, the nurse should use categories listed for each type of equipment to learn as much about the equipment as possible. By using the following outline, the nurse can learn what is necessary in order to care safely for a patient with special equipment needs. The best source to answer questions is the DME company, which has a trained staff and manufacturer's guidelines available, and is required to participate in patient and staff education.
   a. Type of equipment: What is the purpose of the equipment?
   b. Equipment features and general uses
      (1) How is the equipment used for, by, or on the patient?
      (2) Is disposable equipment also required?
   c. Care planning
      (1) How does the equipment affect the other care needs of the patient?
      (2) How will the equipment make other care easier for the patient or caregiver?
      (3) What are the outcome measures that need to be incorporated into a care plan?
      (4) What education on uses, side effects, complications, or untoward effects needs to be given to the patient and caregiver?
      (5) What observations or interventions need to be made?
   d. Safety considerations
      (1) Is electrical safety an issue?
      (2) Can the equipment injure the patient in any way?
      (3) What can happen if the equipment malfunctions?
   e. Infection control: Do universal precautions cover all aspects of infection control for the device?
   f. Documentation
      (1) What needs to be documented about observations, interventions, or other aspects of nursing care that are different as a result of the device?
      (2) How is medical necessity documented?
   g. Reimbursement considerations
      (1) Will Medicare or the patients' third-party payer cover the cost of the device for this patient? If so, for how long and under what conditions?
      (2) Will nursing visits be reimbursed if they are made in relation to care for a patient using this specific device?

(3) If there are disposable items related to the piece of equipment, will the patient have to pay for them?
(4) What is the cost of electricity for use of the device?

STUDY QUESTIONS AND EXERCISES

1. Mrs. Jones has been home for a few days and, because of her deteriorating medical condition, now requires a wheelchair. Her physician has completed the certificate of medical necessity and you are ready to call the DME company. What information do you need before you call the company?
2. You are caring for a patient who is using oxygen at home. You are concerned about safety for the patient. What safety considerations should be taught and documented?
3. The patient you are caring for is at risk for skin breakdown. You need to select a pressure-relieving system for the patient. What needs to be considered in making the correct choice for your patient?
4. List appropriate steps to be taken and to be taught to the caregiver regarding infection control.

BIBLIOGRAPHY

Birmingham, J. 1994. *Discharge planning for case managers.* Palos Verdes Estates, Calif.: Academy Medical Systems.

Health Industries Distributors Associations Educational Foundation. 1990. *Customer service manual for home medical equipment.* Alexandria, Va.

Humphrey, C. 1986. *Home care nursing handbook.* Norwalk, Conn.: Appleton-Century-Crofts.

Jaffe, M. and L. Skidmore-Roth. 1993. *Home health nursing care plans.* St. Louis: Mosby-Year Book, Inc.

Johnston, J.E., and B. Clark. 1991. Orientation to home care: Maximizing Medicare reimbursement. *Home Healthcare Nurse* 8, no. 1:45–50.

Rice, R., and J.U. Jorden. 1992. Infection control education. *Caring* 11, no. 4:54–59.

Webb, L., and S. Berquist. 1991. Standardized care plans for home care. *Home Healthcare Nurse* 8, no. 6:21–29.

Nursing Management of the Patient with Cardiovascular Disease

Part III

11

Coronary Artery Disease/Angina Pectoris

Debra Finley-Cottone and Brenda Stefanik Bartock

A. Incidence of coronary artery disease (CAD): CAD is the leading cause of death in the United States; 6.3 million Americans have CAD.
B. Pathophysiology
   1. Epicardial coronary arteries are highly susceptible to intimal atherosclerotic process.
   2. Fats are deposited in and under the intimal layer (inner lining of arteries).
   3. Gradually fibrous plaque (atheroma) develops (contains lipids, macrophages, collagen, and a proliferation of smooth muscle cells), which reduces the caliber of the arterial lumen.
   4. Plaque can then calcify, hemorrhage, and/or have platelet accumulation (further narrows the vessel).
   5. Process is ongoing, finally resulting in complete arterial occlusion, most frequently by thrombus formation.
   6. Symptomatology based on degree of stenosis is individual and is affected by other characteristics (e.g., presence of coronary artery spasm and/or collateral circulation).
   7. Complications/manifestations of CAD include angina, myocardial infarction (MI), congestive heart failure (CHF), dysrhythmia, and sudden cardiac death.
C. Risk factors
   1. Controllable factors
      a. Cigarette smoking
         (1) Nicotine is a cardiac stimulant (increased heart rate, increased blood pressure, increased stroke volume, increased cardiac output).

(2) Carbon monoxide decreases oxygen-carrying capacity of the blood.
(3) Elevated carbon monoxide levels decrease threshold for ventricular fibrillation.
(4) Smoking cessation significantly reduces future risk for CAD.
 b. Hypertension
  (1) Hypertensive persons have twice the risk for CAD than do normotensive persons.
  (2) Both nonpharmacologic treatment and pharmacologic treatment usually are needed for adequate blood pressure reduction.
 c. Hypercholesterolemia
  (1) Risk increases with cholesterol levels greater than 200 mg/dL.
  (2) Cholesterol intake should not exceed 200 to 300 mg/day.
  (3) Fats should be limited to 30% of daily caloric intake, and only 10% should come from saturated fats.
  (4) Elevated low-density lipoprotein (LDL) levels correlate positively with CAD risk; high-density lipoprotein (HDL) levels reduce CAD risk.
 d. Glucose intolerance: diabetes mellitus potentiates atheroma formation.

2. Uncontrollable factors
   a. Age: Incidence of CAD increases with age.
   b. Gender: CAD is more prevalent in men than in women until menopause, when the female risk rapidly increases to approach male levels.
   c. Race: Black men and women have higher death rates from CAD up to age 75, after which rates equal those of whites.
   d. Heredity
3. Contributing factors: sedentary lifestyle, personality factors, stress, obesity
4. New York Heart Association functional classification system
   a. Class I: no symptoms
   b. Class II: symptoms with ordinary physical activity
   c. Class III: symptoms with less than ordinary physical activity but no symptoms at rest
   d. Class IV: symptoms at rest

D. Angina pectoris
   1. Pathophysiology
      a. See pathophysiology for CAD.
      b. Pain occurs as a result of myocardial ischemia/hypoxia.
         (1) CAD (most commonly)
         (2) Thrombosis or embolism
         (3) Coronary artery spasm
         (4) Severe anemia
         (5) Increased myocardial workload caused by disease (e.g., aortic stenosis, tachydysrhythmia, hypertension, thyrotoxicosis)
   2. Precipitating factors
      a. Activity level: physical exertion
      b. Ingestion of large meals
      c. Emotional stress
      d. Cold temperatures
   3. Signs/symptoms
      a. Discomfort or pain may be described as pressure, tightness, heaviness, squeezing, constricting, aching, or burning.
      b. Discomfort/pain is usually located over the precordium or substernal area with radiation to jaws, neck, shoulders, arms, back, or epigastric area.
      c. Discomfort may be accompanied by shortness of breath, diaphoresis, nausea, vomiting, or anxiety.
      d. Episode usually lasts 1 minute to several minutes.
      e. Discomfort is relieved by rest, removal of the precipitator, and use of nitroglycerin.
   4. Types
      a. Stable angina: predictable pattern, no increase in frequency or severity over a period of time
      b. Unstable angina: increased frequency, severity, duration of symptoms (preinfarction or crescendo angina is a type of unstable angina that usually precedes an MI)
      c. Prinzmetal's angina (vasospastic or variant angina): occurs at rest often during night or early morning in a cyclic pattern; caused by coronary artery spasm; can occur with or without CAD
      d. Intractable angina: chronic, frequent chest discomfort unresponsive to medical intervention

5. Silent ischemia: occurs without chest discomfort
   a. Two theories
      (1) Asymptomatic episodes involve a small amount of myocardium.
      (2) Perception of pain is altered (e.g., as in diabetes mellitus, due to neurologic damage).
6. Diagnosis
   a. Patient history: chief complaint, risk factors, past medical history
   b. Electrocardiogram (ECG): presence of ischemic changes during an anginal episode
   c. Stress test: exercise, pharmacologic or mechanical testing to elicit ischemic changes on ECG
   d. Radionuclide studies: imaging of ischemic areas
   e. Holter monitoring
   f. Cardiac catheterization: definitive for location, extent, and severity of CAD
7. Assessment
   a. History of anginal episodes using disease descriptors
      (1) Location, radiation, intensity
      (2) Quality, description, course, duration
      (3) Precipitating and alleviating factors
      (4) Associated symptoms
   b. Presence of risk factors
   c. Cardiopulmonary assessment
      (1) Vital signs, heart and lung sounds
      (2) Palpitations, dizziness/syncope
      (3) Activity tolerance, fatigue, dyspnea
      (4) Skin color (pallor, cyanosis)
      (5) Jugular vein distention
      (6) Peripheral edema, pulses
      (7) Baseline ECG
8. Treatment: Minimize discrepancy between supply and demand by decreasing myocardial oxygen consumption or increasing myocardial oxygen supply.
   a. Nonpharmacologic intervention
      (1) Pace activity below anginal threshold.
      (2) Encourage and supervise regular exercise below anginal threshold.

(3) Suggest a diet to achieve or maintain ideal weight.
(4) Encourage smoking cessation.
(5) Control hypertension.
b. Pharmacologic intervention: relief or prevention of anginal episodes
  (1) Nitrates (isosorbide dinitrate, nitroglycerin, pentaerythritol tetranitrate, erythrityl tetranitrate) available for administration by sublingual, oral, transdermal, intravenous routes
    (a) Sublingual nitrates: for relief of acute attacks (repeat every 5 minutes for 15 minutes; seek medical attention if relief not obtained after three tablets); may be taken prophylactically in situations likely to cause attacks
    (b) Longer-acting nitrates: for prophylaxis in long-term management
    (c) Potent coronary vasodilators: improve blood flow and oxygen supply to ischemic areas
    (d) Venodilation action: decreases preload; reduces cardiac workload and oxygen consumption
    (e) Arterial/arteriolar dilatation at high doses: reduces afterload
    (f) Indicated for stable, unstable, and vasospastic angina
    (g) Contraindication: low venous filling pressures and low diastolic arterial pressures
    (h) Side effects: headache, flushing, hypotension, dizziness, syncope, nausea, reflex tachycardia, and dermatitis with topical preparations
    (i) Nitrate tolerance: occurs when increased doses are required for desired effect; deal with by giving smallest effective dose, fewest daily doses, or in the case of the transdermal route, a nitrate-free interval of 8 to 12 hours daily (preferably at night)
  (2) Calcium-channel blockers (nifedipine, verapamil, diltiazem, nicardipine, isradipine)
    (a) Block transmembrane influx of calcium across myocardial and smooth muscle cells
    (b) Hemodynamic effects: relaxation of coronary artery smooth muscle (prevents spasm) and reduced peripheral resistance
    (c) Have negative inotropic effect

- (d) Indicated for stable, unstable, and vasospastic angina (preferred agents for vasospastic angina)
- (e) Contraindications: high degree of sinoatrial and atrioventricular block, significant heart failure, sick sinus syndrome
- (f) Side effects: dizziness, headache, flushing, pedal edema, nausea, fatigue, weakness, hypotension, bradydysrhythmias, CHF, constipation, rash (verapamil has the worst side effect profile, diltiazem the best)

(3) β-Blockers (propranolol, metoprolol, atenolol, nadolol, timolol, pindolol, acebutolol, betaxolol, labetalol); available for oral route
- (a) Inhibit $β_2$-receptors in myocardium resulting in decreased contractility, decreased cardiac output, decreased myocardial oxygen consumption
- (b) Depress sinoatrial node, automatically resulting in decreased heart rate
- (c) Inhibit $β_2$-receptor stimulation in pulmonary and vascular smooth muscle, potentially resulting in bronchospasm, peripheral vasoconstriction, and increased peripheral vascular resistance
- (d) Cardioselective β-blockers have predominately $β_1$ effects and the benefit of reduced $β_2$ effects
- (e) Indicated in treatment of angina, MI, hypertension, dysrhythmia related to catecholamine excess
- (f) Contraindications: CHF, symptomatic bradycardia, sick sinus syndrome, severe asthma, bronchospasm, severe peripheral vascular disease, insulin-dependent diabetes mellitus (masks hypoglycemic symptoms)
- (g) Side effects: bradycardia, conduction abnormalities, CHF, hypotension, worsening of peripheral vascular disease, dyspnea, bronchospasm, fatigue, weakness, nightmares, insomnia, dizziness, diarrhea, nausea, rash, impotence, decreased libido
- (h) Abrupt withdrawal of a β-blocker: avoid by slowly tapering the dose to prevent exacerbation of angina, MI, or dysrhythmia

(4) Antiplatelet agents (aspirin, dipyridamole)

             (a) Action: decrease platelet aggregation
             (b) Dipyridamole: use in conjunction with aspirin, as it is an ineffective agent alone
             (c) Proven to decrease incidence of mortality from MI
             (d) Aspirin side effects: gastrointestinal disturbances, tinnitus, hepatotoxicity, renal insufficiency, rash, anemia
          (5) Procedures to provide symptom relief and prolongation of life in selected patients
             (a) Percutaneous transluminal coronary angioplasty (PTCA): nonsurgical invasive procedures; directional coronary atherectomy; stent; percutaneous transluminal coronary rotational atherectomy
             (b) Coronary artery bypass surgery
9. Patient teaching
   a. Disease process
   b. Symptom management
      (1) Proper response to chest discomfort (nitroglycerin sublingually, one tablet every 5 minutes up to three in 15 minutes; alert emergency medical response system if not relieved after three tablets)
      (2) How and when to alert emergency medical response system
      (3) Reporting change in frequency or severity of angina
      (4) Prophylactic use of nitroglycerin in situation likely to cause angina
   c. Medications: action, use, side effects, importance of compliance
   d. Risk factor reduction
   e. Moderate, supervised plan of exercise with physician approval
   f. Diet
      (1) Cholesterol intake: limit to 300 mg/day
      (2) Fat intake: limit to 30% of daily caloric intake, saturated fats to 10% of daily caloric intake
   g. Postprocedure activity
   h. Routine medical follow-up with primary physician
   i. Angina diary: may be helpful assessment tool

STUDY QUESTIONS AND EXERCISES

1. Describe the atherosclerotic process that leads to CAD.
2. List the controllable and uncontrollable risk factors for CAD.
3. Identify five processes that can result in anginal pain from MI.
4. What four classes of drugs are used in the treatment of angina? How do they work?
5. Outline a teaching plan for a patient discharged home with a new diagnosis of unstable angina.

BIBLIOGRAPHY

Calloway, C. 1990. Zeroing in on chest pain. *Nursing '90* 20, no. 4:44–45.

Castelli, W.P. 1983. Cardiovascular disease and multifactorial risk: Challenge of the 1980's. *American Heart Journal* 106:1191.

Chiro, A., and D.G. Curtis. 1988. Asymptomatic coronary artery disease. *Heart and Lung* 17, no. 2:144–149.

Chyun, D., et al. 1991. Silent myocardial ischemia. *Focus on Critical Care* 18, no. 4:295–306.

Goodman, D., et al. 1988. Expert panel on detection, evaluation, and treatment of high blood cholesterol in adults. Bethesda, Md.: NIH publication no. 88-2925.

Kalmar, J. 1990. Nitrate tolerance: A new look at an old problem. *Focus on Critical Care* 17, no. 5:407–409.

Kinney, M., et al. 1991. *Comprehensive cardiac care*. St. Louis: Mosby-Year Book, Inc.

National health and nutrition examination survey II and the American Hospital Association. 1991.

Nurse review: A clinical update system 1. 1989. Springhouse, Pa.: Springhouse Corporation.

Rochester General Hospital, Division of Surgical Nursing. 1992. *Cardiac surgery—A guide for patient and family education*. Rochester, N.Y.

Underhill, S., et al. 1989. *Cardiac nursing*. Philadelphia: J.B. Lippincott Co.

12

Myocardial Infarction

Debra Finley-Cottone and Brenda Stefanik Bartock

A. Pathophysiology of myocardial infarction (MI)
   1. Usually begins with coronary artery disease (CAD) (see Chapter 11)
      a. Blood rushes past roughened plaques
      b. Platelets aggregate
      c. Thrombus forms, occluding the artery
   2. Other causes
      a. Trauma to coronary arteries
      b. Spasm of coronary artery
      c. Emboli
      d. Thyrotoxicosis
   3. Imbalance between oxygen supply and demand results in
      a. Ischemia
      b. Injury
      c. Infarction: cell death/necrosis within 4 hours if adequate blood flow not restored
   4. Location and size of MI depend on
      a. Artery involved
      b. Size and location of lesion
      c. Extent of collateral blood flow to area
      d. Transmural MI: involves full thickness of myocardium
      e. Nontransmural MI (non–Q wave MI): may involve smaller amount of myocardium
      f. Usually left ventricular (anterior, septal, inferior, lateral, or posterior wall)
   5. Pathologic changes
      a. Eight to ten days after an MI: phagocytosis of necrotic tissue (wall is at thinnest point)

    b. Three to four weeks after an MI: scar tissue develops
    c. First few weeks: collateral circulation increases
B. Signs and symptoms
  1. Chest pain
    a. Usually severe but may be mild or absent in some cases
    b. Substernal with radiation to neck, jaws, epigastrium, shoulder blades, arms
    c. Described as constant heaviness, pressure, constriction, squeezing, crushing, burning sensation
    d. Persists for 30 minutes or longer; not relieved with rest or nitroglycerin sublingually
  2. Shortness of breath
  3. Diaphoresis
  4. Nausea or vomiting
  5. Severe anxiety or feeling of "impending doom"
  6. Weakness
  7. Skin: may be cool and clammy or cyanotic
  8. Dysrhythmias
C. Diagnosis
  1. Patient history
  2. Presenting signs and symptoms
  3. Pathologic electrocardiographic (ECG) changes:
    a. ST segment elevation
    b. T wave inversion
    c. Significant Q waves with transmural MI
    d. Non–Q wave MI: cannot be diagnosed by ECG (changes nonspecific)
  4. Laboratory findings
    a. Serial serum enzymes
      (1) Creatine phosphokinase (CPK), serum glutamic-oxaloacetic transaminase (SGOT), lactate dehydrogenase (LDH) elevations
      (2) CPK-MB and LDH_2 isoenzymes: most specific for cardiac muscle damage
    b. Elevated white blood cell count
    c. Elevated erythrocyte sedimentation rate
  5. Radionuclide imaging methods
    a. Thallium Tl 201 scintigraphy

b. Technetium Tc 99m pyrophosphate imaging
c. Dipyridamole: Tl 201 scintigraphy
6. Echocardiography
D. Complications
1. Dysrhythmia and conduction defects
2. Congestive heart failure (CHF) and pulmonary edema
3. Papillary muscle rupture causing mitral insufficiency
4. Cardiogenic shock
5. Thromboembolism
6. Ventricular aneurysm
7. Ventricular rupture
8. Pericarditis: caused by irritation of cellular debris and exudates from infarcted area
   a. Signs/symptoms: typical chest pain; low-grade fever; ECG changes; pericardial friction rub
9. Dressler's syndrome: autoimmune response occurring 1 day to 3 months after MI
   a. Signs/symptoms: fever; chest pain; shortness of breath; ECG changes
   b. May accompany pericarditis, pleurisy
10. Persistent pain and extension
    a. Non–Q wave MI: has higher risk of reinfarction
    b. Survival rates after extension: lower for non–Q wave than Q wave MIs
E. Treatment
1. Reduce or eliminate pain: use of oxygen, intravenous nitrates, intravenous morphine sulfate
2. Control dysrhythmias and conduction defects: intravenous lidocaine hydrochloride or other antiarrhythmics; atropine or temporary pacemakers
3. Preservation and salvage of viable myocardial tissue
   a. Thrombolytic therapy
      (1) Streptokinase
      (2) Urokinase
      (3) Recombinant tissue plasminogen activator (RT-PA)
      (4) Anistreplase
   b. Emergency percutaneous transluminal coronary angioplasty (PTCA)

        c. Emergency coronary artery bypass surgery
    4. Prevention of future MI
        a. Aspirin daily
        b. β-Blocker (metoprolol tartrate [Lopressor]): reduces mortality post-MI
        c. Risk factor reduction
    5. Control complications: CHF; persistent dysrhythmias
F. Home care management
    1. Assess for further myocardial ischemia.
        a. Report chest pain.
        b. Use a 12-lead ECG at home.
    2. Assess for pump failure; report abnormal findings to physician.
        a. Evidence of fluid retention: edema, weight gain greater than 3 to 5 pounds in 1 week
        b. Abnormal breath sounds; crackles
        c. Jugular vein distention
        d. Shortness of breath, orthopnea, paroxysmal nocturnal dyspnea
        e. Increased weakness or fatigue
        f. Heart sounds: new murmur or S_3/S_4 gallop
        g. Oliguria or nocturia
    3. Assess for changes in heart rhythm and rate: less than 60 beats per minute or more than 100 beats per minute.
    4. Establish a bowel regimen to prevent vasovagal stimulation from straining.
    5. Provide emotional support to patient and caregivers.
        a. Role changes/relationships
        b. Fears
        c. Intimacy
        d. Financial concerns
    6. Assess medication effectiveness.
        a. Absence of chest discomfort
        b. Blood pressure and heart rate in desired range
        c. Absence or control of CHF
        d. Absence or control of dysrhythmias
    7. Teach the patient/caregiver about the condition.
        a. Disease process
        b. Risk factor identification and reduction

c. Symptom management
   (1) Chest pain
   (2) Shortness of breath
   (3) Edema and/or weight gain
   (4) Constipation
d. Problems to report
   (1) Chest pain
   (2) Shortness of breath
   (3) Palpitations
   (4) Dizziness or fainting
   (5) Swelling or edema
   (6) Weight gain
e. Medications: actions, use, side effects, importance of compliance
f. Diet: low cholesterol, low fat, low sodium as ordered by physician
g. Postprocedure activity
h. Activity progression
i. Sexuality and resumption of intercourse (usually when able to climb one or two flights of stairs without symptoms, but should check with physician)
j. Postinfarction weakness and depression
k. Community resources
8. Develop a rehabilitation plan with physician's approval and guidance.

STUDY QUESTIONS AND EXERCISES

1. Identify the most common cause of acute MI.
2. Location and size of MI are determined by what factors?
3. List three methods of detecting an acute MI.
4. Identify six potential complications of acute MI.
5. Outline a teaching plan for a patient on home care after an MI.
6. List signs and symptoms that would alert you to complications post-MI.

BIBLIOGRAPHY

Cardiovascular care handbook. 1986. Springhouse, Pa.: Springhouse Corporation.

Kinney, M., et al. 1991. *Comprehensive cardiac care.* St. Louis: Mosby-Year Book, Inc.

Leddy, K.G., and C. Helgenberg. 1989. Myocardial infarction: Assessing the patient in the family setting. *Home Health Care Nurse* 7, no. 3:28–31.

Lewis, R.S. 1992. Clinical implications on non-Q wave (subendocardial) myocardial infarctions. *Focus on Critical Care* 19, no. 1:29–33.

Nurse review: A clinical update system 1. 1989. Springhouse, Pa.: Springhouse Corporation.

13
Congestive Heart Failure

Annette C. Strickland

A. Definition of congestive heart failure (CHF): state in which the heart can no longer pump an adequate supply of blood (cardiac output) to meet the demands of the body
B. Etiology: can result from conditions that cause
   1. Volume overload (e.g., overtransfusion)
   2. Pressure overload (e.g., hypertension)
   3. Myocardial dysfunction (e.g., cardiomyopathy)
   4. Filling disorders (e.g., restrictive pericarditis)
   5. Increased metabolic demand (e.g., fever)
C. Pathophysiology
   1. Compensatory mechanisms to decrease cardiac output
      a. Sympathetic nervous system stimulation: tachycardia
      b. Activation of renin-angiotensin system: sodium and water retention, vasoconstriction
      c. Ventricular hypertrophy: increased contractility
      d. Frank-Starling mechanism: increased preload
   2. Decompensation
      a. Left ventricular failure: pulmonary congestion
      b. Right ventricular failure: systemic venous congestion
D. Clinical manifestations: left and right ventricles can fail separately; left ventricular failure most often precedes right ventricular failure
   1. Left-sided failure: pulmonary congestion
      a. Dyspnea
      b. Cough
      c. Fatigue
      d. Orthopnea
      e. Paroxysmal nocturnal dyspnea

       f. Crackles
       g. Tachycardia with S_3
       h. Anxiety
       i. Restlessness
       j. Confusion
    2. Right-sided failure: systemic venous congestion
       a. Peripheral edema
       b. Weight gain
       c. Hepatomegaly
       d. Jugular vein distention
       e. Ascites
       f. Nocturia
       g. Anorexia
E. Diagnostic evaluation
    1. Clinical signs and symptoms
    2. Electrocardiogram
    3. Chest X-ray
    4. Echocardiogram
    5. Pulmonary artery catheter
F. Medical management
    1. Pharmacologic therapy
       a. Digoxin: positive inotropic action
       b. Diuretic therapy: promotes excretion of sodium and water through kidneys (loop diuretics, thiazide diuretics)
       c. Angiotensin-converting enzyme (ACE) inhibitors: prevent vasoconstriction and sodium and water retention
       d. Vasodilator therapy: reduces afterload and/or preload
       e. Dobutamine: positive inotropic agent
    2. Rest
    3. Diet therapy: sodium restriction
    4. Heart transplant for end-stage disease
G. Nursing management
    1. Pharmacologic therapy
       a. Digoxin
          (1) Teach patient/family to monitor pulse rate.
          (2) Teach signs/symptoms of digoxin toxicity: anorexia, nausea, vomiting, visual disturbances, bradycardia.
          (3) Monitor potassium levels.
       b. Diuretic therapy

        (1) Administer early in the morning.
        (2) Teach patient to weigh daily.
        (3) Teach signs/symptoms of hypokalemia: muscle weakness and cramps.
        (4) Replace potassium.
    c. ACE inhibitors
        (1) Monitor blood pressure.
        (2) Monitor for side effect: dry cough.
    d. Vasodilator therapy
        (1) Monitor blood pressure.
        (2) Monitor for side effects: postural hypotension and headache.
    e. Dobutamine
        (1) Administer via vascular access in home setting.
        (2) Monitor hemodynamic status.
        (3) Monitor for infection at site.
2. Activity and exercise
    a. Assist patient to recognize activity limitations.
    b. Teach patient to space activities of daily living, resting after each.
    c. Teach patient to conserve energy and to plan rest periods.
3. Dietary modifications
    a. Assess compliance with prescribed sodium restrictions.
    b. Utilize resources to assist patient and family in meal planning to maintain adequate nutrition.
4. Management of sleep disturbances
    a. Teach patient to take a diuretic early in the morning to minimize sleep disturbance.
    b. Elevate head of the bed for sleep.
    c. Teach patient relaxation techniques.
5. Teach patient to recognize symptoms to report to the physician.
    a. Any increase in shortness of breath or fatigue with previously tolerated activities
    b. Weight gain of 2 pounds or more overnight
    c. Edema in feet and ankles
    d. Edema in hands
    e. Feeling of abdominal fullness
    f. Persistent cough without other symptoms of cold or flu
6. Provide psychosocial support for patient/family.

STUDY QUESTIONS AND EXERCISES

1. Develop a teaching plan for a patient on a moderate sodium-restricted diet. What resources would you utilize?
2. Mrs. Smith is a 70-year-old patient with a new diagnosis of CHF. She is returning to her home after a brief hospitalization. She lives alone in a two-story house. Develop activity guidelines to assist her at home.
3. Mr. Hall is newly diagnosed with CHF. He has been sent home on the following oral medications: digoxin 0.25 mg daily; furosemide 20 mg daily; enalapril maleate 10 mg twice daily. Develop a teaching plan to assist him in managing his medications at home.

BIBLIOGRAPHY

Ignatavicius, D.D., and M.V. Bayne. 1991. *Medical-surgical nursing*. Philadelphia: W.B. Saunders Co.

Letterer, R.A., et al. 1992. Learning to live with congestive heart failure. *Nursing '92* 22, no. 5:34–41.

Sohl, L.L., and M.M. Applefeld. 1992. A new direction for dobutamine. *Nursing '92* 22, no. 10:42–43.

Wright, S.M. 1990. Pathophysiology of congestive heart failure. *Journal of Cardiovascular Nursing* 4, no. 3:1–16.

14

Hypertension

Sandra L. McClain and Kathy J. Morgan

A. Definition of hypertension: persistent elevation of systolic blood pressure (BP) equal to or greater than 140 mm Hg; a diastolic BP equal to or greater than 90 mm Hg. Hypertension may be diagnosed after two consecutive high BP readings; BP should be taken in both arms.
   1. Systolic hypertension: loss of elastic tissue and arteriosclerotic changes occurring in the large blood vessels (e.g., aorta)
   2. Diastolic hypertension: amount of pressure exerted on arterial wall of small arteries (e.g., pressure caused by contraction of left ventricle)
   3. Major risk factor in cardiovascular disease; most common cause of cerebrovascular accident (CVA)
B. Pathophysiology
   1. Primary (essential) hypertension may result from
      a. Release of epinephrine: increases rate/force of heart contractions, increasing cardiac output and BP
      b. Renin-angiotensin-aldosterone system
         (1) Renal perfusion drops: kidneys release renin
         (2) Renin: activates angiotensin I
         (3) Angiotensin I: converted to angiotensin II
            (a) Constricts blood vessels
            (b) Stimulates adrenal cortex to release aldosterone
         (4) Aldosterone: causes sodium and water retention by kidneys
            (a) Increases intravascular volume
            (b) Increases arterial resistance
   2. Secondary hypertension: develops as a result of other primary diseases (underlying condition)

a. Pregnancy-induced hypertension: preeclampsia and eclampsia
   b. Tumors
   c. Renal or renovascular disorders
   d. Drug induced (e.g., birth control pills or steroids)
   e. Endocrine diseases (e.g., pheochromocytoma or Cushing's syndrome)
C. Symptoms (may be asymptomatic): headache, dizziness, vertigo, fatigue, epistaxis
D. Risk factors
   1. Uncontrollable: age, race, heredity, gender, family history (blacks and elderly at greatest risk)
   2. Controllable: smoking, obesity, diet, exercise, alcohol intake, stress, diabetes, uncontrolled hypertension, hypercholesterolemia, cardiovascular and renal disease
E. Hypertension complications
   1. Atherosclerosis with hypertension: increases workload of heart with potential to result in angina, myocardial infarction, congestive heart failure, and/or sudden death
   2. Transient ischemic attack and/or CVA
   3. Renal disease and/or failure
   4. Retinal abnormalities with resulting blindness
F. Diagnostic studies to determine cause of hypertension (essential or secondary)
   1. Electrocardiogram
   2. Urinalysis: to determine presence of protein, red blood cells, white blood cells, and casts, all evidence of possible renal disease
   3. Hematologic studies, in particular hemoglobin and hematocrit values
   4. Measurement of serum sodium, potassium, chloride, carbon dioxide, calcium, creatinine, and cholesterol levels
G. Treatment modalities: goal is to control, not cure
   1. Non–drug therapy: should be utilized prior to drug therapy because of multiple side effects/adverse reactions to drugs
      a. Weight reduction for obesity
      b. Smoking cessation
      c. Stress reduction
      d. Exercise programs

e. Dietary modification: low salt, low fat, low cholesterol, high fiber, decreased calorie
f. Limitation of alcohol intake to 1 ounce/day
2. Drug therapy
   a. Diuretics: less expensive; effective in reducing BP in elderly patients
      (1) Side effects: hypokalemia, hypomagnesemia, hyperglycemia, hyperuricemia
      (2) Thiazide diuretics: hydrochlorothiazide
      (3) Loop diuretics: furosemide (Lasix)
      (4) Potassium-sparing diuretics: spironolactone (Aldactone)
   b. α-Blockers: doxazosin mesylate (Cardura), prazosin (Minipress)
   c. β-Blockers: metoprolol tartrate (Lopressor), atenolol (Tenormin), nadolol (Corgard)
      (1) Side effects: central nervous system (CNS) disturbances, decreased cardiac output, bradycardia, impotence, confusion, bronchospasm
      (2) Should not be considered first-line treatment in elderly persons
      (3) Cardioprotective, antianginal, decreased hypokalemia
   d. Sympatholytic: clonidine hydrochloride (Catapres), methyldopa (Aldomet)
      (1) Side effects: dry mouth, postural hypotension, CNS disturbances
      (2) Preserve cerebral and renal blood flow
   e. Vasodilators: hydralazine (Apresoline), minoxidil (Loniten)
      (1) Side effects: reflex tachycardia in younger patients and orthostatic hypotension in the elderly
   f. Calcium-channel blockers: diltiazem hydrochloride (Cardizem), nicardipine (Cardene), nifedipine (Procardia), verapamil (Calan, Isoptin)
      (1) Side effects: headache, constipation, peripheral edema, atrioventricular conduction blocking
      (2) Calcium-channel blockers potentiate the effects of digoxin
      (3) With few CNS side effects, antianginal property, and circulation maintenance, good drug for patients with coronary artery disease

g. Angiotension-converting enzyme inhibitors: captopril (Capoten), enalapril maleate (Vasotec), lisinopril (Prinivil, Zestril)
   (1) Side effects: hyperkalemia, rash, cough, taste imbalance, proteinuria, neutropenia
   (2) Safe, well-tolerated, effective for longstanding hypertensives

H. Patient education for the home care RN
   1. Definition of hypertension, to dispel any misconceptions
   2. Asymptomatic progression of disease
   3. Non–drug therapy treatments/interventions
   4. Medication: dose, frequency, route, side effects
   5. Therapy/treatment compliance
   6. Recognition of signs/symptoms of hypertension
   7. Risk factors: controllable/uncontrollable
   8. Complications of hypertension
   9. Measures for controlling hypertension

STUDY QUESTIONS AND EXERCISES

1. Discuss the difference between essential and secondary hypertension. Why it is important?
2. What initial criterion constitutes an initial diagnosis of hypertension?
3. Discuss non–drug therapy treatment modalities in controlling hypertension.
4. Discuss role of the RN in patient education of the hypertensive patient.

BIBLIOGRAPHY

Feury, D., and D.T. Nash. 1990. Hypertension: The nurse's role. *RN* 53, no. 11:54–59.

Luckmann, J., and K. Sorensen. 1987. *Medical-surgical nursing: A psychophysiologic approach.* Philadelphia: W.B. Saunders Co.

Meyers, D. 1989. Cardiovascular diseases teaching guides: Hypertension. In *Client teaching guides for home health care.* Gaithersburg, Md.: Aspen Publishers, Inc.

Rodman, M.J. 1991. Hypertension step-care management. *RN* 54, no. 1:24–30.

Rousseau, P. 1991. Management of hypertension in the elderly. *Home Healthcare Nurse* 9, no. 5:47–49.

Trottier, D.J., and M.S. Kochar. 1992. Hypertension and high cholesterol: A dangerous synergy. *American Journal of Nursing* 92, no. 11:40–43.

15

Cardiomyopathy

Debra Finley-Cottone and Brenda Stefanik Bartock

A. Pathophysiology of cardiomyopathy: disorder involving the structure and function of the myocardium
   1. Three major categories
      a. Hypertrophic cardiomyopathy: also known as idiopathic hypertrophic subaortic stenosis
         (1) Probably a genetically transmitted trait
         (2) Cellular hypertrophy and interstitial fibrosis of myocardium, especially of the upper ventricular septum
         (3) May or may not reflect outflow obstruction interfering with left ventricular ejection
         (4) Contractility: becomes impaired
         (5) Ventricular walls: become rigid and noncompliant, causing increased diastolic filling pressures and ultimately pump failure
      b. Congestive or dilated cardiomyopathy (most common type)
         (1) Causative factors: metabolic disorders, infections (viral myocarditis), toxic agents, alcoholism, hypertension, multiple myocardial infarctions, pregnancy-related factors (including the first 6 weeks postpartum)
         (2) Marked ventricular dilatation and thinning, causing contractility abnormalities and heart failure
         (3) Poor prognosis
      c. Restrictive cardiomyopathy (least common)
         (1) Pronounced ventricular hypertrophy and endocardial fibrosis and thickening
         (2) Extremely limited ventricular filling due to small chamber size, noncompliance

(3) Contractility: reduced, causing cardiac output to drop; congestive failure ensues
B. Diagnosis: chest X-ray, electrocardiogram (ECG), echocardiogram, myocardial biopsy
C. Signs and symptoms
   1. Hypertrophic cardiomyopathy
      a. Dyspnea, shortness of breath
      b. Orthopnea
      c. Paroxysmal nocturnal dyspnea
      d. Angina
      e. Fatigue
      f. Palpitations
      g. Syncope
      h. Peripheral edema
      i. Systolic murmur that increases with Valsalva maneuver
      j. S_4 gallop
      k. Apical thrill and heave
      l. Cardiomegaly (mild)
   2. Congestive or dilated cardiomyopathy
      a. Dyspnea/shortness of breath
      b. Fatigue
      c. Chest pain
      d. Biventricular failure
      e. Normal to low systolic blood pressure
      f. Narrow pulse pressure
      g. Mitral and tricuspid regurgitation: causes systolic murmurs
      h. S_3 and S_4 gallops
      i. Systemic or pulmonary emboli
      j. Cardiomegaly
   3. Restrictive cardiomyopathy
      a. Dyspnea/shortness of breath
      b. Fatigue
      c. Exercise intolerance
      d. Right ventricular failure
      e. Systolic murmur of mitral regurgitation
      f. S_3 and S_4 gallops
      g. Narrow pulse pressure
      h. Cardiomegaly
D. Treatment

1. Hypertrophic cardiomyopathy
   a. Relaxation of ventricles by
      (1) Decreasing heart rate
      (2) Decreasing contractility
      (3) Improving ventricular filling and cardiac output
      (4) Drug of choice: propranolol or verapamil
   b. Dysrhythmia control
   c. Anticoagulant if atrial fibrillation present
   d. Septal myotomy for severe outflow obstruction: surgical resection; removal of hypertrophied ventricular septum beneath aortic cusps
   e. Moderation of activity to avoid physical exertion
2. Congestive or dilated cardiomyopathy
   a. Improved stroke volume and cardiac output: digoxin, diuretics, vasodilator
   b. Dysrhythmia control
      (1) Ventricular ectopy
      (2) Atrial fibrillation
   c. Anticoagulation: for risk of systemic emboli, venous thrombus
   d. Inflammation control: steroids, immunosuppressants
   e. Limitation of physical activity
   f. Cardiac transplantation (only surgical option)
3. Restrictive cardiomyopathy
   a. Congestive heart failure (CHF): control with digoxin, diuretics, vasodilators
   b. Sodium restriction
   c. Anticoagulation to prevent emboli

E. Home care assessment and monitoring
   1. Interview patient for symptomatology.
      a. Shortness of breath
      b. Dyspnea on exertion
      c. Cough
      d. Orthopnea
      e. Paroxysmal nocturnal dyspnea
      f. Fatigue
      g. Nausea, vomiting
      h. Anorexia
      i. Oliguria, nocturia
      j. Edema

2. Monitor vital signs.
3. Palpate peripheral pulses.
4. Auscultate heart for rate, rhythm, gallops, murmurs.
5. Auscultate lungs for crackles, wheezing, diminished breath sounds (could indicate pleural effusion; percussion of flat tone over same area can help confirm finding).
6. Evaluate oxygenation; assess mental status; check for presence of cyanosis; check oxygen saturation if oximeter is available.
7. Assess for jugular vein distention.
8. Palpate right upper quadrant of abdomen.
    a. Liver should not be palpable below right costal margin.
    b. Hepatomegaly is present if edge of the liver is palpable below costal margin.
    c. Note tenderness (usually present with engorgement).
9. Assess for ascites.
    a. Palpate for fluid wave.
    b. Percuss for tone change.
    c. Monitor with abdominal girth measurements.
10. Assess peripheral edema.
    a. Note whether edema is pitting or nonpitting (pitting edema is generally due to CHF).
    b. Look for edema not only in lower extremities but in sacral areas as well.
    c. Note that edema measurements are an objective tool.
11. Monitor weight changes.
    a. A 3- to 5-pound weight gain generally requires intervention.
    b. Ideally, use the same scale; weigh patient on arising, after voiding, with same weight of clothing (pajamas).
12. Assess skin color and turgor.
    a. Cyanosis
        (1) Peripheral: blue nails, digits, lips indicate tissue hypoxia.
        (2) Central cyanosis: blue tongue, oral mucosa, ear lobes indicate hypoxemia.
    b. Pallor: peripheral vasoconstriction
    c. Jaundice: liver involvement may be secondary to CHF
13. Assess urinary patterns.
    a. Check response to diuretics.
    b. Nocturia occurs from increased renal perfusion in supine position.

c. Intake and output records may be helpful in class III or class IV CHF or if patient is on fluid restriction.
14. Assess activity tolerance level and self-care abilities.
15. Assess compliance with medications, diet, and activity limitations.
16. Assess for adverse effects of treatment.
    a. Fluid and electrolyte imbalance
    b. Digoxin toxicity
    c. Dizziness
    d. Cramping
17. Use home laboratory monitoring.
    a. Electrolytes (Sequential Multiple Analyzer 6/60 [SMA6]).
    b. Creatinine
    c. Liver function tests
    d. Hemoglobin/hematocrit
    e. Protein/albumin levels
        (1) Edema unresponsive to diuretic therapy
        (2) Cardiac cachexia
    f. Digoxin level
18. Use additional tools: oximetry; home chest X-ray; ECG (to evaluate change in rate or rhythm).
19. Check effectiveness of treatment plan.
    a. Lungs clear
    b. Reduced or absent peripheral edema, ascites
    c. Eupneic at rest
    d. Reduced dyspnea on exertion
    e. Improved activity tolerance
    f. Weight stable

F. Patient teaching
  1. Instruction in disease process
  2. Signs/symptoms to report
      a. Present written information.
      b. Be specific: e.g., "Call nurse or physician with weight gain of 3 or more pounds."
  3. Self-management
      a. Daily weight log
      b. Sodium-restricted diet: 2 to 4 g/day (read food labels for content)
      c. High-potassium foods: if on potassium-wasting diuretic; caution with

                (1) Patients with renal insufficiency usually will not require potassium supplementation
                (2) Patients on angiotensin-converting enzyme inhibitors: may not require potassium supplementation
            d. Medication compliance
                (1) Workable schedule
                (2) Knowledge of action and side effects to report
            e. Activity paced with rest to keep below CHF threshold
            f. Elevation of feet/legs with edema
            g. Instruction on how to take radial pulse
                (1) Report change in rhythm.
                (2) Report heart rate less than 60 beats per minute or more than 100 beats per minute.
            h. Fluid restriction
                (1) Intake and output record
                (2) Instruction on what constitutes a fluid (e.g., anything that is a liquid at room temperature)
            i. Oxygen administration

STUDY QUESTIONS AND EXERCISES

1. Identify three major categories of cardiomyopathy with pathophysiologic alterations.
2. List signs and symptoms for each type of cardiomyopathy.
3. How does treatment for hypertrophic cardiomyopathy differ from that for congestive or restrictive cardiomyopathy?
4. Outline an assessment plan for a patient with cardiomyopathy.
5. Outline a teaching tool for a patient with congestive cardiomyopathy.

BIBLIOGRAPHY

Canobbio, M. 1990. *Cardiovascular disorders*. St. Louis: Mosby-Year Book, Inc.

Cardiovascular care handbook. 1986. Springhouse, Pa.: Springhouse Corporation.

Feagins, C., and D. Daniel. 1991. Management of congestive heart failure in the home setting: A guide to clinical management and patient education. *Journal of Home Health Care Practitioners* 4, no. 1:31–37.

Kinney, M., et al. 1991. *Comprehensive cardiac care*. St. Louis: Mosby-Year Book, Inc.

Letterer, R.A., et al. 1992. Learning to live with congestive heart failure. *Nursing '92* 22, no. 5:34–41.

Nurse review: A clinical update system 1. 1986. Springhouse, Pa.: Springhouse Corporation.

Solomon, J. 1991. Managing a failing heart. *RN* 54, no. 8:46–50.

Stillwell, S., and E. Randall. 1990. *Pocket guide to cardiovascular care*. St. Louis: Mosby-Year Book, Inc.

Tarkington, S., and G. Raterink. 1987. *Every nurse's guide to cardiovascular care*. New York: John Wiley & Sons, Inc.

Wright, S.M. 1990. Pathophysiology of congestive heart failure. *Journal of Cardiovascular Nursing* 3, no. 3:1–16.

16

Valvular Heart Disease

Debra Finley-Cottone and Brenda Stefanik Bartock

A. Definition of valvular heart disease: a congenital or acquired disorder of one of the four cardiac valves; results in either stenosis (obstruction to blood flow) or degeneration (regurgitation). Valvular heart disease most often is a chronic disease that takes years for symptoms to develop. Acute onset is seen after trauma of myocardial infarction (MI).
B. Incidence: declining over the last 30 years as a result of development/ refinement of diagnostic procedures and use of antibiotic therapies
C. Classification
   1. Congenital
      a. Bicuspid aortic valve
      b. Pulmonary stenosis
      c. Tricuspid atresia
      d. Pulmonary atresia
      e. Mitral valve prolapse (potentially)
      f. Ebstein's anomaly
   2. Acquired (in order of frequency)
      a. Rheumatic fever
      b. Endocarditis
      c. Post-MI
      d. Cardiomyopathy
      e. Trauma to the heart
      f. Marfan's syndrome: connective tissue disorder
      g. Myxomatous degeneration: mitral valve
D. General pathophysiology
   1. Stenosis: rigidity and thickening of the valve orifice, which leads to narrowing of the valvular diameter; causes an obstruction to blood flow across the valve and necessitates a high-pressure gradi-

ent to overcome the obstruction. The higher-pressure gradient leads to increased left ventricular wall thickness and ventricular hypertrophy.
	2. Regurgitation (incompetency, insufficiency): Scarring, calcification, and retraction of the leaflets or surrounding structures lead to incomplete closure of the valves, which causes a portion of the blood to flow retrograde.
E. Diagnostic studies: electrocardiogram (ECG), echocardiogram, radionuclide studies, cardiac catheterization
F. Most common disorders
	1. Mitral stenosis
		a. Cause: Rheumatic valvulitis leads to fibrosis and scarring, which increase rigidity and thickness of the leaflets.
		b. Symptoms: fatigue; palpitations; dyspnea on exertion (DOE); hoarseness; paroxysmal nocturnal dyspnea; orthopnea; hemoptysis
		c. Possible physical assessment findings
			(1) Alterations in pulse: resting tachycardia, irregular beats (atrial arrhythmias most common)
			(2) Jugular vein distention: most prevalent with right-side ventricular failure
			(3) Diastolic murmur
			(4) Lung sounds: crackles
	2. Mitral regurgitation
		a. Causes
			(1) Rheumatic fever: Commissures become fused with the chordae tendineae, which causes the valve leaflets to retract.
			(2) Nonrheumatic
				(a) MI: displacement of papillary muscle due to dilatation of the ventricle
				(b) Dysfunction of papillary muscle: rupture or fibrosis caused by ventricular aneurysms, ischemia, infarction
		b. Symptoms: orthopnea, fatigue, exercise intolerance, palpitations
		c. Possible physical assessment findings
			(1) Alterations in pulse: irregular, impulse displaced downward to left
			(2) Jugular vein distention: most prevalent with right-side ventricular failure

(3) Holosystolic murmur: best auscultated at apical area
(4) Lung sounds: crackles
3. Aortic stenosis
   a. Causes
      (1) Congenital: bicuspid/unicuspid valve
      (2) Degenerative, over age 65 years: calcification and thickening
      (3) Rheumatic (less common): thickening of the cusps and commissural fusion
   b. Symptoms: orthopnea, dyspnea, syncope, fatigue, dizziness, angina
   c. Possible physical assessment findings
      (1) Alteration in pulse: loud/strong apical pulse that is sustained through systole
      (2) Early normal blood pressure (BP); late narrowing pulse pressure; decreased systolic pressure
      (3) Systolic murmur: auscultated at base, second intercostal space to right of sternum
      (4) Lung sounds: crackles
4. Aortic regurgitation
   a. Causes: rheumatic fever; syphilis; infective endocarditis; Marfan's syndrome
   b. Symptoms: palpitations, orthopnea, DOE, exertional angina
   c. Possible physical assessment findings
      (1) Alteration in pulse: bounding, displaced to the left
      (2) Widening pulse pressure
      (3) Skin alterations: flushing, increased warmth, dampness
      (4) Head-bobbing (deMusset's sign)
      (5) Systolic ejection murmur: auscultate at base, diastolic murmur (second intercostal space right of sternal border)
5. Other: Patients can have involvement in one or more valves; also, mixed lesions in which both stenosis and regurgitation exist.
G. Treatment/management
   1. Overall: Management is guided by the severity of the disorder and the symptoms.
   2. Decreased cardiac output: caused by specific mechanical valve dysfunction. Mechanical problems lead to alterations in preload and afterload, and eventually lead to congestive heart failure (CHF).

3. Potential for embolization: related to development of an alteration in the electrical conduction system of the heart. Most common arrhythmia is atrial fibrillation.
   a. Assessment/interventions for arrhythmia
      (1) Auscultate apical pulse rate, rhythm, abnormal heart sounds.
      (2) Perform ECG if available.
      (3) Monitor effects of antiarrhythmic drugs.
         (a) Digoxin
         (b) Verapamil
         (c) Quinidine
         (d) Procainamide hydrochloride (Pronestyl)
         (e) β-Blockers
         (f) Antiarrhythmics
      (4) Toxicity of antiarrhythmic medications: Measure blood levels periodically.
      (5) Objective of antiarrhythmics: control heart rate to between 50 and 100 beats per minute
      (6) Effect of arrhythmia on CHF
   b. Assessment/interventions for embolization
      (1) Symptoms
         (a) Altered mental status
         (b) Restlessness
         (c) Increased BP
         (d) Widened pulse pressure
         (e) Paresthesia
         (f) Aphasia
         (g) Hemiparesis/hemiplegia
         (h) Altered breathing
      (2) Anticoagulation
         (a) Sodium warfarin (Coumadin): needed for periodic laboratory tests (signs and symptoms of bleeding)
         (b) Enteric-coated or baby aspirin
4. Patient teaching
   a. Anxiety
   b. Activity intolerance
   c. Knowledge deficit
   d. Disease process
   e. Medication

    f. Symptoms to report to physician
        (1) Signs and symptoms of CHF
        (2) Palpitations
        (3) Change in activity level
    g. Need to inform all health care providers of valve disease (especially dentists, urologists, gynecologists): prophylactic antibiotic therapy to prevent endocarditis
    h. Activity limitations
    i. If woman of childbearing age: Discuss risk of pregnancy and give information on contraceptives.
H. Procedures to improve blood flow
    1. Mitral valvulotomy (commissurotomy): surgical splitting of fused or stenotic valve leaflets with a dilator (palliative measure to improve blood flow): contraindicated in patients with history of emboli
    2. Valvular annuloplasty: reparative procedure usually performed on mitral and tricuspid valves with regurgitation; can involve valve ring, chordae, or papillary muscle
    3. Valve replacement: stenotic or incompetent valves replaced with mechanical or bioprosthetic devices
    4. Percutaneous balloon catheter dilatation: Balloon catheter is inserted under fluoroscopy into the area of the calcified valve and inflated repeatedly to decrease calcium deposits. Exact mechanism of reduction of the deposits is unknown.
        a. Candidates
            (1) Persons of advanced age, children, women of childbearing age
            (2) Complicated medical history: pulmonary disease, renal insufficiency, coronary artery disease
            (3) Patients who refuse surgical intervention for stenotic valves
I. Nursing management: Refer to postoperative management of open-heart surgery patients (see Chapter 18).

STUDY QUESTIONS AND EXERCISES

1. Disease of the valves results in either of what two conditions?
2. Since valvular disorders cause alteration in the flow of blood from the heart, what is the major problem patients experience?

3. Name two procedures that can be performed to improve flow of blood through diseased valves.
4. What cardiac dysrhythmia do patients with valve disorders most often develop?
5. Discuss the key points you would teach a patient undergoing anticoagulation therapy.

BIBLIOGRAPHY

Canobbio, M. 1990. *Cardiovascular disorders.* St. Louis: Mosby-Year Book, Inc.

Kinney, M., et al. 1991. *Comprehensive cardiac care.* St. Louis: Mosby-Year Book, Inc.

Nurse review: A clinical update system 1. 1986. Springhouse, Pa.: Springhouse Corporation.

Ohler, L., et al. 1989. Aortic valvuloplasty: Medical and critical care nursing perspective. *Focus on Critical Care* 16, no. 4.

Rafalowski, M. 1990. Cardiac valve replacement: The homograft. *Focus on Critical Care* 17, no. 2.

17

Pacemakers

Debra Finley-Cottone and Branda Stefanik Bartock

A. Definition of a pacemaker: a battery-operated generator that initiates and controls the heart rate by delivering an electrical impulse to the myocardium via an electrode
B. Indications for inserting a pacemaker
   1. Bradyarrhythmias (most common)
      a. Complete heart block (third-degree heart block)
      b. Sick sinus syndrome
      c. Second-degree heart block (type II)
      d. Bradycardia-tachycardia syndrome
      e. Sinus arrest
      f. First-degree heart block (only when symptomatic)
      g. Carotid sinus syndrome
      h. Atrial fibrillation with slow ventricular response
   2. Tachyarrhythmias
      a. Sinus tachycardia
      b. Supraventricular tachycardia
      c. Atrial tachycardia
      d. Junctional tachycardia
      e. Ventricular tachycardia
   3. Prophylactic: cardiac surgery
C. Types of pacemakers
   1. Temporary: provides hemodynamic stability after an acute cardiac event (myocardial infarction) or emergency measure for malfunction of a permanent pacemaker
   2. Permanent: for sustained bradycardia or refractory tachyarrhythmia
      a. Components of a permanent pacemaker system

(1) Generator: hermetically sealed unit consisting of an electronic circuit and a power source of lithium batteries; average life of battery is 5 to 8 years
(2) Electrodes (unipolar lead/bipolar leads): conduct electricity from generator to myocardium
3. Transvenous: most common approach for both temporary and permanent pacing
   a. Permanent: electrode is inserted percutaneously or via a cutdown into the internal or external jugular vein; generator is implanted subcutaneously in shoulder or upper left quadrant of abdomen.
4. Epicardial: Electrode is sutured to epicardium of the right ventricle (most often done during open-heart surgery).
5. Transthoracic: Electrode is inserted directly into the heart in emergencies or after open-heart surgery.
D. Modes of pacemakers
 1. Fixed rate: fires at set rate regardless of patient's own underlying heart rate (not commonly used)
 2. Demand (most common): fires only when patient's own heart rate falls below preset rate (e.g., 70 beats per minute). Patients lose atrial contribution to cardiac output with this type of pacing.
 3. Synchronous: A sensing circuit looks at the patient's underlying atrial and ventricular rate. The pacemaker fires only when patient's atrial or ventricular rate falls below preset rate; provides optimal cardiac output.
E. Patient management
 1. Assessment
   a. Infection of pacer site: redness, drainage, increased temperature, stability of generator, increased pain
   b. Vital signs: blood pressure, apical pulse (regular/irregular, number of irregular beats in 1 minute)
   c. Baseline electrocardiogram (ECG) (if available): type of pacemaker, rate, sensing capturing
   d. Signs of decreased cardiac output: shortness of breath, dizziness, lightheadedness, mental status changes, failure to return to baseline activities (activity intolerance)
   e. Signs of pacemaker failure: syncope, chest pain, dizziness, hiccoughing, symptoms of congestive heart failure
   f. Range of motion of the extremity with the generator

g. Incisional pain
2. Teaching
   a. Why the pacemaker was inserted
   b. How it helps the heart
   c. Need for follow-up to assess function of pacemaker
      (1) Visit to cardiologist
      (2) Generator checks via pacemaker clinic visit or via telephone transmission (guidelines: 1 week, 1 month, then every 3 months)
   d. Medic Alert® bracelet
   e. Symptoms of pacemaker failure (call physician)
      (1) Shortness of breath
      (2) Syncope
      (3) Dizziness
      (4) Weight gain greater than 3 pounds in 3 to 5 days
      (5) Edema of feet/ankles
      (6) Chest pain
      (7) Confusion
      (8) Prolonged hiccoughing
      (9) Increased or decreased heart rate
   f. Pacemaker identification card and importance of carrying it at all times
   g. Pulse taking (Newer pacemakers have warning signals when generator is nearing end of its life.)
   h. Changes in medications: can affect pacemaker function
      (1) Corticosteroids
      (2) Type I antiarrhythmics: quinidine, β-blockers, procainamide hydrochloride, disopyramide, calcium-channel blockers
   i. Avoidance of external sources that can interfere with pacemaker function
      (1) Small appliances, hair dryers, electric razors, drills
      (2) TVs/computers
      (3) Microwave ovens: stand 6 feet away when operating
      (4) Car engines: do not lean over distributor
      (5) Airport metal detectors
      (6) Theft-prevention alarms
      (7) Shortwave radios

(8) Magnetic resonance imaging
j. Signs/symptoms of infection
F. Internal cardioverter defibrillator: a device used to prevent sudden cardiac death in patient with ventricular tachycardia or ventricular fibrillation
1. Procedure
    a. Percutaneous or thoracotomy
    b. Single or double leads
    c. Implanted—Epicardial or Endocardial
    d. New models have pacemaker capabilities also
2. Patient population
    a. Patients who have refractory/lethal tachyarrhythmias despite antiarrhythmic therapy
    b. Patients who have survived sudden cardiac death without myocardial infarction
3. Assessment/intervention: signs/symptoms of infection at generator site
    a. Vital signs (ECG, if available)
    b. Lung/heart sounds
    c. Symptoms of ventricular arrhythmia: increased heart rate, syncope, dizziness, blackouts
    d. Anxiety
    e. Psychologic adaptation to "shocking"
    f. Pain level
4. Patient teaching
    a. Avoidance of strong magnetic fields
        (1) Some hospital equipment, airport security systems, construction sites
        (2) Direct contact with alternators
        (3) Magnet: do not place over or near pulse generator
        (4) Beeping from generator: remove self from the area and call physician
    b. Avoidance of contact sports
    c. Avoidance of tight clothing or belts over generator
    d. Family members encouraged to learn cardiopulmonary resuscitation
    e. Medic Alert® tag/identification card

  f. Emergency numbers posted by telephone
  g. Notification of physician
    (1) Fainting, palpitations, dizziness, weakness
    (2) If shock is received (keep diary: date, time, symptoms associated with shock)
  h. Notification of health professionals of presence of device: might need to be turned off for certain procedures
  i. Medications
  j. Dietary restriction
  k. Activity progression
  l. Touch by others during a shock: not harmful; feels like a buzz

STUDY QUESTIONS AND EXERCISES

1. List three indications for the insertion of permanent pacemaker.
2. List three things you would teach a patient after pacemaker insertion.
3. List three assessment parameters used at home to evaluate adequate pacemaker function.
4. What is the most common insertion procedure for a permanent pacemaker?
5. Name two components of a pacemaker.
6. List two indications for the insertion of an internal cardioverter defibrillator.

BIBLIOGRAPHY

Aurrier, D., and D. Packa. 1992. The patient with an implantable cardioverter defibrillator: A case study. *Focus on Critical Care* 19, no. 2.

Brannon, P., and R. Johnsen. 1992 The internal cardioverter defibrillator: Patient family teaching. *Focus on Critical Care* 19, no. 1:41–46.

Canobbio, M. 1990. *Cardiovascular disorders.* St. Louis: Mosby-Year Book, Inc.

Kinney, M., et al. 1991. *Comprehensive cardiac care.* St. Louis: Mosby-Year Book, Inc.

Mercer, M. 1992. Rate responsive pacers. *RN* 55, no. 5:34–37.

Nurse review: A clinical update system 1. 1986. Springhouse, Pa.: Springhouse Corporation.

Riggel, B., and B. Vitello. 1991. Cardiac pacemakers. *Journal of Cardiovascular Nursing* 5, no. 3.

18

Invasive Interventions

Debra Finley-Cottone and Brenda Stefanik Bartock

A. Open-heart surgery: coronary artery bypass grafting
   1. Purpose: improve patient's quality of life through improvement of myocardial oxygen supply by directly increasing coronary blood flow
   2. Candidates
      a. Coronary artery obstruction
         (1) Significantly abnormal electrocardiogram (ECG) in response to exercise
         (2) Greater than 50% obstruction of left main coronary artery
         (3) Obstruction of all three coronary arteries
      b. Chronic angina: class III/IV
      c. Unstable angina (preinfarction angina)
      d. Ongoing ischemia following an acute myocardial infarction (MI)
      e. Ongoing, persistent ventricular arrhythmia after an acute MI
   3. Procedure
      a. Midsternal incision and usually leg incision by which the saphenous vein is removed for grafting
      b. Circulation via heart-lung machine to provide bloodless operative field
      c. Anticoagulation: systemic to reduce chance of embolization
      d. Hypothermia: to decrease metabolic demands
      e. Grafting selection: saphenous vein, internal mammary artery
   4. Home assessment/intervention
      a. Adequate cardiac output
         (1) Vital signs
            (a) Hypo/hypertension

(b) Heart rate more than 100 or less than 50 beats per minute and/or irregularities
(c) Baseline ECG (if available)
  (2) Dizziness, palpitations
  (3) Shortness of breath, mental changes
  (4) Decreased peripheral pulses
  (5) Skin temperature
  (6) Adequate hematocrit/hemoglobin
 b. Fluid volume excess
  (1) Blood pressure increase
  (2) Weight increase, peripheral edema
  (3) Skin turgor; nocturia
  (4) Shortness of breath
  (5) Lung sounds (crackles)
  (6) Jugular vein distention
  (7) Orthopnea; cough; tachypnea
  (8) S_3 heart sound; tachycardia
 c. Potential for infection
  (1) Increased temperature
  (2) Sternal/leg incision
   (a) Palpate for sternal stability.
   (b) Check for increased superficial redness, increased warmth.
   (c) Check for pustule formation on or near incision (regrowing of hair).
   (d) Check for drainage, edema.
  (3) Elevated white blood cell counts with differential shift
 d. Potential for altered gas exchange
  (1) Increased respiratory rate
  (2) Lung sounds
   (a) Crackles: can indicate atelectasis or fluid
   (b) Decreased breath sounds: poor respiratory effort due to pain or pleural effusion
   (c) Pleural friction rub: possible pleurisy
  (3) Oxygen saturation
  (4) Use of incentive spirometer
  (5) Cough/deep breathing

e. Potential for altered coping
   (1) Fear of being home
   (2) Depression over illness, lack of appetite, crying, poor sleep pattern, inability to progress with activities of daily living, lack of concentration
f. Pain management
   (1) Use of pain medication
   (2) Surgical pain distinguished from former anginal pain
   (3) Pain rating (1 to 10)
   (4) Comfort measures: back rub, change in position, warm shower
g. Potential gastrointestinal alteration
   (1) Frequency and consistency of bowel movement
   (2) Nausea/vomiting; appetite changes
   (3) Perception of food taste (often altered)

5. Patient teaching
   a. Refer to Chapter 11 (risk factors, diet, sodium restriction, symptoms to report)
   b. Recall of how procedure was done: instruct if recall poor
   c. Incision care
      (1) Check for initial bruising, swelling, itching, or soreness.
      (2) Back/shoulder soreness is common.
      (3) Edema at top of sternum is common.
      (4) Note slight movement or clicking of sternum with breathing or turning: sternum heals in 4 to 6 weeks.
      (5) Wash incisions gently with soap and water, preferably in shower; do not use lotions.
      (6) Use support stocking to reduce edema from saphenous vein graft removal and prevent embolization.
      (7) Report any signs of infection.
   d. Pain management
   e. Activity/exercise
      (1) No driving until approved by physician, usually 4 to 6 weeks after procedure
      (2) Household chores: setting table, clearing table, light surface dusting, potting plants, minor home repairs
      (3) Lifting: no more than 5 to 10 pounds; no activities that

strain breastbone; no pushing or pulling until cleared by physician
            (4) Rest periods: 20 to 30 minutes/day
            (5) Sex: can resume when incision pain is decreased and can walk one flight of stairs without getting short of breath
            (6) Stair climbing: limit to one or two times per day for first 2 weeks
            (7) Cardiac exercise program (see Chapter 20)
    6. Other potential issues
        a. Management of open sternal/leg wounds
        b. Development of postpericardiotomy syndrome
            (1) Definition: autoimmune response that develops secondary to an increase in antiheart antibodies
            (2) Incidence: as high as 30%; occurs early or late postoperatively
            (3) Duration: 2 to 100 days
            (4) Diagnosis: often elusive because of nonspecific signs/symptoms
            (5) Signs/symptoms (in order of frequency)
                (a) Increase in sedimentation rate
                (b) Pleuritic pain, pericardial rub
                (c) Pleural effusion (usually on left; fluid is lymphocytic)
                (d) Fever, leukocytosis
                (e) Dyspnea, crackles, pleural rub
                (f) Pericardial effusion
                (g) ECG: elevated ST segment
            (6) Treatment
                (a) Decrease inflammation: aspirin, nonsteroidal agents, or steroids.
                (b) Control pain through use of above medications, splinting of chest, and/or positioning.
                (c) Suggest thoracentesis if patient is symptomatic (shortness of breath, increased respiratory rate, orthopnea).
        c. Management of neurologic deficits due to postoperative cerebrovascular accident
B. Percutaneous transluminal coronary angioplasty (PCTA)

1. Restoration of blood flow through a stenotic coronary artery by compression of atheromatous plaque within the vessel by repeated inflation/deflation of a balloon-tipped catheter
2. Patient selection guidelines
   a. Chronic stable angina not controlled by medical therapy
   b. Single-vessel coronary stenosis (most ideal)
   c. Objective evidence of ischemia by exercise treadmill, thallium scintigraphy with exercise, or gated blood pool studies
   d. Lesions in which procedure is easier to perform: those proximal, discrete, concentric, and noncalcified
3. Not considered for more complex patients
   a. Multivessel disease; total occlusions
   b. Complex anatomies of coronary artery (distal disease)
   c. Bifurcation lesions
   d. Diseased saphenous vein bypass grafts
   e. Previous internal mammary artery bypass graft
4. Contraindications: coronary artery spasm, left main coronary artery disease
5. Complications: reocclusion of the vessels; need for emergency bypass surgery
6. Assessment/interventions
   a. Refer to Chapter 11.
   b. Common medications postprocedure
      (1) Aspirin for 6 months
      (2) Nitrates for 3 to 6 months
      (3) Calcium-channel blockers for 3 to 6 months
   c. Insertion site: check for signs/symptoms of infection
7. Patient teaching
   a. Refer to Chapter 11.
   b. Instruction on need for antiplatelet medications
   c. Instruction on activity allowances (general guidelines)
      (1) Avoidance of strenuous activity, exercise, and heavy lifting 1 to 2 weeks after procedure
      (2) No work or driving for 3 to 4 weeks
   d. Instruction on need for periodic treadmill tests to assess patency of arteries

C. New procedures (invasive cardiology laboratories)
   1. Coronary stints
   2. Atherectomy
   3. Laser surgery

STUDY QUESTIONS AND EXERCISES

1. Describe at least two conditions that would benefit from coronary artery bypass surgery.
2. What assessment parameters would you measure for fluid volume excess?
3. List three topics to teach a patient who has undergone open-heart surgery.
4. Name three disorders in which PCTA would be the treatment of choice for stenosis.
5. Describe what points to teach a post-PCTA patient on activity limitations.

BIBLIOGRAPHY

Barbiere, C. 1991. PTCA: Treating the tough cases. *RN* 54, no. 2:38–42.

Canobbio, M. 1990. *Cardiovascular disorders*. St. Louis: Mosby-Year Book, Inc.

Cella, A., et al. 1994. Same day admission for cardiac surgery: A benefit to patient, family and institution. *Journal of Cardiovascular Nursing* 7, no. 4:14-29.

Culligan, M., et al. 1990. Preventing grafting complications in CABG patients. *Nursing '90* (June):59-61.

Horneffer, P., et al. 1990. The effective treatment of postpericardium syndrome after cardiac operations. *Journal of Cardiovascular Surgery* 100, no. 2:292–295.

Kahn, J. MD. 1993. Caring for patients after coronary bypass surgery. *Postgraduate Medicine* 93, no. 4:249-262.

Kim, K., et al. 1988. Lymphocytic pleural effusion in postpericardiotomy syndrome. *American Heart Journal* 115, no. 5:1077–1079.

Kinney, M., et al. 1991. *Comprehensive cardiac care*. St. Louis: Mosby-Year Book, Inc.

Nurse review: A clinical update system. 1986. Springhouse, Pa.: Springhouse Corporation.

Stillwell, S., and E. Randall. 1990. *Pocket guide to cardiovascular care*. St. Louis: Mosby-Year Book, Inc.

19

Cardiac Transplantation

Debra Finley-Cottone

A. Indications
 1. End-stage cardiac disease (prognosis 6 to 12 months)
 2. Patients must meet the New York Heart Association class III or class IV status
 3. Inability to be treated by conventional therapies or surgeries
B. Common diagnoses in which transplantation is performed
 1. Cardiomyopathy
 2. Congenital defect
 3. Ischemic heart disease
 4. Valvular heart disease
C. Contraindications for transplantation
 1. Active infection
 2. Pulmonary hypertension
 3. Hepatic abnormalities
 4. Active ulcer
 5. Compromised renal system
 6. Recent pulmonary embolism
 7. Insulin-dependent diabetes
 8. Cerebrovascular accident
 9. Severe psychologic instability
 10. Alcohol or drug abuse
D. Transplantation procedures
 1. Heterotopic: the native heart is left in and the donor heart is "piggybacked" onto it
 2. Orthotopic: the native heart is removed and replaced with the donor heart
E. Major complications of transplantation

1. Rejection
2. Infection
3. Immunosuppression
4. Accelerated atherosclerosis

F. Assessment/interventions: All patients who undergo cardiac transplantation are closely monitored by a transplant center; therefore the information provided is a general guideline. The home care nurse's role is to follow up the teaching initiated at the center and to monitor the patient's understanding and compliance.
   1. Cardiovascular
      a. Vital signs
         (1) Blood pressure: tendency toward hypertension related to immunosuppression
         (2) Resting pulse: usual range 90 to 110 (lower heart rate not achievable because of denervation of the donor heart)
      b. Chest pain (angina)
         (1) Initially the patient is unable to perceive chest pain because of denervation.
         (2) Perceived chest pain is related to incisional healing, muscle spasm, and muscle strain.
         (3) Now, evidence shows that months after transplantation sensory afferent reinnervation of the donor heart occurs. This is important because the patient should be able to perceive angina, which is a good indicator of accelerated atherosclerosis that can occur post-transplantation.
      c. Electrocardiogram (ECG): can show remnant P wave if orthotopic procedure
      d. Follow other assessment parameters outlined in Chapter 11 and Chapter 18.
   2. Infection
      a. Pulmonary (common):
         (1) Productive cough
         (2) Shortness of breath
         (3) Increased temperature
      b. Wounds: pain, swelling, redness, and/or drainage at site; increased temperature
   3. Rejection
      a. Physical symptoms and changes in ECG are unreliable indications

        b. Endomyocardial biopsy is the only way of detecting rejection.
    4. Response to immunosuppressants
        a. Prevents body from rejecting transplanted heart, but at the same time decreases defenses against infection
        b. Common immunosuppressant medications
            (1) Azathioprine (Imuran): suppresses bone marrow
                (a) Can lead to decreased white blood cells (WBC)
                (b) Medication adjusted by WBC counts
            (2) Cyclosporine: allows for a lower dose of corticosteroids; side effects:
                (a) Renal dysfunction
                (b) High blood pressure (very common)
                (c) Liver dysfunction
                (d) Increased susceptibility to infections
                (e) Headache
                (f) Shaking and trembling of hands
                (g) Leg cramps
                (h) Swollen gums
                (i) Nausea and vomiting
            (3) Prednisone: anti-inflammatory
                (a) Increased appetite that could lead to weight gain
                (b) Cushingoid appearance
                (c) Muscle weakness
                (d) Increased oiliness of skin that may lead to acne on the upper body
                (e) Fragile skin that tears and bruises easily
                (f) Greater sensitivity to sun
                (g) Increased potassium excretion
                (h) Osteoporosis
                (i) Sodium and fluid retention (higher doses)
                (j) Mood changes and impaired concentration (higher doses)
                (k) Tendency for gastrointestinal bleeding
                (l) Glucose intolerance
    5. Bleeding (if patient continues on anticoagulation therapy after surgery)
    6. Monitor response to antihypertensive medication.
G. Patient teaching
    1. Refer to Chapter 11.

2. Refer to Chapter 18.
3. Monitor pulse. Note change in rate and regularity.
4. Monitor blood pressure via automated monitoring machine; keep log. (Recommended by some centers)
5. Record weight daily, weighing the same time every day with the same amount of clothing.
6. Monitor compliance with monitoring vital signs and weight.
7. Signs and symptoms of infection
    a. Take temperature every day, or at times when you think you have a fever.
    b. Report an elevation in temperature for several hours that is greater than 100° F.
    c. Do not take aspirin or acetaminophen (Tylenol) products for a fever because it could mask the symptoms of an infection.
    d. Report presence of a sore throat, cough, respiratory congestion, shortness of breath, inflamed or draining sores, or pain or burning with urination.
    e. Avoid persons with obvious contagious infection.
    f. Do not change litter boxes because cat feces may contain the pathogen that causes toxoplasmosis.
    g. Report gastrointestinal symptoms.
    h. Report cutaneous lesions.
8. Obtain a Medic Alert® tag.
9. Keep phone numbers of your physicians and transplant center near your phone.
10. Activity
    a. Avoid contact sports or any other activity that has potential for injury.
    b. Avoid extremes in pressure changes, such as during hang gliding, scuba diving, skydiving, or flying in unpressurized aircraft (denervated heart).
    c. Recommend a cardiac rehabilitation program for progressive activity and exercise.
11. Demonstrate an understanding of follow up care
    a. Lab and office visits
    b. Biopsy schedules
12. Verbalize signs and symptoms of rejection.
    a. Hypotension
    b. Symptoms of congestive heart failure
    c. Arrhythmias

STUDY QUESTIONS AND EXERCISES

1. For what patients is cardiac transplantation indicated?
2. List three contraindications for transplantation.
3. List the four major complications of transplantation.
4. Outline what you would teach a patient regarding immunosuppression.
5. Describe the main role of the home care nurse in caring for the transplant patient.

BIBLIOGRAPHY

Canobbio, M. 1990. *Cardiovascular disorders.* St. Louis: Mosby-Year Book, Inc.
Kinney, M., et al. 1991. *Comprehensive cardiac care.* St. Louis: Mosby-Year Book, Inc.
Seifert, P. 1994. *Cardiac surgery.* St. Louis: Mosby-Year Book, Inc.
Stillwell, S., and E. Randall. 1990. *Pocket guide to cardiovascular care.* St. Louis: Mosby-Year Book, Inc.

20

Cardiac Rehabilitation and Support

Debra Finley-Cottone and Brenda Stefanik Bartock

A. Goals
 1. Improve functional work capacity.
    a. Improve functional abilities and self-care.
    b. Limit need for long-term care.
 2. Improve psychologic outlook: sense of well-being; quality of life.
 3. Reduce risk factors for recurrent cardiovascular event.
B. Benefits
 1. Increased sense of well-being
 2. Improved self-image
 3. Reduction of anxiety and/or depression
 4. Improved flexibility and strength
 5. Increased efficiency of heart pump
 6. Reduced resting heart rate and blood pressure
 7. Increased ability to tolerate stress
 8. Improved sleep
 9. Improved digestion and nutritional status
C. Indications
 1. Reversal of physical deconditioning related to
    a. Adverse effects of bed rest
       (1) Hypovolemia
       (2) Increased blood viscosity, which predisposes to thromboemboli
       (3) Orthostatic hypotension
       (4) Impaired wound healing
       (5) Decreased musculoskeletal functioning
       (6) Increased heart work; tachycardia

(7) Decreased digestion
    b. Sedentary lifestyle
        (1) Without pre-existing cardiovascular disease
        (2) As a result of chronic cardiovascular disease
    c. Improvement of cardiovascular fitness: improve fitness and maintenance
D. Candidates
    1. After myocardial infarction
    2. After open-heart surgery: coronary artery bypass or valve surgery
    3. After percutaneous transluminal coronary angioplasty
    4. Possible candidates (with caution)
        a. Controlled congestive heart failure (CHF)
        b. Controlled angina
        c. Controlled dysrhythmia
        d. Controlled hypertension
        e. Pacemaker insertion
    5. Contraindicated
        a. Unstable angina
        b. Pulmonary embolism
        c. Anemia
        d. Uncontrolled CHF, hypertension, dysrhythmia, metabolic illnesses (diabetes or thyrotoxicosis)
        e. Active noncardiac illnesses
E. Phases of rehabilitation
    1. Phase I
        a. Inpatient–based: begins immediately after acute cardiac event has stabilized
            (1) Gradual progression of self-care activities and ambulation
            (2) Initial educational efforts
                (a) Disease process and symptom management
                (b) Medication instruction
                (c) Physical activity
                (d) Sexual counseling
                (e) Risk factor identification and reduction
        b. Risk stratification
            (1) Diagnostic testing
                (a) Exercise testing
                (b) Radionuclide studies

(c) Holter monitoring
(d) Cardiac catheterization
(2) Identification of those at high risk for future cardiac event
2. Phase II
   a. Immediate postdischarge period: continuing for approximately 8 weeks (convalescence)
      (1) Patient and significant other: anxious, depressed, and fearful about resumption of activity levels
      (2) Critical time for rehabilitative process
      (3) Period of highest mortality
   b. Outpatient-based: cardiac rehabilitation facility
      (1) Team approach/multidisciplinary
      (2) Medical supervision
      (3) Usually continuous electrocardiographic (ECG) monitoring during exercise
      (4) Components
         (a) Physical conditioning program
         (b) Psychosocial support
         (c) Education regarding disease process, symptom management, risk factor reduction, medications, safe activity progression
3. Phase III
   a. Community-based exercise program
      (1) Usually not monitored
      (2) Less supervision
      (3) Emergency equipment and protocols available
   b. Patients at least 6 to 12 weeks posthospitalization and medically stable
   c. Ongoing maintenance exercise program
4. Home-based program
   a. Supervised programs generally are recommended and have several advantages over home-based programs.
   b. Unfortunately, supervised programs are not always feasible because of geography, economics, homebound status, patient motivation, and age.
   c. Home health nurse is in a unique position to promote cardiac rehabilitation objectives.
      (1) Psychosocial assessment and support
      (2) Education

(3) Physical assessment
(4) Clinical supervision of selected cardiac home care patients on approved low-level exercise program in the home
(5) Guidance with safe activity progression
F. Exercise prescription
  1. Prescription is based on results of graded exercise testing.
  2. Prescription includes four characteristics of an exercise program.
     a. Type of activity
        (1) Isometric exercise: development of muscle tension with little or no change in muscle length or joint movements (e.g., weight lifting); cardiac patients should avoid
        (2) Isotonic exercise: rhythmic muscle contraction and relaxation, and joint movement (e.g., walking, swimming, bicycling); promotes cardiovascular conditioning; recommended for cardiac patients
     b. Intensity of activity: may be prescribed based on
        (1) Relative perceived exertion by Borg: This is an indicator of the level of physical exertion felt at a given work level; rated on a scale from 0 (being none) to 10 (maximal).
        (2) Heart rate: There are several methods for calculating the target heart rate for conditioning effect; for home exercise, a safe guide is for the heart rate to increase no more than 20 beats over the resting rate, not to exceed a maximal heart rate of 120 beats per minute.
        (3) Metabolic equivalents of a task (MET) (Table 20–1)
            (a) Energy cost or requirement as determined by oxygen consumption of basal body function at rest
            (b) Equal to 3.5 mL of oxygen per kilogram of body weight per minute
            (c) Physical activities: vary in degree of workload placed on cardiovascular and pulmonary systems
     c. Duration of conditioning (stimulus) period of exercise
        (1) The lower the intensity, the longer the duration required for conditioning; inversely, the stronger the intensity, the lower the duration required.
        (2) Warm-up before the conditioning period is imperative.
            (a) Head-to-toe range of motion and light calisthenics for 5 to 10 minutes
            (b) Prepares the body for higher levels of activity and pre-

Table 20–1 Metabolic Equivalent of a Task (MET)

MET	Daily Living and Home Activities	Occupational Activities	Recreational Activities
1–2	Sleeping, bedrest, sitting, eating, reading, combing hair, shaving, bathing at bedside or sink, brushing teeth	Paperwork, typing (electric)	Walking 1 mph on level ground, handicrafts (knitting, needlepoint, crocheting, rug hooking), picture painting, card games
2–3	Shower standing, sexual intercourse, cooking, general housework (windows, dusting, sweeping, washing dishes, making beds, ironing), light gardening, mowing with power/riding mower	Office work, plastering, brick laying, driving a truck, some assembly line work	Walking 3 mph, bicycling 6 to 7.5 mph, riding a motorcycle, hammering, golfing (with pull cart), fly-fishing, badminton, shuffleboard
4–5	Stair climbing, changing linen on bed, grocery shopping, vacuuming, mopping, carrying light objects, lifting up to 25 lb, weeding, raking leaves	Painting, paper hanging, light carpentry, auto repair	Walking 4 mph, dancing, fishing, bowling, golf (carrying clubs), ping-pong
5–6	Crutch walking, lifting (25–30 lb), garden digging, light shoveling, washing car	Using heavy tools	Bicycling 10 mph, skating, hiking, hunting, horseback riding, sailing

Note: This chart is meant only to be a guide. The vigor and other mediating circumstances under which any of these activities are performed can alter the energy cost (MET) significantly.

Source: Courtesy of authors and the Visiting Nurse Service of Rochester and Monroe County, Inc., Rochester, New York.

vents many untoward effects (e.g., musculoskeletal injuries, dysrhythmias, angina)

(3) Stimulus period lasts for 20 to 40 minutes when heart rate is maintained in the target range (may need to build slowly to this duration).

            (4) Cool-down after the stimulus period is imperative.
                (a) Lower-intensity work for 5 to 10 minutes, similar to warm-up
                (b) Adjusts body back to lower level of work and prevents adverse effects (e.g., dizziness, dysrhythmias)
            (5) Try interval training.
                (a) Alternating periods of exercise with rest
                (b) Permits exercise for longer periods
        d. Frequency of exercise
            (1) Depends on intensity and duration
            (2) Usually three times per week, but low levels of intensity or duration require higher frequency to obtain conditioning effect
G. Home exercise guidelines
    1. Instruct patient and/or significant other in how to take and monitor radial pulse with exercise.
        a. Take pulse before, midway through, and immediately after exercise.
        b. Stay within target heart rate; report any drop in pulse with exercise.
    2. Stay with patient to monitor exercise response until patient is knowledgeable of exercise regimen and self-monitoring, and it is well documented how patient tolerates activity.
    3. Stress importance of warm-up before and cool-down after exercise.
    4. Monitor for abnormal exercise response.
        a. Systolic blood pressure (BP) increase >20 mm Hg
        b. Diastolic BP decrease >10 mm Hg
        c. Heart rate increase >20 beats per minute over resting rate
        d. Heart rate decrease >10 beats per minute below resting rate
        e. Change in rhythm of pulse
        f. Severe shortness of breath (should be able to talk comfortably with exercise)
        g. Angina
        h. Palpitations
        i. Dizziness/syncope
        j. Excessive fatigue
        k. If ECG available, monitor for
            (1) Change in rhythm
            (2) Development of dysrhythmia

                (3) ST segment elevation or depression >1 mm
        5. Avoid exercise 1 hour before and 2 hours after a meal.
        6. Do not exercise in extreme hot or cold temperatures (good range is 40° to 80°F).
        7. Dress properly to avoid overheating by allowing for evaporation of perspiration.
        8. Do not shower for at least one-half hour after exercise.
        9. Curtail exercise if any acute illness develops.
        10. Keep primary physician informed at all times of patient response, progress, and any adverse effects.
        11. If patient is an insulin-dependent diabetic, monitor blood glucose; may require adjustment in insulin dose with change in activity level; avoid injection sites involving large exercising muscles.
        12. Keep in mind the patient's prescribed drugs, as they may affect response to exercise.
        13. Involve significant others.
    H. Support through resources
        1. American Heart Association
        2. Mended Hearts: support group for open-heart surgery patients
        3. Any educational materials patient received in the hospital; use to assist with your teaching
        4. Hospital-sponsored support groups

STUDY QUESTIONS AND EXERCISES

1. Identify the goals and five benefits of cardiac rehabilitation.
2. What are the two indications for rehabilitation of a cardiac patient?
3. Describe the three phases of rehabilitation.
4. An exercise prescription includes what four characteristics of an activity?
5. Outline guidelines for a safe home exercise program.

BIBLIOGRAPHY

American College of Sports Medicine. 1986. *Guidelines for exercise testing and prescription.* Philadelphia: Lea and Febiger.

Borg, G. 1985. *An introduction to Borg's R.P.E. scale.* Ann Arbor, Mich.: McNaughton and Gunn, Inc.

Cardiovascular Care Handbook. 1986. Springhouse, Pa.: Springhouse Corporation.

Kinney, M., et al. 1991. *Comprehensive cardiac care.* St. Louis: Mosby-Year Book, Inc.

Nurse review: A clinical update system 1. 1989. Springhouse, Pa.: Springhouse Corporation.

Peterson, L. 1983. *Cardiovascular rehabilitation.* New York: Macmillan Publishing Co.

Sirles, A., and C. Selleck. 1989. Cardiac disease and the family: Impact, assessment, and implications. *Journal of Cardiovascular Nursing* 3, no. 2.

Stillwell, S., and E. Randall. 1990. *Pocket guide to cardiovascular care.* St. Louis: Mosby-Year Book, Inc.

Talkington, S., and G. Raterrink. 1987. *Every nurse's guide to cardiovascular care.* New York: John Wiley & Sons, Inc.

Part IV

Nursing Management of the Patient with Respiratory Disease

21

Asthma/Bronchitis

Jeannette F. Levy

A. General etiology
   1. Chronic irritation to lungs
   2. Limitation to airflow on expiration
      a. Cigarette smoking: primary factor
      b. Infection
      c. Inhaled irritants
   3. Variable development depends on
      a. Host susceptibility
      b. Nature and severity of exposure to irritant
B. Pathogenesis
   1. Asthma: reversible
      a. Structural changes
         (1) Increased responsiveness of trachea and bronchi to various stimuli: hypersensitivity reaction
         (2) Bronchospasm
         (3) Inflamed airways; mucosal edema
         (4) Chronic inflammatory process
      b. Symptomatology: cough, dyspnea, chest tightness, wheezing
   2. Chronic bronchitis: irreversible
      a. Structural changes
         (1) Exposure to irritant and/or infection
         (2) Inflamed airways; mucosal edema
         (3) Hypersecretion of mucus
      b. Symptomatology
         (1) Frequent, productive cough
         (2) Variable dyspnea (relatively late)
         (3) Frequent respiratory infections

         (4) "Blue bloater," cyanosis
         (5) Slight to marked increase in anteroposterior diameter of chest
         (6) Scattered crackles (rales), rhonchi, wheezing
C. Assessment
    1. Current symptoms and previous disease manifestation
    2. Current level of functioning
    3. Psychologic status
    4. Family support and ability to assist with care
    5. Physical environment of the home
    6. Oxygen and home medical equipment needs
    7. Techniques used for bronchial hygiene; respiratory therapy visits
    8. Exercise status/tolerance
    9. Rest and sleep status
    10. Nutrition status
    11. Elimination status
    12. Financial needs/concerns
    13. Diagnostic tests
        a. Chest X-ray
        b. Arterial blood gases
        c. Sputum culture and sensitivity
        d. Hemoglobin and hematocrit
        e. White blood cell count
        f. Theophylline level
        g. Lung volumes
           (1) Tidal volume
           (2) Residual volume
           (3) Vital capacity
           (4) Forced expiratory volume in 1 second (FEV_1)
           (5) FEV_1/forced vital capacity (FVC)
D. Management
    1. Improvement in gas exchange
        a. Drugs for relief of airflow obstruction
           (1) Bronchodilators
               (a) β-agonists/sympathomimetics
               (b) Methylxanthine derivatives
           (2) Anticholinergics
           (3) Anti-inflammatory agents
           (4) Mucolytics

                (5) Mast-cell inhibitors
            b. Home oxygen therapy
                (1) Noninvasive monitoring during home visits
                    (a) Pulse oximetry for spot checks
                    (b) Peak-flow meter readings
                    (c) Lung sounds
                    (d) Palpation and percussion of chest
                    (e) Vital signs
                    (f) Ventilatory pattern
                    (g) Sputum volume, color, consistency
                    (h) Patient's appearance and presentation
                    (i) Compliance with oxygen therapy, self-care measures
                (2) Home medical equipment needs
                (3) Teaching
                    (a) Safety with equipment
                    (b) Signs/symptoms of oxygen toxicity
                    (c) Knowledge about hypoxic drive and caution related to amount of oxygen received
    2. Removal of bronchial secretions
        a. High fluid intake
        b. Percussion, vibration, postural drainage
        c. Education related to smoking cessation and avoidance of pulmonary irritants
        d. Education related to effective breathing and coughing techniques
    3. Prevention of bronchopulmonary infections
        a. Education related to early detection of signs/symptoms of infection
        b. Education to avoid contact with persons who have respiratory infection
        c. Education to avoid significant pollutants
        d. Immunization against *Haemophilus influenzae* and *Streptococcus pneumoniae*
    4. Improvement in nutritional intake
        a. Vitamin and between-meal supplementation
        b. Smaller, more frequent meals
        c. Consideration of ethnic and financial background
    5. Promotion of breathing exercises and physical conditioning
        a. Recognition of times when exercise tolerance is decreased

        b. Education related to diaphragmatic breathing and inspiratory muscle training
        c. Education related to pursed-lip breathing
        d. Graded exercise and physical conditioning programs
    6. Promotion of self-care activities
        a. Patient participation in planning
        b. Rest periods
    7. Promotion of coping measures
        a. Recognition of behavioral/mood changes
        b. Recognition of sexual function changes
        c. Education related to remaining active to the level of symptom tolerance
        d. Support groups
E. Patient education
    1. Knowledge of illness or disability
    2. Perceived view of changes in physical and interpersonal environment
    3. Physical independence
        a. Use of energy-conservation measures
        b. Use of preventive, reconditioning, and adjustment measures
        c. Compliance with necessary environmental changes
    4. Therapeutic competence
        a. Bronchial hygiene
        b. Breathing retraining
        c. Conditioning exercises
        d. Oxygen therapy
        e. Smoking cessation
        f. Diet
        g. Elimination
        h. Self-assessment
        i. Medications
            1) Oral
            2) Inhalers, i.e., metered-dose inhalers (MDI) and spacers (inhalation aids)
    5. Psychosocial competence
        a. Own awareness/acceptance/desire to cope
        b. Response/support of significant others
    6. Financial resources
        a. Disability benefits

b. Retirement funds
   c. Social Security benefits
   d. Medicaid
   e. Medicare
   f. Food stamps
7. Community resources
   a. Smoking cessation programs
   b. American Lung Association
   c. Prescribed exercise programs
   d. Support groups
   e. Meals on Wheels

STUDY QUESTIONS AND EXERCISES

1. Differentiate the symptomatology for chronic bronchitis and asthma.
2. List the physical and environmental assessments that should be performed by the home health nurse when he or she visits the patient with asthma or bronchitis.
3. What are the goals of home management for patients with asthma or bronchitis?
4. Identify at least three areas of patient education.

BIBLIOGRAPHY

Bella, L.A. 1992. Steroidphobia and the pulmonary patient. *American Journal of Nursing* 92:26-32.

Brucia, J., et al. 1991. Management of persons with problems of the lower airways. In *Medical-surgical nursing: Concepts and clinical practice*, eds. W. Phipps and B. Long, 871–951. St. Louis: Mosby-Year Book, Inc.

Brunner, L., and D. Suddarth. 1992. Management of patients with conditions of the chest and lower respiratory tract. In *Textbook of medical-surgical nursing*, eds. L. Brunner and D. Suddarth, 559–603. Philadelphia: J.B. Lippincott Co.

Fitzgerald, S.T. 1992. National asthma education program expert panel report-guidelines for the diagnosis and management of asthma. *AAOHN Journal* 92:376-382.

Hoffman, L.A., and S.W. Wesmiller. 1988. Home oxygen—transtracheal and other options. *American Journal of Nursing* 88:464–469.

Kacmarck, R. 1990. Noninvasive monitoring of respiratory function outside of the hospital. *Respiratory Care* 35:719–723.

Openbrier, D., et al. 1988. Home oxygen therapy—evaluation and prescription. *American Journal of Nursing* 88:192–197.

Petty, T. 1987. Drug strategies for airflow obstruction. *American Journal of Nursing* 87:180–184.

Reinke, L., and L. Hoffman. 1992. Breathing space: How to teach asthma co-management. *American Journal of Nursing* 92:40-51.

Sexton, D. 1990. *Nursing care of the respiratory care patient.* Norwalk, Conn.: Appleton & Lange.

Weaver, T., and T. Van Sciver. 1992. Nursing role in management: Obstructive pulmonary diseases. In *Medical-surgical nursing: assessment and management of clinical problems,* eds. S. Lewis and I. Collier, 557–601. St. Louis: Mosby-Year Book, Inc.

22

Chronic Obstructive Pulmonary Disease

Rebecca C. Clark

A. Chronic obstructive pulmonary disease (COPD): a group of respiratory disorders that produce obstruction of small airways
   1. Includes bronchial asthma, chronic bronchitis, pulmonary emphysema
   2. Patients may exhibit more than one of these diseases
   3. Incidence: fifth leading cause of death in the United States; affects 17 million Americans
   4. Risk factors: cigarette smoking; recurring respiratory infections; genetic factors; allergens; inhaled irritants (e.g., air pollution, occupational irritants)
B. Emphysema: abnormal, permanent enlargement of airspaces beyond terminal bronchioles with destruction of alveolar walls
   1. Pathophysiology
      a. Destruction of supporting structures of lung with air trapping; distention and hyperinflation of alveoli
      b. Alveoli coalesce, with decrease in amount of surface area available for diffusion of oxygen and carbon dioxide
      c. Loss of elastic recoil of lungs
   2. Clinical course: slow, progressive course of dyspnea on exertion with decreasing exercise tolerance
   3. Symptoms
      a. Early: dyspnea becomes increasingly severe; minimal cough with little or no sputum
      b. Later: accessory muscles used for respiration; may be thin with muscle wasting (barrel chest); no cyanosis; "pink puffer"; finger clubbing; hypercapnia

C. Complications of COPD
   1. Hypoxemia
      a. Decreased level of blood oxygen ($PO_2 < 80$ mm Hg)
      b. Symptoms: changes in mentation, restlessness, confusion, drowsiness, tachycardia, hyperventilation
   2. Hypercapnia
      a. Increased level of blood carbon dioxide ($PCO_2 > 45$ mm Hg)
      b. Symptoms: depression of central nervous system with drowsiness, loss of concentration, irritability, inability to sleep, headache
   3. Cor pulmonale
      a. Right ventricular hypertrophy with or without heart failure, generally due to pulmonary hypertension
      b. Symptoms: distended neck veins, hepatomegaly, epigastric distress, peripheral edema, weight gain
   4. Acute respiratory failure
      a. $PO_2 < 50$ mm Hg; $PCO_2 > 50$ mm Hg.
      b. May be due to acute respiratory infection, excessive use of oxygen, use of sedatives, improper use of medications
      c. Symptoms: increased cough and sputum production, difficulty in coughing up sputum, progressive dyspnea, confusion, increasing drowsiness
   5. Peptic ulcer disease
   6. Increased risk of pneumonia, upper respiratory infections
D. Goals of care for the patient with COPD
   1. Improve ventilation.
   2. Manage symptoms.
   3. Prevent progression of disease.
   4. Promote comfort and self-care abilities.
E. Nursing assessments (focused on respiratory components)
   1. General condition of patient: weight for height, skin color, level of consciousness, energy
   2. Respirations: quality, character, rate, and depth; abnormal breath sounds, dyspnea, shortness of breath on exertion, use of accessory muscles, cough
   3. Sputum: character, amount, color, changes
   4. Activity tolerance, ability to manage activities of daily living
   5. Complete home assessment: factors that affect respiratory status; physical structure of the home (stairs, bathroom arrangements, etc.)

6. Family assessment: sources of support, anxiety
7. Use of community resources
F. Nursing interventions
 1. Ineffective airway clearance
    a. Encourage smoking cessation.
    b. Teach patient to avoid exposure to environmental irritants or infectious agents.
    c. Teach patient to maintain adequate hydration; humidify air; advise fluid intake of 2 to 3 L/day (unless contraindicated).
    d. Teach patient effective coughing technique.
       (1) Forward-leaning posture, arms supported
       (2) Diaphragmatic breathing/pursed-lip exhalations, two or three times to mobilize secretions
       (3) Prior to initiating cough, deep inhalation, then cough three or four times with exhalation
    e. Consider chest physical therapy.
    f. Teach patient signs/symptoms of infection.
    g. Recommend immunizations for pneumonia, influenza.
 2. Ineffective breathing pattern
    a. Teach patient energy-conserving breathing patterns.
       (1) Forward-leaning position with support
       (2) Pursed-lip/diaphragmatic breathing
       (3) Exhalation with activity
       (4) Prolonged expiratory phase
 3. Impaired gas exchange: hypercapnia/hypoxemia
    a. Assess/teach family to assess for signs hypoxemia/hypercapnia.
    b. Teach patient appropriate use of oxygen therapy.
       (1) Avoid excessive levels of oxygen (>1 to 2 L/minute): depress hypoxic drive for respirations.
       (2) Stress that oxygen is a drug; it should be used as prescribed.
       (3) Use of oxygen at night may be adequate to provide increased activity tolerance during the day.
    c. Teach patient to use medications appropriately, avoiding sedatives, central nervous system depressants, and over-the-counter medications without consulting physician.
 4. Activity intolerance
    a. Teach patient to alternate periods of rest and exercise, to avoid fatigue and shortness of breath.

    b. Teach patient energy-conservation measures.
        (1) Arrange chores/tasks to allow sitting as much as possible during an activity (e.g., while shaving, cooking).
        (2) Do lifting while exhaling.
        (3) Avoid stair climbing; organize activities on one floor of home as much as possible.
    c. Assist patient to establish an exercise pattern to regain and maintain exercise capacity; walking is beneficial.
    d. Refer patient to occupational therapist/physical therapist for work simplification/muscle reconditioning programs.
 5. Health maintenance
    a. Make sure that patient knows names of medications and treatments, and understands rationale for use.
    b. Instruct in use of medications, purpose, dose, frequency, side effects.
    c. Teach patient side effects to report to physician.
G. Management of medication therapy
 1. Bronchodilators
    a. Inhaled/oral β-adrenergic agonists
        (1) Primarily administered by metered-dose inhaler (MDI) or nebulizer; allows for lower dose of medication for therapeutic effect than if given orally; lower incidence of side effects
        (2) Includes isoetharine, metaproterenol sulfate, albuterol, isoproterenol, terbutaline sulfate
        (3) Primarily stimulates $β_2$-adrenergic receptors, causing bronchodilatation
        (4) Side effects: tachycardia, tremors, nervousness, palpitations
    b. Methylxanthine derivatives
        (1) Less effective than β-agonists
        (2) Given orally (theophylline) or intravenously (IV) (aminophylline)
        (3) Therapeutic range, 10 to 20 mg/mL
        (4) High incidence of side effects: gastrointestinal distress, central nervous system stimulation, cardiovascular stimulation
 2. Anti-inflammatory agents/corticosteroids
    a. Anti-inflammatory; immunosuppressive; decreases mucus secretion and edema in bronchial airways

b. Inhaled routes effective for patients requiring less than 15 mg/day
   c. Include prednisone (oral); hydrocortisone (IV); beclomethasone (MDI); triamcinolone (MDI)
   d. Oral administration
      (1) Take entire dose in the morning to mimic natural secretion of hormone. Do not discontinue suddenly: can cause acute steroid withdrawal symptoms.
      (2) Side effects include mood swings, hematologic changes with bruising, hypokalemia, diabetes, nausea, vomiting, increased appetite, weight gain, immunosuppression with increased susceptibility to infection, muscle wasting, osteoporosis, fluid retention, and redistribution of fat (buffalo hump and moon face).
   e. Inhaled administration
      (1) Primary side effect is oral infection with *Candida;* avoid by using mouthwash after treatment. Clean home inhalation equipment after use.
      (2) Medication is not intended for use during an acute attack of bronchospasm but is a long-acting maintenance medication.
3. Cromolyn sodium (mast cell stabilizer)
   a. Used primarily with asthma
   b. Prevents allergic response; rarely used to treat bronchospasm associated with COPD
4. Mucolytics: acetylcysteine (nebulizer), iodinated glycerol (oral)
   a. Act as irritant; liquefy mucus
   b. Side effects: gastrointestinal irritation, bronchospasm

STUDY QUESTIONS AND EXERCISES

1. Mr. Jones is a 68-year-old patient with a history of COPD. On the initial home visit, what symptoms would the nurse expect to assess?
2. Mrs. Andrew is a 74-year-old patient with COPD. Following discharge from the hospital for pneumonia, she complains of dyspnea on exertion that is more severe than her dyspnea before hospitalization. Develop a care plan for Mrs. Andrew that will help her manage this problem.

3. Mr. Neal has COPD and is managed on theophylline 200 mg orally twice daily. What side effects should he be aware of to report to his physician?

BIBLIOGRAPHY

Gould, E., and J. Wargo. 1987. *Home health nursing care plans.* Gaithersburg, Md.: Aspen Publishers, Inc.

Lewis, S., and I. Collier. 1992. *Medical-surgical nursing.* St. Louis: Mosby-Year Book, Inc.

Malloy, C., and J. Hartshorn, eds. 1989. *Acute care nursing in the home.* Philadelphia: J.B. Lippincott Co.

Patrick, M., and S. Woods. 1991. *Medical-surgical nursing.* Philadelphia: J.B. Lippincott Co.

Whitney, L. 1992. Chronic bronchitis and emphysema: Airing the differences. *Nursing '92* 22, no. 3:34–42.

23

Pneumonia

Mary Tracy Parsons

A. Background information
   1. Most common cause of death among infectious diseases
   2. Fifth leading cause of death overall
   3. Second most common reason for antibiotic therapy
   4. Can be classified as hospital-acquired or community-acquired
B. Risk factors
   1. Alcoholism: decreases white blood cell mobilization and increases risk for aspiration
   2. Chest trauma or surgery: may impair respiration
   3. Malnourished individuals: may have a diminished immune response
   4. Smoking: damages the respiratory tract and lungs
   5. Lower states of consciousness: contribute to diminished cough reflex
   6. Immunosuppression: places the patient at greater risk
   7. Aged persons: experience variety of normal and abnormal physiologic changes that place them at risk
      a. Weakened respiratory muscles
      b. Decreased chest expansion
      c. Increased residual volume
      d. Decreased respiratory reserve
      e. Decreased cough effectiveness
      f. Decreased ciliary activity
   8. Obesity: impairs lung expansion
   9. Pre-existing respiratory problems: predispose individuals to complication
   10. Narcotic analgesics: depress respirations and cough reflex

11. Muscle weakness/muscular disorders: may impair respiration or make it impossible for the individual to cough effectively
12. Fatigue and chilling
13. Frequent upper respiratory infections
14. Limited mobility, especially bed rest: impairs effective lung expansion

C. Types of pneumonia
   1. Bacterial (accounts for 70% to 90% of cases)
      a. Most common type is caused by *Streptococcus pneumoniae.*
      b. Pneumonia may result from other bacteria: opportunistic; often complicated by an abscess or pleural effusion.
   2. Aspiration: caused by inhaling a foreign substance and/or gram-negative bacteria colonized in posterior pharynges (especially aged persons)
   3. *Histoplasma capsulatum:* caused by a fungus found in bat or bird feces
   4. *Legionella* pneumonia: caused by a bacterium spread through contaminated water
   5. Mycoplasmal: caused by a bacterium; typically afflicts the younger population
   6. *Pneumocystis carinii:* thought to be caused by a simple fungus or related to a fungus
   7. Viral pneumonia: caused by a variety of viruses; usually more severe when it afflicts children

D. Pathophysiology of pneumococcal pneumonia (*S. pneumoniae*)
   1. Bacteria enter lungs.
   2. Plasma proteins and excess water move to the most dependent areas of the lungs.
   3. Alveoli are converged upon by fibrin, red blood cells, and polymorphonuclear neutrophil (PMN) leukocytes (red hepatization).
   4. Affected area of the lung becomes consolidated (semisolid); alveoli become airless.
   5. Hyperemia occurs where alveoli are engorged with fluid and blood exudate; exudate coagulates.
   6. Red blood cells decrease: neutrophils invade the alveoli (gray hepatization).
   7. PMN leukocytes are replaced by macrophages.
   8. Exudate is absorbed or removed by coughing (resolution).

E. Assessment of bacterial pneumonia

1. Signs and symptoms (frequently of sudden onset)
    a. Elevated temperature and pulse
    b. Chilling
    c. Productive cough (may be blood-streaked or rust-colored)
    d. Pleuritic chest pain
    e. Dyspnea
    f. Diaphoresis
    g. Elevated white blood cell count
    h. Pale or cyanotic skin
    i. Hypoxemia
    j. Diminished breath sounds
    k. Crackles
    l. Pleural friction rub
    m. Aged person's symptoms may be different: temperature elevation delayed, anorexia, changes in mental status, weight loss, diminished activity
2. Diagnostic studies
    a. Sputum culture and sensitivity: identify organisms and determine appropriate antibiotic
    b. Sputum gram stain: identify organism, examine for neutrophilia and number of epithelial cells
    c. Blood cultures: for septicemia
    d. White blood cell count: will be elevated
    e. Arterial blood gases: may demonstrate a PO_2 below normal, and respiratory acidosis
    f. Chest X-ray: evidence of density changes
    g. Pulse oximetry spot-check: identify deterioration or improvement in status
3. Complications: lung abscess; pleural effusion; meningitis; congestive heart failure; paralytic ileus
F. Management of bacterial pneumonia
    1. Drug therapy
        a. Antibiotic therapy is single most important intervention.
            (1) Administer at appropriately spaced intervals to maintain therapeutic serum level.
            (2) Improvement should be seen within 48 hours.
            (3) Complete entire prescription course.
            (4) Observe for signs and symptoms of side effects and sensitivity.

(5) Monitor drug levels and renal function tests.
b. Administer antipyretics for temperature higher than 39°C (102°F).
c. Administer narcotic analgesics for chest pain.
(1) Monitor for respiratory depression.
(2) Give at correct dosage and frequency.
d. Avoid cough suppressants (coughing is natural, protective mechanism); if necessary, administer at night only.
2. Patient and/or family teaching
a. Teach pathophysiology of pneumonia; risk factors, correlation with treatments.
b. Teach effective coughing: several deep abdominal breaths followed by a strong double cough.
c. Force fluids up to 2 to 3 L/day (unless contraindicated); fruit juices and water are preferred to liquefy secretions.
d. Teach correct method to take temperature, and frequency; show where to record it.
e. Splint patient's chest when coughing to reduce pain.
f. Describe purposes of oxygen therapy, correct flow rate, how to use and care for equipment, and safety factors; patient should keep record of when oxygen is used.
g. Demonstrate percussion, vibration and/or postural drainage, and intermittent positive pressure breathing as ordered.
h. Change patient's position every 1 to 2 hours; set up a schedule; with bilateral lung disease may do better on right side; with unilateral lung disease may do better if positioned with healthy lung dependent.
i. Elevate head of the bed with pillows.
j. Use a humidifier to help liquefy secretions.
k. Use proper hygiene (wash hands if they come in contact with mucus, and dispose of tissues promptly).
l. Encourage patient to stop smoking; provide support and appropriate referrals to assist; instruct family members to avoid smoking around patient.
m. Demonstrate proper oral hygiene with performance every 2 hours.
n. Schedule rest periods to avoid fatigue.
o. Serve high-protein, well-balanced diet divided into six small meals.

p. Notify physician in case of increased dyspnea; temperature over 104°F; decreased urine output; decreased level of consciousness.
G. Prevention of bacterial pneumonia
1. Alter risk factors.
2. Administer influenza vaccine: must be taken annually; administered intramuscularly; epinephrine should be available; recommended for anyone over 65 years of age; contraindicated if allergy to eggs.
3. Administer pneumococcal vaccine.
   a. It provides protection against most types of pneumococci.
   b. It is believed to give lifetime immunity.
   c. It can be administered subcutaneously or intramuscularly.
   d. Epinephrine should be available.
   e. Recommended for anyone over 65 years of age.
4. Teach components of a well-balanced diet.

STUDY QUESTIONS AND EXERCISES

1. What is the single most important intervention for pneumonia?
2. Identify five risk factors for pneumonia.
3. What is the most common type of pneumonia?
4. What is the purpose of the sputum culture and sensitivity?
5. What information does the patient/family need to be able to administer safely narcotic analgesics for chest pain?

BIBLIOGRAPHY

Bullock, B.L. 1992. *Pathophysiology: Adaptations and alterations in function.* Philadelphia: J.B. Lippincott Co.

Caruthers, D.D. 1990. Infectious pneumonia in the elderly. *American Journal of Nursing* 90, no. 2:56–60.

Frasier, D. 1993. Patient assessment: Infection in the elderly. *Journal of Gerontological Nursing* (July):5-11.

Wilson, S.F., and J.M. Thompson. 1990. *Respiratory disorders.* St. Louis: Mosby-Year Book, Inc.

Yeaw, E.M.J. 1992. How position affects oxygenation: Good lung down? *American Journal of Nursing* (March):26-32.

24
Pulmonary Edema
Antoinette Laguzza

A. Pathophysiology: most severe form of pulmonary congestion; usually results from left-sided heart failure caused by prolonged strain on a diseased heart
   1. Cardiogenic origin (most common cause)
      a. Hypertensive heart disease
      b. Arteriosclerotic heart disease (coronary artery disease, myocardial infarction)
      c. Valvular heart disease
   2. Noncardiogenic origin
      a. Aspiration pneumonia
      b. Fluid overload from intravenous fluids
      c. Inhalation of caustic agents (smoke, toxic chemicals)
      d. Hypoalbuminemia (nephrotic syndrome, hepatic disease, malnutrition)
      e. Near-drowning syndrome
      f. Malignancies
      g. Shock
      h. Sepsis
      i. Narcotic overdose
      j. Fat embolism
      k. Oxygen toxicity
      l. Acute respiratory distress syndrome
   3. Pathogenesis
      a. Cardiogenic
         (1) Overwork of myocardium
         (2) Decline in cardiac output of left side of heart
         (3) Increased left atrial and ventricular pressures

(4) Increased pulmonary vein and capillary pressures
(5) Serous fluid: escapes from intravascular spaces into alveolar spaces
    b. Noncardiogenic
       (1) Increased capillary permeability
       (2) Protein-rich molecules: escape from vascular space to interstitium
       (3) Increased oncotic pressure: pulls fluid into interstitial and alveolar spaces
       (4) Impaired ventilation: results in diminished oxygen and carbon dioxide exchange
B. Symptomatology
  1. Initial
    a. Paroxysmal nocturnal dyspnea
    b. Slight dyspnea with exertion
    c. Orthopnea
    d. Persistent cough
    e. Weakness, fatigue, exercise intolerance
    f. Restlessness, anxiety, insomnia
  2. Acute
    a. Rapid, labored respirations
    b. Audible wheezes, rales
    c. Cough more intense, producing blood-tinged, frothy sputum
    d. Tachycardia, dysrhythmias
    e. Pallor; cyanosis; cold, clammy skin
    f. Hypotension
    g. Reduced urine output
  3. Advanced
    a. Decline in level of consciousness (impaired memory, confusion)
    b. Diminished breath sounds
    c. Progressive changes in vital signs (shock)
C. Assessments
  1. Cardiovascular
    a. Auscultate rate and rhythm of heart.
    b. Locate the point of maximal impulse or apical pulse.
    c. Palpate precordium for heaves.
    d. Palpate peripheral pulses.
    e. Auscultate heart sounds to detect S_3 or S_4 gallops.

- f. Check capillary refill of extremities.
- g. Note color and temperature of extremities.
- h. Locate and grade edema.
- i. Check for jugular vein distention.
2. Respiratory:
    - a. Monitor rate and rhythm of respirations.
    - b. Auscultate lungs for rales (crackles), wheezing, and diminished breath sounds, especially in bases.
3. Other signs of fluid retention
    - a. Hepatomegaly
    - b. Reduced urine output and concentration
    - c. Rapid gain in weight
    - d. Tightness of clothing and jewelry
4. Laboratory data: digitalis levels; levels of electrolytes, arterial blood gases, blood urea nitrogen

D. Management
1. Reduce workload of heart.
    - a. Ensure physical and mental rest.
        - (1) Control environment to minimize stress.
        - (2) Relieve anxiety by allowing verbalization and answering all questions.
        - (3) Encourage gradual return to normal activities.
        - (4) Plan frequent rest periods (especially 1 hour after meals and sustained activity).
        - (5) Assess response to activity; monitor pulse and respiratory rates and blood pressure before and after activity.
    - b. Maximize oxygenation status of the body.
        - (1) Give 2 to 6 L of oxygen by nasal cannula.
        - (2) Have patient sit in upright position.
        - (3) Instruct patient to deep breathe to ventilate distal alveoli.
    - c. Decrease venous return.
        - (1) Elevate head of bed (even at night).
        - (2) Administer vasodilators: hydralazine (Apresoline); nitrates (isosorbide dinitrate); captopril (Capoten).
    - d. Eliminate accumulated body fluids.
        - (1) Reduce sodium intake: usually to 2 g/day.
        - (2) Restrict fluids to 1.5 to 2 L/day (as low as 1 L/day in most severe cases).

(3) Monitor for signs of electrolyte depletion, especially hypokalemia: muscle weakness, apathy, lethargy, abdominal distention, anorexia, nausea, hypotension, arrhythmias.
(4) Monitor for dehydration: dry mucous membranes, dry skin, thirst, hypotension, skin tenting (turgor).
(5) Administer diuretics: furosemide (Lasix), bumetanide (Bumex).
(6) Replace potassium.
2. Enhance myocardial contractility with digitalis.
   a. Ensure compliance.
   b. Monitor for signs of toxicity: cardiac signs are bradycardia, tachycardia, arrhythmias; noncardiac signs are anorexia, nausea, vomiting, vision changes.

STUDY QUESTIONS AND EXERCISES

1. Identify the most common causes of pulmonary edema.
2. List the early and more advanced respiratory symptoms that are present in patients with pulmonary edema.
3. Develop a comprehensive teaching plan for patients/family that will assist them with living with the chronicity of heart failure that leads to pulmonary edema.

BIBLIOGRAPHY

Bousquet, C.L. 1990. Congestive heart failure: A review of nonpharmacologic therapies. *Journal of Cardiovascular Nursing* 4, no. 3:35–46.

D'Addio-Wilson, D. 1989. Acute pulmonary edema: How to respond to a crisis. *Nursing '89* 19, no. 10:34–42.

Ellstrom, K. 1990. What's causing your patient's respiratory distress? *Nursing '90* 20, no. 11:57–61.

Luckmann, J., and K.C. Sorensen. 1987. *Medical-surgical nursing: A psychophysiologic approach.* Philadelphia: W.B. Saunders Co.

Phipps, W.J., et al. 1991. *Medical-surgical nursing: Concepts and clinical practice.* St. Louis: Mosby-Year Book, Inc.

Van Parys, E. 1987. Assessing the failing state of the heart. *Nursing '87* 17, no. 2:42–49.

25

Pulmonary Embolus

Mary Tracy Parsons

A. Background information
   1. Approximately one third of patients who develop pulmonary embolus die.
   2. Embolus is the most common pulmonary perfusion abnormality.
   3. The vast majority of emboli come from thrombi (usually in the thigh and pelvis).
   4. Defined: Pulmonary embolism is blockage of a pulmonary vessel by material from somewhere other than lung.
B. Risk factors
   1. Any conditions leading to injury of a vein, increased clotting of blood, or venous stasis
   2. Patients who have a history of embolus
   3. Increased risk with some specific diseases (e.g., infection, diabetes mellitus)
   4. History of smoking or oral contraceptive use
   5. Aged patients
C. Pathophysiology
   1. Initial event is injured vein, increased clotting of blood, or venous stasis.
   2. Any of the above, or a combination, establishes location for clot to begin.
   3. The clot becomes an embolus when it dislodges from the vein wall.
   4. Usually the clot breaks off in several pieces that travel to different parts of the lung; they stop somewhere in the pulmonary capillary bed.
   5. Blood flow beyond the clot is blocked.
   6. Small obstructions may cause no changes.

7. Cor pulmonale can result if larger obstruction increases resistance to blood flow.
8. A larger embolus in main pulmonary artery can cause death.
9. Simultaneously with clot release, histamine, serotonin, catecholamine, and prostaglandin are released; thrombin is activated.
10. Bronchoconstriction occurs.
11. Lung absorbs embolus; fibrosis occurs.

D. Assessment
   1. Diagnostic tests
      a. Electrocardiographic changes: assist in differentiating an embolus from a myocardial infarction
      b. Ventilation/perfusion lung scan
      c. Pulmonary angiography: diagnostic, but risky
      d. Arterial blood gases: decreased PO_2 and O_2 saturation
      e. Venous blood flow studies: document presence of deep vein thrombosis
   2. Signs and symptoms
      a. Sudden onset of shortness of breath and/or dyspnea on exertion
      b. Coughing, hemoptysis, chest pain
      c. Cyanosis, tachycardia, hypotension
      d. Positive Homans' sign
      e. S_3 or S_4 gallop rhythms; murmurs
      f. Pulmonic heart sound accentuated
      g. Decreased breath sounds/rales/wheezing
      h. Anxiety, fear of suffocation
      i. Diminished activity tolerance
   3. Complications
      a. Right-sided heart failure (cor pulmonale)
      b. Chronic pulmonary hypertension
      c. Cardiac arrhythmias
      d. Alveolar necrosis, hemorrhage, or infection

E. Management
   1. Drug therapy
      a. Heparin: Maintain partial thromboplastin time at 2 to 2.5 times control level.
      b. Sodium warfarin (Coumadin): Initiate before heparin is discontinued
         (1) Usually maintained for 3 to 6 months

(2) Monitoring of prothrombin time or the International Normalized Ratio (INR)
(3) INR now recommended by World Health Organization (WHO)
(4) Recommended therapeutic INR range is 2.0 to 3.0
2. Patient/family education/instruction
   a. Instruct on side effect of bleeding (e.g., bleeding gums; black, tarry stools; hematuria).
   b. Avoid use of aspirin.
   c. Avoid foods high in vitamin K (e.g., bananas, dark vegetables).
   d. Instruct in method for applying antiembolic stockings: Apply in morning before rising; inspect skin daily; remove at least twice daily for 15 minutes; keep wrinkle-free.
   e. Avoid hazardous activity (use electric razor, soft-bristled toothbrush).
   f. Obtain Medic Alert® bracelet.
   g. Notify other health care providers of anticoagulant therapy.
   h. Take anticoagulant at same time each day.
   i. Instruct in measures to avoid constipation.
   j. Instruct in problems that require notification of physician (e.g., evidence of bleeding, forgetting to take medication).
   k. Explain purpose of bed rest (if ordered).
   l. Plan a program to increase activity safely.
3. Prevention teaching/instruction
   a. Describe signs/symptoms of thrombophlebitis.
   b. Teach measures to avoid venous stasis (e.g., avoid standing in one position, crossing legs, or wearing constrictive clothing); instruct patient to walk 5 minutes every hour during travel.
   c. Caution patient never to rub or massage sore calf muscles.
   d. Instruct patient to elevate legs when sitting.
   e. Encourage patient to cease smoking because of the vasoconstrictive effect.
4. Vena cava filters
   a. Indicated for patients with contraindications for anticoagulant therapy (e.g., patients receiving chemotherapy and/or radiation therapy typically are not candidates for anticoagulation therapy)
   b. Placed in the inferior vena cava (IVC) via the internal jugular or femoral vein

c. Measures to prevent filter dislodgment include avoiding
   (1) Abdominal trauma
   (2) Significant valsalva maneuvers
   (3) Excessive coughing
d. Signs and symptoms of vena cava occlusion/penetration include:
   (1) Localized pain
   (2) Lower extremity edema
   (3) Venous stasis ulcers

STUDY QUESTIONS AND EXERCISES

1. Identify three conditions that may lead to pulmonary embolus.
2. What causes bronchoconstriction to occur during clot release?
3. List five signs and symptoms of a pulmonary embolus.
4. Identify three areas of teaching necessary for the patient on sodium warfarin therapy.

BIBLIOGRAPHY

Bullock, B.L., and P.P. Rosendahl. 1992. *Pathophysiology: Adapting and alteration in function.* Philadelphia: J.B. Lippincott Co.

Fahey, V.A. 1988. *Vascular nursing.* Philadelphia: W.B. Saunders Co.

Sticklin, L.A., and M. Walkenstein. 1993. Vena cava filters: A nursing perspective. *Oncology Nursing Forum* 30, no. 3:507-513.

Swearingen, P.L., and J.H. Keen. 1991. *Manual of critical care.* St. Louis: Mosby-Year Book, Inc.

Wilson, S.F., and J.M. Thompson. 1990. *Respiratory disorders.* St. Louis: Mosby-Year Book, Inc.

26

Pleural Effusion

Antoinette Laguzza

A. Definition of pleural effusion: accumulation of fluid in pleural space with compression of lung tissue, usually secondary to other diseases
B. Etiology
 1. Increased pulmonary capillary pressure (e.g., during left-sided heart failure)
 2. Decreased capillary oncotic pressure (e.g., when liver or kidneys fail)
 3. Inflamed pleura, pleural spaces, and underlying structure (e.g., due to infection or tumor)
 4. Impaired lymphatic system function (e.g., due to obstruction)
C. Types
 1. Transudate: filtrates of plasma that move across intact capillary walls due to imbalances in hydrostatic or oncotic pressures; occurs when factors influencing formation and reabsorption of pleural fluid are altered
   a. Causes
    (1) Congestive heart failure
    (2) Renal failure
    (3) Hypoproteinemia
    (4) Nephrotic syndrome
    (5) Myxedema
    (6) Cirrhosis with ascites
    (7) Peritoneal dialysis
    (8) Acute atelectasis
 2. Exudate: high-specific-gravity substances that escape from the blood vessels; occurs in conditions that increase capillary permeability

a. Causes
    (1) Collagen vascular conditions
    (2) Rheumatoid pleuritis: systemic lupus erythematosus
3. Drug hypersensitivity: nitrofurantoin; procainamide hydrochloride
4. Gastrointestinal conditions: hepatic abscess; pancreatitis; subphrenic abscess
5. Infections: bacterial (e.g., tuberculosis); fungal; parasitic; viral
6. Neoplasms: mesotheliomas; metastatic disease
7. Trauma: chylothorax; hemothorax
8. Other conditions: pulmonary infarction; asbestos exposure; postmyocardial infarction syndrome; congenital lymphatic abnormalities

D. Symptomatology and assessments (dependent on amount and rate of accumulation)
    1. Tachypnea
    2. Dyspnea
    3. Orthopnea
    4. Coughing
    5. Shortness of breath
    6. Tachycardia
    7. Diminished breath sounds over the effusion
    8. Egobronchophony above the effusion
    9. Bronchial breath sounds above the effusion
    10. Pleuritic chest pain

E. Diagnosis
    1. Chest X-ray: visualized if effusion is more than 200 to 300 mL
    2. Ultrasound
    3. Thoracentesis
    4. Pleural fluid analysis: Gram stain; acid-fast bacillus stain; red and white blood cell count; blood chemistry; pH; cytology

F. Management
    1. Determine cause by thoracentesis and pleural fluid analysis.
    2. Remove fluid by thoracentesis and chest tube drainage.
    3. Obliterate the pleural space.
        a. Pleurectomy: surgical stripping of parietal pleura away from visceral pleura, which produces severe inflammatory reaction with formation of adhesion
        b. Pleurodesis: instillation of sclerosing substance (tetracycline, nitrogen mustard, radioactive isotopes) into pleural space via

thoracotomy tube, resulting in adhesion of parietal and visceral pleura
4. Treat the cause.
5. Institute nursing interventions.
   a. Prepare for diagnostic and treatment procedures.
   b. Promote comfort: positioning, oxygen therapy, analgesia.
   c. Offer emotional support.
   d. Teach patient about therapy.
   e. Monitor closely for recurrence.

STUDY QUESTIONS AND EXERCISES

1. Differentiate between effusions classified as transudates and exudates and describe the pathogenesis of each.
2. Identify common symptoms of pleural effusion and correlated assessments necessary to detect and monitor its status.

BIBLIOGRAPHY

Connor, P., et al. 1989. Two stages of care for pleural effusion. *RN* 52, no. 5:30–34.

Hewitt, J.B., and W.R. Janssen. 1987. A management strategy for malignancy-induced pleural effusion: Long-term thoracostomy drainage. *Oncology Nursing Forum* September/October:17–22.

Luckmann, J., and K.C. Sorensen. 1987. *Medical-surgical nursing: A psychophysiologic approach.* Philadelphia: W.B. Saunders Co.

Pleural effusions without symptoms. 1990. *Emergency Medicine* 22, no. 9:55–56.

Smeltzer, S., and B.G. Bare. 1992. *Brunner and Suddarth's textbook of medical-surgical nursing.* Philadelphia: J.B. Lippincott Co.

27

Tuberculosis

Elizabeth A. Guba and Kathy J. Morgan

A. Definition: airborne communicable disease
   1. Cause: *Mycobacterium tuberculosis* (tubercle bacillus [TB]) causes vast majority of cases
      a. *M. tuberculosis* has three closely related species (known as *M. tuberculosis* complex) that can cause disease
         (1) *M. bovis* and *M. africanum:* rare in United States
         (2) *M. microti:* does not cause human disease
      b. Nontuberculous mycobacteria: mycobacteria that do not cause TB
   2. Primary transmission: droplet-nuclei airborne transmission by infectious person with pulmonary or laryngeal TB
      a. Tubercle bacilli multiply in alveolar macrophages with spread through bloodstream
      b. Immune system response within 2 to 10 weeks usually prevents disease development
      c. Three factors for transmission to occur
         (1) Infectiousness of person with TB
         (2) Duration of exposure
         (3) Environment in which exposure occurs
   3. Infection progresses to disease when immune system can no longer handle tubercle bacilli and bacilli reactivate and multiply.
      a. Infection progresses to disease rapidly or very slowly over many years.
      b. Lymphocytes omit toxins as TB organisms are ingested; toxins liquefy and destroy lung tissue; cavities form.
      c. Ten percent of infected persons develop disease.
      d. Ninety percent of infected persons remain disease free.

4. Primary sites of TB
   a. Lungs (85% of all cases diagnosed)
   b. Genitourinary system (especially kidneys)
   c. Central nervous system
   d. Pleura
   e. Disseminated (miliary TB)
   f. Lymphatic
5. Risk factors
   a. Close contact with person with infectious TB: family members, friends, co-workers, etc.
   b. Drug-resistant TB: patients usually infectious for longer periods with potential to infect more people
6. Serious national health problem with 14% increase in incidence from 1985 through 1993 (25,313 new cases); factors attributed to increase:
   a. Immigrants entering the United States from countries that have high incidence of TB (e.g., Asia, Africa, Latin America)
   b. Residents of long-term care facilities (homeless shelters, correctional institutions, low-rent housing, nursing homes, mental facilities, etc.)
   c. Homeless population
   d. Human immunodeficiency virus (HIV) epidemic
   e. Decreased funding to federal/state health programs
7. Certain medical conditions increase risk of infection progressing to disease: HIV, diabetes mellitus, silicosis, head and neck cancer, end-stage renal disease, substance abuse, prolonged corticosteroid therapy, immunosuppressive therapy, intestinal bypass, gastrectomy, chronic malabsorption syndrome, Hodgkin's disease, leukemia, body weight 10% or more below ideal weight
8. Signs/symptoms (that last longer than 3 weeks)
   a. Persistent cough
   b. Hemoptysis
   c. Hoarseness
   d. Fever
   e. Chills
   f. Night sweats
   g. Anorexia
   h. Unexplained weight loss
B. Screening

1. High-risk groups should be screened for infection
    a. HIV-infected persons
    b. Persons with risk factors for HIV but HIV status is not known
    c. Health care workers
    d. Contacts of a person with infectious TB
    e. Immigrants from countries with increased incidence of TB
    f. Intravenous (IV) drug users
    g. Residents and staff of long-term care facilities
    h. Homeless persons
    i. Migrant farm workers
    j. Persons with certain medical conditions
    k. Low-income, medically underserved population, especially where overcrowded living quarters exist
2. Mantoux TB skin test is preferred screening method
    a. Intradermal injection of 0.1 mL of purified protein derivative (PPD) tuberculin that contains 5 tuberculin units (TU)
        (1) Reaction is read 48 to 72 hours after injection; measure only induration; results are recorded in millimeters.
        (2) Injection produces a 6- to 10-mm diameter, pale elevation of the skin (a wheal).
    b. Classification of tuberculin reaction
        (1) A wheal greater than or equal to 5 mm is positive in
            (a) Persons with known or suspected HIV infection
            (b) IV drug users
            (c) Persons with chest X-ray suggestive of previous TB
            (d) Persons with close contacts with a person with infectious TB
        (2) A wheal greater than or equal to 10 mm is positive in
            (a) Children younger than 4 years of age
            (b) Residents of long-term care facilities
            (c) Immigrants from countries with high incidence of TB
            (d) Persons with other medical conditions
            (e) Other groups with increased rate of TB (e.g., homeless, migrant farm workers, residents of long-term care facilities, medically underserved, low-income groups)
        (3) A wheal greater than or equal to 15 mm is positive in any individual with no known risk factors for TB
3. Anergy: delayed-type hypersensitivity response (e.g., tuberculin reaction) may decrease or disappear

180 CORE CURRICULUM FOR HOME HEALTH CARE NURSING

   a. Causes: HIV infection, measles or other viral infections, corticosteroids or immunosuppressive medications, sarcoidosis, Hodgkin's disease, febrile or severe illnesses
   b. 10% to 25% of persons with TB have negative skin tests
   c. Test for anergy: Administer at least two other delayed-type hypersensitivity antigens (e.g., mumps, tetanus toxoid, or Candida) along with TB skin test. Reaction of greater than or equal to 3 mm to any of the antigens: not anergic.
  4. Two-step testing: Differentiates between boosted reactions and reactions caused by new infection.
   a. Person infected with *M. tuberculosis* for many years may develop delayed-type hypersensitivity.
    (1) When skin tested years later, may have negative reaction, but test may boost (stimulate) ability to react to tuberculin.
    (2) Subsequent skin tests may be positive and interpreted as new infection.
   b. Method/interpretation
    (1) If first test positive, person considered infected
    (2) If first test negative, administer second test 1 to 3 weeks later
    (3) If second test positive, person considered infected
    (4) If second test negative, person considered not infected
   c. Utilized for initial skin testing of adults who will be retested periodically
C. Diagnosis
  1. Medical history and physical examination for signs/symptoms
  2. Mantoux TB skin test
  3. X-ray
   a. Abnormalities may or may not be present
   b. Cannot confirm diagnosis, but used to rule out pulmonary TB
  4. Sputum cultures and smears
   a. At least three early-morning specimens collected on different days
   b. Detection of acid-fast bacilli (AFB) in stained smears; results usually available in 24 hours; negative smear does not exclude infection
   c. Positive culture for *M. tuberculosis* confirms diagnosis
    (1) Results can take 10 to 14 days or 6 to 12 weeks depending on testing methodology

(2) Positive cultures must be tested for drug susceptibility
D. Treatment
1. Must treat for 6 to 24 months or patient can become infectious and symptomatic again
2. Multiple drug therapy
   a. Single medication use can cause drug-resistant strains to that drug
   b. Adding a single medication to regimen that is failing can cause drug-resistant strains
3. First-line drugs: four drugs initially for 2 months (dosing may be daily, two times per week, or three times per week)
   a. Isoniazid (INH): 300 to 900 mg/day orally
      (1) Adverse reactions: hepatitis, peripheral neuropathy, mild central nervous system (CNS) effects, drug interactions
      (2) Monitoring: baseline hepatic enzymes; repeat if patient has symptoms of or is at high risk for adverse reactions or if baseline results abnormal
         (a) Pyridoxine can prevent peripheral neuropathy.
         (b) Hepatitis risk increases with alcohol use and age.
   b. Rifampin (RIF): up to 600 mg/day orally
      (1) Adverse reactions: gastrointestinal (GI) upset, hepatitis, bleeding, rash, flulike symptoms, drug interactions
      (2) Monitoring: baseline complete blood count (CBC), platelets, and hepatic enzymes; repeat if abnormal results or if patient has symptoms of adverse reaction
      (3) Colors body fluids orange (e.g., urine, tears, saliva)
      (4) Significant interactions (e.g., methadone, birth control pills, many other drugs)
   c. Pyrazinamide (PZA): 15 to 70 mg/day orally
      (1) Adverse reactions: rash, hepatitis, GI upset, joint pain, hyperuricemia, gout (rare)
      (2) Monitoring: baseline uric acid and hepatic enzymes; repeat if abnormal results or if patient has symptoms of adverse reactions
      (3) Treat hyperuricemia only if patient has symptoms
   d. Ethambutol (EMB): 15 mg/kg per day orally
      (1) Adverse reaction: optic neuritis
      (2) Monitoring: baseline and monthly tests for color vision and visual acuity

        (3) Not recommended for children too young to be monitored for vision changes unless drug-resistant TB
    e. Streptomycin (SM): 30 mg/kg per day orally
        (1) May be used instead of EMB
        (2) Adverse reactions: ototoxicity and renal toxicity
        (3) Monitoring: baseline (and repeat as indicated) hearing tests and renal function
        (4) Avoid or decrease dose in adults 60 years of age or older
    f. Adjustments to medications when susceptibility results received
    g. INH, RIF, and PZA may be adequate for initial therapy if drug resistance not likely
    h. If INH and RIF demonstrate susceptibility, continue two to three times per week for 4 months
4. Second-line drugs: used when drug-resistant TB diagnosed and/or patient cannot tolerate first-line drugs; side effects more pronounced with second-line drugs
    a. Capreomycin: 15 to 30 mg/kg per day orally
        (1) Adverse reactions: toxicity (auditory, vestibular, and renal)
        (2) Monitoring: assess vestibular and hearing function, blood urea nitrogen, and creatinine
    b. Kanamycin: 15 to 30 mg/kg per day orally
        (1) Adverse reactions: toxicity (auditory, vestibular, and renal)
        (2) Monitoring: assess vestibular and hearing function, blood urea nitrogen and creatinine
    c. Aminosalicylic acid (PAS): 150 mg/kg per day orally
        (1) Adverse reactions: sodium load, GI upset, hypersensitivity, hepatotoxicity
        (2) Monitoring: hepatic enzymes and volume status (especially in cardiac patients)
    d. Ethionamide: 15 to 20 mg/kg per day orally
        (1) Adverse reactions: GI upset, metallic taste, bloating, hypersensitivity, hepatotoxicity
        (2) Monitoring: hepatic enzymes
        (3) May cause hypothyroid condition, especially if used with PAS
    e. Cycloserine: 15 to 20 mg/kg per day orally
        (1) Adverse reactions: psychosis, convulsions, depression, headache, rash, drug interactions

(2) Monitoring: serum drug levels and mental status
   f. Ciprofloxacin: 500 to 1000 mg/day orally
      (1) Adverse reactions: headache, restlessness, dizziness, GI upset, hypersensitivity
      (2) Monitoring: drug interactions (avoid antacids, iron, zinc, sucralfate)
   g. Amikacin: 15 mg/kg per day orally
      (1) Adverse reactions: renal toxicity, hearing loss, dizziness
      (2) Monitoring: hearing function, renal function, serum drug levels
      (3) Not approved by Food and Drug Administration (FDA) for treatment of TB
   h. Clofazimine: 100 to 300 mg/kg per day orally
      (1) Adverse reactions: severe organ damage and abdominal pain secondary to crystal deposits, GI upset, skin discoloration (avoid sunlight, dose at mealtime)
      (2) Monitoring: drug interactions
      (3) Not approved by FDA for treatment of TB; efficacy unproven
   i. Ofloxacin: 400 to 800 mg/day orally
      (1) Adverse reactions: restlessness, headaches, dizziness, GI upset, hypersensitivity, drug interactions (avoid antacids, iron, zinc, sucralfate)
      (2) Monitoring: drug interactions
      (3) Not approved by FDA for treatment of TB
E. Preventive therapy
   1. Persons in high-risk groups with positive skin test results regardless of age
      a. Close contacts of person with infectious TB (positive reaction greater than or equal to 5 mm)
      b. IV drug users known to be HIV negative (positive reaction greater than or equal to 10 mm)
      c. Persons with certain medical conditions (positive reaction greater than or equal to 10 mm)
      d. Persons with chest X-ray findings suggestive of previous TB who received inadequate or no treatment (positive reaction greater than or equal to 5 mm)
      e. Persons with known or suspected HIV (positive reaction greater than or equal to 5 mm)

f. Conversion of skin test from negative to positive within past 2 years (greater than or equal to 10 mm increase if younger than 35 years; greater than or equal to 15 mm increase if 35 years of age or older)
  2. Persons in high-prevalence groups with positive reaction greater than or equal to 10 mm
     a. Residents of long-term care facilities
     b. Medically underserved, low-income populations with high-risk racial/ethic groups (Native Americans, Hispanics, Pacific Islanders, Asians, blacks)
     c. Immigrants from countries in which TB is common
     d. Children younger than 4 years of age
  3. Persons with occupational exposure to TB if positive tuberculin tests
     a. Health care workers and staffs of correctional institutions, drug/alcohol treatment centers, etc.
     b. Employees' individual risk factors for TB and prevalence of TB must be considered
  4. Treatment: typically INH preventive therapy daily for 12 months
F. Home care nursing management
  1. Adherence to drug therapy
     a. Nonadherence is major problem in TB control
        (1) 25% of patients do not complete recommended regimen within 12 months
        (2) Inadequate treatment: relapse, continued transmission, and/or drug-resistant strains
     b. Directly observed therapy (DOT): ensures adherence
        (1) Nurse or another designated person watches patient swallow each dose of medication
        (2) Should be considered for all patients secondary to typical poor adherence
        (3) Reduces frequency of relapse and drug-resistant strains
     c. Use incentives/enablers to increase adherence
  2. Education to medications
     a. Adherence and dosing
     b. Adverse reactions
     c. Monitoring according to suggested drug protocols
     d. Response to treatment
        (1) If sputum cultures positive before treatment: cultures every month until cultures negative

(a) When sputum cultures negative for *M. tuberculosis* after treatment for 2 months, perform at least one sputum culture and smear at completion of therapy
(b) Multidrug-resistant TB: cultures monthly throughout treatment
(2) Chest X-ray: at completion of treatment for future baseline comparison
(3) Positive cultures after 2 months of therapy: evaluate for medication nonadherence or drug-resistant disease
(4) Adding a drug to a failing regimen: may produce drug-resistant strains
(5) If negative sputum cultures before treatment: chest X-rays and clinical evaluation
3. Infection control
   a. Patient not infectious if three criteria met:
      (1) Favorable clinical response to therapy (symptoms improve)
      (2) Three consecutive negative sputum smears (collected on different days)
      (3) Adequate drug therapy for at least 2 to 3 weeks
   b. Extrapulmonary TB patient usually not infectious (draining skin or tissue abscess can contain *M. tuberculosis* and be infectious)
   c. Patient education
      (1) Transmission: Limit contacts while infectious.
      (2) Cover mouth/nose with tissue when coughing/sneezing.
      (3) Wash hands frequently.
      (4) Cleanse equipment and utensils.
      (5) Practice other infection control measures as appropriate.
   d. Cough-inducing procedures should not be performed on patient with infectious TB unless absolutely necessary.
      (1) Perform in well-ventilated area away from other family members (e.g., open window or perform outside home).
      (2) Nurse should wear respiratory protection during procedure.
   e. Respiratory protection for home care staff
      (1) National Institute for Occupational Safety and Health (NIOSH)-approved high-efficiency particulate air (HEPA) particulate respirator
      (2) To be worn by staff entering patient's home until patient not infectious

4. Coordination with public health department
   a. Screening and reporting
   b. Management of preventive therapy
5. Potential nursing diagnoses
   a. Ineffective airway clearance/breathing pattern
   b. Altered nutrition: less than body requirements
   c. Fear related to disease transmission and chronic disease
   d. Potential for infection (patient and close contacts)
   e. Knowledge deficit
6. Screening high-risk groups
7. Initial and ongoing patient assessment
8. Recognition of association of TB with other diseases (e.g., HIV)
9. Assessment of close contacts and arranging follow-up
10. Multidrug-resistant TB (MDR TB): difficult to treat
    a. Resistant to RIF and INH
    b. Individualized, prolonged treatment based on drug susceptibility and medication history
    c. May need expert consultation with TB specialist if unfamiliar with MDR TB treatment
11. Bacille Calmette-Guérin (BCG) vaccine: not usually recommended in United States
    a. Low risk of infection with *M. tuberculosis*
    b. Effectiveness varies substantially
    c. Can cause a positive skin test result
    d. Given only to infants and children with negative skin test results in certain situations (per Centers for Disease Control [CDC] recommendations)
       (1) Infant/child exposed continuously to patient with infectious TB that is resistant to RIF and INH
       (2) Infant/child exposed continuously to patient with infectious TB and infant/child cannot be given INH preventive therapy
       (3) Infant/child belongs to high-risk groups with new infection rates of 1% or greater and usual surveillance/treatment programs have failed

STUDY QUESTIONS AND EXERCISES

1. Describe the first-line drugs used for treating TB.
2. How is TB diagnosed?
3. List signs/symptoms of infectious TB.
4. Describe the preferred screening method for TB, and actual administration and interpretation of results.
5. Develop a nursing plan of care for a patient newly diagnosed with TB.

BIBLIOGRAPHY

Cantwell, M.F., et al. August 17, 1994. Epidemiology of tuberculosis in the United States, 1985 through 1992. *Journal of the American Medical Association* 272, no. 7:535-539.

Centers for Disease Control and Prevention. October 28, 1994. Guidelines for preventing the transmission of Mycobacterium tuberculosis in health-care facilities, 1994. *Morbidity and Mortality Weekly Report* 43, no. RR-13:1-132.

Centers for Disease Control and Prevention. May 21, 1993. Initial therapy for tuberculosis in the era of multidrug resistance: Recommendations of the advisory council for the elimination of tuberculosis. *Morbidity and Mortality Weekly Report* 42, no. RR-7:1-8.

Centers for Disease Control and Prevention. May 18, 1990. Screening for tuberculosis and tuberculous infection in high-risk populations: Recommendations of the advisory committee for elimination of tuberculosis. *Morbidity and Mortality Weekly Report* 39, no. RR-8:1-7.

Ismeurt, R.L., and C.O. Long. 1993. Tuberculosis: A new threat from an old nemesis. *Home Healthcare Nurse* 11, no. 4:16-23.

3M Occupational Health and Environmental Safety Division. January 1994. OSHA enforcement procedures for occupational exposure to TB. *3M Regulation Update.* no. 16.

United States Department of Health and Human Services, Public Health Service. 1994. *Core curriculum on tuberculosis: What the clinician should know.* Atlanta: Centers for Disease Control and Prevention.

United States Department of Health and Human Services, Public Health Service. 1994. *Improving patient adherence to tuberculosis treatment.* Atlanta: Centers for Disease Control and Prevention.

28

Cystic Fibrosis

Kathleen Cummings

A. Definitions/points of emphasis
 1. Cystic fibrosis (CF) is a fatal inherited genetic disease; it involves multiple organ systems; it is an autosomally recessive disease.
 2. CF occurs without warning. Since carriers have no symptoms, they usually do not know they are carriers until they have a child with the disease.
 3. Most common complications:
    a. Recurrent pneumonia
    b. Chronic diarrhea
    c. Failure to maintain weight
    d. Nasal polyps
    e. Enlarged fingertips and toes
 4. Intellectual ability is not impaired; CF does not affect the brain.
 5. CF patients are living longer. Since 1938, life expectancy has risen from 6 months to 28 years; many survive into their 30s, 40s, and 50s, but still suffer from a chronic terminal disease.
 6. Rapid advances in genetic research have paved the way for gene-therapy treatments that would replace defective CF cells with healthy ones.
 7. Psychosocial needs of both individuals with CF and their families require particular attention.
    a. Nurse's role: directed toward enhancing the parent's ability to cope
    b. Focus on the individual's developmental needs
B. Pathophysiology
 1. Genetic defect is in chromosome 7, which is responsible for the defect in chloride transport.

Cystic Fibrosis

2. There is a dysfunction of the exocrine (mucus-producing) glands and an increase in the serum sodium/chloride content in sweat.
3. Genetically, CF requires the affected offspring to have two CF genes: parents are heterozygote carriers of the disease; each has only one CF gene.
   a. 25% chance that a child will inherit one CF gene from each parent and have CF
   b. 50% chance that a child will inherit only one CF gene from either parent and be a carrier
   c. 25% inherit normal genes; will be completely free of CF
4. Chloride channel (gate through which chloride ions move into and out of the cell) is present but closed in cells affected by CF.
5. When chloride ions cannot leave the cell, they affect the movement of other ions, including sodium, which in turn affects the movement of water into and out of the cell.
   a. Ion-clogged cells pull water from the body's secretions, leaving behind the very thick, sticky mucus characteristic of CF.
      (1) Sweat has too much salt in it.
      (2) Mucus does not have enough water.
   b. Secretions obstruct pancreatic and pulmonary passages.
6. Viscous mucous gland secretions cause mechanical obstruction that results in major clinical manifestations.

C. Demographics
   1. Leading, fatal inherited disease in the United States; affects some 30,000 children and young adults
   2. Commonly carried; 1 in 20 Americans—about 12 million people—carries the defective CF gene
   3. Affects one in 2,000 white babies and 1 in 17,000 black babies; rarely found in Asians and American Indians
   4. Survival rate has increased: median life expectancy is 29 years of age

D. Diagnosis
   1. Usually shortly after birth or in early childhood
      a. Three to four percent of patients are not diagnosed until age 18 or older.
      b. Evaluation should be considered for any child presenting with meconium ileus; failure to thrive; large, frothy, foul-smelling stools; intestinal obstruction due to atresia; fecal inspissation; intussusception; rectal prolapse; repeated respiratory infections; or chronic sinusitis.

2. Diagnosis requires usually two of the following: positive family history for CF, chronic obstructive pulmonary disease, abnormal sweat test, and/or pancreatic enzyme deficiencies.
3. Use of pilocarpine iontophoresis in a sweat test reveals a sweat chloride concentration.
    a. A finding of a sweat chloride concentration greater than 60 mEq/L in a patient whose clinical picture is consistent with CF is confirmatory.
    b. Parents will report a salty taste after they have kissed the child.
4. Classic presentation of CF in early infancy: failure to thrive
    a. Decreased appetite
    b. Distended abdomen
    c. Reduced muscle mass
    d. Poor soft tissue development, especially in the thighs, buttocks, and upper arms
    e. Primary growth failure is in weight
E. Clinical manifestations
   1. Pancreas
      a. 85% to 95% of CF patients have pancreatic involvement
         (1) Thick secretions block ducts in pancreas, leading to cystic dilations of the small lobes
         (2) Eventually degenerate and progress to diffuse fibrosis
      b. Deficiencies of trypsin, amylase, lipase: result in impaired digestion of nutrients, especially fats and protein
      c. Pancreatic fibrosis occurs and progresses.
         (1) Hyperglycemia may occur because of a reduction in the number of island of Langerhans cells.
         (2) With advanced pancreatic disease, diabetes mellitus may ensue.
      d. As undigested fats and proteins are excreted, bulk of stool is increased two to three times the normal amount.
         (1) Excessive stool fat
         (2) Stools extremely frothy and foul smelling
      e. Inability to absorb fats leads to deficiency of fat-soluble vitamins A, D, E, and K.
   2. Respiratory system
      a. Pulmonary involvement: most common and severe clinical manifestation; over 90% of CF patients die of severe pulmonary disease

b. Lungs normal at birth
   (1) Bronchiolar obstruction by thick, tenacious mucus soon develops
   (2) Because of the viscosity of the mucus, ciliate action reduced, hindering effective expectoration
c. With appropriate interventions at early stages, most lung disease can be controlled or at least halted
   (1) If not prevented, usually see increased moist coughs, yellow or green sputum, barrel chest, coarse crackles and wheezes throughout the lungs
   (2) Chronic infections lead to very significant inflammatory changes in the airways
   (3) *Staphylococcus aureus:* most frequently the initial pathogen isolated
   (4) Later infections caused by *Haemophilus influenzae,* Streptococcus *pneumoniae,* and finally *Pseudomonas aeruginosa* and *P. cepacia*
       (a) *Pseudomonas* infections tend to persist
       (b) Organism rarely removed regardless of antibiotic therapy
3. Gastrointestinal (GI) tract: meconium ileus in the newborn: one of the earliest manifestations; later in life intestinal obstruction (meconium ileus equivalent) can occur
4. Liver: obstruction of bile ducts causing biliary cirrhosis in 4% of patients clinically and 25% on autopsy
   a. Decreased secretion of bile salts: may lead to biliary stasis
   b. Portal hypertension and esophageal varices: may occur in adulthood
   c. Biliary fibrosis: may occur and contribute to cirrhosis
5. Reproductive system
   a. Male patients: 95% are sterile as result of maldevelopment or obstruction of the epididymis, vas deferens, and seminal vesicles
   b. Female patients: able to reproduce, although increased viscosity and dehydrated cervical mucus acts as a barrier to sperm
F. Treatments
   1. Medications
      a. Enzyme therapy: to prevent malnutrition, decrease symptoms, and increase weight gain

(1) Pancreatin and pancrelipase: dosage to start is one to three capsules with meals and half that number with snacks; should not be taken without food; administer after an antacid; capsules should not be crushed or chewed
 (a) Low-fat diet preferred to decrease GI symptoms
 (b) Adjustments made depending on signs of fat malabsorption (steatorrhea, abdominal cramping, flatulence, and fullness)
 (c) Children under 6 years old: initial dose is up to one capsule per meal or snack; typical doses are 1,500 to 3,000 U.S.P. lipase units/kg per meal
(2) Both medications contain three primary pancreatic enzymes
 (a) Protease: protein digestion
 (b) Lipase: fat digestion
 (c) Amylase: starch digestion
b. Vitamin therapy: two multivitamin tablets a day, one containing iron
 (1) Vitamin E: supplemented in dosages of 100 to 400 IU/day
 (2) Vitamin K: not necessary in children under 1 year of age
  (a) Normal dose of Vitamin K supplementation in children 2 to 5 years of age: 50 to 100 g daily
  (b) Older children: 1 to 5 mg twice weekly
c. Antibiotics: Positive culture alone does not indicate a need for treatment due to colonization. Signs and symptoms of infection should also be present before instituting antibiotic therapy.
 (1) *S. aureus*
  (a) Cloxacillin (Cloxapen)
   1) Adult dose: 1 to 4 g/day orally in divided doses every 6 hours
   2) Child dose: 50 to 100 mg/kg per day orally in divided doses every 6 hours; needs to be taken on an empty stomach
   3) Need to complete entire course of medication as ordered
  (b) Dicloxacillin (Dycill)
   1) Adult dose: 0.5 to 4 g/day orally in divided doses every 6 hours

2) Child dose: 12.5 to 25 mg/kg per day orally in divided doses every 6 hours
 (c) Cephalexin (Keflex)
  1) Adult dose: 250 to 500 mg orally every 6 hours
  2) Child dose: 25 to 50 mg/kg per day orally in four equal doses
 (d) Cefprozil (Cefzil)
  1) Adult dose (13 years and older): 500 mg orally every 12 to 24 hours
  2) Child dose (2 to 12 years old): 7.5 mg/kg orally every 12 hours
  3) Infant dose (6 months to 2 years old): 15 mg/kg orally every 12 hours
 (f) Cefaclor (Ceclor)
  1) Adult dose: 250 to 500 mg orally every 8 hours, not to exceed 4 g/day
  2) Child dose (>1 month old): 20 to 40 mg/kg per day orally in divided doses every 8 hours, not to exceed 1 g/day
 (g) Cefpodoxime proxetil (Vantin): recommended dosages, durations of therapy, and applicable patient populations vary
(2) *P. aeruginosa:* must be treated aggressively; preferably with two intravenous agents
 (a) Piperacillin (Pipracil): adult and child older than 12 years of age: 100 to 300 mg/kg per day intramuscularly (IM) or intravenously (IV) in divided doses every 4 to 6 hours
 (b) Ticarcillin (Ticar)
  1) Adult dose: 12 to 24 g/day IM or IV in divided doses every 3 to 6 hours; if IV, infuse over ½ to 2 hours
  2) Child dose: 50 to 300 mg/kg per day IM or IV in divided doses every 4 to 8 hours
  3) Neonate dose: 75 to 100 mg/kg per day IV infusion every 8 to 12 hours
 (c) Azlocillin (Azlin)
  1) Adult dose: 100 to 350 mg/kg per day IV in four to six divided doses, maximum dose of 24 g/day
  2) Child dose: 75 mg/kg IV every 4 hours, maximum dose of 24 g/day

(d) Ceftazidime (Fortaz)
   1) Adult dose: 1 g IM or IV every 8 to 12 hours for 5 to 10 days
   2) Child dose: 30 to 50 mg/kg per day IV every 12 hours, not to exceed 6 g/day
   3) Neonate dose: 30 mg/kg IV every 12 hours
(e) Ciprofloxacin (Cipro)
   1) Adult dose: 250 to 500 mg orally every 12 hours
   2) Fluoroquinolone that has been studied most in patients with CF.
   3) Penetrates into tissues and fluids
   4) Active against many strains of *P. aeruginosa*
(f) An aminoglycoside for 10 to 14 days is usually second drug used in combination with one of previously named drugs.
   1) Tobramycin: first choice of aminoglycosides
   2) Gentamicin may also be used
   3) Amikacin: when isolates are resistant to tobramycin and gentamicin
   4) When using aminoglycosides, drug levels should be monitored
(3) Inhalation
   (a) Most helpful "new" drug: Pulmozyme (deoxyribonuclease [DNase] manufactured by Genentech)
       1) Usually used daily as an inhalation solution; kept in the refrigerator
       2) When opened, if the entire ampule is not used, must be discarded
       3) Drug cannot be diluted or mixed with other drugs in the nebulizer
       4) Safety and effectiveness in children under 5 years of age: not yet been studied
       5) Reduces viscosity of lung and airway secretions by chopping up long strands of deoxyribonucleic acid (DNA) enmeshed in a gummy substance
       6) Lung function improved
       7) Reduction in respiratory infections when used daily with other standard therapies

            8) Side effects: inflammation of the throat, chest pain, voice alteration, and laryngitis
          (b) Aerosolized form of the diuretic Amiloride (Viscaid)
            1) Administered to block cells' absorption of sodium
            2) Decreases viscosity of secretions
    d. Bronchodilators: used usually in conjunction with pulmonary drainage
        (1) Albuterol (Proventil): (adult dose)
          (a) One or two puffs every 4 to 6 hours
          (b) 2 to 4 mg orally three times daily or four times daily, not to exceed 8 mg/day
        (2) Terbutaline (Brethine)
          (a) Adult and child older than 12 years of age:
            1) Two puffs minute apart, then every 4 to 6 hours
            2) 2.5 to 5 mg orally every 8 hours
            3) 0.25 mg subcutaneously every 8 hours may facilitate drainage
        (3) Theophylline: decreases airway obstruction through bronchodilation; should be reserved for those individuals who do not respond satisfactorily to other bronchodilators.
        (4) Patient/caregiver education
          (a) Wash inhaler with warm water daily.
          (b) Avoid smoking and smoke-filled rooms, especially when using bronchodilators.
          (c) Correct use of an inhaler: After shaking container, exhale, then place mouthpiece in the mouth, inhale slowly as container is pumped one time (one puff), hold breath, remove mouthpiece, and exhale slowly.
    e. Prednisone: as a corticosteroid, may be effective in decreasing inflammation associated with pulmonary exacerbations of CF
        (1) Adult dose: 2.5 to 15 mg orally twice daily to four times daily, then every day or every other day maintenance
        (2) Child dose: 0.14 to 2 mg/kg per day orally in divided doses four times daily
2. Nutrition
    a. Ideally, calorie consumption: 120 to 150% of the recommended daily allowance (RDA); protein consumption should be 200% of the RDA.

(1) Assess dietary preferences and dental status.
(2) Take daily dietary intake history.
(3) Understand elimination status and any changes in bowel pattern.
b. Dietary supplements may be required.
(1) Sixteen to twenty-four ounces of dietary supplements daily will provide 480 to 720 additional kilocalories to a patient's diet.
(2) Examples: Osmolite, Sustacal, Ensure Plus, ScandiShake
3. Pulmonary therapy
a. Goal: Prevent infections by removing secretions, improving aeration, and administering antimicrobial agents.
b. Postural drainage coupled with inhalation therapy by nebulization: Perform several times a day; segmental postural drainage is the clapping and vibrating of a cupped hand over a lung segment.
(1) Postural drainage for 5 to 10 minutes
(2) Followed by nebulization with prescribed medication
(3) Followed by another 10 to 20 minutes of postural drainage
(4) Routine is appropriate to be done twice a day
(5) Currently, hand-held vibrators are used on some lung areas to assist the patient to be more independent
4. Psychosocial interventions
a. Patients have been referred to as the "invisibly handicapped"; chronic disease may produce unique psychologic and social problems in patients and families.
b. Family of the patient with CF, perhaps more than any other factor, determines the quality of the patient's life.
c. Nursing interventions
(1) Assist parents in using positive coping mechanisms; marital stress is increased in families of children with CF.
(2) Nursing assessments: Include parents' perceptions of the illness, what is threatening in dealing with the illness, how they are coping with demands of the illness, and to whom they can turn for socioemotional and instrumental support.
(3) Support the family in what they should talk about with others regarding CF.
(a) Stress the need for openness and honesty to deal directly with implications of CF in all conversations.

(b) This is a specific disease even though there are many adjustments that have to be made.
(4) Health care team: Take a unified approach to all aspects of care to the child. Encourage parents to make no major changes in their lives for at least 1 full year after the diagnosis of CF is made for one of their children.
(5) Management of psychosocial issues raised by CF: an ongoing process
   (a) The nurse needs to understand developmental issues depending on the age of the CF patient.
   (b) Assess the need for a home treatment program.
   (c) Various ages have their developmental concerns.
      1) Toddler and preschool-aged children must learn to reconcile the demands of the treatment regimen (i.e., medications and postural drainage) with their need for autonomy.
      2) Adolescence provides a period of great challenge and major frustration for health care providers.
         a) Perhaps there is no other age group in which personal interactions between patient and staff assume such importance.
         b) Intense peer pressure is also present.
         c) Patients are ashamed of their bodies (i.e., clubbing of extremities, barrel chest), expectorating mucus in public, and delayed sexual development.
         d) High risk-taking behavior, which can be part of this age group's role, is particularly detrimental to the individual with CF.
         e) Adolescents also grow up with the awareness of their compromised future.

G. Other nursing interventions/patient teaching
  1. Instruct patient/caregiver on the correct dosage of the medication and its frequency.
     a. Teach the intravenous delivery of those medications given IV.
     b. Teach and educate about the side effects of all the medications prescribed, including over-the-counter medications.
  2. Provide information about the illness.
     a. Information leads to a sense of control by parents about the demands that may be made upon them.

b. Encourage parents to maintain or develop healthy rest and sleep patterns, proper nutritional habits, and a form of exercise routine to help them to cope physically and emotionally with all the demands.
3. Refer parents to a support group or provide them with an opportunity to meet other parents in similar situations.
   a. Nurse's role should be directed toward enhancing each parent's ability to cope.
   b. Positive feedback is essential.
4. Understand that preventive health care is the goal. The nurse must recognize that the provision of quality care requires a multidisciplinary approach; documentation should reflect this.
5. Be aware that acute exacerbations and deteriorating physical conditions threaten the hopes of the parents and the CF patient that they will survive this disease longer. When needed, hospice services may be provided to assist families who have chosen to have terminal care provided in their home rather than in the hospital.

STUDY QUESTIONS AND EXERCISES

1. Identify three major symptoms of cystic fibrosis, and define a therapy for each of these.
2. Describe two goals of nursing interventions that involve the psychosocial aspects of cystic fibrosis.
3. New to your caseload is a 17-year-old woman with cystic fibrosis diagnosed at age 2. She lives alone, has dropped out of high school, and works in a warehouse for a company that produces wood chips. Her job is box lifter on the 3 to 11 PM shift.. The referral to you defines the need for an in-home pulmonary drainage program. She has been hospitalized three times in the last 2 months. Develop a plan of care for this patient and explain why you have identified the problems you have.

BIBLIOGRAPHY

Gibson, S. 1988. Perspective in parental coping with a chronically ill child: The case of cystic fibrosis. *Comprehensive Pediatric Nursing* 11:33-41.

Greig, J. February 23, 1994. Growing demand. *Nursing Times* 90, no. 8:20.

Kuhn, R. February 1994. Cystic fibrosis: Current treatment and promise for the future. *American Druggist V* 209:51.

Physicians' desk reference. 49th ed. 1995. Montvale, N.J.: Medical Economics Data Production Co., Inc.

Skidmore-Roth, L. 1993. *Mosby nursing drug reference 1993.* St. Louis: Mosby-Year Book, Inc.

Starr, C. August 16, 1993. Promising new therapies in the works for cystic fibrosis. *Drug Topics.*

Tausisg, L. 1984. *Cystic fibrosis.* New York: Thieme-Stratton Inc.

Walker, C. December 1988. The clinical challenge of cystic fibrosis. *Journal of Intravenous Nursing* 11, no. 6:373-381.

29
Mechanical Ventilation at Home

Merry Mosier Foyt

A. Disorders that may lead to chronic ventilator dependence
   1. Neuromuscular disorders may affect respiratory drive or disrupt communication between respiratory centers and muscles (e.g., central nervous system, spinal cord, lower motor neuron, muscle and peripheral nerve disease or injury).
   2. Primary pulmonary disorders increase work of breathing, promote fatigue of respiratory muscles, and lead to inefficient gas exchange (e.g., emphysema, chronic bronchitis, other tracheal/bronchopulmonary ailments, and chronic aspiration).
   3. Thoracic and diaphragmatic disorders impair the efficiency of the respiratory pump (e.g., kyphoscoliosis and post-thoracoplasty).
B. Signs/symptoms of respiratory failure (commitment to mechanical ventilation may be necessary if patient presents with all or a combination of issues below and conventional oxygen supply devices do not meet patient's needs)
   1. Permanent neuromuscular injury or progressive disease producing apnea or nocturnal desaturation
   2. Abnormalities in arterial blood gases (ABGs): hypoxia, hypercarbia, alkalosis, acidosis
   3. Fatigue and weakness unrelieved by rest
   4. Apnea, bradypnea, or tachypnea
   5. Decreased vital capacity and inadequate results of pulmonary function tests
   6. Uncoordinated breathing patterns
   7. Hemodynamic instability

8. Confusion, headache
9. Anorexia and weight loss
10. Dyspnea on exertion, orthopnea
11. Reduction in functional status: unable to work; unable to carry out own activities of daily living (ADL); irritability; anxiety
12. Hypersomnolence
13. Retention of secretions and poor cough
C. Ventilator dependence (unweanability)
   1. Oxygen supply does not meet demand when attempt is made to withdraw ventilatory support.
   2. Patient is psychologically dependent on ventilatory support.
D. Selection of candidate for home ventilation
   1. Patients with neuromuscular or thoracic disorders do best.
   2. Usually noninvasive ventilatory support is used.
   3. Ventilation and oxygen requirements do not change very rapidly.
   4. Ventilation may only be needed at night.
   5. Ventilation is usually elective.
   6. As a rule, such patients adjust better to disability than do patients with chronic obstructive pulmonary disease (exception: in patients with amyotrophic lateral sclerosis, the disease progresses more rapidly than many other neuromuscular diseases).
E. Criteria for home mechanical ventilation
   1. Failure to wean; may be required only at night
   2. Clinical stability
      a. Maximal treatment of underlying respiratory disease
      b. Stable ventilatory requirement
      c. Adequate ABGs, minimal or no dyspnea, and acid-base stability on fraction of inspired oxygen (FiO_2) less than or equal to 40% and little or no positive end-expiratory pressure (PEEP)
      d. A manageable care routine (best if patient can help)
      e. Absence of pulmonary or other infection
      f. Absence of significant coexisting symptoms or disease (e.g., dysrhythmia or exacerbated congestive heart failure)
      g. Tracheostomy if artificial airway necessary
      h. Ability to manage secretions
      i. Other organ systems stable
      j. Adequate nutritional provision and status

3. A safe and accommodating home environment
4. Qualified caregivers: properly educated; always available (rarely will patients be able to spend time unattended)
5. Available community resources: durable medical equipment (DME) suppliers; emergency services; home health agencies
6. Financial support
7. Psychologic stability
    a. Absence of extreme depression and anxiety
    b. Ability to cope with stress
    c. A sense of humor helps!
8. Informed consent

F. Goals of care
   1. Rehabilitative
      a. Allow participation in ADL
      b. Partially or totally wean
   2. Custodial
      a. Comfort
      b. Acceptance of permanence.
      c. Acceptance of deterioration
      d. Satisfying self-sufficiency

G. Types of mechanical support
   1. Portable volume-cycled ventilator providing intermittent positive pressure ventilation (IPPV) via tracheostomy
      a. Generates pressure necessary to overcome airway resistance to deliver the prescribed volume of air.
      b. May be constant or periodic support.
      c. Advantages: Machine provides easier management of secretions; better control of volumes, FiO_2, and rate; and more efficient alarms.
      d. Disadvantages: Machine is associated with barotrauma pneumothorax and atelectasis; associated with tracheostomy (e.g., infection, bleeding, aspiration, structural changes, increased secretions, and difficulties with communication).
   2. IPPV via nasal, nasal-mouth, or mouth mask
      a. IPPV with mask is used with those with no need for artificial airway and secretion management, but who need help with airway patency, and those whose need is nocturnal and periodic (e.g., postpolio airway collapse and sleep apnea syndromes).
      b. Disadvantages: There is lack of airway and secretion management.

3. Negative pressure ventilators: tank respirator, iron lung, chest cuirass, body suit
   a. Negative pressure pulls diaphragm down, chest wall out, and decreases intrathoracic pressure, allowing for initiation of respiration.
   b. Negative pressure alternates with periods of no pressure to allow for inhalation and passive exhalation.
   c. Negative pressure ventilators are useful with patients who require nocturnal or periodic respiratory support.
   d. Advantages: Complications associated with tracheostomy and positive pressure ventilation are not an issue.
   e. Disadvantages: There remain problems with fit and comfort, synchronization with spontaneous breaths, position requirements (supine or semirecumbent), decreased mobility, lack of airway and secretion management, and pulmonary parameter control.
   f. Negative pressure ventilators are not indicated for those with airway patency problems (e.g., postpolio and sleep apnea syndromes).
4. Pneumobelt
   a. Pneumobelt is applied around abdomen and connected to positive pressure generator.
   b. Inflation of the belt compresses abdominal contents, causing the diaphragm to rise and exhalation to occur.
   c. Deflation allows the diaphragm to descend, decreasing intrapulmonary pressure and allowing inhalation to occur.
   d. The belt is used during waking hours, when the patient is upright at 75 degrees or greater.
5. Rocking bed
   a. Rocking of bed shifts abdominal contents, altering intrathoracic and intrapulmonary pressure, facilitating ventilation cycles.
   b. The bed works best in the presence of diaphragmatic paralysis and the absence of primary pulmonary disease.
   c. It may be used in combination with other devices.
   d. It assists in the mobilization of secretions.
H. Diagnostic monitoring
   1. Requirements are controversial and limited; patients should be medically stable and should not require continuous monitoring other than alarms indicating apnea, consistently low pressure, or equipment malfunction.

2. Do clinical assessment of pulmonary status.
   a. Vital signs
   b. Chest assessment
   c. Ventilatory assessment
   d. Sputum characteristics and management
3. Monitor patient on ventilator system periodically.
   a. Equipment function
   b. Static compliance and system resistance
   c. Airway pressure changes
   d. Work of breathing
4. Spot-check pulse oximeter and end-tidal CO_2 value.

I. Nursing management/teaching
  1. Tracheostomy care: stoma and cuff care; changing tube, inner cannula, dressing, and ties; suctioning
  2. Chest physical therapy techniques
  3. Importance of hydration
  4. Personal care/hygiene/self-care as tolerated
  5. Diet, including feeding tube care if necessary
  6. Rest and exercise
  7. Elimination and bowel care
  8. Foley catheter care as applicable
  9. Intravenous site care as applicable
  10. Bed-to-chair and chair-to-bed transfers
  11. Safety
  12. Diversional activities
  13. Universal precautions and sterile technique
  14. Signs and symptoms of cor pulmonale
  15. Schedules: personal care, respiratory hygiene, medications
  16. Importance of respite care
  17. Troubleshooting ventilator alarms
  18. DME procurement, maintenance, and DME supplier's telephone number
  19. Emergency measures
     a. Ventilator or power failure: use of manual resuscitator, backup ventilator, battery-powered as well as electrically powered ventilator and suction
     b. Telephone numbers of power company, emergency paramedical service, and fire department

       c. Dislodged tracheostomy tube
       d. Obstructed airway
       e. Cuff leaks
       f. Dyspnea or shortness of breath
       g. Signs and symptoms of infection
       h. Falls
       i. Bleeding
       j. Cardiac arrest
    20. Communication techniques
       a. Cuff deflation if tolerated
       b. Use of "talking" tracheostomy tube
       c. Electrolarynx
       d. Pneumatic voice apparatus
       e. "Sip and puff" communicators
       f. Computers with voice synthesizers
       g. Writing, sign language, communication boards, alphabet keyboards
       h. Lip reading
    21. Relaxation techniques
J. Assessment and reassessment of patient and home environment
    1. Accessibility
    2. Adequacy of equipment
    3. Safety
    4. Comfort
    5. Adjustment of patient and family members
    6. Functional status
    7. Pulmonary status

STUDY QUESTIONS AND EXERCISES

1. List three causes of ventilator dependence.
2. Describe the types of ventilators that may be used by ventilator-dependent patients in the home.
3. List the assessments, physical and environmental, that should be performed by the home health care professional when he or she visits the patient who is ventilator-dependent.

BIBLIOGRAPHY

Bach, J., et al. 1989. Management alternatives for post-polio respiratory insufficiency: Assisted ventilation by nasal or oral-nasal interface. *American Journal of Physical Medicine and Rehabilitation* 68, no. 6:264–271.

Frye, B., and T. Hilton. 1988. Preparing the caregiver to manage the ventilator-dependent patient at home. *Rehabilitation Nursing* 13, no. 1:38, 42.

Gilmartin, M. 1991. Long-term mechanical ventilation: Patient selection and discharge planning. *Respiratory Care* 36, no. 3:205–216.

Goldberg, A., et al. 1991. Combined nasal intermittent positive-pressure ventilation and rocking bed in chronic respiratory insufficiency: Nocturnal ventilatory support of a disabled person at home. *Chest* 99, no. 3:627–629.

Goldstein, R., and M. Avendano. 1991. Long-term mechanical ventilation as elective therapy: Clinical status and future prospects. *Respiratory Care* 36, no. 4:297–304.

Haynes, N., et al. 1990. Discharging ICU ventilator-dependent patients to home health care. *Critical Care Nurse* 10, no. 7:39–47.

Kacmarek, R. 1990. Noninvasive monitoring of respiratory function outside of the hospital. *Respiratory Care* 35, no. 7:719–727.

Martinez, M., and A. Mitchell. 1989. Home planning and discharge for the ventilator-dependent patient: A case study. *Critical Care Nurse* 9, no. 7:79–82.

Nochomovitz, M., et al. 1991. Placement alternatives for ventilator-dependent patients outside the intensive care unit. *Respiratory Care* 36, no. 3:199–204.

Peters, S., and R. Viggiano. 1988. Subspecialty clinics: Critical care medicine—home mechanical ventilation. *Mayo Clinic Proceedings* 63, no. 12:1208–1213.

Stoller, J. 1991. Establishing clinical unweanability. *Respiratory Care* 36, no. 3:186–198.

Swearingen, P., and J.H. Keen, eds. 1991. *Manual of critical care*. St. Louis: Mosby-Year Book, Inc..

Thompson, C., and M. Richmond. 1990. Teaching home care for ventilator-dependent patients: The patients' perception. *Heart and Lung* 19, no. 1:79–83.

Part V

Nursing Management of the Patient with Neurologic/Mental Disorders

30

Cerebrovascular Accident

Linda Rickabaugh

A. Definition of cerebrovascular accident (CVA): sudden interruption of blood flow and oxygen to brain cells; results in disturbed neurologic functioning
B. Etiology: may result from one of the following cerebral events
   1. Thrombosis (most frequent cause)
   2. Embolus (usually following cardiac disease)
   3. Hemorrhage (intracerebral or subarachnoid)
   4. Ischemia (transient ischemic attack)
C. Pathophysiology
   1. Anoxia
      a. Brain cells have no reserve oxygen.
      b. Permanent alteration of cerebral metabolism and cellular damage result within minutes of disrupted cerebral perfusion.
      c. Site of lesion is critical in producing pathologic signs.
      d. Vessels most commonly involved are middle cerebral artery and internal carotid artery.
D. Primary risk factors
   1. Cardiovascular disease: hypertension and peripheral vascular disease
   2. Diabetes mellitus
   3. Cigarette smoking
   4. Age greater than 65
   5. Male gender
   6. African-American descent
   7. Hematopoietic disorders
E. Common clinical picture: function and effect (effects vary depending on whether dominant or nondominant hemisphere is involved)

1. Language: aphasia (receptive, expressive, or both)
2. Speech: dysarthria
3. Sensation
   a. Contralateral diminished awareness of pain and temperature
   b. Decreased proprioception
   c. Contralateral homonymous hemianopsia
4. Perception
   a. Disturbed visual spatial relationships
   b. Neglect of paralyzed side
   c. Altered level of consciousness
5. Movement
   a. Contralateral hemiplegia
   b. Dysphagia
   c. Apraxia
6. Behavior
   a. Impaired judgment
   b. Emotional liability
   c. Withdrawal
7. Memory
   a. Short-term or long-term loss
   b. Decreased ability to concentrate

F. Diagnostic evaluation
   1. Clinical findings
   2. Computed tomographic scan or magnetic resonance imaging (MRI)
   3. Carotid angiography or digital subtraction angiography
   4. Lumbar puncture
   5. Doppler studies

G. Medical management goal: increase cerebral perfusion
   1. Initial
      a. Assess neurologic status for change or complications.
      b. Maintain airway and ventilation if level of consciousness is altered.
   2. Pharmacology
      a. Stabilization of blood pressure
      b. Anticoagulants (sodium warfarin)
      c. Steroidal anti-inflammatory agents (dexamethasone or diuretics to decrease cerebral edema)

Cerebrovascular Accident

        d. Platelet inhibitors (e.g., acetysalicylic acid [ASA], dipyridamole)
        e. Thrombolytic agents (e.g., tissue plasminogen activator [TPA] being used experimentally)
    3. Surgical interventions
        a. Carotid endarterectomy
        b. Microvascular bypass
    4. Rehabilitation
        a. Multidisciplinary team approach
H. Nursing management
    1. Impaired communication
        a. Provide alternative means of communicating.
        b. Provide a patient, supportive approach.
        c. Involve speech therapy.
    2. Sensory perceptual alteration
        a. Teach safety precautions: falls, burns, etc.
        b. Teach visually impaired patient to scan field of vision.
    3. Impaired mobility/self-care deficit
        a. Encourage independence in activities of daily living.
        b. Involve occupational therapy and physical therapy.
        c. Perform active and passive range of motion.
        d. Utilize assistive devices.
        e. Encourage ambulation and activity.
        f. Try dietary modifications for dysphagia.
        g. Manage bowel and bladder function.
        h. Teach preventive measure for immobility complications (e.g., impaired skin integrity, constipation, etc).
    4. Altered thought processes
        a. Apply cognitive retraining.
        b. Foster acceptance of limitations.
    5. Altered family processes
        a. Provide psychosocial support for family.
        b. Utilize available community resources.
        c. Teach the following:
            (1) Side effects of medications (e.g., bleeding with sodium warfarin)
            (2) Modification of risk factors
            (3) Signs of recurrence (e.g., headache, drowsiness, confusion)
            (4) Importance of follow-up care

STUDY QUESTIONS AND EXERCISES

1. Devise a teaching plan to assist patient to modify risk factors for CVA.
2. How would you assist the family to care for a patient at home who has severe expressive aphasia after a CVA?
3. Mr. Terry is a 65-year-old patient being discharged home with his wife after a left hemisphere CVA. His medications include clonidine hydrochloride (Catapres), 0.2 mg orally twice daily; aspirin, one tablet twice daily; and docusate sodium (Colace), one capsule daily. Develop a plan to assist Mr. Terry and his wife to manage his medications.

BIBLIOGRAPHY

Moore, K., and E. Trifiletti. 1994. Stroke. The first critical days. *RN* 57, no. 2:22-28.

Moore, K. 1994. Stroke. The long road back. *RN* 57, no. 3:50-55.

Phipps, W.J., et al. 1993. *Medical-surgical nursing: Concepts and clinical practice*. St. Louis: Mosby-Year Book, Inc.

Smeltzer, S.C., and B.G. Bare. 1992. *Brunner and Suddarth's textbook of medical-surgical nursing*. Philadelphia: J.B. Lippincott Co.

31

Seizure Disorder

Susan C. Nolt

A. Definitions/points of emphasis
 1. A paroxysmal disorder of cerebral function manifested by changes in consciousness, motor activity, or sensory phenomena
 2. Epilepsy: another term for seizure; used primarily for idiopathic seizures
 3. More common terminology: seizure or convulsive disorder rather than epilepsy
 4. Status epilepticus: a state of repetitive seizure activity with no recovery between attacks
 5. Tonic/clonic movements: alternating contraction and relaxation of muscles
 6. Myoclonic: a spasm or twitching of a muscle or muscle group
 7. Ictus: an attack or seizure
 8. Postictal: the period following an attack or seizure
B. Pathophysiology
 1. Intrinsic characteristics of nerve cells are excitability and inhibition.
 2. Normally, a balance exists between excitatory and inhibitory transmission of electrical impulses.
 3. When balance is disrupted, neurons discharge electrical impulses in a disorganized, paroxysmal manner, causing seizure activity.
 4. Pattern of seizure depends on area of the brain from which seizure activity begins.
 5. It is unknown why a seizure begins or ends.
C. Demographics
 1. All races
 2. Males and females affected equally

3. No specific geographic distribution
D. Etiology
    1. Given the right circumstances, any person can have a seizure.
        a. Fever, fatigue, stress, and/or trauma
        b. Electrolyte imbalance
        c. Metabolic abnormality
        d. Alcohol/drug use, poison
        e. Infectious diseases
        f. Pregnancy
        g. Vascular disorders
    2. Most common causes in children are idiopathic and congenital factors.
    3. Most common causes in adults are as follows:
        a. Young adults/middle-aged adults: injury or tumor
        b. Elderly adults: occlusive vascular disease (stroke) or possibly advancing stages of Alzheimer's disease
E. Diagnosis
    1. Required components of diagnostic work-up.
        a. Thorough medical history of patient
        b. Observation and/or accurate description of preseizure, seizure, and postseizure activity
        c. Complete physical examination with appropriate laboratory work
        d. Electroencephalogram
        e. Cerebral imaging (computed tomography, magnetic resonance imaging, arteriogram)
    2. By the time patient is accepted on home care services, the diagnostic work-up should have been completed.
F. Types of seizures
    1. Partial seizures
        a. Initial activity: occurs in neurons in one part of one cerebral hemisphere
        b. Activity: may remain localized to this area or spread to other parts of brain and evolve to generalized seizure activity
        c. Simple partial seizures
            (1) Generally no loss of consciousness
            (2) Focal motor signs on contralateral side (e.g., jacksonian epilepsy: seizure activity begins at one site then progresses throughout extremity or one side of body)

(3) Focal sensory signs on contralateral side
(4) Focal somatosensory signs (visual or auditory signs, unusual taste)
(5) Autonomic signs (pallor, pupil dilation, sweating)
(6) Psychic signs (distorted memory, dreamy states)
            d. Complex partial seizure
                (1) Impairment of consciousness
                (2) Consciousness impaired at onset: may involve automatisms
                    (a) Involuntary motor activity manifested during and after a seizure (chewing, random ambulation, repetitive vocalization)
        2. Generalized seizures
            a. Three key characteristics
                (1) May or may not be convulsive
                (2) Involve both cerebral hemispheres at onset
                (3) Loss of consciousness
            b. Variety of manifestations
                (1) Absence or staring spell
                (2) Myoclonic
                (3) Atonic or drop attack
                (4) Tonic
                (5) Clonic
                (6) Tonoclonic: commonly called grand mal
        3. Unclassified: includes all seizures that cannot be defined as partial or generalized
        4. Seizure activity: may vary from patient to patient; however, each patient will develop own particular pattern that will be repeated during periods of seizure activity
    G. Treatment
        1. Treat underlying cause, if possible
        2. Medication
        3. Psychosocial adaptations of lifestyle
    H. Medications
        1. Goals
            a. To attain therapeutic serum levels
            b. To have patient free of seizure activity
        2. Seven commonly used medications
            a. Phenytoin (Dilantin)
                (1) Used for tonic/clonic activity and partial seizures

(2) Recommended dose
  (a) Children: 250 mg orally daily
  (b) Adults: 300 mg orally daily
b. Carbamazepine (Tegretol)
  (1) Used for tonic/clonic activity and partial seizures
  (2) Recommended dose
    (a) Children under age 12: 10 to 20 mg/kg orally daily
    (b) Children age 12 and older: 200 mg orally twice daily
c. Primidone (Mysoline)
  (1) Used for tonic/clonic activity and partial seizures
  (2) Recommended dose
    (a) Children under age 8: 125 mg orally daily
    (b) Children age 8 and older: 250 mg orally daily
d. Valproate (Depakene)
  (1) Used for tonic/clonic activity, partial seizures, generalized absence, or myoclonic activity
  (2) Recommended dose
    (a) Adults and children: 60 mg/kg orally daily
e. Phenobarbital
  (1) Used for tonic/clonic activity, partial seizures, and myoclonic activity
  (2) Recommended dose
    (a) Children: 4 to 6 mg/kg orally daily
    (b) Adults: 100 to 200 mg orally daily
f. Clonazepam (Klonopin)
  (1) Used for myoclonic seizures and may help tonic/clonic, partial, and absence seizures
  (2) Recommended dose
    (a) Children under age 10: 0.1 to 0.2 mg/kg orally daily
    (b) Children age 10 and older: up to 20 mg orally daily
g. Ethosuximide (Zarontin)
  (1) Used for generalized absence seizures
  (2) Recommended dose
    (a) Children age 3 to 6: 250 mg orally daily
    (b) Children age 6 and older: 500 mg orally daily
3. Nursing interventions/patient teaching
  a. Instruct patient on appropriate dosage and frequency of medication.

(1) Initial dosing may be at a low dose, increasing gradually until maintenance level is reached
(2) Emphasis is on strict adherence to medication regimen, as sudden withdrawal can increase seizure activity and could lead to status epilepticus
(3) If unable to take medication, patient to inform physician
b. Monitor for drug interactions (alcohol, narcotics, barbiturates, antidepressants, antipsychotics); some anticonvulsant drugs may lower serum level of anticoagulants, haloperidol, theophylline, quinidine, digoxin, and antidepressants.
c. Monitor for side effects.
(1) Common to most anticonvulsants: nausea, vomiting, drowsiness, dizziness, gait disturbance, diplopia, agitation
(2) Gingival hyperplasia (phenytoin)
(3) Potential hematologic problems (carbamazepine)
(4) Potential for liver failure (valproate)
d. Obtain blood sample to determine when therapeutic levels of anticonvulsant are reached or whether anticonvulsant is affecting therapeutic levels of other medications.
I. Management of seizure patient at home
1. Goals
a. To instruct patient/caregiver in management of a seizure
b. To facilitate patient's/caregiver's adaptation to a chronic health problem by
(1) Instruction in patient-specific pathology causing seizure
(2) Instruction in safety issues
(3) Referral to appropriate support systems/community resources
2. Seizure management
a. Seizure activity: usually does not require emergency care
b. During seizure activity: provide support and prevent injury
c. Seizure: observed from beginning to end, reporting activity at onset, progression of seizure, and postseizure behavior
d. Observe and report
(1) Presence of aura, cry at onset
(2) Where seizure began and its sequence
(3) Phases of seizure and length of each phase
(4) Bladder incontinence

(5) Vomiting
(6) Changes in vital signs, pupils
(7) Level of consciousness
(8) Response to stimuli
(9) Cyanosis
(10) Deviation of eyes
(11) Postseizure behavior: aphasia, weakness of extremities, headache, confusion, level of consciousness, other neurologic deficit, or injury
  e. Accurate observations: assist in identifying the seizure focus within cerebral hemisphere(s)
  f. Seizures do not cause death
  g. Status epilepticus: requires medical attention; transport patient to nearest emergency room for treatment
3. Safety issues in seizure management
  a. Turn patient's head to side to prevent aspiration of secretions.
  b. Loosen clothing at neck and waist.
  c. Do not try to limit or stop seizure activity.
  d. Protect patient from injury.
  e. If patient's teeth are clenched, do not try to insert padded tongue blade into mouth.
4. Other safety issues
  a. Assess home for sharp objects that may harm patient if falls occur.
  b. Instruct patient not to operate heavy equipment.
  c. Know state laws regarding a seizure-prone person's operating a car; usually the person must be seizure-free for 1 year before driving.
  d. Instruct patient to carry a medical identification card.
5. Psychosocial issues
  a. People with seizures, regardless of age, may experience some or all of the following:
    (1) Job loss
    (2) Fear/anxiety
    (3) Social isolation/peer rejection
    (4) Frustration; anger; denial; depression
    (5) Changes in self-image, especially if patient experiences residual neurologic deficit
    (6) Changes in family dynamics

b. Make intra-agency referrals for therapy or social work as appropriate.
   c. Coordinate interdisciplinary care to address patient problems identified during each professional discipline's assessment.
   d. Make referrals to community resources (e.g., Family Services, Epilepsy Service Unit, Mental Health Association, etc.) as appropriate.
   e. Maintain patient confidentiality.
6. Patient/caregiver: should keep written notes regarding any seizure activity, medication compliance, and any problems that occur between nursing visits
7. Information should be reviewed and appropriate interventions taken during each nursing visit
8. Nursing documentation
   a. Any seizure activity
   b. Compliance with medication regimen
   c. Any instructions given and patient's/caregiver's level of understanding
   d. Psychosocial assessment/interventions
   e. Communications with other agency staff, patient's physician, and community agencies

STUDY QUESTIONS AND EXERCISES

1. List two goals of nursing interventions when managing seizure patients at home.
2. You are admitting to the agency a 45-year-old man who periodically has generalized seizures. His wife, his primary caregiver, states that she has seen only one seizure and at that time called 911. She is concerned about what to do in the event her husband has another seizure. Develop a plan of care for this patient.

BIBLIOGRAPHY

Hackey, J.V. 1984. *Quick reference to neurological nursing.* Philadelphia: J.B. Lippincott Co.
Johnston, M.V., et al. 1992. *Principles of drug therapy in neurology.* Philadelphia: F.A. Davis Co.

Katzman, R., and J.W. Rocve. 1992. *Principles of geriatric neurology.* Philadelphia: F.A. Davis Co.

Mitchell, P.H., et al. 1988. *AANN's neuroscience nursing.* Norwalk, Conn.: Appleton & Lange.

Nursing '92 drug handbook. 1992. Springhouse, Pa.: Springhouse Corporation.

Phipps, W.J., et al. 1991. *Medical-surgical nursing: concepts and clinical practice.* St. Louis: Mosby-Year Book, Inc.

Raimond, J., and J.W. Taylor. 1986. *Neurological emergencies: effective nursing care.* Gaithersburg, Md.: Aspen Publishers, Inc.

32

Multiple Sclerosis

Susan C. Nolt

A. Definitions/points of emphasis
   1. Multiple sclerosis (MS) is a chronic disease of the central nervous system (CNS).
   2. CNS includes the brain and spinal cord.
   3. Myelin is a fatty substance that surrounds and protects nerve fibers of the CNS.
   4. Myelin insulation is essential for proper conduction of signals to and from the CNS to muscles and sensory organs.
B. Pathophysiology
   1. Inflammation and breakdown occur in the myelin sheath surrounding the nerve fibers.
   2. Myelin is destroyed and replaced by hardened patches called plaques. Plaques may occur in multiple places within the CNS.
C. Demographics
   1. MS strikes young adults aged 20 to 40.
   2. Women develop MS more frequently than do men.
   3. The white race develops MS more frequently than do the black or Oriental races.
   4. MS is found more frequently among people in colder climates.
D. Etiology
   1. Exact cause unknown
   2. Areas of research
      a. Immunology
         (1) Autoimmune disease in which immune system is misdirected and attacks a component of the body
         (2) In MS, the target of the misdirected immune system is the myelin sheath of nerve fibers

(3) Research focus: understanding specific immune system problem contributing to MS
  b. Genetics
    (1) MS is not directly inherited but does occur in people genetically susceptible.
    (2) Rationale
      (a) MS occurs frequently in multiple cases in families.
      (b) MS does not occur in some world populations, possibly because of inbred resistance.
      (c) The way in which the immune system functions is genetically determined.
      (d) MS is believed to be a multigenetic disease.
  c. Virology
    (1) No viral causative agent found
    (2) MS may be triggered by something in the environment
    (3) Research focus:
      (a) Understanding the way a genetically predisposed immune system handles virus infections
      (b) Learning to control this inappropriate autoimmune response
  d. Biology of glial cells
    (1) Myelin is manufactured and maintained by glial cells.
    (2) CNS can remyelinate from cells existing within CNS.
    (3) The demyelination process is more aggressive and faster than the remyelination process.
    (4) Research focus: Understanding the myelination process, which will assist in understanding how remyelination can be enhanced after the myelin is destroyed.
E. Forms of MS
  1. Benign: mild form; patient may have initial attack with no recurrence
  2. Relapsing/remitting
    a. Exacerbations of symptoms followed by partial or complete recovery
    b. Exacerbations occur on average of one every 2 to 3 years
  3. Relapsing/progressive
    a. Exacerbations with some recovery with significant residual impairment
    b. Slow deterioration of function

4. Chronic/progressive
    a. Continuous functional deterioration over months or years
    b. Patient at risk for life threatening complications
F. Symptoms
    1. Highly individual; dependent on location of areas of plaque
    2. May vary in severity and duration
    3. Symptoms may include, but are not limited to
        a. Unusual fatigue
        b. Blurred or double vision
        c. Tingling sensations or numbness
        d. Slurred speech
        e. Loss of muscle coordination and balance
        f. Tremors
        g. Muscle cramps or spasms
        h. Bowel and bladder problems
        i. Gait disturbance
        j. Partial or complete paralysis
G. Diagnosis
    1. To establish a diagnosis of MS, the patient must demonstrate the following:
        a. More than one area of CNS malfunction
        b. These episodes must have appeared at least two separate times
    2. Definitive diagnosis can take several months to years
    3. Components of diagnostic work-up
        a. Clinical examination
        b. History
        c. Special procedures (performed only if further corroboration needed to establish diagnosis)
            (1) Evoked potentials: measure rate of response of CNS to rapidly repeated stimuli
            (2) Computer-assisted tomography
            (3) Magnetic resonance imaging
            (4) Lumbar puncture
            (5) Myelography
    4. By the time the patient is accepted on home care services, diagnostic work-up should have been completed.
H. Treatment
    1. There is no specific treatment to cure MS.
    2. Treatment should be directed toward symptomatic relief of acute

attacks, as appropriate; prevention of complications; and management of physical and psychosocial problems.
    3. Occasionally nontraditional treatments become available. Before recommending a treatment to patients, verify that treatment with the National Multiple Sclerosis Society, 733 Third Avenue, New York, NY 10017-3288; 1-800-LEARN MS.
I. Home management of the MS patient
    1. Goals:
       a. To develop a home management treatment program that will
          (1) Provide symptom relief,
          (2) Prevent/treat complications, and
          (3) Maintain the patient's functional level.
    2. When the patient is accepted in the home care program, most likely he or she will have either the relapsing/progressive or chronic/progressive form of MS.
    3. When appropriate, care should be provided using a team approach.
    4. The team should appoint a case manager preferably the nurse or rehabilitation staff.
    5. The team: members and functions
       a. Nurse
          (1) The nurse establishes a baseline neurologic assessment; updates each certification period or in accordance with the patient's symptoms.
          (2) The nurse assesses patient for exacerbations and potential complications. These may be, but are not limited to
             (a) New neurologic signs/symptoms
             (b) Skin breakdown
             (c) Bowel and bladder dysfunction
             (d) Respiratory problems
          (3) The nurse provides treatment and support as required by patient's need(s).
             (a) Intramuscular (IM)/intravenous (IV) administration of medications required during exacerbations
             (b) Development of bowel and bladder programs
             (c) Patient teaching regarding aspects of care (e.g., self-catheterization)
             (d) Referral to other therapeutic disciplines and assistance with therapy as required

b. Physical therapist (PT)/occupational therapist (OT)
    (1) The PT or OT establishes baseline assessment of patient's functional status; updates each certification period or in accordance with patient's condition.
    (2) These programs may overlap but preferably are complementary to one another.
    (3) Generally the PT focuses on gross motor function and the OT focuses on fine motor skills.
    (4) Ultimately, both disciplines will be developing programs that address muscle strength, coordination, balance, dexterity, energy conservation, and prevention of contractures.
    (5) Goals of therapy are to assist the patient in reaching and maintaining highest level of independent function in exercise program, transfers, ambulation/wheelchair mobility, and activities of daily living. These activities may be done with or without assistive devices.
c. Speech-language pathologist (SLP)
    (1) The SLP establishes a baseline assessment of communication skills; updates each certification period or in accordance with the patient's condition.
    (2) Generally, speech-language pathology services for the MS patient is directed toward strengthening the tongue and muscles essential for speech.
d. Medical social worker
    (1) The medical social worker establishes a baseline of psychosocial needs; updates each certification period in accordance with the patient's need(s).
    (2) The medical social worker develops a plan of care to meet these needs, which may include, but are not limited to, the following:
        (a) Understanding stresses of MS on patient and family
        (b) Sexuality
        (c) Understanding and improving (as appropriate) coping abilities of patient and family
        (d) Financial burdens (medication costs, medical needs, general living expenses)
        (e) Self-esteem
        (f) Referral to community agencies when appropriate (local branch of national MS society, Blind Association, etc.)

e. Home health aide (HHA)/support services (SS)
   (1) HHA assists with personal hygiene and activities of daily living.
   (2) HHA may assist with aspects of PT/OT/SLP programs.
   (3) HHA/SS perform limited homemaking activities.
   (4) SS perform unskilled activities; provide companionship.
6. The team should meet periodically to address the patient problems identified during each professional discipline's assessment. Care should be coordinated accordingly.
7. Patient confidentiality should be maintained.
8. Documentation
   a. Patient's functional status
   b. Patient compliance with care plan (medication, home exercise program, etc.)
   c. Related patient teaching
   d. Assessments and interventions
   e. Patient response to teaching, treatments, and other interventions
   f. Communication among disciplines, physicians, and other community agencies
   g. Ability to achieve discipline specific goals

STUDY QUESTIONS AND EXERCISES

1. Your patient stated that a friend of hers also has MS. This friend said that she started on a treatment that originated outside the United States and that the Food and Drug Administration has not yet approved of this treatment for MS. Your patient wants you to get more information about this treatment. How would you handle this request?

2. You are assigned a new admission, a 56-year-old female who has had MS for the last 20 years. During the initial assessment, there were the following findings:
   a. Decreased strength in extremities, now needs the assistance of another person for mobility
   b. Cried frequently during interview
   c. Increased frequency of constipation

d. Urinary frequency with occasional incontinence
   e. Reported a recent fall in the bathroom while trying to get in the tub (She also stated she was alone at the time and had to wait 2 hours until her family came home.)

Develop a comprehensive care plan for this patient.

BIBLIOGRAPHY

Blanck, R. 1985. The ABC's of diagnosing MS. In *MS facts and issues*. Reprinted from the Summer 1985 issue of *Inside MS*. New York: National Multiple Sclerosis Society.

Brunner, L.S., and D.S. Suddarth. 1984. *Textbook of Medical-Surgical Nursing*. Philadelphia: J.B. Lippincott Co.

Brunner, L.S., and D.S. Suddarth. 1982. *The Lippincott manual of nursing practice*. Philadelphia: J.B. Lippincott Co.

Giesser, B. 1992. Compendium of multiple sclerosis information. In *National Multiple Sclerosis Society research and medical program*. New York: National Multiple Sclerosis Society.

Reingold, S.C. 1992. *Research directions in multiple sclerosis*. New York: National Multiple Sclerosis Society.

National Multiple Sclerosis Society. 1992. Check your multiple sclerosis facts. In *Multiple sclerosis fact sheet*. New York: National Multiple Sclerosis Society.

National Multiple Sclerosis Society. 1992. *What is multiple sclerosis*. New York: National Multiple Sclerosis Society.

33
Muscular Dystrophy

Sharron Smitherman-González

A. Definition of muscular dystrophy (MD)
   1. A number of neuromuscular disorders of genetic origin in which a slow degeneration of muscle fibers occur
   2. Each form has its own distinct characteristics in regard to muscle groups affected, age at onset, rate of progression, and inheritance patterns
   3. All are progressive
   4. List of MD diseases: entities that are included in the Muscular Dystrophy Association program
      a. Duchenne muscular dystrophy (pseudohypertrophic)
      b. Becker's muscular dystrophy
      c. Facioscapulohumeral muscular dystrophy (Landouzy-Dejerine)
      d. Limb-girdle muscular dystrophy (including juvenile dystrophy of Erb)
      e. Myotonic dystrophy (Steinert's disease)
      f. Congenital muscular dystrophy
      g. Ophthalmoplegic muscular dystrophy
      h. Distal muscular dystrophy
      i. Muscular dystrophy of late onset
B. Demographics
   1. Duchenne muscular dystrophy (DMD): the most common of the muscular dystrophies
      a. A progressive hereditary disease that is a X-linked MD caused by a mutation of Xp21 in the gene coding for protein dystrophin
      b. Gene defects at Xp21 that result in a total absence of dystrophin usually lead to DMD

c. In all X-linked disorders, males are affected almost exclusively, but there is some evidence of heart muscle problems affecting female carriers; a heart biopsy is required for diagnosis
2. Pseudohypertrophy is muscle enlargement—especially of the thighs and upper arms—from fatty infiltration and feel unusually firm or woody on palpation.
3. Age at onset: usually before the age of 3 years old

C. Pathophysiology of DMD: three theories have evolved regarding the cause of MD
1. Membrane theory: the most popular; states that a cell membrane has altered genetically, compromising the integrity of the cell and making it vulnerable to degeneration
2. Neurogenic theory: disturbance in nerve-muscular interaction
3. Vascular theory: lack of blood flow causes muscle and tissue degeneration

D. Characteristics of DMD
1. Increased muscle weakness in the pelvic and shoulder girdles
a. Difficulty in running, climbing stairs, rising from a sitting or supine position
b. Develops Gowers' sign: walking hands up legs to achieve upright position
c. Waddling gait
d. Lordosis: abnormally exaggerated concave lumbar curvature
2. Later in disease process, abnormal gait on level surfaces
3. Profound muscular atrophy, contractures, and deformities involving large and small joints as the disease progresses
4. Ambulation is impaired usually by the age of 12 years
5. Respiratory or cardiac failure the usual cause of death

E. Diagnosis of DMD
1. Confirmed by elevated levels of serum enzyme creatine phosphokinase (CPK)
2. Abnormal muscle biopsy results
3. Abnormal electromyogram (EMG)

F. Treatment of DMD
1. Exercise programs to maintain function in unaffected muscles, also including breathing exercises for respiratory decompensation due to weakness of inspiratory muscles
2. Bracing (leg and spinal)
3. Performance of activities of daily living

G. Medications for DMD
   1. Prednisone is the only treatment shown to modify the progressive course of DMD.
      a. Classification: corticosteroid
      b. Action: decreased inflammation
      c. Dosage and research information:
         (1) Studies show that prednisone improves strength in DMD.
         (2) This improvement begins within 10 days and requires a dosage of 0.75 mg/kg per day orally; improvement reaches a plateau after 3 months.
      d. The reason for improvement of strength and muscle mass with prednisone use has not been established, but these studies suggest that prednisone might improve DMD by suppressing immune attacks on necrotic fibers.
      e. In 1993, studies were conducted with prednisone and azathioprine (an immunosuppressant) with the thought that if prednisone affects DMD through immunologic mechanisms then perhaps other immunosuppressant drugs, with fewer side effects than prednisone, should have similar benefits. The studies showed that the immunosuppressants had no clinical benefits, either alone or in combination with prednisone.
      f. Nursing interventions with prednisone
         (1) Assess
            (a) Adrenal insufficiency
            (b) Nausea/vomiting
            (c) Hypotension
            (d) Confusion
            (e) Weight gain: notify the physician if weekly gain greater than 5 pounds
            (f) Urinary output
            (g) Edema
            (h) Cardiac symptoms
            (i) Laboratory evaluation: potassium, blood sugar, urine glucose
         (2) Instruct patient and family/caregiver
            (a) Not to discontinue prednisone abruptly or adrenal crisis can occur
            (b) To avoid over-the-counter medications, e.g., salicylate and cough products containing alcohol

(c) To report any signs and symptoms of infection
2. Antibiotics: patients are susceptible to respiratory tract infections, and antibiotics have helped to prolong life.
H. Nursing considerations
1. Major emphasis is to assist patient and family/caregiver in coping with progressive, incapacitating, and fatal nature of DMD.
2. Assist patient and family/caregiver in developing a plan for greater independence with the limitations the disease imposes on daily living, such as developing self-help skills.
3. Develop a home program related to physical limitations of housing and mobility.
4. Be alert to potential alteration in nutrition due to dysphagia and chewing difficulties.
5. Be alert to ineffective airway clearance due to impaired ability to cough.
6. Be alert to need for referrals for community services when supplementary services are indicated, including genetic counseling services for the family.
I. Prognosis: depends on the type and severity of the disease
1. In DMD, affected individuals rarely survive to maturity.
2. Death is usually due to respiratory weakness or heart failure.

STUDY QUESTIONS AND EXERCISES

1. Develop a plan of care for a patient with DMD with emphasis on an exercise program (functional and breathing) and nutrition program.
2. Why is a good nutrition and weight control program so important for a patient with DMD?
3. List potentials for injury related to the following muscle dysfunctions:
   a. Unsteady gait
   b. Weakness
   c. Uncontrolled movements
4. How is the body affected by DMD?
5. How is DMD diagnosed?

BIBLIOGRAPHY

Carpenito, L.J. 1984. *Handbook of nursing diagnosis*, 110–112. Philadelphia: J.B. Lippincott Co.

Carpenito, L.J. 1994. *Nursing diagnosis: Application to clinical practice*, 603. Philadelphia: J.B. Lippincott Co.

Dorland's illustrated medical dictionary. 1994. Philadelphia: W.B. Saunders Co.

Griggs, R.C., et al. 1993. Duchenne dystrophy: Randomized, controlled trial of prednisone (18 months) and azathioprine (12 months). *Journal of the American Academy of Neurology* March:520-526.

Kissel, J.T., et al. 1993. Mononuclear cell analysis of muscle biopsies in prednisone and azathioprine—treated Duchenne muscular dystrophy. *Journal of the American Academy of Neurology* March:532-536.

McGriff, S.E. November 1985. *Learning to live with neuromuscular disease: A message for parents*, 9. New York: Muscular Dystrophy Association.

Muscular Dystrophy Association. 1994. *Quest 1*, no. 1:11.

Roth, L.S. 1995. *Mosby's 1995 nursing drug reference.* St. Louis: Mosby-Year Book, Inc.

Whaley, L.F., and D.L. Wong. 1982. *Essentials of pediatric nursing*, 858–859. St. Louis: Mosby-Year Book, Inc.

34

Parkinson's Disease

Keltie Baker Kerney

A. Definitions/points of emphasis
   1. "Involuntary tremulous motion with lessened muscular power with a propensity to bend the trunk forward and to pass from a walking to running pace; the senses and intellects being uninjured" (Abley 1991)
   2. A progressive neurologic disorder affecting the brain centers responsible for control and regulation of movement
   3. Characterized by the classic motor features of bradykinesia (slowness of movement), tremor, muscle rigidity, and impaired postural reflexes
   4. Postural instability in disordered gait as well as disorders in the fine motor movement
B. Pathophysiology
   1. A deficiency of dopamine in the substantia nigra of the brain
   2. Degeneration of the dopaminergic nigrostriatal pathway: Severity of the disease is associated with the degree of neuronal loss in the midbrain at the level of the substantia nigra.
   3. The balance of dopamine and acetylcholine is responsible for normal motor function; a deficiency in dopamine (the balance of neurotransmitters is upset) results in a decrease in the inhibitory effect of dopamine and an increase in the excitatory effect of acetylcholine, causing symptoms of the disease.
C. Demographics
   1. Approximately 1 million Americans are currently diagnosed.
   2. Men have a slightly higher incidence.
   3. Whites are disproportionately affected when compared with other races.

4. Typically, Parkinson's disease is a disease of the "aged," with a mean onset at 60 years of age (although cases have been identified in individuals as young as 30 years of age).
5. The chance of developing this disease by 65 years of age is approximately 1%.
6. There is no socioeconomic preference.

D. Etiology
1. Unknown
2. Current genetic research focusing on mitochondrial defects in family linage
3. Genetic susceptibility (positive family history)
4. Viral theory: first suggested with the outbreak of encephalitis lethargica, which resulted in postencephalitic parkinsonism
5. Cerebral vascular disease
6. Poisoning or toxicity (manganese, carbon monoxide, and other environmental toxins)
7. For secondary parkinsonism: tumors, stroke, chemicals, medication, or viruses; if the cause can be removed, the disease may be cured

E. Diagnosis/evaluation
1. Observation of characteristic signs and symptoms
2. In an older patient: diagnosis may be missed, as early symptoms may be regarded as part of "aging"
3. Assess:
   a. Extent of tremor(one hand at rest and/or decreased during active movement)
   b. Rigidity as evidenced by resistance to passive movement (example: when elbow is bent and straightened)
   c. Bradykinesia as evidenced by hesitation in starting movement, slowness in movement, and rapid fatigue
   d. Complaints of falling
   e. Retropulsion (patient tends to move backward following minor pressure from the front)
   f. Difficulty with fine movements, rigidity, and autonomic dysfunction
   g. Micturition

F. Clinical manifestations
1. Motor features

a. Tremor (resting tremor)
   (1) The most classic and visible sign; 70% of patients present with this as their chief complaint
   (2) Described as having a pill-rolling quality and can affect all four limbs and the head
   (3) Subsides with action; therefore described as a resting tremor
b. Rigidity
   (1) A plastic resistance to passive movement, often described as stiffness
   (2) Can be detected as a coglike release of muscle resistance in the wrists, elbows, neck, and knees as the limb is moved through passive range of motion
   (3) Can cause the face to take on a masklike quality, where the face appears fixed and rigid
   (4) Previously recognizable nonverbal messages are misinterrupted or lost in communication. Families find this difficult to deal with because the patient no longer has a change of facial expression.
c. Bradykinesia
   (1) Difficulty with initiating and continuing movement
   (2) Movements are slow and performed with conscious effort
   (3) Patient describes bradykinesia as feeling as if "my brain is sending the message to my body, but my body won't listen"
d. Postural instability and gait disorders
   (1) Patient demonstrates difficulty in maintaining erect posture.
   (2) Forward flexion of the neck, hips, knees, and elbows
   (3) Posture abnormalities greatly reduce the patient's ability to be ambulatory and place the patient at high risk for injury; lead to reliance on assistive devices.
   (4) Rigidity and postural changes also cause the patient to develop a shuffling quality to the gait and to use small steps.
   (5) Propulsion develops
      (a) A disturbance in which the patient goes from a slow walking pace to running with an inability to stop
      (b) Can stop only by grabbing stationary objects (i.e., the door frame)

e. On/off phenomenon
      (1) The on/off phenomenon is a syndrome in which the patient is freely ambulatory one minute and then unable to move the next.
      (2) Patients describe the "off" period as if someone has turned off the switch and their feet have sprouted roots.
   f. Swallowing and speech defects (dysphagia)
      (1) Difficulty with chewing or moving food to the back of the mouth
      (2) Significant weight loss
   g. Dysarthria
      (1) A form of speech disturbance characterized by deviations in phonation
      (2) Prosodic disturbances: speech may be slow or extremely fast
      (3) An articulatory disorder: vocal sounds are distorted
   h. Handwriting
      (1) Difficulty in handwriting can be an early sign of the disease.
      (2) Typically, the patient will initiate handwriting with normal sized penmanship and then trail off words and sentences with smaller illegible words ("micrographia").
2. Non-motor features
   a. Depression
      (1) Accounts for the majority of psychiatric referrals in patients with parkinsonism
      (2) Can be the initial feature of parkinson's disease
      (3) Patients may become demoralized with the diagnosis; experience a reactive depression linked to exterior events; depression is of short duration
      (4) Patient may have endogenous depression caused by a biochemical imbalance in the brain; can be life threatening if not treated
   b. Dementia: a common feature
      (1) It is estimated that 20% of the patients will become demented.
      (2) An acquired persistent impairment of intellectual function that would cause compromise in at least three of the following areas of mental activity:
         (a) Language

(b) Memory
(c) Visuospatial skills
(d) Emotionality
(e) Personality
(f) Cognition in the presence of clear conscience
   c. Sleep disturbances: frequent complaints in patients; disorders of sleep initiation, sleep fragmentation, early morning awakening, excessive daytime somnolence, and parasomnias
   d. Sexual dysfunction
      (1) Sexual function has received inadequate attention, as it is a complex issue.
      (2) Dysfunction of the autonomic nervous system, depression, medication, and interpersonal issues all play a role in sexual dysfunction.
      (3) A thorough assessment may lead the clinician to treat the dysfunction adequately.
   e. Driving performance
      (1) Motor manifestations of the disease as well as a decline in cognition may impair the patient's ability to function safely as a driver of a motor vehicle.
      (2) Evaluation of driving skills by a driving instructor may provide a nonthreatening approach to assist automobile safety.

G. Treatment
  1. Rehabilitation therapy (speech-language pathologist [SLP], occupational therapy [OT], physical therapy [PT])
  2. Medication
  3. Psychosocial adaptations of lifestyle
  4. Patient/family education

H. Medication
  1. Goals:
    a. To obtain compliance in taking prescribed medications
    b. To have successful management of disease
    c. To help ameliorate some of the symptoms to achieve maximal functioning
  2. Commonly used medications
    a. Antihistamines (Benadryl)
      (1) Used for anticholinergic and sedative effects
      (2) Indications: tremor, rigidity, insomnia

        (3) Side effects: dry mouth, lethargy, confusion
    b. Anticholinergics (Artane, Cogentin)
        (1) Indications: tremors, rigidity, insomnia
        (2) Side effects: dry mouth, constipation, blurred vision, confusion, visual hallucinations
    c. Dopaminergics (Symmetrel, Carbidopa/Levodopa, Sinemet)
        (1) Indications: rigidity, bradykinesia, tremor
        (2) Side effects: leg edema, reticularis, hallucinations, orthostatic hypotension, nausea, confusion
    d. Dopamine agonists (Parlodel, Permax)
        (1) Indicators: motor fluxion
        (2) Side effects: hallucinations, mental cloudiness, orthostatic hypotension, confusion
3. Nursing interventions/patient teaching
    a. Instruct patient on appropriate dosage and frequency of medication.
        (1) Initial dosing may be a low dose, increasing gradually until maintenance level reached
        (2) Emphasis on strict adherence and compliance
        (3) If patient unable to take medication, inform physician
    b. Monitor for drug interactions.
    c. Monitor for side effects.
    d. Obtain blood samples to determine therapeutic level.
    e. Goal: maintain patient on conservative level of medication while maintaining mobility. As disease progresses, the patient becomes less responsive to medications and experiences end-of-dose failure, peak dose dyskinesias, and painful dystonic cramps.
    f. Assess the patient at home.
        (1) Ask the patient about slowing of body movement, difficulty with equilibrium, muscle aching and soreness, weakness, fatigue, and insomnia.
        (2) Monitor patient during activities (i.e., arising from bed/chair, walking, dressing and eating).
        (3) Listen to patient's speech.
        (4) Discuss with the patient how the disease is affecting his or her quality of life.
        (5) Assess for signs of depression.

I. Surgical treatment
   1. Implantation of autologous adrenal medullary tissue to the caudate nucleus of the brain
   2. Adrenal gland of patient removed via laparotomy; medullary grafts (dopamine-making cells) transplanted onto right caudate nucleus via craniotomy to restore nigrostriatal function
   3. Laparotomy and craniotomy done simultaneously
   4. Purported to relieve signs and symptoms, particularly tremor; considered investigational
J. Other nursing interventions
   1. Improve mobility and functioning
      a. Encourage patient to continue exercise in physical therapy program to increase muscle strength, improve coordination and dexterity, treat muscular rigidity, prevent contractions, and compensate for lack of automatic movements.
      b. Emphasize importance of a daily exercise program to maintain joint mobility.
      c. Advise and instruct the patient in stretching exercises to loosen the joint structures.
      d. Teach postural exercise and walking techniques to offset shuffling gait and tendency to lean forward.
      e. Encourage warm baths, massage, and passive and active exercises to help relax muscles and relieve painful muscle spasms that accompany rigidity.
      f. Advise frequent rest periods as the patient becomes more fatigued and frustrated by symptoms.
   2. Assist patient to gain independence in self-care.
      a. Teach patient how to turn and get out of bed.
      b. Instruct in assistive devices in helping with bathing and grooming.
   3. Facilitate bowel elimination.
      a. Encourage patient to establish a regular bowel routine.
      b. Encourage intake of foods with a moderate fiber content.
      c. Encourage patient to drink more water.
      d. Encourage patient to secure and use a raised toilet seat.
   4. Improve nutritional status.
      a. Instruct patient in the proper swallowing sequence (close lips, and with teeth together, place food on tongue, lift the tongue

up and then back, and swallow while tilting the head forward).
   b. Encourage the patient to make a conscious effort to chew and to chew first on one side and then the other.
   c. Instruct patient to hold the head in the upright position and make a conscious effort to swallow saliva often (to control the buildup of saliva).
   d. Procure assistive device (i.e., a stabilized plate, nonspill cup, flexible plastic straw) to allow patient to rest during prolonged eating time.
   e. Instruct in supplemental feeding.
   f. Maintain a weekly weight chart.
5. Prevent injury.
   a. Secure safety aides (i.e., grabrails on tub, raised toilet seat, handrails on both sides of steps, etc.).
   b. Secure a knotted rope to the foot of bed to allow patient to pull self to a sitting position.
   c. Minimize effect of the orthostatic hypotension.
   d. Secure a form of a call system.
6. Maximize residual communication ability.
   a. Encourage patient to take prescribed medication (e.g., Levodopa), which appears to improve overall speech intelligibility.
   b. Remind patient to take a deep breath before speaking (increases the volume of sound and the number of words spoken per breath) and to follow exercises recommended by speech-language pathologist.
   c. Encourage patient to practice reading aloud in front of a mirror to improve speech.
   d. Have patient speak into a tape recorder to monitor progress.
   e. Consider use of electronic devices for problems with weak voice.
7. Develop positive, achievable goals.
   a. Help patient establish achievable goals.
   b. Encourage patient to be an active participant in therapy and in social/recreational events.
   c. Instruct patient to participate in a planned program of activity throughout the day to prevent daytime sleep, disinterest, or apathy.

d. Offer realistic reassurance.
   e. Try to dispel anxiety and fears that the patient may have, which may be as disabling to patient as the disease.
   f. Provide care and support for family (also vulnerable to emotional stresses and anxiety from living with a progressively disabled person).
K. Psychosocial issues
   1. Regardless of age, patient may experience some or all of the following:
      a. Job loss
      b. Fear/anxiety
      c. Social isolation
      d. Depression, anger, denial
      e. Changes in self-image
      f. Changes in family dynamics
   2. Referrals for SLP, PT, OT, home health aide, or social worker may be appropriate.
   3. Multidisciplinary care coordination must occur and address patient problems.
   4. Referrals to community resources may be indicated.

STUDY QUESTIONS AND EXERCISES

1. To assist the patient with Parkinson's disease to achieve maximum functioning, the following nursing care should include (list supportive justification of your answer):
   a. Assessment
   b. Intervention
   c. Evaluation of physical and psychosocial aspects of care
   d. All of the above
2. The classic triage of symptoms of Parkinson's disease includes resting tremor, rigidity, bradykinesia, and masklike face. This collection of symptoms, rather than one distinct clinical picture, can be difficult to assess in the early stages of the disease. True or false?

BIBLIOGRAPHY

Abley, C. 1991. Learning to live with Parkinson's: A teaching program to boost patient understanding. *Professional Nurse* May:458-461.

Baker, M., and B. McCaul. 1990. Meeting the needs of people with Parkinson's disease and their families appropriately. *Care of the Elderly* 2, no. 6:221-223.

Calne, S. June 15, 1994. Nursing care of patients with idiopathic parkinsonism. *Nursing Times* 90, no. 24:38-39.

Frances, T. 1992. Facilitating self-care in clients with Parkinson's disease. *Home Health Care Nurse* 10, no. 4:23-27.

Fritzsimmons, B., and L. K. Bunting. December 1993. Parkinson's disease quality of life issues. *Nursing Clinics of North America* 28, no. 4:807-819.

Suddarth, D.S. 1991. *The Lippincott manual of nursing practice.* Philadelphia: J.B. Lippincott Co.

Whitehouse, C. April 1994. A new source of support, the nurse practitioner role in Parkinson's disease in dystonia. *Professional Nurse,* 9 no. 7. 448-451.

35
Amyotrophic Lateral Sclerosis

Tecla K. Webber

A. Definition
   1. Amyotrophic lateral sclerosis (ALS) is a progressive degenerative disorder of the motor neurons in the spinal cord, brain stem, and motor cortex.
   2. ALS is characterized by atrophy of the muscles of the hands, forearms, and legs that eventually spreads to involve most of the body.
B. Points of emphasis
   1. ALS usually occurs between 40 and 70 years of age.
   2. The disorder has an incidence of 2 to 7 cases per 100,000 people in the United States; 95% of the cases are sporadic, and 5% are familial.
   3. Men are affected approximately three times more frequently than women.
   4. ALS is sometimes called Lou Gehrig's disease, since the famous New York Yankee ballplayer died of the disease.
C. Pathophysiology
   1. ALS is characterized by degeneration of the upper and lower motor neurons.
   2. Myelin sheaths are destroyed and are replaced by scar tissue, causing blockage of nerve impulses.
   3. Loss of upper motor neurons results in spasticity and reduced muscle strength while lower motor neuron involvement results in flaccidity, paralysis, and muscle atrophy.
   4. Cause of the disease is unknown.
D. Clinical manifestations
   1. Early symptoms of the disease:

a. Muscle weakness
 b. Wasting
 c. Atrophy, especially involving the muscles of the hand, shoulder, and upper arm.
 2. The lower limb muscles are affected last; they feel heavy, are subject to fatigue, and cramp easily.
 3. Dysarthria and dysphagia occur when the muscles of speech, chewing, and swallowing are affected.
 4. Dyspnea will occur if respiratory muscles are affected.
 5. There is no sensory loss with the disease; the patient remains alert.
 6. Death usually occurs as a result of aspiration, infection, or respiratory failure.
E. Diagnostic studies
 1. There is no definitive test for ALS.
 2. Initial testing for ALS may include electromyography (EMG), to rule out other muscle diseases, and fibrillation studies, which indicate muscle wasting and denervation.
 3. Serum creatine phosphokinase may be twice the normal value.
 4. Cerebrospinal fluid may have a slight elevation of total protein with normal cell count.
 5. Computed tomography (CT) scan (brain): may show possible cerebral atrophy, but usually normal.
F. Treatment
 1. There is no known treatment to cure or arrest this fatal disease.
 2. Management is based on treating the symptoms of the disease as they occur.
G. Nursing diagnosis/interventions
 1. Impaired physical mobility
 a. Instruct patient/family in routine of alternating physical activity with rest periods.
 b. Instruct the patient about the importance of physical activity and physical therapy to maintain motor function.
 c. Encourage the greatest degree of physical independence possible.
 d. Teach actions of muscle-relaxant drugs given to reduce spasticity.
 e. Demonstrate proper use of assistive aids (e.g., walker, splints, etc.).

2. Impaired swallowing
   a. Instruct patient/family to have patient in upright position when eating, to facilitate swallowing.
   b. Be aware that soft foods are easier to swallow than liquids.
   c. Give crushed pills in gelatin or custard; instruct in use of adaptive equipment to facilitate independence when eating.
   d. Instruct in use of suction equipment.
3. Impaired verbal communication
   a. Ask questions that can be answered easily.
   b. Maintain calm atmosphere and allow patient time to answer questions.
   c. Inform the entire health team of the established communication method (e.g., communication board, etc.).
4. Potential of impairment of skin integrity
   a. Instruct patient/family of potential for injury to skin from spasticity, impaired sensation, or development of decubitus ulcers.
   b. Reposition patient frequently.
   c. Protect patient from injury (e.g., mechanical, thermal).

H. Therapy management
   1. Physical therapy
      a. Range of motion exercises to control or improve weakness or spasticity
      b. Assistance with gait training
      c. Instruction in use of assistive devices (e.g., cane, walker, etc.)
      d. Instruction on proper transfer techniques
   2. Occupational therapy
      a. Assistance in performing activities of daily living
      b. Assistance with selecting special adaptive equipment (e.g., eating utensils, safety equipment)
   3. Speech-language pathology services
      a. Teaching patient muscle control
      b. Breathing to help with dysarthria and dysphagia
   4. Medical social worker
      a. Patient/family counseling in dealing with problems associated with debilitating, fatal disease

I. Drug therapy
   1. Antianxiety: diazepam (Valium) used for its muscle-relaxant effect

2. Muscle relaxant: baclofen (Lioresal)
3. Anticholinergic drugs: amitriptyline (Elavil) or clonidine hydrochloride (Catapres) used to reduce oral secretions

STUDY QUESTIONS AND EXERCISES

1. List three signs and symptoms of amyotrophic lateral sclerosis.
2. Identify three nursing diagnoses and the appropriate intervention when treating the ALS patient.
3. What are the home safety concerns that should be identified in caring for the patient with ALS?

BIBLIOGRAPHY

Bruno, P.M., et al. 1986. *Medical-surgical nursing: Pathophysiological concepts.* Philadelphia: J.B. Lippincott Co.

Chipps, E.M., et al. 1992. *Neurologic disorders.* St. Louis: Mosby-Year Book, Inc.

Evans, M.J. 1989. *Neurological-neurosurgical nursing.* Springhouse, Pa.: Springhouse Corporation.

Hickey, J. 1987. *The clinical practice of neurological and neurosurgical nursing.* Philadelphia: J.B. Lippincott Co.

36

Alzheimer's Disease

Elizabeth B. Runyon and Patricia A. Wernert

A. Prevalence
   1. Some 6 million people in the United States have been diagnosed as having Alzheimer's disease or related dementias.
   2. It is anticipated that the numbers will rise as the population ages.
   3. More than 100,000 people die of Alzheimer's disease annually.
   4. Cause of the disease is unknown, but it is under intense scientific investigation.
B. Pathophysiology
   1. Alzheimer's disease is a dementing disorder marked by certain brain changes; it was first described by Alois Alzheimer in 1906.
      a. Alzheimer's disease is not a normal part of aging.
      b. Most people affected are over age 65 years.
      c. Of population aged 65 to 74, 1% have severe dementia.
      d. Of those aged 75 to 84, 7% are affected.
      e. Of adults aged 85 or older, 25% develop dementia.
   2. Microscopic studies of brain tissue reveal certain changes.
      a. Senile or neuritic plaques that are degenerating nerve cells combined with a form of protein called amyloid
      b. Neurofibrillary tangles that are nerve cell malformations
   3. Computed tomographic scans may reveal an atrophied brain with widened sulci and enlarged cerebral ventricles.
   4. Nerve cells degenerate in the brain's nucleus basalis of Meynert.
   5. There are reduced levels of acetylcholine (neurotransmitter) in the brain.
   6. There is no specific test. Diagnosis can be certain only by examination of brain tissue obtained at autopsy. Diagnosis for living persons is made by exclusion of other possible causes.

C. Research to find the cause of Alzheimer's disease
   1. Chemical theories
      a. Diminished levels of neurotransmitters
      b. Increased levels of aluminum in brains of victims
   2. Genetic theory: inconclusive
      a. May occur more frequently in some families
      b. Apparent association between Down's syndrome and Alzheimer's disease in some families: when patients with Down's syndrome survive into middle age in some families, they have dementia indistinct from that of Alzheimer's disease
      c. Genetic risk factors for late-onset Alzheimer's disease has been linked to a specific version of apolipoprotein (Apo) E, a protein that transports cholesterol through the blood stream.
         (1) Apo E-IV is also linked to high cholesterol and heart disease.
         (2) Senile plaques of Alzheimer's disease may be side effect of this disease and effects of Apo E-IV on metabolism.
   3. Autoimmune theory: immune system may attack own tissue, producing antibodies to its own cells
   4. Slow virus theory: slow virus has not been isolated
      a. No comparable immune virus found in patients with other dementias
      b. Theory not discounted or confirmed
   5. Blood vessel theory: potential defects in the blood-brain barrier
D. Symptoms progressive and relate to alterations in cognitive functioning
   1. Symptoms
      a. Restlessness and agitation
      b. Disorientation; memory impairment
      c. Judgment impaired
      d. Alteration in manner of relating to others
      e. Ability to perform activities of daily living (ADL) and instrumental ADL
      f. Withdrawal; easily fatigued
      g. Alterations in sleep/wake cycle, nutritional status, elimination patterns.
      h. Hallucinations and delusions
   2. Goals
      a. Improved orientation, memory, judgment

b. Decreased incidence of or response to delusional thoughts
c. Decreased restlessness and agitation
d. Improved behavioral control
e. Increased ability to relate to others
f. Improved ability to perform self-care
g. Improved sleep/wake cycle, nutrition, elimination
h. Ability to perform daily exercise routine
3. Interventions
   a. Weigh weekly.
   b. Obtain history of behavioral patterns.
   c. Assess behavioral pattern during every home visit.
   d. Develop behavioral goals with patient/family.
   e. Apply behavior therapy to increase functional behavior.
   f. Reality test as patient able to tolerate.
   g. Offer noncritical feedback about behavior displayed.
   h. Limit setting as appropriate.
   i. Teach ways to maintain adequate sleep/wake cycle, nutrition, elimination.
   j. Teach simple exercise routine.
   k. Teach relaxation technique.
   l. Refer to occupation therapy as appropriate.
   m. Enhance memory by the following techniques:
      (1) Use usual visual and verbal cues.
      (2) Use simple phrases and language.
      (3) Expect one action at a time (e.g., "Put on your socks," not "Put on your socks and shoes.").
   n. Tacrine (Cognex) is a medication used in earlier stages of Alzheimer's disease.
      (1) For some patients there is an improvement in cognitive functioning.
      (2) Requires lab work for alamine aminotransferase levels.
      (3) Effectiveness should be assessed by observation and family support.
E. Family education to maximize ability to care for patient at home
   1. Goals
      a. Verbalize purpose, side effects, how and when to administer medications.
      b. Verbalize when to contact physician, nurse, emergency medical services (EMS), police.

c. Verbalize understanding of management of dementia/Alzheimer's disease, to include safety measures, exercise/relaxation routine, behavioral control, nutritional needs, effective elimination regimen (bowel/bladder training), and adequate sleep/wake cycle.
d. Verbalize available community resources.
e. Improve communication between family members.
f. Demonstrate effective problem-solving skills.
g. Identify the primary caregiver.
2. Interventions
a. Assess family dynamics, coping skills, and problem-solving ability.
b. Assess safety measures.
c. Teach disease process and medication regimen.
d. Teach care/management of dementia/Alzheimer's disease.
  (1) Safety measures; exercise
  (2) Nutritional needs, diet changes
  (3) Behavioral control
  (4) Bowel/bladder training
  (5) Management of memory impairment (e.g., lists, calendars, labeling)
  (6) Consistent route
  (7) When to call physician, nurse, EMS, police
e. Provide information about available community resources.
f. Refer to social worker.
g. Provide family therapy to increase communication among family members.

STUDY QUESTIONS AND EXERCISES

1. Explain the microscopic brain changes present in victims of Alzheimer's disease.
2. How is Alzheimer's disease diagnosed?
3. List the five major avenues of research being conducted to find the cause of Alzheimer's disease.
4. List 10 symptoms of Alzheimer's disease.
5. List five nursing interventions.

6. What are the goals of family education in caring for the patient with Alzheimer's disease?

BIBLIOGRAPHY

Hall, G.R. 1988. Care of the patient with Alzheimer's disease living at home. *Nursing Clinics of North America* 23, no. 1:31–45.

Harris, K.A. 1990. Care plan approach to dementia. *Geriatric Nursing* 11, no. 2:76–78.

National Institute of Mental Health. 1990. *Alzheimer's disease*. Rockville, Md.: DHHS publication no. ADM, 90–1696.

Sanders, A.M., and A.D. Roses. 1989. Apolipo protein E4, A genetic risk factor for late-onset Alzheimer's disease. *Caring* 8, no. 13:24-28.

Wernert, P.A., and E.B. Runyon. 1991. Enabling caregivers to care for Alzheimer's patients at home. *Caring* 10, no. 12:28–34.

37

Mental Illness

Elizabeth B. Runyon

A. Because of deinstitutionalization over the last 30 years, most seriously mentally ill individuals remain in the community.
   1. Individuals also develop medical illnesses that may require home care.
   2. Assessment of strengths as well as problem identification is extremely important.
B. Determining mental status will indicate patient's ability to learn medical regimen.
   1. Intellectual functioning: attention span, abstract thinking, reasoning ability
   2. Orientation: person, place, time
   3. Insight
      a. Ability to acknowledge presence of psychologic problems
      b. Blames others or circumstance for problems
   4. Judgment
      a. Ability to manage daily living activities
      b. Ability to make reasonable life decisions
   5. Memory: recent, remote, immediate recall of recently provided information
   6. Thought content/speech patterns: logical, coherent, normal rhythmics
   7. Perception (absence of hallucinations or delusions)
      a. Hallucinations: seeing, hearing, smelling, tasting, feeling things not really there
      b. Delusion: false ideas or beliefs maintained in spite of evidence
   8. Mood, posturing, facial expression
   9. Response to interviewer: appearance and behavior

C. Schizophrenia: group of mental disorders that present with alterations in thinking (content and process) as well as behavior
  1. Incidence: about 1% of the total United States population.
     a. Onset usually in late adolescence and early adulthood and continues through life
     b. Frequent rehospitalization for psychotic symptoms not unusual
     c. Cause thought to be a combination of biologic and environmental factors
  2. Symptoms
     a. Hallucinations: usually auditory
     b. Delusions, especially of grandeur or persecution, or odd beliefs
     c. Blunting or inappropriateness of affect
     d. Incoherence or little continuity of thought
     e. Lack of initiative
  3. Treatment
     a. Medication (e.g., fluphenazine dihydrochloride [Prolixin], haloperidol [Haldol])
     b. Problem-solving/supportive counseling
     c. Teaching of illness management
     d. Array of outpatient services
D. Bipolar disorder (manic-depressive illness): involving episodes of extreme mood changes.
  1. Moods swing from overly elated and irritable to sad and hopeless.
  2. Periods of normal moods occur in between.
  3. Illness begins in late adolescence or early adulthood.
  4. Some 2 million people suffer from disorder in the United States.
  5. Bipolar disorder is believed to be inherited.
  6. Symptoms of mania are denial that anything is wrong; obnoxious or intrusive behavior; substance abuse; increased sexual tension; irritability; distractibility; decreased sleep; increased energy, agitation, racing thoughts; poor judgment.
  7. Symptoms of depression are feelings of sadness, hopelessness, helplessness; excessive worrying; guilt; loss of interest in ordinary activities; feeling fatigued; restlessness; irritability; sleep disturbances; change in appetite/weight; chronic pain; thoughts of suicide or death; impaired thinking or concentration.
  8. Treatment

a. Lithium carbonate for controlling mania
b. Medications and on occasion electroconvulsive therapy to treat depression
c. Counseling with problem-solving/supportive focus
d. Education of illness management
e. Hospitalization, especially if the person is in danger of harming self

E. Depressive illness: symptoms can last for months or years.
  1. Causes
     a. Some families display genetic predisposition.
     b. Appears to be relationship between malfunctioning of neurotransmitters at synapse between nerve cells and the presence of depression.
  2. Symptoms: see bipolar disorder
  3. Treatment
     a. Medication: antidepressants (e.g., amitriptyline hydrochloride [Elavil], fluoxetine hydrochloride [Prozac])
     b. Psychotherapy: including cognitive therapy to introduce more effective ways of thinking
     c. Electroconvulsive therapy
     d. Hospitalization, especially if the person is in danger of harming self
  4. Medical illnesses that frequently precipitate depression: diabetes, cerebrovascular accident, cardiac drugs that cross blood-brain barrier
  5. Depressed patients: have a potential for suicide
     a. Factors that increase risk
        (1) Suicide statements or threats
        (2) Definite plan for suicide
        (3) Readily available means for suicide
        (4) History of previous suicide attempt(s)
        (5) Sudden marked changes in behavior or personality
        (6) Neglect of responsibilities
        (7) Selection of reading material about death
        (8) Making final arrangements
        (9) Requests for sleeping pills
        (10) Divorced, separated, or widowed
        (11) Socially isolated
        (12) Drug or alcohol use

(13) Chronic or terminal illness
    b. Urgent need for psychiatric follow-up of patients felt to be at risk for suicide
F. Substance use and abuse by patients
    1. Symptoms: incoherent speech, aggressive behavior, agitation/restlessness or lethargy, impaired coordination, health problems, sleep disturbance, incontinence, alterations in nutrition, impaired judgment, fear, memory disturbance, self-neglect, accident prone, financial problems, family problems, problems with the law
    2. Treatment: detoxification; supportive communities (e.g., Alcoholics Anonymous); education
G. Role of the home health nurse
    1. Patients with psychiatric symptoms
        a. Develop rapport.
        b. Encourage patient to accept and utilize medications as prescribed.
        c. Teach as much of treatment regimen as is practical.
        d. Work with family members.
        e. Encourage outpatient follow-up for mental health needs when possible.
        f. Facilitate hospitalization when necessary.
    2. Patients without psychiatric symptoms
        a. Assess level of tolerable stress.
        b. Assist patient to develop reasonable expectations.
        c. Encourage self-care to the extent patient has ability.
    3. Patient compliance with medication
        a. Make regimen as simple as possible.
        b. Use meals or other regularly recurring events as reminders of times.
        c. Give specific advice on how to take medication.
    4. Recognize nurse's reaction to patient's behavior so he or she can respond to the patient more effectively.

STUDY QUESTIONS AND EXERCISES

1. What are three symptoms of schizophrenia?
2. What are three symptoms of mania?
3. List five symptoms of depression.

4. List two medical illnesses that may precipitate depression.
5. List five risk factors in assessing for suicide potential.
6. List five symptoms of substance abuse.

BIBLIOGRAPHY

American Psychiatric Association. 1987. *DSM III R*. Washington, D.C.

Baumann, A., et al. 1990. *Decision making in psychiatric and psychosocial nursing.* Toronto: B.C. Decker, Inc.

Lessing, D. 1987. Home care for psych problems. *American Journal of Nursing '87* 87, no. 10:1317–1320A.

National Institute of Mental Health. 1989. *Bipolar disorder.* Rockville, Md.: DHHS publication no. ADM, 89–1609.

Nursing Management of Other Patient Disorders

Part VI

38
Diabetes Mellitus

James A. Fain

A. Definition of diabetes mellitus (DM): chronic disorder characterized by abnormalities in metabolism of carbohydrates, proteins, and fats; encompasses a group of genetically and clinically heterogenous disorders in which glucose intolerance is a common denominator
B. Classifications: developed in 1979 by the National Diabetes Data Group; includes three clinical classes
   1. DM: further classified into three mutually exclusive subclasses
      a. Insulin-dependent DM (IDDM): also called type I diabetes
         (1) Patients with IDDM are dependent on injected insulin to prevent ketoacidosis.
         (2) IDDM is characterized by an abrupt onset of symptoms associated with hyperglycemia (e.g., fatigue, blurred vision, weight loss, polydipsia, polyuria, glycosuria, polyphagia).
         (3) IDDM accounts for approximately 2% of all cases of diabetes diagnosed each year in the United States.
         (4) Incidence increases with age until puberty, and peaks around age 12 to 14 years.
         (5) IDDM is three or four times more common than other chronic childhood diseases.
      b. Non–insulin-dependent DM (NIDDM): also called type II diabetes
         (1) Patients with NIDDM are not insulin-dependent or ketosis-prone.
         (2) NIDDM can occur at any age but usually is diagnosed after age 40 years.
         (3) NIDDM accounts for 98% of all cases of DM in the United States.

(4) It is estimated that approximately 5 million individuals with NIDDM remain undiagnosed; 75% to 90% are obese or had a history of obesity at time of diagnosis (>20% above ideal body weight).
(5) In some patients, insulin levels may be normal, mildly depressed, or elevated.
(6) Use of insulin by injection may be required for correction of symptomatic or persistent hyperglycemia.

    c. About 6.5 million people in the United States (approximately 3%) report having diagnosed DM. This number underestimates the true number of cases because half of all adult diabetes are underdiagnosed. Counting diagnosed and underdiagnosed, the true prevalence of DM may be as high as 13 million people.

    d. DM: may occur secondary to other conditions (e.g., pancreatic disease, insulin receptor abnormalities, drug and chemical agents, and/or genetic syndromes).

2. Impaired glucose tolerance (IGT): fasting glucose levels are higher than normal but lower than those considered diagnostic for DM.
3. Gestational DM (GDM)
   a. Patients with GDM have glucose intolerance that is first detected during pregnancy (women who become pregnant with known DM are not part of this classification).
   b. GDM occurs in approximately 2% to 3% of pregnant women during the second or third trimester.
   c. Screening of all pregnant women should take place between the 24th and 28th weeks of pregnancy.
   d. After parturition, patients should be reclassified as having DM, IGT, or previous abnormality of glucose tolerance.

C. Pathophysiology
   1. IDDM
      a. Insulin deficiency occurs as a result of destruction of beta cells within the pancreatic islets.
      b. Islet cell antibodies are found in many patients with IDDM and have been responsible for the destruction of beta cells.
      c. An autoimmune attack on beta cells diminishes the effective circulating insulin level.
      d. With continued destruction, patients ultimately will require insulin within 3 to 12 months.

2. NIDDM
   a. Patients experience reduction in number of insulin receptors and/or binding to receptors on surfaces of cells in various tissues.
   b. Insulin resistance occurs in most patients.
   c. Insulin resistance tends to be a direct correlation between severity of insulin resistance and fasting blood glucose levels.
   d. Discussion has been raised as to whether impaired beta cell function or diminished tissue sensitivity occurs first.
   e. Weight gain and obesity are important factors in the pathogenesis of NIDDM.
   f. Additionally, increasing age, family history of diabetes, and ethnic/racial groups (e.g., Hispanics, blacks) are considered important risk factors.
D. Treatment modalities: major goals of diabetes management are to achieve normal biochemical indices of metabolic control and to prevent acute and chronic complications. Recommended treatment modalities include the following:
   1. Nutritional management
      a. Current nutritional goals: improve blood glucose and lipid levels while providing adequate nutrition throughout the life cycle. Striving for euglycemia delays and/or prevents onset of complications.
      b. Difference between IDDM and NIDDM
         (1) Patients with IDDM should strive for consistency in day-to-day food intake, set aside a specific time for meals, and incorporate an exercise snack if appropriate.
         (2) Patients with NIDDM need to focus on weight management, paying particular attention to caloric restrictions and fat modification.
      c. Nutritional requirements for patients with IDDM and/or NIDDM: similar to those of the American Heart Association and American Cancer Society
         (1) Recommendations are developed to meet physical, metabolic, and lifestyle requirements.
         (2) Success depends on tailoring the diet to meet unique needs of the individual and incorporating them into their lifestyles.
      d. Distribution of calories in the meal plan:

(1) Of total calories, 55% to 60% come from carbohydrates, 15% to 20% come from proteins, and 20% come from fats.
(2) Calories should be distributed throughout the day.
(3) Adding between-meal snacks can help prevent hypoglycemia and the need for insulin to cover large meals.
  e. Food exchange system
    (1) A food exchange system is recommended for patients because of its uniformity in meal planning, incorporating a variety of caloric equivalency.
    (2) Two versions are available through the American Diabetes Association (ADA).
      (a) "Healthy Food Choices" (simpler)
      (b) "Exchange Lists for Meal Planning" (more expanded form)
2. Exercise
  a. Patients with IDDM and/or NIDDM: experience benefits from exercise similar to those experienced by nondiabetics
    (1) Improved fitness and psychologic state
    (2) Weight loss
    (3) Improved physical work capacity
  b. Benefits of exercise for those with DM
    (1) Improved insulin sensitivity due to an increase in the number of insulin receptors on target cells
    (2) Improved glucose tolerance
    (3) Potential reduction in insulin dosage
    (4) Reduction of risk factors associated with cardiovascular disease
  c. Exercise strategies for patients with IDDM
    (1) Patients should self-monitor blood glucose.
      (a) Always check blood glucose levels before, during, and after exercise.
      (b) Review of logs/records is an effective way to interpret particular patterns of response to exercise.
      (c) Blood glucose levels may drop for up to 4 to 10 hours after exercise.
    (2) A snack may be needed before prescribed activity/exercise: 10 to 15 g of carbohydrates (e.g., one fruit or bread exchange) should be eaten before 1 hour of moderate exercise (e.g., swimming, tennis, cycling, jogging).

（3) Strenuous exercise over an extended period may require a decrease in insulin: general rule of thumb is to decrease insulin by 10% in relation to total insulin dose per day.
(4) Patients are particularly prone to dehydration: fluid intake during exercise is important.
(5) Patients should carry some form of identification and source of readily available carbohydrate.
   d. Exercise strategies for patients with NIDDM
(1) Exercise should be performed at least three times per week to achieve continuous improvement. If weight reduction is the major goal, patients may need to exercise five times per week and burn 250 calories per session.
(2) Aerobic exercises are recommended (e.g., brisk walking, jogging, swimming, cycling).
(3) Muscle-strengthening exercises may lead to improved glucose disposal.
3. Pharmacologic interventions
   a. Instituted when normal to near-normal glycemic control cannot be reached
(1) Insulin regimens are required for the treatment of IDDM.
(2) Oral hypoglycemic agents and/or insulin are used when patients with NIDDM cannot achieve normal to near-normal blood glucose levels with dietary modifications and regular exercise.
   b. Insulin: three sources of insulin currently utilized—beef, pork, and human
(1) All animal insulin preparations are highly purified, in contrast to those available before 1970.
(2) Human insulin has a shorter duration of action than does animal insulin.
   c. Injection sites
(1) Rotate injection sites from one anatomic site to another: prior to the production of human insulin, this practice minimized problems with lipoatrophy.
   d. Insulin absorption
(1) Absorption is fastest in the abdomen, followed by arm, thigh, and buttocks.
(2) Avoid administering insulin in areas to be exercised (e.g., in thigh before jogging).

e. Mixed insulin
   (1) Mixed insulin is the most common regimen used for patients with IDDM.
   (2) Mix regular insulin with NPH (Neutral Protamine Hagedorn) or Lente and administer.
   (3) Mixtures may be in ratios of 90:10, 80:20, 70:30, or 50:50.
f. Duration of action: see Table 38-1.
g. Insulin concentrations
   (1) The insulin of choice for all patients in the United States is U-100 insulin.
   (2) Less than 2% of all patients use U-40 insulin; U-500 insulin is used among patients requiring large doses.
h. Oral hypoglycemic agents (sulfonylureas)
   (1) Sulfonylureas: divided into two categories—first and second generations. Second-generation agents introduced after 1984 have few side effects, interact less frequently with other drugs, and have alternate excretion routes.

Table 38-1 Time Course of Action of Insulin Preparations.*

Insulin Preparation	Onset of Action	Peak Action	Duration of Action
Short-acting			
Regular Iletin II (crystalline-zinc)	15–30 min	2–4 h	5–7 h
Novolin R	30 min	2.5–5 h	5–8 h
Velosulin	30 min	2–5 h	5–8 h
Humulin R	30 min	2–4 h	6–8 h
Intermediate-acting			
Lente	1–2 h	6–12 h	18–24 h
NPH	1–2 h	6–12 h	18–24 h
Novolin L	2.5–5 h	7–15 h	18–24 h
Humulin N	1–3 h	6–12 h	14–20 h
Novolin 70/30	30 min	7–12 h	24 h
Long-acting			
Ultralente (beef/pork)	4–6 h	14–24 h	28–36 h
Humulin U	4–6 h	8–20 h	24–28 h

*Average values. Considerable variation is found in individual diabetic patients.

Source: Reprinted from *Physician's Guide to Non–Insulin-Dependent (Type II) Diabetes: Diagnosis and Treatment*, 2nd ed., p. 43, with permission of American Diabetes Association, Inc., © 1989.

(2) Contraindications of sulfonylurea therapy
  (a) Patients with IDDM
  (b) During pregnancy/lactation
  (c) Patients known to be allergic to sulfonylurea compounds
(3) Complications of sulfonylurea therapy
  (a) Hypoglycemia is a serious complication (e.g., dizziness, blurred vision, confusion, sweats, nervousness, and/or numbness and tingling around mouth).
  (b) A patient usually is considered hypoglycemic with a blood glucose level <60 mg/dL.
  (c) Hypoglycemia may induce cardiac arrhythmias or even myocardial infarction and result in permanent brain damage.
  (d) Chlorpropamide (Diabinese) has been responsible for over 50% of reported cases of hypoglycemia.
     1) Agent with longest history of use and longest duration of action
(4) Characteristics of sulfonylurea agents: see Table 38-2

E. Nursing assessment
  1. Self-monitoring of blood glucose (SMBG): has influenced quality of care patients received; provides health care professionals with immediate response to treatment parameters
    a. SMBG is recommended for all people with IDDM. It is likewise recommended by most endocrinologists/diabetologists for people with NIDDM. SMBG is essential for adjusting doses of insulin or oral hypoglycemic agents; adjusting the overall meal plan; and recognizing the effect of activity and exercise on glycemic control.
      (1) Results of the Diabetes Control and Complications Trial (DCCT) have established that intensive blood glucose control in patients with IDDM resulted in decreased rates of development and progression of retinopathy, neuropathy, and nephropathy.
      (2) Major components of the DCCT: more frequent blood glucose monitoring (SMBG); smaller, more frequent insulin injections; and more frequent contact with health care professionals.
    b. Advantages of SMBG
      (1) SMBG is especially useful in diagnosing hypo- and hyperglycemia.

Table 38-2 Characteristics of Sulfonylurea Agents

Generic Name	Brand Name	Daily Dosage Range (mg)	Duration of Action (h)	Comments
Tolbutamide	Orinase	500–3,000	6–12	Metabolized by liver to an inactive product; given 2–3 times/day
Chlorpropamide	Diabinese	100–500	60	Metabolized by liver (approx. 70%) to less-active metabolites and excreted intact (approx. 30%) by kidneys; can potentiate antidiuretic hormone action; given once daily
Acetohexamide	Dymelor	250–1,500	12–18	Metabolized by liver to active metabolite; given 1–2 times/day
Tolazamide	Tolinase	100–1,000	12–24	Metabolized by liver to both active and inactive products; given 1–2 times/day
Glipizide	Glucotrol	5–40	12–24	Metabolized by liver to inert products; given 1–2 times/day
Glyburide	Diabeta Micronase	2.5–20	16–24	Metabolized by liver to mostly inert products; given 1–2 times/day

Source: Reprinted from *Physician's Guide to Non–Insulin-Dependent (Type II) Diabetes: Diagnosis and Treatment,* 2nd ed., p. 38, with permission of American Diabetes Associations, Inc., © 1989.

      (2) SMBG is critical when adjusting insulin dosage and levels of activity.
      (3) SMBG ensures prompt adjustment of insulin during periods of stress (e.g., illness, pregnancy, postoperatively).
  c. Disadvantages of SMBG
      (1) Strips and meters are costly.
      (2) There is discomfort from sticking finger with needle.
      (3) Meter use is complex.
  d. Older adults at home who might have cataracts or decreased ability to distinguish colors: generally not good candidates for

visual methods of blood glucose monitoring; meters that are more user-friendly and less technique-dependent are more appropriate
2. Urine testing
   a. Urine testing was original method of monitoring diabetes.
   b. It is no longer the preferred method for testing glucose values.
   c. It is valuable for testing ketones and protein excretion.
   d. Testing for ketones determines impending ketosis.
   e. Urine ketone testing should be done when blood glucose values are elevated (>250 mg/dL), during pregnancy, and at time of illness.
   f. Ketones are tested for those involved in weight-loss programs.
   g. Ketones are waste products of fat metabolism.
   h. Presence of protein in the urine may be an indication of microvascular changes in the kidneys.
3. Glycosylated hemoglobin: clinical chemistry assessment that validates results of SMBG.
   a. Glucose in plasma attaches to the hemoglobin molecule.
   b. The process is irreversible.
   c. Hemoglobin molecules have life span of 120 days; test reflects average blood glucose concentration over that period of time.
   d. Glycosylated hemoglobin (HbA$_{1c}$) is the measurement of glycosylation; normal value is usually in the range of 4% to 7%.
4. Educational considerations
   a. Patients on home care tend to be older adults; education of this age group has been neglected.
   b. Difficulty in comprehension increases with age, and other cognitive deficits may be present; older adults need special attention because of the high incidence of diabetes in those aged 65 years and older.
   c. Patient counseling suggestions
      (1) Inform patients that any lowering of blood glucose, even a little, can help reduce the risk of developing diabetes-specific complications.
      (2) Encourage patients to discuss any changes in therapy.
      (3) Emphasize the need for more frequent SMBG and the use of results in making changes in therapy.
      (4) Suggest that patients keep a diary that includes diet, exercise, diabetes medication, and blood glucose levels.

            (5) Encourage patients and families to join local affiliate of the American Diabetes Association (ADA).
        d. Assess diabetes knowledge and beliefs.
            (1) Older adults frequently have had experience with diabetes through dialogue with their spouses, family members, and/or friends; such experiences will have an impact on the educational plan and their willingness to care for themselves.
            (2) Misconceptions need to be clarified with correct information provided over a period of time that meets the needs of each individual.
        e. Assess physical function and sensory ability.
            (1) Older adults' inability to perform activities of daily living and diminished visual acuity may interfere with their ability to administer insulin and perform SMBG.
            (2) Diminished hearing may affect their ability to hear and understand information needed to care for themselves.
        f. Assess the patient's educational and literacy levels.
            (1) It is extremely important to determine literacy levels and match educational materials to reading and/or cognitive ability.
                (a) For some patients, reading versus listening versus looking at illustrations will be more advantageous as a method of learning.
                (b) Printed material should be in large type and be written at an eighth-grade reading level.
                (c) Clear, nontechnical language and good illustrations enhance effectiveness of printed material.

STUDY QUESTIONS AND EXERCISES

1. Describe the various subclasses of diabetes mellitus with respect to epidemiology and pathophysiology.
2. What are the nutritional guidelines for patients with type I and type II diabetes?
3. List and differentiate insulin preparations on the basis of type, source, concentration, onset of action, peak, and duration.

4. Compare and contrast oral hypoglycemic agents in their clinical application. What is the major complication associated with sulfonylurea therapy?
5. Discuss some of the advantages and disadvantages of SMBG.
6. Describe several techniques that could be used to enhance patient learning.

BIBLIOGRAPHY

American Diabetes Association. 1989. *Physician's guide to insulin-dependent (type I) diabetes: Diagnosis and treatment.* Alexandria, Va.

American Diabetes Association. 1989. *Physician's guide to non–insulin-dependent (type II) diabetes: Diagnosis and treatment.* Alexandria, Va.

American Diabetes Association. 1994. Standards of medical care for patients with diabetes mellitus. *Diabetes Care* 18:8–15.

American Diabetes Association. 1990. Consensus statement: Self monitoring of blood glucose. *Diabetes Care* 13:41–46.

American Diabetes Association. 1993. *Diabetes 1993 vital statistics.* Alexandria, Va.

Anderson, L.A., and C.M. Jenkins. 1994. Educational innovations in diabetes: Where are we now? *Diabetes Spectrum* 7:90-125.

Anderson, R.M., and R.W. Genther. 1990. A guide for assessing a patient's level of personal responsibility. *Patient Education and Counseling* 16:2699–2790.

Brodows, R.G. 1992. Benefits and risks with glyburide and glipizide in elderly NIDDM patients. *Diabetes Care* 15:75–80.

Diabetes Control and Complications Trial Research Group. 1993. The effects of intensive treatment of diabetes on the development and progression of long-term complications in insulin-dependent diabetes mellitus. *New England Journal of Medicine* 329:977-986.

Fain, J.A. 1993. National trends in diabetes: An epidemiologic perspective. *Nursing Clinics of North America* 28:1-7.

Graham, C. 1991. Exercise in the elderly patient with diabetes. *Practical Diabetology* 10:8–11.

Grundy, S. 1991. Dietary therapy in diabetes mellitus: Is there a single best diet? *Diabetes Care* 14:796–801.

Haire-Joshu, D. 1992. *Management of diabetes mellitus: Perspectives of care across the life span.* St. Louis: Mosby-Year Book, Inc.

Hirsch, I.B., and R. Farkas-Hirsch. 1993. Type I diabetes and insulin therapy. *Nursing Clinics of North America* 28:9-23.

National Diabetes Data Group. 1979. Classification and diagnosis of diabetes mellitus and other categories of glucose intolerance. *Diabetes* 28:1039–1057.

39

Hyperthyroidism

Keltie Baker Kerney

A. Definitions/points of emphasis
   1. Excessive activity of the thyroid gland (diffuse toxic goiter)
   2. Characterized by excessive production of thyroid hormone
   3. A generalized, extremely hypermetabolic state that occurs in response to excessive levels of circulating thyroid hormones
B. Pathophysiology
   1. Characterized by hypertrophy and hyperplasia of the thyroid gland, accompanied by increased vascularity and blood flow and enlargement of the gland
   2. A hypermetabolic condition resulting from excessive secretion of thyroid hormone resulting in exaggerated metabolic processes
   3. Most cases: due to an autoimmune reaction, in which circulating autoantibodies mimic the action of thyroid-stimulating hormone (TSH) and increase the secretion of thyroid hormone
   4. An increased metabolic rate, excessive heat production, increased neuromuscular and cardiovascular activity, and hyperactivity of the sympathetic nervous system produce most of the clinical manifestations.
   5. May be mild or extreme, resulting in severe hyperactivity (known as thyrotoxicosis, thyroid storm, or thyroid crisis).
C. Demographics
   1. More common in women than in men
   2. Occurs in about 2% of the female population
   3. Graves' disease (most prevalent form of hyperthyroidism): most commonly seen in women during the third and fourth decades of life.

D. Etiology
   1. Unknown
   2. Immunologic origin is likely
   3. Viral
   4. Hyperplastic
   5. Familial
   6. Neoplastic
   7. An acute systemic illness (excessive thyroid hormone results in enhanced sympathetic tone)
   8. Other possible causes:
      a. Thyroid-stimulating antibody: long-acting thyroid stimulator that correlates very closely with the clinical course of Graves' disease
      b. Thyroid-stimulating antibody is capable of reacting with the receptor for TSH on the thyroid plasma membrane and stimulating glandular function.
      c. May appear after an emotional shock, surgery, infection, or other emotional stressors.
      d. Genetic predisposition; female sex
      e. B and T lymphocytes (immunologic factors) have been implicated.
   9. Less common causes: toxic multinodular goiter, thyroiditis, drug-induced thyrotoxicosis, and (rarely) thyroid carcinoma
E. Diagnosis/evaluation
   1. Assessment of clinical manifestations
   2. Simple blood tests
      a. Elevated serum triiodothyronine (T_3) resin uptake
      b. Elevated serum thyroxine (T_4) levels
   3. Physical exam reveals a hypermetabolic state.
   4. A thrill or bruit over the thyroid often can be detected because of the increased blood flow.
   5. The thyroid gland may be palpable on examination, indicating further need for assessment.
   6. Ultrasonograms/scans can assist in making a differential diagnosis.
   7. Successful diagnosis is attributed to a clinician who maintains a high degree of suspicion for the diagnosis of a thyroid dysfunction.

8. Prompt diagnosis and treatment of early thyroid dysfunction usually prevents episodes of life-threatening thyroid storm or myxedema coma.
F. Clinical manifestations
   1. Neurologic
      a. Hyperthyroidism
         (1) Irritability/nervousness
         (2) Tremors
         (3) Insomnia
         (4) Emotional lability
         (5) Diplopia
         (6) Headache
         (7) Large, protruding eyes (exophthalmos), which produce a startled expression
         (8) Periorbital edema
         (9) Tremor of eyelids
         (10) Weakness or paralysis of extraocular muscles
         (11) Brisk deep-tendon reflexes
         (12) Muscle fatigability and weakness or atrophy
      b. Thyroid storm
         (1) Extreme restlessness
         (2) Confusion or disorientation
         (3) Frank psychosis
         (4) Apathy
         (5) Stupor or delirium
         (6) Coma
   2. Cardiovascular
      a. Hyperthyroidism
         (1) Palpitations
         (2) Rapid bounding pulses (at rest as well as on exertion)
         (3) Wide pulse pressure
         (4) Irregular pulse/dysrhythmias
         (5) Systolic cardiac murmur
         (6) Congestive heart failure
         (7) Edema
      b. Thyroid storm
         (1) Profuse diaphoresis
         (2) Tachycardia disproportionate to change in blood pressure
         (3) Atrial fibrillation

(4) Weak pulses
(5) Hypotension
3. Respiratory
    a. Hyperthyroidism
        (1) Dyspnea
        (2) Increased depth of respiration
        (3) Pulmonary edema
    b. Thyroid storm: pulmonary edema
4. Gastrointestinal
    a. Hyperthyroidism
        (1) Weight loss
        (2) Increased thirst and/or appetite
        (3) Diarrhea
        (4) Nausea
        (5) Abdominal pain
        (6) Hyperactive bowel sounds
        (7) Frequent stools
    b. Thyroid storm
        (1) Anorexia
        (2) Protracted vomiting
        (3) Severe abdominal pain
        (4) Hepatomegaly
        (5) Jaundice
5. Metabolic
    a. Profuse sweating
    b. Sensitivity to heat; heat intolerance
    c. Increased tolerance to cold
    d. Enlarged thyroid gland
    e. Bruit over neck
6. Integumentary
    a. Skin: soft, warm, moist, shiny, reddened, hyperpigmented
    b. Hair: thinning, fine, straight; oily scalp
    c. Separation of nails from nail beds
7. Sexuality/reproductive function
    a. Changes in menstruation; amenorrhea
    b. Changes in sexual activities or desires
    c. Gynecomastia in male patients
8. Difficulty in sitting quietly
9. Course may be mild, characterized by remissions and exacerba-

tions; may progress to emaciation, extreme nervousness, delirium, disorientation, thyroid storm or crisis, and death.
   10. Thyroid storm or crisis: an extreme form of hyperthyroidism
       a. Hyperpyrexia
       b. Diarrhea
       c. Dehydration
       d. Tachycardia
       e. Dysrhythmia
       f. Extreme irritation
       g. Delirium
       h. Coma
       i. Shock
       j. Death, if not adequately treated
       k. May be precipitated by stress or inadequate preparation for surgery in a patient known to have hyperthyroidism
G. Treatment
   1. Antithyroid drug therapy
   2. Irradiation
   3. Surgery
   4. Factors influencing treatment: causes, age of patient, severity of disease, and complications
   5. Remission of hyperthyroidism
       a. Spontaneously within 1 to 2 years
       b. Relapse can be expected in half the patients
       c. All three forms of treatment are appropriate
   6. Nodular toxic goiter: extreme amounts of thyroid hormone secreted; surgery or use of radioiodine is preferred.
   7. Carcinoma: surgery or irradiation indicated
   8. According to age of patient
       a. Radioiodine therapy: may be used in all patients regardless of age when other forms of therapy are contraindicated
       b. Radioiodine: used in older patients for whom surgery is contraindicated; surgery is recommended for younger patients
       c. Radioiodine therapy: contraindicated in pregnancy and in women of childbearing age
   9. According to severity
       a. Drug therapy is administered before proceeding with radioiodine or surgery.
       b. Radioiodine or surgery may be preferred when the patient does not take medication regularly and is not compliant.

c. Surgery may also be indicated for patients living in remote areas without access to satisfactory medical care.
10. Surgery
   a. Indicated for patients with large or medium-sized goiters (greater than 80 g)
   b. Antithyroid drugs are given to patients with a small goiter (less than 40 g)
H. Medications
1. Goals
   a. Use medications that inhibit hormone formation.
   b. Bring the metabolic rate to normal as soon as possible and maintain at this level.
2. Commonly used medications
   a. Thionamides (propylthiouracil, methimazole [Tapazole]): used to depress the synthesis of thyroid hormone by inhibiting peroxidase)
   b. Propranolol (Inderal)
      (1) Acts as a β-adrenergic blocking agent
      (2) Indicated for tachycardia, tremor, excessive sweating, nervousness
      (3) Controls hyperthyroid symptoms until antithyroid drugs or radioiodine can take effect.
   c. Glucocorticoids: indicated to decrease the peripheral conversion of T_4 to T_3.
   d. Radioactive iodine
      (1) Indicated to limit secretion of thyroid hormone by destroying thyroid tissue
      (2) Side effect: permanent hypothyroidism can be produced in patients treated with radioiodine
3. Surgery
   a. An effective treatment in selected patients with very large goiters or those for whom the use of radioiodine or thionamides is contraindicated
   b. Subtotal thyroidectomy involves removal of most of the thyroid gland.
4. Nursing interventions/teaching related to medications
   a. Instruct patient in appropriate dosage and frequency of medication.
   b. Monitor patient's response to pharmacologic therapy and prescribed fluids and electrolytes.

c. Instruct patient, once started on a particular brand of medication, to continue because a different brand will have a different bioavailability.
d. Instruct patient to report side effects of medication to physician.
e. Instruct patient in the frequency of obtaining blood samples to determine therapeutic levels.
f. Instruct patient not to take aspirin.
   (1) Aspirin competes with thyroid hormone.
   (2) When thyroid hormone is produced, it binds to a protein called thyroid-binding globulin (TBG).
   (3) A small amount of hormone is left as free functioning, with most binding to TBG.
   (4) Aspirin competes with thyroid hormone for a binding site on TBG, and aspirin wins.
   (5) Large amounts of thyroid hormone are released, with increase in amount of free functioning thyroid hormone (may lead to thyrotoxic crisis).

I. Other nursing interventions
   1. Goal: improve nutritional intake.
      a. Assess patient's food and fluid preferences.
      b. Instruct in high-caloric foods and fluids consistent with patient requirements and preferences.
      c. Encourage a quiet, calm environment at mealtimes.
      d. Encourage patient to restrict stimulants (tea, coffee, alcohol, anything with caffeine); explain rationale of restrictions.
      e. Encourage patient to eat alone if embarrassed or disturbed by increased appetite.
      f. Instruct patient to weigh daily and keep accurate weight chart and keep accurate intake and output records during times advised by physician.
      g. Monitor vital signs to detect changes in fluid volume status.
      h. Assess skin turgor, mucous membranes, and neck veins for signs of increased or decreased fluid volume
   2. Goal: maintain skin integrity.
      a. Assess skin frequently for abnormalities or diaphoresis.
      b. Instruct patient to bathe frequently with cool water and to change damp linen.

c. Instruct patient to protect and relieve pressure from bony prominences when and if immobilized, or while hypothermia or other mattress is used.
3. Goal: relieve anxiety. Encourage patient to verbalize concerns and fears about illness, treatment, and therapies.
4. Goal: maintain sufficient energy to perform activities of daily living.
   a. Instruct patient to restrict activity to level of tolerance.
   b. Instruct in adequate rest periods and to discontinue activity at onset of signs of intolerance (i.e., dyspnea, tachycardia, or fatigue).
5. Goal: maintain patient's eyes moist and free from abrasions.
   a. Encourage use of sunglasses during sunlight.
   b. Instruct patient to use lubricants as ordered.
   c. Instruct patient to avoid getting foreign bodies in eyes (i.e., dirt or dust).

STUDY QUESTIONS AND EXERCISES

1. Describe the early signs/symptoms of hyperthyroidism versus signs/symptoms of thyroid storm/crisis.
2. Discuss home care nursing interventions for the patient with hyperthyroidism.
3. Describe treatment protocols for patients with hyperthyroidism.

BIBLIOGRAPHY

Halloran, T.H. 1990. Nursing responsibilities in endocrine emergencies. *Critical Nursing Quarterly* 13, no. 3:74-81.

Neff, J.A., et al. July/August 1989. Patient care guidelines—hypothyroidism: Thyroid crisis, storm, thyrotoxic crisis. *Journal of Emergency Nursing* 15, no. 4:352-355.

Piziak, V.K. April 15, 1992. Thyroid disease—some considerations in later life. *Emergency Medicine:* 67-74.

Spittle, L. May 1992. Diagnoses in opposition: Thyroid storm and myxedema coma. *AACN Clinical Issues* 3, no. 2.

Suddarth, D.S. 1991. *Lippincott manual of nursing practice.* Philadelphia: J.B. Lippincott Co.

University of Toronto Facility of Medicine. February 1994. *Health News* 12, no. 1:1-4.

40

Hypothyroidism

Keltie Baker Kerney

A. Definitions/points of emphasis
   1. Primary hypothyroidism results from the inability of the thyroid gland to secrete a sufficient amount of hormone.
      a. Directly attributed to thyroid gland dysfunction
      b. Hashimoto's thyroiditis or autoimmune thyroiditis: most common cause of primary hypothyroidism in adults
      c. Ablative therapy for hyperthyroidism and endemic iodine deficiency: other causes of primary hypothyroidism
   2. Secondary hypothyroidism
      a. Failure of the pituitary gland to secrete an adequate amount of thyroid-stimulating hormone (TSH)
      b. Attributed to pituitary disease and a lack of TSH
   3. Tertiary hypothyroidism
      a. Failure of the hypothalamus to release thyroid-releasing hormone (TRH)
      b. Hypothalamic failure when the production of TSH is inhibited or diminished
   4. Cretinism: a severe form of hypothyroidism; a result of a deficiency of thyroid function during fetal life or shortly after birth
B. Pathophysiology
   1. Characterized by an inadequate secretion of thyroid hormone (leads to a general slowing of all physical and mental processes)
   2. General depression of most cellular enzyme systems and oxidative processes
   3. Metabolic activity of all cells of the body decreases, resulting in decreased oxygen consumption and decreased oxidation of nutrients for energy (which produces less body heat).

4. Clinical manifestations range from vague, nonspecific complaints to severe symptoms that may be life threatening, if untreated.
C. Demographics
 1. Endemic iodine deficiency (primary hypothyroidism) is not a major problem in North America).
 2. Hashimoto's thyroiditis usually affects women.
 3. Tertiary causes of hypothyroidism: relatively uncommon and account for less than 1% of all patients with hypothyroidism.
 4. The incidence of clinical hypothyroidism in people over the age of 60 is 0.8%.
   a. About 9.7% are men in that age group.
   b. About 15% of women have elevated levels of TSH.
   c. Hypothyroidism affects almost 7 million North Americans.
   d. Prevalence rises to 10% or more among the elderly.
D. Etiology
 1. May be idiopathic in origin
 2. May be result of chronic immunologic dysfunction (as in Hashimoto's thyroiditis)
 3. Primary hypothyroidism: most common form; generally due to removal, destruction, or suppression of all or some of the thyroid tissue by thyroidectomy, use of radioactive iodine, or overtreatment with antithyroid drugs
 4. Secondary causes: attributed to pituitary disease and a lack of TSH
 5. Tertiary causes: hypothalamic failure when the production of TSH is inhibited or diminished
 6. Medications (e.g., Lithium) can cause hypothyroidism
E. Diagnosis/evaluation
 1. Assessment of clinical manifestations over a period of time; disease develops insidiously and sometimes manifestations are unrecognized.
 2. Low serum triiodothyronine (T_3) resin uptake and serum thyroxine (T_4) levels
 3. Elevated TSH levels in primary hypothyroidism
 4. Elevation of serum cholesterol
 5. Abnormal electrocardiogram (ECG) (sinus bradycardia)
 6. Prolonged deep-tendon reflex response, especially ankle jerk
 7. Possible previous treatment with radioactive iodine
 8. General suppression and depression of organs and symptoms
F. Clinical manifestations

1. Central nervous system
   a. Fatigue
   b. Cold intolerance (especially hands and feet); patient desires room temperature increased
   c. Hyporeflexia
   d. Slowed mental responses
   e. Generalized aching
   f. Increased sensitivity to narcotics and barbiturates
   g. Lethargy
   h. Temperature and pulse become subnormal
   i. Reduced attention span
   j. Impaired short-term memory
   k. Polyneuropathy
   l. Cerebellar ataxia
   m. Clumsiness
   n. Muscle aches and weakness
2. Cardiovascular
   a. Bradycardia
   b. Pericardial effusion
   c. Anemia
   d. Weak myocardial contractility
   e. Predisposition to congestive heart failure
   f. Enlarged heart on chest X-ray
3. Pulmonary: slowed respiratory movement/dyspnea
4. Gastrointestinal
   a. Weight gain
   b. Constipation
   c. Diminished bowel sounds
   d. Abnormal distention
5. Integumentary
   a. Dry skin
   b. Myxedema
   c. Dry, coarse hair; thinning hair
   d. Loss of a lateral one third of eyebrows
6. Sexuality/reproductive function
   a. Menorrhagia or amenorrhea
   b. May have difficulty conceiving or may experience spontaneous abortion
   c. Decreased libido

7. In severe hypothyroidism
    a. Hypotension
    b. Unresponsiveness
    c. Bradycardia
    d. Hypoventilation
    e. Hyponatremia
    f. Possible convulsions
    g. Hypothermia
    h. Cerebral hypoxia
    i. Myxedema
8. Other
    a. Generalized appearance of thick, puffy skin
    b. Subcutaneous swelling in hands, feet, and eyelids

G. Treatment
  1. Depends on the severity of the symptoms
     a. In mild cases: replacement hormone therapy with synthetic products
     b. Severe hypothyroidism and myxedema coma: provide lifesaving support and treatment.
  2. Restore normal metabolic state as rapidly as possible through replacement of thyroid hormone.

H. Medications
  1. Goal: replace thyroid hormone and restore normal metabolic state as rapidly as possible but not to a suppressed level.
  2. Commonly used medications
     a. Levothyroxine (Synthroid, Levothroid): Synthroid is indicated to restore thyroxine level.
     b. Thyroglobulin (Proloid)
     c. Liotrix (Euthroid, Thyrolar)
  3. Nursing interventions: teaching related to medications
     a. Monitor patient to assess medication effects.
        (1) Diuresis, decreased puffiness
        (2) Improved reflexes and muscle tone
        (3) Accelerated pulse rate
        (4) Slightly higher level of total serum thyroxine
     b. Patient instructions
        (1) Explain that signs of hypothyroidism should disappear 3 to 12 weeks after treatment is initiated.
        (2) Do not stop taking medications, even when feeling better

(if patient stops too soon, or without medical advice, symptoms may return in a few weeks).
    (3) Explain appropriate dosages, side effects, and frequency of medication.
    (4) Report side effects of medication to physician.
    (5) Remember frequency of obtaining blood samples to determine therapeutic levels as ordered by the physician.
    (6) Once started on a particular brand of medication, continue with that brand (a different brand may have a different bioavailability).
I. Other nursing interventions: the nursing care of the patient with profound thyroid dysfunction (i.e., myxedema coma) presents other nursing challenges to assess signs and symptoms of alternations in function.
   1. Goal: improve cardiac output.
      a. Control factors that increase metabolic rate and threaten cardiovascular status.
         (1) Monitor vital signs.
         (2) Monitor ECG.
         (3) Prevent chilling.
         (4) Administer fluids cautiously as ordered, even though hyponatremia may be present.
         (5) Give prescribed glucose in concentrated amounts to prevent fluid overload.
      b. Administer prescribed medications with caution (some patients are more susceptible to the effects of sedatives, narcotics, anesthetics, and other medications, once thyroid therapy is started).
      c. Report angina and the signs and symptoms of other myocardial distress or cardiac failure.
      d. Monitor arterial blood gases to assess cardiopulmonary function.
   2. Goal: increase activity and tolerance.
      a. Limit visitors during acute stage of illness to prevent excessive stimulation
      b. Assist patient in activities of daily living as much as possible to reduce the energy output
      c. Assist patient in turning and encourage patient to cough and deep breathe.

d. Provide good skin care to prevent skin breakdown.
3. Goal: improve nutritional status.
   a. Assess gastrointestinal function.
   b. Encourage frequent intake of fluids and dietary fiber to prevent constipation.
   c. Administer stool softener, if necessary and as ordered.
   d. Consult dietitian to offer appetizing, low-calorie meals (patient is usually overweight; however, appetite is poor).

STUDY QUESTIONS AND EXERCISES

1. The classic symptoms of hypothyroid disease frequently go undetected and undiagnosed as they are insidious and are sometimes considered early symptoms of the aging process. True or false?
2. Describe the early signs/symptoms of hypothyroidism versus the signs/symptoms of myxedema.
3. Discuss home care nursing interventions for the patient with hypothyroidism.
4. Describe treatment protocols for patients with hypothyroidism.

BIBLIOGRAPHY

Halloran, T.H. 1990. Nursing responsibilities in endocrine emergencies. *Critical Nursing Quarterly* 13, no. 3:74-81.

Neff, J.A., et al. July/August 1989. Patient care guidelines—hypothyroidism: Thyroid crisis, storm, thyrotoxic crisis. *Journal of Emergency Nursing* 15, no. 4:352-355.

Piziak, V.K. April 15, 1992. Thyroid disease—some considerations in later life. *Emergency Medicine*:67-74.

Spittle, L. May 1992. Diagnoses in opposition: Thyroid storm and myxedema coma. *AACN Clinical Issues* 3, no. 2.

Suddarth, D.S. 1991. *Lippincott manual of nursing practice*. Philadelphia: J.B. Lippincott Co.

University of Toronto Facility of Medicine. February 1994. *Health News* 12, no. 1:1-4.

41

Arthritis

Kevin L. Ross

A. Definitions/points of emphasis
   1. Arthritis: "joint inflammation"; also includes approximately 100 inflammatory and noninflammatory diseases that affect the joints, connective tissue, and other supportive tissue
   2. Osteoarthritis (OA): a disorder of hyaline cartilage and subchondral bone in which all tissue in and around involved joints are hypertrophic
   3. Rheumatoid arthritis (RA): a chronic syndrome characterized by nonspecific inflammation of the peripheral joints, resulting in progressive destruction of articular and periarticular structures.
   4. Infectious arthritis: results from infection of the synovial tissue; pathogenic microbes infecting a joint may be bacterial, viral, or fungal.
   5. Crystal-induced arthritis (gout): a recurrent acute arthritis resulting from crystals of monosodium urate (MSU) in and around peripheral joints and tendons
B. Pathophysiology
   1. Osteoarthritis
      a. A roughening and pitting of the hyaline cartilage resulting in diffuse areas of loss of cartilage surface
      b. Characteristic spur formation around the periphery of the joints
      c. Bony proliferations (Heberden's nodes) occur at the distal interphalangeal joints
   2. Rheumatoid arthritis
      a. Rheumatoid factors (antiantibodies) form immune complexes in the blood, causing inflammation.

b. Increased numbers and size of synovial lining cells with colonization by lymphocytes and plasma cells, causing chronic inflammation and swelling
   c. Widespread inflammatory processes may involve other tissue (e.g., skin, muscles, nerves, heart, and lungs)
  3. Infectious arthritis
   a. When pathogenic microbes infect a joint, acute arthritis may result.
   b. Microbes may reach the joint hematogenously, through direct inoculation during surgery or drug injection, or secondary to trauma.
  4. Crystal-induced arthritis (gout)
   a. Supersaturated hyperuricemic body fluids result in needle-shaped MSU crystals to deposit in cartilage, tendons, and ligaments around distal peripheral joints
   b. May be precipitated by trauma, ingestion of certain foods or alcohol, fatigue, or stress.
C. Demographics
  1. OA affects men and women equally, with onset earlier in men.
  2. RA affects women two or three times more often than men.
  3. Approximately one in seven Americans displays some form of arthritis.
  4. There is no specific geographic distribution
D. Etiology
  1. Unknown for OA and RA
  2. Infectious arthritis
   a. Bacteria: staphylococci, gram-negative bacilli, gonococci, streptococci, or pneumococci
  3. Gout: dietary purines resulting from overindulgence of rich foods and alcoholic beverages
E. Diagnosis
  1. Complete medical history
  2. Complete physical examination, including serologic testing
  3. Cultures of blood, sputum, spinal fluid, and synovial fluid
  4. Biopsy of subcutaneous nodules
  5. X-ray studies
F. Treatment
  1. Medication
  2. Treatment of underlying cause, if applicable

3. Psychosocial adaptation to physical limitations
4. Physical and occupational therapies
5. Dietary counseling
6. Exercise
7. Surgery

G. Medication
   1. Goals:
      a. Reduction of inflammation
      b. Freedom from pain
      c. Freedom from infection
      d. Prevention of deposition of MSU crystals
      e. Inhibition of synthesis of prostaglandin
   2. Commonly used medications
      a. Aspirin: initial dosing, 0.6 to 1.0 g four times daily orally with meals and bedtime snack, increasing gradually until reaching maximal effectiveness or mild toxicity (e.g., tinnitus)
      b. Ibuprofen: 400 to 800 mg four times daily orally
      c. Indomethacin: 25 mg three to four times daily orally with food
      d. Gold compounds: initially weekly dosing of 10 mg intramuscularly (IM) for week 1, 25 mg IM for week 2, and 50 mg/week IM thereafter until a total of 1.0 g has been given. Administration is contraindicated for patients with significant hepatic or renal disease or blood dyscrasia.
   3. Nursing intervention/patient teaching
      a. Instruct patient on appropriate dosage and frequency of medications.
         (1) Initial dosing: may be at low dose, increasing gradually until desired level is reached
         (2) Emphasis: many anti-inflammatory drugs should be taken with meals or snacks, as gastrointestinal (GI) upset/bleeding could result
         (3) If excess GI upset/bleeding is detected, patient to inform physician and/or nurse
      b. Monitor for side effects.
         (1) Common to nonsteroidal anti-inflammatory drugs (NSAID): GI upset, GI bleeding, drowsiness, dizziness, blurred vision, tinnitus
         (2) Common to gold compounds: pruritus, rash, stomatitis, indigestion, metallic taste

H. Management of arthritis patient at home
    1. Goals:
        a. To instruct patient/caregiver in management of arthritis
        b. To educate patient/caregiver regarding the achievement of and maintenance of an optimal level of physical fitness through:
            (1) Appropriate exercise (e.g., range of motion, isometric, isokinetic, strengthening)
            (2) Nutrition
            (3) Rest (including the use of splints to provide local joint rest)
        c. To facilitate patient/caregiver's adaptation to a chronic health problem:
            (1) Instruction in safety issues
            (2) Referral to support systems/community resources
    2. Safety issues in arthritis management
        a. Protect patient from injury.
        b. Assess home for objects that may result in falls or joint injury.
    3. Psychosocial issues
        a. Patients with arthritis may experience some or all of the following:
            (1) Changes in self-image
            (2) Fear/anxiety
            (3) Frustration, anger, denial, depression
            (4) Social isolation
            (5) Changes in family dynamics
        b. Intra-agency referrals for therapy or social services may be indicated.
        c. Interdisciplinary care coordination should occur and address patient problems identified during each professional discipline's assessment.
        d. Referrals to community resources (e.g., Arthritis Foundation, local support groups) may be indicated.
    4. Patient/caregiver should keep written notes regarding location and level of pain, changes in joint mobility, medication complication, and any problems that occur between nursing visits.
    5. Information should be reviewed by the nurse and appropriate interventions taken during each nursing visit.
    6. Nursing documentation should reflect
        a. Location and level of patient's pain

    b. Complications and compliance with patient's medication
    c. Instructions given to the patient/caregiver, including level of understanding
    d. Psychosocial assessment, including any intervention
    e. Communications with other staff members, patient's physician, community resources

STUDY QUESTIONS AND EXERCISES

1. List two goals for medication use in the treatment of arthritis.
2. List two goals the nurse may develop when planning the care of an arthritis patient at home.
3. List three educational interventions that the nurse should instruct the patient to monitor and report.

BIBLIOGRAPHY

Berkow, R., and A. Fletcher. 1992. *The Merck manual of diagnosis and therapy.* Rahway, N.J.: Merck and Co.

Kelly, W.N., et al. 1993. *Textbook of rheumatology.* Philadelphia: W.B. Saunders Co.

McCarthy, D.J., and W.J. Koopman. 1993. *Arthritis and allied conditions: A textbook of rheumatology.* Vol. 2. Philadelphia: Lea and Febiger.

Olin, B.R., et al. 1994. *Drug facts and comparisons.* Philadelphia: J.B. Lippincott Co.

Schumacher, R., et al. 1988. *Primer on rheumatic disease.* Atlanta: Arthritis Foundation.

42

Ostomies

Kathleen Calitri Brown

A. Colostomy: a surgically created opening into the large intestine, or colon
   1. Functions of the large intestine: storage area for stool; absorb water and digestive enzymes from stool; helps make formed stool
   2. Sites for colostomy stomas: can be made anywhere in large intestine
      a. Ascending colostomy: rare
      b. Transverse colostomy
      c. Descending colostomy
      d. Sigmoid colostomy: most common type; creates a stoma in the left lower abdominal quadrant
   3. Reasons for colostomies
      a. Disease: cancer, Crohn's disease, diverticulitis.
      b. Congenital: imperforate anus, Hirschsprung's disease, volvulus
      c. Traumatic: gunshot wounds, motor vehicle accidents
   4. Types of colostomy stomas
      a. End colostomy stoma: a single, budded, matured stoma; has resected end of colon everted, or cuffed back on itself and sutured to skin. Innermost lining of gastrointestinal (GI) tract, or mucosa, is visible when looking at the stoma; distal colon is removed or oversewn and left inside (if left inside is a Hartmann's pouch).
      b. Double-barrel colostomy stomas: both proximal and distal ends of colon are brought out through abdominal wall as stomas. Proximal stoma is the functioning one; distal, nonfunctioning stoma is called mucous fistula.

- c. Loop colostomy stoma: a loop of bowel brought out with anterior wall opened, usually transversely, along teniae coli muscles. Posterior wall of bowel is left intact with support device or red rubber catheter inserted through bowel's mesentery. Rod is used to support stoma for first 5 to 7 days after surgery. Loop stomas are usually oval-shaped and most commonly done in transverse colon; also called diverting (temporary) colostomies.
5. Irrigation: managing a colostomy stoma
   a. Irrigation is for descending and sigmoid colostomy stomas only.
   b. An enema is given into the stoma on a daily or an every-other-day basis to clean out distal colon.
   c. Enema is given to make stoma stool-free between irrigations.
   d. Good candidates for successful irrigations are patients who are well-motivated and dexterous, willing to spend the 45 to 60 minutes/day it takes to irrigate, and have preoperative bowel habits of one or two movements per day.
   e. Irrigation as a method of management is contraindicated in patients receiving pelvic or abdominal radiation; those with Crohn's disease, temporary stomas, diarrhea, stomal prolapse, or parastomal hernia; and in children with colostomies.
   f. Irrigation procedure: With patient sitting on toilet, a maximum of 1000 mL of warm tap water is hung in a water bag at patient's shoulder height; water is infused into stoma via cone tip over 5 to 8 minutes. Patient wears an irrigation sleeve that belts on or is snapped onto a flange and empties into the toilet.
   g. After infusion of water, most of the stool and water return within 15 to 20 minutes. Patient can then clamp bottom of irrigation sleeve and walk around; this will help speed up return of remaining water and stool.
   h. People who are successful with irrigation can wear a closed-end or security pouch, BandAid, or small gauze dressing over stoma; should put out only mucus until the next irrigation.
   i. Common problems with irrigation
      (1) "The water won't go in": try raising water bag; do digital examination of stoma to check for a fecal impaction and to see which way the colon angles as it comes through the abdominal wall; adjust angle of the cone to match angle of the colon.

(2) "The water won't come out": Patient is dehydrated and colon is absorbing irrigation water. Instruct patient to increase fluids by mouth before irrigating.
(3) "Stool spillage hours after irrigating": Try to identify and avoid offending foods that trigger stool output from stoma. Increase amount of irrigation to 1000 mL of water; make sure entire amount of irrigation is infused before allowing return of water and stool.
(4) Cramping or feeling faint during irrigation: Make sure water bag is at shoulder height, water temperature is warm, and that rate of water infusion is slow (5 to 8 minutes).
6. Specific to colostomies
   a. No dietary restrictions
   b. Treatment of constipation: Patients who tended toward constipation before colostomy surgery may still get constipated after a sigmoid colostomy, especially if not irrigating; may prevent with plenty of fluids by mouth and a high-fiber diet (bran, fresh fruits, and vegetables). A stool softener or bulk agent is appropriate; gentle over-the-counter laxatives (e.g., Milk of Magnesia) can be taken occasionally. Irrigation can be done as treatment for constipation or as part of bowel preparation before surgery or a diagnostic procedure.

B. Ileostomy: a surgically created opening into the ileum, or third part of the small intestine
   1. Functions of the small intestine: digestion of food; absorption of nutrients
   2. Reasons for ileostomies
      a. Disease: ulcerative colitis, Crohn's disease, necrotizing enterocolitis
      b. Congenital: familial polyposis
      c. Traumatic: rare
   3. Types of ileostomy stomas
      a. End ileostomy stoma or Brooke ileostomy: a single, budded, matured stoma, usually in right lower abdominal quadrant
      b. Double-barrel ileostomy stomas: proximal and distal ends of small bowel brought out as stomas; rare in adults; usually in infants
      c. Loop ileostomy stoma: a loop of ileum is brought out and held in position with a red rubber catheter or other support device inserted through mesentery of loop of ileum; loop of bowel is

opened distal to midline, and both ends are matured; distal limb can be stapled shut. This procedure commonly is done in patients with an ileoanal anastomosis to provide a temporary diversion.
4. Specific to ileostomies
   a. Hydration needs: Stool is usually watery to toothpaste-thick consistency; at least 10 to 12 glasses of fluids per day are needed to replace fluid lost in stool and avoid dehydration; fluids that contain sodium and potassium are best.
   b. Food obstructions: mechanical obstruction caused by high-residue, poorly chewed food lodged in distal small bowel, usually adjacent to stoma where small intestine goes through fascia. Kinking or narrowing in intestine caused by stenosis or scarring is another likely spot for undigested food to lodge.
      (1) Symptoms: abdominal cramping; liquid, foul-smelling output; high-pitched, tinkling bowel sounds; and swollen stoma. Symptoms progress to the point where there is no stomal output; patient has a silent, atonic bowel with abdominal distention, nausea, and vomiting.
      (2) Measures to prevent: Chew food thoroughly and drink plenty of fluids. Some patients may need to avoid high-residue foods that precipitate a food obstruction for them.
      (3) Foods that can cause a food obstruction: popcorn, nuts, coconut, mushrooms, high-fiber vegetables (e.g., corn, broccoli, snow peas, or celery), or high-fiber fruits.
      (4) If it is thought that patient is getting a food obstruction: Instruct patient to take a warm bath, assume a knee-chest or fetal position, and press in and around the stoma in an attempt to dislodge blockage.
      (5) Contact physician or nurse if patient has nausea or vomiting or has progressed to no stomal output, or if above measures have been tried with no success.
   c. Absorption of oral medications: transit time from mouth to stoma is short; may have an erratic absorption of large pills (e.g., vitamins, coated tablets [especially enteric coated], timed-release medications, and capsules). Physicians prescribing medication should be aware of ileostomy. Patient should be instructed to look for pieces of pill or tablet when emptying pouch.

C. General care of a fecal diversion: colostomy and ileostomy
   1. Characteristics of a healthy GI tract stoma: made from innermost lining of GI tract. Stomas are
      a. Moist, because they secrete mucus
      b. Red, because they are so vascular; may bleed with even gentle cleansing or rubbing
      c. Without sensory nerve endings, so are insensitive to touch or to pain
      d. Swollen for first 6 to 8 weeks after surgery
      e. Placed in a site that was marked preoperatively. Site is marked in appropriate abdominal quadrant; in a spot patient can see; within rectus abdominal muscle; and away from creases, fat folds, umbilicus, belt line, old scars, and anything else that might interfere with pouch adherence.
      f. Budded, or standing up from the skin so that stool ends up in pouch instead of undermining pouch's faceplate.
   2. Characteristics of stool from a fecal diversion
      a. The higher in the GI tract, the more liquid and irritating the stool is to skin.
      b. The pH of the gut, once past the stomach, is alkaline and full of digestive proteolytic enzymes that can actually digest the skin if stool is allowed to come into contact with it.
      c. Stool from an ileostomy is liquid to toothpaste-thick consistency.
      d. Stool from a transverse colostomy is soft and mushy.
      e. Stool from a sigmoid colostomy is very close to normal stool consistency.
      f. All fecal diversions should have an odorproof pouch with a skin barrier that can be karaya gum or pectin- and gelatin-based; skin barriers melt slowly in the presence of stool.
      g. No odor should be noted when pouch is on, except when it is being emptied into toilet. If odor is noted, check pouch's seal, as it may be leaking; check clamp and part of pouch distal to the clamp, as they may be soiled. Some foods act as an internal, natural deodorant, such as orange juice and parsley. Oral medications can help with stool odor (e.g., bismuth subgallate and chlorophyllin copper). External pouch deodorants in the form of pills or drops can be placed inside the pouch; a few

drops of mouthwash on a piece of toilet paper placed inside the pouch may be an easier, less expensive way to deodorize.
3. Teaching goals for patients with fecal diversions
   a. Pouch emptying: The very least a patient should learn is to empty pouch when it is one-third to one-half full to prevent the weight of a full pouch from breaking the seal and pulling pouch off. Patient should learn to empty pouch in the bathroom, sitting on toilet. Toilet paper or a baby wipe can be used to clean the tail of the pouch before putting the pouch clamp back on; a nonstick cooking spray or commercial peristomal skin cleanser can be sprayed inside the pouch to make it slippery so that stool will slide out more easily.
   b. Pouch changing: Perform on a routine basis, before pouch leaks, so that patient has control over ostomy. Best time for a routine pouch change is first thing in the morning or whenever stoma is quiet (e.g., usually just before a meal). In addition to routine pouch changing, pouch should be changed whenever it leaks, to prevent stool from irritating the peristomal skin.
   c. Minor peristomal skin irritation should be treated whenever irritated skin is noted during the pouch change. Refer to item 4 below.
4. Pouch change procedure for colostomy and ileostomy patients
   a. Assemble all supplies: pouch with hole for stoma sized or cut to fit snugly around stoma, water, paper towels, skin sealant, skin barrier paste, and karaya gum powder (or other skin barrier in powdered form).
   b. Take off old pouch: unstick patient from pouch to avoid mechanical stripping of epidermis; save pouch clamp.
   c. Clean stool from peristomal skin with warm water; there is no need to remove old paste; let dry.
   d. Look at peristomal skin; if any redness or irritation is noted, sprinkle on karaya gum powder.
   e. Use skin sealant on peristomal skin wherever pouch will stick; if any karaya gum powder is used, the skin sealant will seal it in; let dry.
   f. Spread skin barrier paste up close to stoma like caulk; use a wet finger to spread paste; let paste dry.
   g. It is fine for any of the products used in pouching to touch the stoma.

h. Center pouch over stoma and apply; hold pouch in place for a few minutes to help it stick.
i. Put clamp on bottom of pouch.
j. Tape down edges of pouch with paper or waterproof tape if desired.
5. Hints for increasing pouch's seal
   a. Make sure to dry skin well after each step; use hairdryer on low or cool setting to speed up drying process.
   b. Apply pouch with patient standing up or lying down.
   c. Make sure size of opening fits snugly around stoma with a minimal amount of peristomal skin showing; skin barrier in paste form will protect the immediate peristomal skin.
   d. Pouches cannot adhere to raw, severely irritated, denuded skin. Crust skin with repeated applications of karaya gum powder (or pectin-based powder) and either water or a silicone-based adhesive spray; use of karaya gum powder and skin sealant is not wrong, but a skin sealant contains alcohol and will sting if applied to denuded skin.
   e. Make sure pouch is being emptied whenever it is one-third to one-half full; otherwise weight of a too-full pouch will break the seal.
   f. Add a belt or binder to pouching system.
   g. Evaluate style of pouch with pouch off and patient in a sitting position; note appearance of peristomal skin: Does it crease or dimple in around stoma? Is stoma still budded or does it retract when patient sits? Does shape of stoma change? Does it go from round to oval? Are there any different creases or skin folds that appear when patient sits up? The faceplate, or part of pouch that adheres to body must match peristomal skin contours.
6. Types of pouches for fecal diversions: Drainable pouches have a clamp at bottom of pouch and are meant to be drained or emptied before becoming overfull with patient sitting on toilet; all should have a skin barrier that adheres to the skin immediately around stoma.
   a. One-piece pouches: There are three basic types: all-flexible styles, pouches with a firm ring or gasket around the stoma, and pouches with varying degrees of convexity. They are sized by several methods that differ from company to com-

pany and from one style to another within the same company. The most common way to size is to have the diameter of the stoma at its widest part be the pouch size. There are also custom-cut pouches that are cut to fit the stoma with every pouch change; these are most often used in the postoperative period when the stoma is changing size and shape, or with irregularly shaped stomas.
    b. Two-piece pouches: The part that adheres around the stoma is called a flange; a drainable pouch usually snaps or sticks onto flange. Pouch and flange size must match in order to be able to snap them together successfully. The numerical size of a two-piece system usually refers to the diameter of the flange's plastic snap-on ring or to the diameter of the flange's cutting surface and not to the size of stoma. Most two-piece systems must have the flange cut out by hand to fit the stoma before each pouch change, although some flanges are now precut. Patient must be sized again whenever changed from one style of pouch to another or from one brand-name pouch to another.
D. Urinary diversion: surgical technique used to establish a continuous, unimpeded flow of urine
  1. Reasons for urinary diversions
    a. Disease: cancer, usually transitional cell carcinoma of the bladder
    b. Congenital: exstrophy of the bladder, myelomeningocele
    c. Traumatic: crushing injuries or those resulting in a neurogenic bladder
  2. Types of urostomy stomas
    a. Pyelostomy: an opening into the renal pelvis, done with a tube
    b. Nephrostomy: an opening into the back side of the kidney, done with a tube
    c. Ureterostomy: one or both of the ureters are brought out to the skin; makes for flush stomas that stenose often; difficult to pouch
    d. Vesicostomy: an opening directly into the bladder
    e. Ileal conduit: most common urinary diversion; a 6- to 8-inch segment of terminal ileum is isolated with its blood supply intact; both ureters are anastomosed into the segment of ileum, the proximal end of which is closed and the distal end brought out to the right lower abdominal quadrant as a stoma.

f. Colon conduit: similar to an ileal conduit, except that an isolated section of large intestine is used as the passageway for urine. Used mostly in patients who have received radiation to their small intestine.
g. Continent urinary diversions: a variety of surgical procedures that leave the patient with an internal reservoir for urine and a continent or dry abdominal stoma that is catheterized to drain the urine. An antirefluxing anastomosis between the ureters and the reservoir for urine helps protect the kidneys from deteriorating (e.g., the Kock continent urostomy, the Indiana reservoir, and the ileocecal reservoir); helps free the patient from having to wear an external pouch to collect the urine.
3. Specific to urinary diversions
   a. Hydration needs: 10 to 12 glasses of fluid per day are needed to keep urine acidic. Acidic urine is less likely to have a foul odor or to encourage stone formation or bacterial growth leading to a urinary tract infection (UTI), compared to alkaline urine. Patients should refrain from drinking large amounts of milk or citrus juices daily, as these are excreted as alkaline urine once metabolized.
   b. Signs and symptoms of a UTI: Patients with urinary diversions will not have frequency, urgency, or dysuria as symptoms of an infection; the only symptoms are fever and kidney pain. Sometimes foul-smelling urine is a symptom of an infection; other times it is a sign of concentrated urine or poor hydration habits or results from something the patient has eaten. Certain foods (e.g., fish, eggs, asparagus, onions, or other spicy foods) can temporarily change the way the urine smells. There are no dietary restrictions for urinary diversions as such.
   c. Obtaining urine specimens from urinary diversions: Urine for urinalysis can be obtained from the bottom of a freshly changed, disposable pouch. Urine for culture and sensitivity or urine for cytology must be obtained by sterile catheterization of the stoma.
4. Catheterizing the urinary stoma
   a. Explain procedure to patient, especially the fact that it is a painless procedure; make sure that you have another pouch to apply.
   b. Place waterproof pads under the patient and across lap; may be easier to collect the specimen if the patient is sitting up.

c. Set up sterile field with dry gauze, water-soluble lubricant, three povidone-iodine swabs, a specimen cup, and an appropriately sized sterile catheter. Ileal conduits usually accommodate a #14 French catheter; ureterostomy stomas need a #8 or a #10 French catheter.
d. Take off old pouch and wipe stoma clean.
e. Put on sterile gloves.
f. Using a circular motion, swab stoma with each of the three povidone-iodine swabs.
g. Using dry sterile gauze, wipe the stoma free of povidone-iodine.
h. Insert lubricated catheter gently into stoma; try to get the catheter past the fascia, about 1 to 2 inches. Never force catheter.
i. Wait for urine to come through the catheter into the specimen cup.

E. General care of a urinary diversion
1. Characteristics of a healthy genitourinary tract stoma: Stomas made from any part of the urinary system are usually pink to white or purple in color, once the initial edema has gone down. Ileal conduits, colon conduits, and continent urinary diversion stomas made from any part of the GI tract look like intestinal stomas (red, moist, insensitive to touch, bleed with gentle cleansing, swollen for first 6 to 8 weeks, budded, and marked preoperatively).
2. Characteristics of urine from a urinary diversion
   a. Chemical makeup and appearance of urine are the same once it has been formed in kidneys, regardless of at what level in the urinary tract it is diverted. Only with ileal conduits, colon conduits, and any other type of urinary diversion that "borrows" a section of small or large intestine is it normal to have mucus in the urine; mucus is secreted by the lining of gut and will always be present to some degree.
   b. Urine contains no digestive proteolytic enzymes, so no skin barrier is needed routinely when pouching a urinary diversion. Because urine can macerate or waterlog the skin around the stoma, all urinary diversions should be pouched, using a skin sealant. All urinary diversions should have an odorproof pouch with an antireflux valve that prevents the urine from pooling on the stoma and breaking the pouch's seal when pa-

tient is when lying down; it also decreases chance of urine refluxing back to kidneys.
  c. No odor should be noted when pouch is on or when pouch is being emptied, unless patient has eaten something that has temporarily affected the smell of the urine. Although there are commercial pouch deodorants and internal deodorizers, foul-smelling urine can signal an impending infection and should never be just deodorized away. The best way to avoid a problem with foul-smelling urine is to drink an adequate amount of fluids, which makes for a dilute urine with an acidic pH and no odor.
3. Teaching goals for patients with urinary diversions
  a. Pouch emptying: taught first because it is performed the most number of times during the day. Empty the pouch whenever it is one-third to one-half full. Women can sit on toilet and men can stand while emptying.
  b. Attaching the pouch to bedside drainage at night: pouch should have some urine in it to prevent a suction vacuum from being formed in the pouch, in which case no urine will drain out of it. There are a variety of bedside drainage collection containers, from bags into which Foley catheters drain, to plastic bottles or jugs made by manufacturers of ostomy supplies. Some pouches have very specific connectors that hook pouch to tubing of drainage collection device, usually one or two connectors to a box of urinary pouches; connectors are meant to be reused. The bedside drainage device itself will last for months if cleaned properly; white vinegar and water are an inexpensive solution for cleaning and deodorizing the bedside drainage bag, although there are commercial cleaners available.
    (1) At night, patient can run tubing down inside of pajama leg, or secure tubing to leg with a catheter strap in order to prevent the tubing from getting wrapped around waist.
    (2) If patient does not wish to use a bedside drainage collector, the pouch must be emptied during the night.
  c. Pouch changing: routinely done during a time when the stoma will not be active (e.g., first thing in the morning before patient has had much to drink) and whenever pouch leaks.
  d. Treatment of minor peristomal skin irritations: same procedure as used with a fecal diversion, using karaya gum powder (or a synthetic pectin-based powder) and a skin sealant.

4. Pouch change procedure for urinary diversions
    a. Assemble all supplies: pouch with the opening cut to bypass any skin folds or creases that are immediately peristomal, skin sealant, paper towels and water, karaya gum powder, and wicks to absorb any urine that is excreted during the pouch change. Wicks can be made from any absorbent material (e.g., a paper towel or washcloth); a short length of the material is rolled up and taped together so that it can be placed on top of the stoma to wick away the urine.
    b. Take off the old pouch: use a wet paper towel to help gently unstick pouch; use of adhesive removers is not recommended, as they are difficult to remove thoroughly and may interfere with the next pouch's seal.
    c. Clean urine from peristomal skin with a wet paper towel; let dry, using a wick on top of the stoma if stoma starts to put out urine.
    d. Look at the peristomal skin; if any redness or irritation is noted, dust the skin with karaya gum powder.
    e. Use a skin sealant on peristomal skin wherever pouch will stick and immediately peristomal, to protect skin from urine; it will seal in karaya gum powder, if used; let dry; use wicks.
    f. Center pouch over stoma and apply; make sure skin is dry. Hold pouch in place to help it stick; close spout on pouch.
    g. If desired, "picture-frame," or put tape around edges of pouch; use paper or waterproof tape and make sure skin covered by tape is also protected by skin sealant.
5. Hints for increasing the pouch seal
    a. Opening in pouch does not have to fit up close to stoma as long as immediate peristomal skin is protected by a skin sealant. Especially in cut-to-fit style pouches, it is appropriate to have opening for the stoma cut back from the stoma itself to avoid creases or skin folds.
    b. Refer to C.5. for more suggestions.
6. Types of pouches for urinary diversions: spouts on bottom for easy emptying and should also come equipped with an antireflux valve. For one- and two-piece pouching systems, refer to C.6. for more information on the different styles.

STUDY QUESTIONS AND EXERCISES

1. Which type of diversion can be managed by irrigation? Discuss why this is so.
2. What are the signs and symptoms of a UTI in a patient with an ileal conduit urinary diversion?
3. Discuss various diseases that might require surgical placement of an ileostomy.
4. List foods most likely to cause a food obstruction in a patient with an ileostomy. Discuss why this is so.
5. Discuss the various pouching techniques used with fecal diversions. What one item should be used in all cases? Why?

BIBLIOGRAPHY

Broadwell, D.C., and B.S. Jackson. 1982. *Principles of ostomy care*. St. Louis: Mosby-Year Book, Inc.

Hampton, B.G., and R.A. Bryant 1992. *Ostomies and continent diversions: Nursing management*. St. Louis: Mosby-Year Book, Inc.

International Association for Enterostomal Therapy. 1989. *Standards of care: Patient with a colostomy*. Irvine, Calif.

International Association for Enterostomal Therapy. 1989. *Standards of care: Patient with an ileostomy*. Irvine, Calif.

International Association for Enterostomal Therapy. 1989. *Standards of care: Patient with a urinary diversion*. Irvine, Calif.

43

Cancer

Constance R. Ziegfeld and Monica Fulton

A. Cancer overview
   1. Definition: group of diseases resulting from uncontrolled growth of abnormal cells
   2. Causes
      a. Environmental: chemicals, radiation, viruses
      b. Host: genetic mutations, immune deficiencies
      c. Multiple factors: may sequentially or concurrently initiate cancers
   3. Risk factors: age, gender, environmental exposure, life style
   4. Incidence of disease
      a. Second leading cause of death in the United States
      b. Men and women: each has increased risk for certain diagnoses
         (1) Men: increased incidence of prostate, lung, colorectal cancer
         (2) Women: increased incidence of breast, colorectal, lung cancer
      c. Diagnosed in all age groups with increased prevalence in the elderly (>65 years)
      d. Increased incidence in urban areas
      e. Increased mortality in: lower socioeconomic populations; men; certain sites of disease (lung, esophagus, pancreas); late stage at diagnosis
   5. Survival rate: varies with age, gender, race, and diagnosis; 5-year survival rate is 51%
B. Screening, prevention, and detection
   1. Primary prevention: avoidance of factors that may lead to development of cancer

a. Smoking
   (1) Cigarette smoking is responsible for 90% of lung cancer among men and 79% among women.
   (2) Smoking accounts for 30% of all cancer deaths.
   (3) Smokeless tobacco: Use of chewing tobacco or snuff increases risk of cancer of the mouth, larynx, throat, and esophagus.
b. Sunlight
   (1) Almost all the 600,000 cases of basal and squamous cell skin cancer diagnosed each year in the United States are considered to be sun-related.
   (2) Avoid sun exposure between 10:00 A.M. and 3:00 p.m.
   (3) Use a sunscreen (minimum sun protective factor 30 [SPF30]).
c. Nutrition
   (1) Obesity may be a risk factor for colon, breast, and uterine cancers.
   (2) Maintain low-fat/high fiber-diet.
   (3) Avoid smoked, salt-covered, or nitrite-covered foods; limit alcohol intake.
d. Estrogen
   (1) Treatment to control menopausal symptoms increases risk of endometrial cancer.
   (2) Including progesterone in estrogen replacement therapy helps minimize risk.
   (3) Contraindications are related to individual risk factors.
e. Occupational hazards
   (1) Exposure to various industrial agents increases risk of various cancers.
   (2) Assess for history of personal exposure.
   (3) Assure worker awareness of occupational risks and personal protection behaviors.
2. Secondary prevention/early detection: actions to diagnose cancer or precursor to cancer as early as possible, following recommendations based on American Cancer Society guidelines and appropriate to individual risk factors.
   a. Breast cancer screening and detection
      (1) Perform breast self-examinations.
      (2) Have physical examination by health care provider.

(a) Women aged 20 to 40 years: every 3 years
(b) Women aged 41 years and older: yearly
  (3) Assess for family history of breast cancer; mother, daughter, or sister with breast cancer increases individual risk.
  (4) Mammography
(a) Women aged 35 to 40 years: baseline mammogram
(b) Women aged 41 to 49 years: mammogram every 1 or 2 years, depending on physical and mammographic findings
(c) Women aged 50 years and older: mammogram yearly
(d) Mammography is appropriate as a diagnostic procedure whenever a mass is identified.
  b. Colorectal cancer screening and detection
    (1) Age 40 and older: Have digital examination yearly.
    (2) Age 50 and older: Have stool blood test yearly and proctosigmoidoscopy examination every 3 to 5 years based on individual risk.
    (3) Assess for family history of colon or rectal cancers or polyps.
  c. Cervical cancer screening and detection
    (1) Women aged 18 years and older, or those younger who have been or are sexually active: Have Papanicolaou test and pelvic examination yearly.
    (2) After a woman has had three or more consecutive, normal yearly examinations: Papanicolaou test may be performed less frequently based on individual risks.
  d. Prostate screening and detection
    (1) Men over age 50: have digital rectal examination yearly.
    (2) Prostatic specific antigen (PSA) screening remains controversial, but is widely used.

C. Cancer treatment
  1. Potential goals of various treatment modalities
    a. Cure: eradicate the entire cancer
    b. Control: arrest tumor growth
    c. Palliate: alleviate symptoms of disease
  2. Surgery
    a. Used to establish tissue diagnosis or achieve goals listed
    b. Effective as local treatment for limited disease, or as an adjunct to other therapies

c. Side effects/complications
   (1) Disfigurement; loss of function
   (2) Surgical complications (e.g., infection, fistulas, wound dehiscence)
   (3) Decreased with limb sparing and laser techniques
d. Nursing care of surgical oncology patient
   (1) Preoperative care: assess preoperative needs.
      (a) Provide patient and family education: preoperative procedures; surgical procedures; expected outcome.
      (b) Assist with preoperative procedures/preparation.
      (c) Provide emotional support.
   (2) Postoperative care: assess postoperative status.
      (a) Nutrition, elimination, comfort, respiratory, and circulatory functions
      (b) Report signs of complications (e.g., infection, bleeding, thrombophlebitis)
      (c) Assist with coping/adaptation/rehabilitation, or refer as appropriate.
   (3) Review discharge instructions.
      (a) Follow-up visits, contact person(s)
      (b) Wound/site care
      (c) Medication administration
      (d) Nutrition/activity/comfort
      (e) Emergency procedures; signs and symptoms
   (4) Refer to appropriate resources.
3. Radiation therapy
   a. Local therapy to achieve goals of cancer treatment
   b. Used alone or in combination with other therapy
   c. Approximately 50% of cancer patients receive radiation therapy
   d. Types of radiation
      (1) External beam therapy
         (a) Delivered by various types of equipment in an outpatient setting
         (b) May require one or multiple treatments over several weeks
         (c) Does not result in radioactive host
         (d) Treatment experience
            1) There is no pain or sensation.

2) Actual treatment time is in minutes.
3) Machine may move and make humming or clicking sounds.
4) Exact position must be replicated for each treatment; permanent dye marks, casts, and field blocks ensure accurate treatment field. Treatment marks should not be removed.
5) Children may require sedation.
   (2) Internal therapy
   (a) High-energy radiation source placed in or on the body
   (b) Brachytherapy: a sealed source causing patient to be radioactive while source is in place
   (c) Radioisotope therapy: an unsealed source, usually ingested; body fluids (blood, urine, intraperitoneal, intrapleural, and intraventricular fluids) temporarily radioactive
e. Side effects
   (1) General (may be increased with recent chemotherapy treatment): skin reaction, fatigue, anorexia, bone marrow depression
   (2) Site-specific: mild to severe dysfunction or alteration of the treatment site
      (a) Cranial: alopecia, erythema, edema
      (b) Head/neck: mucositis, xerostomia, taste change, esophagitis, cataracts
      (c) Chest: esophagitis, pneumonitis, nausea, distortion of breast tissue
      (d) Abdominal: nausea/vomiting, diarrhea, cystitis, sexual and reproductive dysfunction
      (e) Bone growth: may be inhibited in children
f. Nursing care of radiation oncology patient
   (1) Assess current physical/psychosocial status.
   (2) Monitor for side effects of treatment.
   (3) Reinforce patient education.
      (a) Nutrition and hydration
      (b) Rest and activity
      (c) Skin care: keep clean and dry; avoid irritation, soaps, powders, and sun exposure; do not remove treatment markings or use unapproved topical agents

(d) Infection and bleeding precautions
(e) Emergency care; signs and symptoms
(f) Medication administration
(g) Management of side effects
(h) Follow-up appointments/contacts
(i) Safe disposal of body fluids and exposure to radioactive patients
(4) Refer to appropriate resources.
(a) Home care services
(b) Local and community agencies
4. Chemotherapy
   a. Systemic therapy to achieve goals of cancer treatment
   b. Used alone or in combination with other therapy
   c. Routes of administration: oral (PO); intramuscular (IM); subcutaneous (SQ); intravenous (IV); central venous catheters; venous access devices; intra-arterial; intraperitoneal; intrapleural; intrathecal; intraventricular
   d. Administration: continuous or cycled
   e. Side effects
      (1) Onset: immediate (I = 2 to 24 hours) or delayed (D = days to weeks)
      (2) Duration: usually reversible within several weeks of treatment completion
      (3) General
         (a) Bone marrow suppression: mild to severe; usually occurring 7 to 14 days after treatment; duration varies with dose and drugs
         (b) Fatigue: mild to severe; immediate or cumulative
      (4) Assess and document patient tolerance and response
      (5) Drug specific
         (a) Stomatitis/mucositis (D)
         (b) Esophagitis (D)
         (c) Nausea/vomiting (I)
         (d) Anorexia/taste change (I/D)
         (e) Constipation/diarrhea (I)
         (f) Paresthesias (D)
         (g) Alopecia (D)
         (h) Sexual/reproductive dysfunction (D)
         (i) Photosensitivity of skin (D)

(j) Renal function (D)
(k) Cardiovascular function (I/D)
f. Nursing care of chemotherapy patient
(1) Assess current physical/psychosocial status (include site of administration/vascular access device).
(2) Monitor for side effects of chemotherapy.
(3) Reinforce patient/family education.
(a) Nutrition and hydration
(b) Rest and activity
(c) Infection and bleeding precautions
(d) Emergency care; signs and symptoms
(e) Medication administration
(f) Management of side effects
(g) Follow-up appointments, contacts
(h) Instructions for safe disposal of administration equipment and body secretions
(i) Safe disposal of equipment and body fluids
(4) Refer to appropriate resources.
5. Biotherapy
a. Adjunct systemic therapy to stimulate immune response to treatment or disease
b. Dose, frequency, and route of administration: vary; include IM, IV, and SQ administration given by patient, caregiver, or health care provider
c. Classifications
(1) Active specific: toxic to tumor cells
(2) Active nonspecific: augments host response
(3) Passive: modifies tumor host factors
d. Frequently used agents: interferon; tumor necrosis factor; interleukin-2; monoclonal antibodies; colony-stimulating factors (GCSF, GMCSF); adoptive immunotherapy (lymphokine-activated killer [LAK], TILS); vaccines
e. Side effects: dose-, route-, and agent-related and may include
(1) Mental status changes; anxiety
(2) Headache; fatigue; fever/chills/rigor
(3) Dysrhythmias
(4) Fluid retention/renal dysfunction
(5) Anorexia; nausea; diarrhea
(6) Rash/itching/local irritation

(7) Allergy symptoms; arthralgias
(8) Less commonly: cardiac dysfunction, angina, respiratory distress, hepatic dysfunction, taste aversions, aplasia, myalgias, bone pain
  f. Nursing care of the oncology patient receiving biotherapy
   (1) Assess current physical/psychosocial status.
   (2) Monitor side effects of treatment.
   (3) Implement appropriate symptomatic relief measures.
   (4) Reinforce patient/caregiver education.
      (a) Symptom relief
      (b) Emergency care; signs and symptoms
      (c) Medication administration
      (d) Follow-up appointments/contacts
      (e) Safe storage and disposal of medication and equipment
   (5) Refer to appropriate resources.
6. Bone marrow transplantation (BMT)
  a. Curative treatment for malignant and nonmalignant conditions (e.g., leukemias, lymphomas, selected solid tumors, aplastic anemia)
  b. Types of BMTs
   (1) Syngeneic: donor is identical twin
   (2) Allogeneic: donor is related, usually a sibling, or unrelated, but human lymphocyte antigen (HLA) matched
   (3) Autologous: patient's marrow or stem cells are treated and reinfused
  c. Treatment process
   (1) Chemotherapy treatment to stabilize or arrest disease
   (2) Patient evaluation and eligibility
      (a) Discussion of risks/benefits/treatment
      (b) Medical history
      (c) Histocompatibility testing (patient and donor)
      (d) Tumor staging
      (e) Evaluation of major organ function
      (f) Reproductive risks
   (3) Donor identification from family or bone marrow donor registry
   (4) Marrow harvest from patient or donor; aseptically aspirated from iliac crests (under general anesthesia in operating room)

(5) Patient preparation
    (a) Eliminates residual malignancy, immunosuppresses host to allow engraftment
    (b) Treated with chemotherapy or radiation and chemotherapy (varies with goal of therapy)
(6) Bone marrow infusion: IV over several hours
(7) Potential complications
    (a) Early onset (within 60 days): mucositis; veno-occlusive disease; acute graft-versus-host disease (GVHD) in allogeneic BMT; bacteremia; herpes simplex virus; interstitial pneumonia; disseminated fungal infection
    (b) Late onset (60 days to 1 year)
        1) Restrictive lung disease
        2) Chronic GVHD in allogeneic BMT
        3) Pneumococcal sepsis
        4) Varicella zoster
        5) Interstitial pneumonia
    (c) Long-term
        1) Failure to engraft, or of graft to function
        2) Disease relapse
        3) Complications of GVHD in allogeneic BMT
        4) Infertility
        5) Growth and development disorders
        6) Cataracts (secondary to radiation)
        7) Secondary malignancy risks increase with some treatments
        8) Psychosocial/body image maladjustment
d. Postdischarge care
    (1) Medical condition is stable and granulocyte count is usually >500 mm^3.
    (2) Requires intensive outpatient follow-up.
e. Care of the post-BMT patient at home
    (1) May require intravenous antibiotics or antiviral agents, blood components, hyperalimentation, physical and psychosocial support.
    (2) Monitor for signs of complications.
        (a) Temperature >38°C, chills
        (b) Changes in catheter site
        (c) Changes in bowel pattern (greater or less volume or frequency)

           (d) Skin rash; mouth sores
           (e) Cough or respiratory complaint
           (f) Anorexia, nausea, or vomiting
           (g) New onset of pain
           (h) Bleeding, bruising, petechiae, or hematuria
       (3) Reinforce patient/family education
           (a) Wear a mask outside of home for 6 months.
           (b) Practice good hand washing.
           (c) Practice "safe sex" (platelets >50,000 use condoms to prevent infection).
           (d) Avoid contact with infectious persons, pets, and human urine and feces.
           (e) Avoid crowds (work, school) for 6 months to 1 year.
           (f) Avoid hot tubs, public pools.
           (g) Do not have live viral vaccines for 1 year.
           (h) Teach medication administration.
           (i) Teach symptom control.
           (j) Teach emergency care; signs and symptoms.
           (k) Keep follow-up appointments/contacts.
D. Supportive therapies
   1. Blood product home transfusion
       a. Advantages
           (1) Decreased cost compared with inpatient administration
           (2) Maintaining familiar home, family, and friend environment
           (3) Convenience for patient and family
           (4) Elimination of pain/discomfort involved in transporting patient to hospital
       b. Disadvantages
           (1) Lack of skilled personnel for emergency
           (2) Lack of sophisticated equipment should the need arise
           (3) Dependence on telephone for emergency assistance
           (4) Time delays in obtaining emergency assistance and transportation to emergency facility
           (5) Coordination required for safe transport of products
           (6) Additional environmental requirements
       c. Patient selection criteria
           (1) Physical/medical status: makes transportation painful for the patient
           (2) Stable cardiorespiratory status

(3) No prior history of a transfusion reaction
(4) Patient able to respond to verbal commands and to report symptoms of any adverse transfusion reactions
(5) Presence of a responsible adult both during and after the transfusion
(6) Telephone access for medical advice and/or ambulance
(7) Appropriate diagnosis for transfusion, including anemia or thrombocytopenia
d. Nursing responsibilities
   (1) Patient assessment/screening (information should be obtained pretransfusion)
      (a) Patient's full name, address, telephone and identification numbers
      (b) Contact person in case of emergency
      (c) Name, location, and telephone number of emergency facility if need occurs
      (d) Telephone number of ambulance company
      (e) Patient's physician's name and telephone number(s)
      (f) Appropriate medical information
         1) Patient diagnosis and reason for transfusion; allergies
         2) Other medical problems
         3) Current medications
         4) Patient's transfusion history, including date of last transfusion; blood products transfused; pre-medications; and any history of transfusion reaction, including description of symptoms and any interventions implemented to address the symptoms
      (g) Signed informed consent, if required
   (2) Blood product administration
      (a) Ensure that temperature of blood product is maintained during transport to home.
      (b) Follow agency's blood product administration policy (should include frequency of vital signs and documentation requirements).
      (c) Assess for signs of potential transfusion reaction (e.g., hives, temperature elevation, shaking chills, shortness of breath, facial flushing, or anaphylaxis).

(d) Have emergency drug box/kit available to treat any transfusion reactions according to agency protocol (epinephrine, diphenhydramine hydrochloride [Benadryl], furosemide [Lasix]).
(e) Patient education regarding post-transplant care.
2. Pain management
   a. Pharmacologic interventions
      (1) Narcotics
         (a) Oral: convenient, practical, self-administered; slow onset; unpredictable absorption
            1) Short-acting drugs given at more frequent intervals (every 3 to 4 hours) (e.g., oxycodone and acetaminophen [Tylox], codeine, hydromorphone hydrochloride [Dilaudid], liquid morphine)
            2) Sustained-release drugs given in less frequent intervals (every 8 to 12 hours) (e.g., Morphine Sulfate Contin)
         (b) Intermittent IM or SQ
            1) Requires no venous access
            2) Faster onset than oral but causes trauma to tissues
            3) Potential for abscess formation
            4) Increased risk of bleeding with low platelets
            5) Continuous subcutaneous infusions provide steady blood level of narcotic
            6) Venous access not required; avoids need for repeated injections; requires infusion device
            7) May cause local tissue irritation
         (c) IV
            1) Bolus rapid onset
            2) Requires venous access
            3) Shorter duration; peak and trough effect
            4) Continuous IV infusions: provide steady blood level of narcotic
               a) Avoids need for repeated injection.
               b) Requires special infusion pump.
               c) Need for greater patient monitoring.
               d) Potential for infection, sepsis.
         (d) Intrathecal route

                1) Lower doses of narcotics required
                2) Longer duration of analgesic
                3) Fewer side effects than with systemic narcotic
                4) Requires special subcutaneous implantable reservoir or rebolus device
                5) Risk of respiratory depression
            (2) Non-narcotics
                (a) Nonsteroidal anti-inflammatory agents: potential for gastrointestinal disorders (e.g., aspirin, naproxen)
                (b) Acetaminophen
            (3) Refer to and implement the Agency for Health Care Policy and Research federal guidelines on cancer pain.
        b. Nonpharmacologic interventions
            (1) Distraction; hypnosis
            (2) Relaxation and guides imagery
            (3) Music and art therapy
            (4) Massage; position; heat/cold
            (5) Transcutaneous nerve stimulation (TENS)
        c. Anesthetic and neurosurgical treatment: nerve blocks
        d. Nursing responsibilities
            (1) Provide ongoing assessment for adequate pain control, especially when any change in pain medication type, route, or frequency occurs. Pain assessment tools are available and provide a standard comparison over time.
            (2) Give patient education related to potential side effects of narcotics.
                (a) Constipation: concurrent use of cathartic agent and adequate amount of fiber and roughage oral intake in daily diet recommended
                (b) Sedation: no driving, operating heavy machinery
                (c) Potential synergistic effect if combined with other medications (e.g., analgesics, antihistamines, psychotropic drugs)
                (d) Pharmacist referral for further information
            (3) Document nursing assessment, interventions, and evaluation of each intervention, and subsequent follow-up communication with patients' primary health care provider.
    3. Total peripheral nutrition (see Chapter 48)
    4. Physical rehabilitation

            a. Provision of appropriate prosthetic devices
            b. Speech training
            c. Ostomy care
            d. Physical and/or occupational therapy
            e. Support for reintegration into life
            f. Referral to cancer survivor support groups
    E. Patient education and support
        1. Disease and treatment-specific information
            a. Written information (pamphlets, discharge instructions, books, PDQ [physician's data query])
            b. Audiovisual materials
            c. Group instruction (e.g., I Can Cope)
            d. Computer-assisted instruction (requires that the patient have access to a compatible computer).
        2. Resource management
            a. Financial and insurance issues
                (1) Assessment of third-party payer benefits
                (2) Negotiation with third-party payers to expand benefits for nonacute care services as indicated
                (3) Information and referral for disability benefits, public assistance, Medicare, Medicaid
                (4) Community assistance program
                (5) Encourage patients and families to be knowledgeable about insurance benefits.
            b. Home care and personal needs
                (1) Assessment of home physical environment for patient safety and comfort
                (2) Information/referrals for meals, transportation, skilled professional care, durable medical equipment and supplies, homemaker services
                (3) Identification of patient contact person(s) and phone number(s) for questions, problems, or emergencies during daytime, evening, and/or weekend hours
        3. Legal/ethical issues
        4. Psychologic issues
            a. Assessment of normal coping mechanisms
            b. Family counseling
            c. Peer support programs
            d. Sexuality concerns

    e. Clergy
    f. Resources
F. Nursing role in home care of the oncology patient
  1. Nursing goals
    a. Achieve maximal desired self-care.
    b. Attain maximal physical and psychosocial function.
    c. Develop and utilize appropriate resources.
    d. Help with planning and decision making by providing information and support.
  2. Nursing interventions
    a. Participate in discharge planning.
    b. Assess home environmental resources needed for care: utilities; equipment; physical design; safety; community resources/agencies.
    c. Assess patient's/family's/caregiver's ability to meet needs: knowledge; skills; motivation; physical status; mental/emotional status; support/assistance.
    d. Assess patient status/needs.
      (1) Diagnosis and extent of disease
      (2) Past, current, and anticipated treatment
      (3) Patient prognosis/goals
      (4) Other existing medical conditions
      (5) Level of function
      (6) Level of knowledge
      (7) Physical assessment: comfort; nutrition; protective mechanisms; mobility; elimination; sexuality; ventilation
      (8) Psychosocial status: coping mechanisms; social/family roles; financial resources
    e. Coordinate/provide required care
      (1) Provide patient/family education.
        (a) Cancer prevention and detection
        (b) Home care treatment and needs
      (2) Adjust visits and care as needed.
      (3) Make appropriate referrals.
    f. Evaluate home care.
      (1) Process of care delivery
      (2) Compliance with home care and oncology standards of care and regulatory requirements.
      (3) Patient/family satisfaction
      (4) Patient outcome

3. Nursing resources
   a. Primary care provider: for specific information concerning history, treatment, and goals
   b. Regional cancer centers: for information on treatment or nursing protocols
   c. Local and national Oncology Nursing Society
      (1) Information on special interest groups, including home and hospice care
      (2) Local, regional, and national workshops and conferences
   d. Local American Cancer Society: provides professional education and publications
   e. National Cancer Institute: provides professional education and publications (1-800-4-CANCER)

STUDY QUESTIONS AND EXERCISES

1. Identify the American Cancer Society standards for screening and detection of the following cancers: breast; prostate; colorectal; cervical.
2. Describe the nursing management of the following side effects of cancer treatment:
   a. Nausea and vomiting related to chemotherapy
   b. Skin irritation related to radiation therapy
   c. Body image changes secondary to a colostomy
3. Describe the nursing assessment and plan of care for a person receiving a continuous infusion of morphine for pain control.

BIBLIOGRAPHY

Clark, J., and R. McGee. 1992. *Oncology Nursing Society Core Curriculum for Oncology Nursing*. Philadelphia: W.B. Saunders Co.

Department of Health and Human Services. 1994. *Cancer pain guidelines United States*. AHCPR Publication no. N.94-0594, Rockville, Md.

Groenwald, S., et al. 1993. *Cancer nursing principles and practice*. Boston: Jones and Bartlett Publishers, Inc.

Whedon, M. 1991. *Bone marrow transplantation: Principles, practice, and nursing insights*. Boston: Jones and Bartlett Publishers, Inc.

44

Acquired Immunodeficiency Syndrome

Jeannee Parker Martin

A. Historical overview of acquired immunodeficiency syndrome (AIDS)
   1. 1981
      a. First cases of AIDS were reported to the Centers for Disease Control (CDC) in Atlanta, Georgia.
         (1) Previously healthy homosexual men in New York and Los Angeles presented with rare diseases: Pneumocystis carinii pneumonia and Kaposi's sarcoma.
         (2) Soon after, similar cases were reported among intravenous drug users, Haitians, and hemophiliacs.
      b. Additional cases were identified in other major cities around the United States.
   2. 1982
      a. The CDC developed their initial case definition for surveillance purposes.
         (1) Definition was based on the presence of opportunistic infections and malignancies in persons with no other known causes for these diseases.
         (2) Case definition was controversial and was felt by many leading AIDS advocates and scientists to touch only the "tip of the iceberg" of possible cases.
      b. Modes of transmission were believed to be sexual contact; sharing needles or syringes used in injecting drugs; transfusion or injection of infected blood or blood products; and perinatal transmission, by an infected mother to her fetus or newly born baby. (In 1994, there was still no scientific evidence to indicate other modes of transmission.)

3. 1984
   a. First AIDS home care and hospice program in the United States was established by the Visiting Nurses and Hospice of San Francisco: average daily census of 18 patients per day.
      (1) Program became a model for other home health and hospice programs throughout the United States, as well as for the Robert Wood Johnson Foundation AIDS demonstration projects and the federal Ryan White CARE funding.
      (2) Staff had been panelists at the local, state, federal, and international levels, providing expertise to government agencies for policy and funding decisions, as well as to the World Health Organization for guidance in nations around the world.
      (3) Discovery of hepatitis C virus. Hepatitis C is widespread among persons with AIDS and causes often fatal liver damage.
4. 1986
   a. Virus believed to cause AIDS was described simultaneously by three different researchers and was known by three names.
   b. At the International AIDS Conference held in Paris in June 1986, a common name for the virus, human immunodeficiency virus (HIV), was accepted.
   c. HIV was believed to be a retrovirus, meaning that its genetic code is carried in ribonucleic acid.
5. 1987: CDC revised case definition to incorporate HIV-related encephalopathy and wasting syndrome.
6. 1989
   a. More than 115,000 people since 1981 were diagnosed with AIDS in the United States.
   b. 13.58 cases per 100,000 population in the United States.
   c. More than 1 million people were believed to be infected with HIV.
   d. San Francisco scientists determined the average incubation period to be approximately 11 years.
7. 1992
   a. CDC proposed a new case definition to "emphasize the clinical importance of the CD4+ lymphocyte count in the categorization of HIV-related clinical conditions."

      b. Reportable as AIDS cases to the CDC:
         (1) CD4+ cells <500/mm^3 and have acute HIV as primary HIV infection; characterized by flulike or mononucleosis-like illness or meningitis; generally occurring within 6 weeks of a documented exposure to HIV; or persistent generalized lymphadenopathy.
         (2) CD4+ cells <500/mm^3 and have symptomatic conditions occurring in an HIV-infected adolescent or adult that meet at least one of the following criteria:
            (a) Attributed to HIV infection and/or indicate a defect in cell-mediated immunity.
            (b) Considered by physicians to have a clinical course/management that is complicated by HIV infection.
      c. More than 225,000 cases of AIDS identified in the United States from 1981 to 1992.
      d. 17.83 cases per 100,000 population in the United States.
      e. At Visiting Nurses and Hospice of San Francisco, average daily AIDS census exceeds 240 patients.
      f. Most home health and hospice programs throughout the United States have cared for some AIDS patients; many dedicated programs developed to specialize in the home and hospice care of persons with AIDS/HIV disease.
8. 1993
      a. 103,691 cases reported for 1993 alone.
      b. 40.20 cases per 100,000 population in the United States.
      c. Large increase in cases in 1993, due to CDC revised case definition effective January 1, 1993.
9. 1994
      a. More than 325,000 cases of AIDS identified in the United States from 1981 to 1994.
      b. CDC revised classification system for human immunodeficiency virus infection in children less than 13 years of age.
         (1) Infected children are classified into mutually exclusive categories according the three parameters: infection status, clinical status, and immunologic status.
         (2) Reflects the stage of the child's disease.
         (3) Establishes mutually exclusive classification categories.
         (4) Balances simplicity and medical accuracy in the classification process.
      c. Vaccine trials fail; will try with other products.

d. Scientists at Columbia College of Physicians and Surgeon's identify herpes-like virus as the potential cause of Kaposi's sarcoma. Discovery could lead to early diagnostic test, and development of antiviral treatments for Kaposi's sarcoma.
B. AIDS indicator conditions
  1. AIDS indicator conditions: those conditions outlined in the 1987 CDC AIDS surveillance definition
     a. Candidiasis of the bronchi, trachea, or lungs
     b. Esophageal candidiasis
     c. Coccidioidomycosis, disseminated or extrapulmonary
     d. Cryptococcosis, extrapulmonary
     e. Cryptosporidiosis, chronic intestinal (more than 1 month duration)
     f. Cytomegalovirus (CMV) disease (other than liver, spleen, or nodes)
     g. Cytomegalovirus retinitis (with loss of vision)
     h. HIV encephalopathy
     i. Herpes simplex: chronic ulcers (more than 1 month duration), or bronchitis, pneumonitis, or esophagitis
     j. Histoplasmosis, disseminated or extrapulmonary
     k. Isosporiasis, chronic intestinal, more than 1 month
     l. Kaposi's sarcoma
     m. Lymphoma, Burkitt's (or equivalent term)
     n. Lymphoma, immunoblastic (or equivalent term)
     o. Lymphoma, primary in brain
     p. *Mycobacterium avium* complex (MAC) or *M. kansasii,* disseminated or extrapulmonary
     q. *Mycobacterium tuberculosis,* disseminated or extrapulmonary
     r. *Mycobacterium,* other species or unidentified species, disseminated or extrapulmonary
     s. *Pneumocystis carinii* pneumonia (PCP)
     t. Progressive multifocal leukoencephalopathy
     u. *Salmonella* septicemia, recurrent
     v. Toxoplasmosis of brain
     w. Wasting syndrome
C. Nursing management of the patient with AIDS
  1. Continuum of disability
     a. AIDS/HIV disease typically has a variable course over many weeks, months, or years.
     b. A continuum of disability helps to conceptualize degrees of

disability and appropriateness for home care services.
(1) Apparently well individual
   (a) HIV positive
   (b) Requires little, if any, medical intervention
   (c) Usually would not be homebound or require home care services
   (d) May benefit from counseling or peer support groups
   (e) Should consider advance directives
      1) Identify durable power of attorney
      2) Living will
      3) Treatment decisions if mentally unable to decide
(2) Acutely ill individual
   (a) May be experiencing first opportunistic infection
   (b) May require hospitalization; however, many of these patients are now cared for in homecare setting with intensive IV therapy or other nursing and pharmaceutical management regimen
   (c) Should be entered into case management program for appropriate assignment and utilization of resources
   (d) Patient likely to regain pre-illness level of function
   (e) Patient, family, other caregivers should be instructed in the care of the patient at home and symptoms to be aware of to prevent further exacerbation of illness.
   (f) Goals of care at home: resolve acute symptoms; return to pre-illness state or maximal level of function. Ensure that the patient/support system is knowledgeable about the care required by the patient at home.
(3) Chronically ill individual
   (a) Represents the majority of persons diagnosed with AIDS
   (b) Experiences multiple infections, or relapse of an opportunistic infection (e.g., *P. carinii* pneumonia)
   (c) May exhibit progressive or deteriorating physical and neurologic function
   (d) Requires home care nursing intervention to monitor the patient's physical and neurologic status for signs of new or recurrent infection, response to medications, symptom management, nutrition, safety, and activities of daily living; instruct the patient and caregivers re-

garding required care skills, including infection control, disease progression, and anticipated problems and care plans; administer IV medications and care of venous access devices.
- (e) Goals of care at home: maximize the patient's level of functional ability; detect signs and symptoms of new or recurrent infection; detect deterioration of neurologic function; educate patient/family regarding care regimens; recognize maladaptive coping mechanisms; intervene in order to prevent a crisis; mobilize community resources.

(4) Terminally ill individual
- (a) Prognosis of 6 months or less
- (b) Profound body disfigurement and wasting.
- (c) Decision making occurs regarding treatment goals.
- (d) Goals of care: assess patient's physical and neurologic status and level of deterioration; provide relief and comfort for symptoms related to opportunistic infections; educate patient/family regarding comfort, care regimens, and signs of impending death; offer spiritual and emotional support to patient/family; assist family with final arrangements (e.g., will, funeral planning); provide bereavement support after patient's death.

2. Ten most common symptoms and their possible etiologies in the care of the patient with AIDS (for detailed interventions and suggested medications, see Martin et al., *The AIDS Home Care and Hospice Manual,* and section below on clinical management.)
   a. Diarrhea: cryptosporidiosis, cytomegalovirus, Kaposi's sarcoma, *M. avium* complex, lymphoma, lymphoid hyper-plasia, other bowel pathogens, medications, unknown etiology
   b. Dysphagia and/or odynophagia: oral or pharyngeal candidiasis, herpes simplex, neurologic impairment, dying process
   c. Dyspnea: *P. carinii* pneumonia, bacterial pneumonia, pulmonary Kaposi's sarcoma, *M. avium* complex, cytomegalovirus, persistent coughing
   d. Edema: Kaposi's sarcoma, hypoalbuminemia
   e. Fever: cryptococcal meningitis, cryptosporidiosis, cytomegalovirus, *M. avium* complex, *M. tuberculosis, P. carinii* pneumonia, other bacterial or viral pneumonia, unknown etiology

- f. Nausea and vomiting: cryptococcal meningitis, cryptosporidiosis, cytomegalovirus, *M. avium* complex, adrenal insufficiency, general deterioration, medication induced
- g. Nutritional deficiency: anorexia, volume depletion
- h. Skin or mucous membrane lesions: Kaposi's sarcoma, herpes simplex, herpes zoster, candidiasis, hairy leukoplakia, molluscum contagiosum
- i. Cognitive impairment: AIDS dementia complex, other central nervous system infection/neoplasm
- j. Dependence in activities of daily living: weakness and fatigue, disease progression, cognitive impairment, visual loss due to cytomegalovirus retinitis

3. AIDS dementia complex (ADC)
    - a. ADC is an irreversible primary progressive subcortical dementing process characterized by cognitive, motor, and behavioral symptoms.
    - b. ADC is the most common neurologic clinical presentation of HIV disease.
    - c. Approximately 65% of patients will demonstrate moderate to severe dementia.
    - d. There is no active treatment for ADC.
    - e. Home management is complex.
        - (1) Plan carefully, with clear management strategies.
        - (2) Close communication and cooperation between the home care team, the patient's support network, and community agencies are necessary.
        - (3) Balance must be achieved between maintaining the patient's independence and autonomy, and providing structure, safety, and control to accommodate lost functions.
        - (4) Expectations must be realistic.
        - (5) Assess and evaluate the patient's functional status during each home visit; subtle or dramatic changes may occur.
            - (a) Include a regular evaluation of the patient's motor functions, ability to perform self-care activities, and safety issues.
            - (b) Make modifications in the care plan and in the home environment as a result of these regular evaluations.
    - f. Communicate with the ADC patient.

(1) Be aware of the need to be relaxed and calm.
(2) Communication can be frustrating for patient and caregiver.
(3) Patient often will not comprehend.
(4) Choose words carefully.
(5) Be aware of body language.
(6) Maintain dignity of the patient as an adult.
4. Clinical management of the person with HIV disease
   a. May vary depending on the stage of the illness, prognosis, and available treatments in a particular geographic region of the United States.
   b. The following list is intended to inform you about potential interventions used to manage certain manifestations of HIV disease.
   c. Treatments change periodically in the care of persons with HIV disease and should be added to this list to guide clinical staff members in advising or intervening with the patient's plan of care.
   d. In addition, experimental therapies may be available, and some may be consistent with the plan of care. Local hospitals, medical schools, or AIDS service organizations often are familiar with experimental uses of new or existing medications.
   e. The goal of therapy may determine the medications or interventions used in treating a particular manifestation of the disease.
      (1) Goals of therapy may include prophylaxis (such as rifubutin in *M. avium* complex), suppression (ganciclovir or foscarnet for cytomegalovirus), acute treatment (trimatrexate for *P. carinii* pneumonia), and palliation (appetite stimulants for wasting or intrathecal chemotherapy of CNS lymphoma).
      (2) Medication dosages and treatment regimens should be considered in relation to the identified goals of care and discussed with the patient's primary physician and the hospice medical director, if applicable.
   f. Candidiasis: *Candida albicans*
      (1) Type:
         (a) Oral
         (b) Pharyngeal

                (c) Esophageal
                (d) Proctal
            (2) Medications/treatments:
                (a) Nystatin oral suspension and/or vaginal suppositories
                (b) Clotrimazole troches (Mycelex)
                (c) Ketoconazole
                (d) Fluconazole
                (e) If resistant to fluconazole, itraconazole (Sporanox)
                (f) Amphotericin-B oral suspension or infusions
        g. Cryptococcosis: *Cryptococcus neoformans*
            (1) Type:
                (a) Meningitis
                (b) Disseminated
            (2) Medications/treatments:
                (a) Amphotericin-B infusions sometimes given in conjunction with flucytosine
                (b) Fluconazole
        h. Cryptosporidiosis: *Cryptosporidium*
            (1) Type:
                (a) Enteritis
            (2) Medications/treatments:
                (a) Octreotide (Somastatin)
                (b) Atropine (Lomotil)
                (c) Loperamide (Imodium)
                (d) Tincture of opium
                (e) Some narcotics may cause constipation and provide some relief
        i. Cytomegalovirus (CMV)
            (1) Type:
                (a) Retinitis
                (b) Disseminated
            (2) Medications/treatments:
                (a) Foscarnet (Foscavir) infusion
                (b) Ganciclovir (DHPG) infusion
                    1) With ganciclovir only, patient may need colony stimulating factors such as GCSF (granulocyte colony-stimulating factor)
        j. Herpes simplex virus
            (1) Type:

(a) Oral
(b) Perirectal
(2) Medications/treatments:
(a) Acyclovir (Zovirax) oral or infusions
(b) If resistant, foscarnet (Foscavir) infusions
k. Herpes zoster virus (shingles)
(1) Type:
(a) Skin lesions
(2) Medications/treatments:
(a) High dose acyclovir (Zovirax) oral or infusions
(b) If resistant, foscarnet (Foscavir) infusions
l. HIV Encephalopathy
(1) Type:
(a) Dementia
(2) Medications/treatments:
(a) Zidovudine (AZT)
(b) Psychotropic medications: perphenazine (Trilaphon), thorazine (low dose), clonazepam (Klonopin)
m. Kaposi's sarcoma (KS)
(1) Type:
(a) Vascular tumors
(b) Disseminated
(2) Medications/treatments:
(a) Vinca alkaloids: vincristine, vinblastine, etopside (VP-16)
(b) For pulmonary KS only: adriamycin + bleomycin + vincristine = ABV; patient may need colony stimulating factors such as GCSF
(c) Doxil (experimental; liposomal adriamycin)
n. *M. avium* complex (MAC)
(1) Type:
(a) Disseminated
(1) Medications/treatments:
(a) Clarithromycin (Biaxin)
(b) Azithromycin
(c) Rifubutin
(d) Clofazimine
(e) Rifampin, ethambutol, pyrazinamide
(f) Other combinations of agents may be available

o. *P. carinii* pneumonia (PCP)
   (1) Type:
       (a) Pulmonary
   (2) Medications/treatments:
       (a) Trimethoprim-sulfamethoxazole (Septra, Bactrim)
       (b) Pentamidine isethionate (aerosol, infusions)
       (c) Dapsone
       (d) Atovaquone (Mepron)
       (e) Clindamycin
       (f) Trimetrexate
       (g) Steroids
       (h) Primaquine
p. Primary lymphoma of the brain
   (1) Type:
       (a) Burkitt's
       (b) Non–Hodgkin's disease
   (2) Medications/treatments:
       (a) Irradiation
       (b) Intrathecal chemotherapy (experimental)
q. Progressive multifocal leukoencephalopathy (PML)
   (1) Type:
       (a) Brain
   (2) Medications/treatments:
       (a) Intrathecal chemotherapy (experimental)
r. Toxoplasmosis: *T. gondii*
   (1) Type:
       (a) Encephalitis
   (2) Medications/treatments:
       (a) Clindamycin
       (b) Sulfadiazine
       (c) Pyrimethamine
s. Tuberculosis: *Mycobacterium* tuberculosis
   (1) Type:
       (a) Pulmonary
   (2) Medications/treatments:
       (a) Isoniazid (INH)
       (b) Rifampin, ethambutol, pyrazinamide
       (c) If resistant, other agents may be required
t. Wasting

(1) Type:
    (a) Disseminated
(2) Medications/treatments:
    (a) Appetite stimulants:
        1) Megace
        2) Marinol
    (b) Experimental: tumor necrosis factor

STUDY QUESTIONS AND EXERCISES

1. Identify three AIDS indicator diseases.
2. Discuss the continuum of disability and its relevance to home care nursing.
3. State three common symptoms in AIDS and their possible causative agents.
4. What is the most common neurologic clinical presentation of HIV disease?
5. What is AIDS dementia complex?

BIBLIOGRAPHY

Amenta, M.D., and C.B. Tehan. 1991. *AIDS and the hospice community.* Binghamton, N.Y.: Haworth Press.

Goldschmidt, R.H., and B.J. Dong. 1993. Current report—HIV treatment of AIDS and HIV-related conditions. *Journal of the American Board of Family Practice.* 6:297-315.

Kaye, P. 1989. *AIDS. Symptoms control in hospice and palliative care.* Essex, Conn.:Hospice Education Institute. 8-14.

Lemp, G.F., et al. 1990. Projections of AIDS morbidity and mortality in San Francisco. *Journal of the American Medical Association* 263:1497–1501.

Levy, M.H., and R.B. Catalano. 1985. Control of common physical symptoms other than pain in patients with terminal disease. *Seminars in Oncology* 12, no. 4:411-430.

Martin, J.P., et al. 1990. *The AIDS home care and hospice manual.* San Francisco: Visiting Nurses and Hospice of San Francisco. 85-113.

Martin, J.P. 1991. Issues in the current treatment of hospice patients with HIV disease. In *AIDS and the hospice community.* New York: Harrington Park Press (Haworth Press, Inc.). 31-40.

McMahon, K.M., and N. Coyne. 1989. Symptom management in patients with AIDS. *Seminars in Oncology Nursing* 5, no. 4:289-301.

Sande, M.A., and P.A. Volberding. 1995. *The medical management of AIDS*. 4th ed. Philadelphia: W.B. Saunders Co. 367-401, 416-436, 460-493.

Schietinger, H. 1986. A home care plan for AIDS. *American Journal of Nursing* 86:1021–1028.

United States Department of Health and Human Services, Public Health Services, Agency for Health Care Policy and Research. January, 1994. *Evaluation and management of early HIV infection.* AHCPR Publication No. 94-0572:101-107, 139, 144.

United States Public Health Service. 1994. 1994 Revised classification system for human immunodeficiency virus infection in children less than 13 years of age. *MMWR* 1994, 43 (No. RR-12):1-10.

United States Public Health Service. 1992. 1993 Revised classification system for HIV infection and expanded AIDS surveillance case definition for adolescents and adults. *MMWR* 1992, 41 (No. RR-17):1-19.

Author's Note: Special thanks to Anne Hughes, RN, MN, CFNP, HIV Clinical Nurse Specialists, San Francisco General Hospital, San Francisco, California, and Thomas Grothe, RN, MFCC, Charge Nurse, Coming Home Hospice, San Francisco, California, for their assistance in developing the clinical management guidelines in Section C.4.

45

The Terminally Ill Patient

Brenda E. Yeadon

A. Assessment of patient and family
   1. History of illness; treatment options; and patient's/family's understanding of disease, its progression, and prognosis
   2. Biophysical status
   3. Mental and emotional status
   4. Family dynamics
   5. Economic, environmental, and social factors affecting current illness
   6. Cultural and religious factors affecting patient and family
   7. Patient's and family's expectations
   8. Coping strategies and support systems of patient and family
   9. Learning needs, skill/ability level of primary caregiver
   10. Bereavement risk factors related to family members
B. Pain and symptom management
   1. Pain
      a. Assessment
         (1) Characteristics of pain: location, onset, frequency, duration, quality, alleviating factors
         (2) Patient's self-description
         (3) Use accepted pain assessment scales or visual or numerical rating systems
         (4) Ongoing subjective and objective data collection
         (5) Exploration of pain experience
         (6) Effects of pain on patient and family
         (7) Attitude of attending physician and other professionals involved in patient care

(8) Nonjudgmental communication
   b. Management
      (1) Pharmacologic intervention, including pharmacokinetics of commonly used analgesics, bioequivalencies, and recommended dose intervals
         (a) Advantages and disadvantages of routes of administration
         (b) Myths related to addiction, tolerance
         (c) Side effects of narcotics
         (d) Concurrent bowel management
         (e) Adjuvant medications
      (2) Nonpharmacologic interventions
         (a) Application of heat/cold
         (b) Massage
         (c) Immobilization, traction
         (d) Transcutaneous electrical nerve stimulation (TENS)
         (e) Relaxation
         (f) Hypnotherapy
 2. Other common symptoms requiring planned interventions may include
    a. Anorexia/cachexia
    b. Elimination dysfunctions
    c. Impaired activities of daily living
    d. Problems with oral hygiene
    e. Impaired skin integrity
    f. Disturbed fluid balance
    g. Disturbed respiration/ventilation
    h. Disturbed rest/sleep patterns
C. Communication skills
 1. Basic communication skills
    a. Attending behaviors: active listening, eye contact, posture, accurate verbal response
    b. Encourage verbal communication
       (1) Minimize interruptions, avoid judgmental evaluative responses.
       (2) Ensure privacy.
       (3) Use open-ended questions; expect/give brief responses.
    c. Paraphrasing: accurate restatement of factual information given

The Terminally Ill Patient   333

   d. Reflection: accurate restatement of what patient/family feels
   e. Summarizing: a technique to tie together major points; a review
   f. Self-disclosure: sharing by nurse of own feelings in order to benefit patient/family
   g. Support and reassurance: demonstration through words/behaviors to indicate acceptance and understanding reflective of reality
 2. Knowledge and skills in patient/family teaching
   a. Assessment of knowledge level and/or deficit
   b. Instruction with appropriate teaching tools
   c. Facilitation of discussion, participation, interchange of ideas
   d. Modeling desired outcome(s)
   e. Monitoring, evaluation of effectiveness of teaching
   f. Feedback: specific, constructive observations
   g. Reteaching as necessary
D. Family dynamics
 1. Concepts related to family functioning
   a. Family system: open, closed, subsystems, enmeshed, disengaged
   b. Adaptive, less adaptive
   c. Family homeostasis; roles, rules
 2. Special needs of families of dying patients
   a. To understand anticipated sequence of events
   b. To know that patient is receiving the best possible care
   c. To know roles of each health care provider
   d. To be involved actively in patient's care
   e. To be acknowledged and supported
   f. To manage logistics related to impending death
   g. For information related to available resources
   h. To complete unfinished business
E. Concepts of death, dying, grief, and loss
 1. Death and dying
   a. Impact of philosophic and cultural attitudes toward death
   b. Impact of death on life
   c. Values of patient, family, and home care nurse
 2. Grief: the reaction to loss
   a. Cultural/social factors affecting grief
   b. Multiple losses: real and symbolic

- c. Grieving and fears of the dying patient
- d. Manifestations of grief
- e. Denial and other defense mechanisms
- f. Grief and the family; children; relationships
- g. Anticipatory grief
- h. Atypical grief

F. Spiritual issues
  1. Self-awareness for the home care nurse
     a. Understanding of major concepts such as suffering, meaning, transcendence, hope, guilt, forgiveness
     b. Exploration of own belief system
     c. Tolerance of other belief systems
     d. Need for support/education
  2. Patient and family
     a. Assess needs of patient and family.
     b. Identify interfamily conflict.
     c. Interventions may include the following:
        (1) Refer to source(s) of spiritual support.
        (2) Facilitate life review through active listening, prompting, etc.
        (3) Examine through self-disclosure.
        (4) Utilize meditation, prayer.
        (5) Avoid problem solving, giving advice, proselytizing.
        (6) Use literature, music, the arts as activities for reminiscence, inspiration, communication.

G. Process of dying and the death event
  1. Physiologic changes resulting in somatic death
     a. Be aware of signs and symptoms of impending death.
  2. Planned death at home
     a. Recognize and support family strengths.
     b. Have available a written teaching tool for families that explains common symptoms.
     c. Provide appropriate interventions preceding death.
     d. Provide nursing support for family immediately postmortem.
     e. Acknowledge faith, religious practices, and rituals that underpin the family system.

H. Community resources
   1. Referrals within home health agency
      a. Social worker
      b. Therapists
   2. Referrals to other organizations
      a. Disease related (e.g., American Cancer Society)
      b. Self-help groups (e.g., I Can Cope, Make Today Count)
      c. Grief and bereavement groups (e.g., Theos, Compassionate Friends)
      d. Churches, service organizations
      e. Local, state, national hospice organizations
I. Ethical issues
   1. Ethical theories and their application: Assist the home care nurse to
      a. Clarify and refine issues and dilemmas.
      b. Help make reflective, rather than reactive, decisions.
      c. Provide a language or framework to facilitate discussion with patients, families, and other health care professionals.
   2. Dilemmas that may be confronted in care of the terminally ill patient and family
      a. Informed consent
      b. Right to refuse treatment
      c. Withholding/withdrawal of nutrition/hydration
      d. Ordinary/extraordinary treatment
      e. Unorthodox therapies
      f. Resuscitation
      g. Suicide
      h. Allocation of scarce resources

STUDY QUESTIONS AND EXERCISES

1. Discuss three tasks to be accomplished through grief work.
2. Explore the cultural, social, and professional values that have an impact on the home care nurse's attitude toward pain management in terminal illness.

3. Describe ways in which the home care nurse can provide spiritual support to the dying patient.

BIBLIOGRAPHY

American Nurses' Association. 1987. *Standards and scope of hospice nursing practice.* Washington, D.C.

Doyle, D., et al., eds. 1993. *Oxford textbook of palliative medicine.* Oxford: Oxford University Press.

Johanson, G.A. 1993. *Physicians handbook of symptom relief in terminal care.* Sonoma County, Calif.: Academic Foundation for Excellence in Medicine.

Saunders, C. 1988. Spiritual pain. *Journal of Palliative Care* 4, no. 3:29–32.

United States Department of Health and Human Services. 1994. *Management of cancer pain. Clinical practice guideline.* no. 9.

Walsh, T.D. 1990. Symptom control in patients with advanced cancer. *American Journal of Hospice and Palliative Care* 7, no. 6 (November/December):20–29.

Worden, W. 1982. *Grief counseling and grief therapy.* New York: Springer Publishing Co.

Part VII
Nursing Management of the Perinatal Patient

46

Perinatal Home Care

Roberta Kempfer-Kline

A. Definition of perinatal home care: home care to the antepartum, postpartum, and newborn patient
   1. Obstetric patient with high-risk condition that may require bed rest or homebound status
   2. Postpartum patient: discharged from hospital within 24 to 48 hours after delivery
   3. Newborn: discharged from hospital within 24 to 48 hours after birth; apnea of prematurity; hyperbilirubinemia
B. Vocabulary
   1. Estimated date of confinement (EDC): due date
   2. Effacement: thinning of cervix
   3. Fundus: top of uterus
   4. Gestational age: number of completed weeks of pregnancy
   5. Gravida: number of times pregnant
   6. Para: number of pregnancies that have reached viability
   7. Quickening: patient's perception of first fetal activity; usually between 18 and 20 weeks of gestation
C. Physical examination of the pregnant patient
   1. Uterus
      a. Fundal height: measured from symphysis pubis to top of uterus; in centimeters should correlate with gestational age after 22 weeks
      b. Leopold's maneuvers: palpate uterus to assess fetal position and heart tones
      c. Fetal heart tones: normal rate 120 to 160 beats per minute, with increased heart rate noted with fetal activity

        d. Fetal movement: assessed by asking patient; in third trimester is indication of fetal well-being
        e. Uterine palpation: assess for uterine contractions and/or for fetal movement
    2. Cervix: examination done by specially trained obstetric nurses; assess for dilatation and effacement
    3. Cardiovascular assessment
        a. Heart sounds to detect any changes from baseline
        b. Heart rate elevation over 15 beats per minute are normal during third trimester
        c. Changes due to increased blood volume in pregnancy
    4. Respiratory assessment
        a. Lung sounds to detect any changes from baseline
        b. Respiratory rate can increase in third trimester due to enlarging uterus and increased oxygen demands
    5. Urinary system assessment
        a. Frequent urination normal in first and third trimesters
        b. Urine for clarity; dipstick for protein, ketones, glucose
        c. Pregnancy predisposes patient to urinary tract infections
    6. Bowel: pregnancy can predispose patient to constipation, especially if patient on activity restrictions
    7. Nutrition
        a. Normal weight gain 25 to 35 pounds over course of pregnancy; first trimester, 3 pounds; second and third trimesters, 1 pound/week
        b. Assess patient's weight gain pattern and discuss well-balanced meals
            (1) Milk: 4 servings
            (2) Protein: 4 servings
            (3) Fruits and vegetables: 4 or more servings
            (4) Breads or grain products: 4 servings
            (5) Fluid: 6 to 8 glasses per day
        c. Patients should be cautioned in
            (1) Alcohol: can be harmful to fetus
            (2) Heavy caffeine intake: not established as safe
            (3) Drugs: can affect the fetus; take only those prescribed by obstetrician
D. Preterm labor: occurs prior to completion of 36 weeks of gestation; may cause cervical change

1. Physical examination
   a. Monitor vital signs and perform physical assessment.
   b. Monitor fetal heart tones and fundal height.
   c. Palpate uterus for uterine activity.
   d. Assess for signs/symptoms of preterm labor.
   e. Assess compliance with activity restrictions and medical management if applicable.
   f. Evaluate nutritional status and assess weight.
2. Treatment: bed rest; force fluids; keep bladder empty. Physician may order home uterine activity monitoring (transmit information over telephone lines to monitoring center; information read by nurses).
3. Patient instruction: signs/symptoms
   a. Menstrual-like cramps; backache
   b. Pelvic pressure
   c. Intestinal cramps with/without diarrhea
   d. Change in vaginal discharge
   e. Gush or trickle of fluid
   f. Regular uterine contractions; may be either painless or painful
4. Additional teaching
   a. No sexual intercourse
   b. Nothing in vagina
   c. No breast manipulation or breast preparation for breast-feeding
   d. Encourage frequent urination
   e. Rest in left lateral position
5. Assessment of uterine contraction
   a. Preterm labor contractions are mostly painless; therefore, they usually are not felt.
   b. Teach patient to put hand on fundus of uterus; if contracting, patient will feel uterus get hard.
   c. Uterus is a muscle; it will contract irregularly.
6. Nutrition: well-balanced meals with increased fiber and fluids; fluids: 10 to 12 glasses per day
7. Prenatal education
8. Medication: beta-mimetics (orally, subcutaneously, or by continuous infusion)
   a. Side effects: tachycardia, fidgetiness, nervousness, flushing, sweating, nausea

b. Instructions to patient: take as ordered; take pulse before each dose; if heart rate over 120 beats per minute, wait 15 minutes and retake pulse
  c. Contact physician if: chest pain; heart rate over 120 beats per minute; palpitations; shortness of breath; rupture of membranes; vaginal bleeding
E. Incompetent cervix
  1. Manifests as painless cervical dilatation without uterine contractions, usually between 16 and 20 weeks of gestation.
  2. Treatment: Physician may place a cerclage or stitch around cervix early in pregnancy; bed rest may be ordered in last trimester.
  3. Patient instruction: Explain incompetent cervix; give same instruction as for preterm labor.
F. Hypertension of pregnancy
  1. Classification
    a. Mild preeclampsia
      (1) Diastolic pressure of at least 90 mm Hg or 15 mm Hg rise over baseline; systolic pressure of at least 140 mm Hg or 30 mm Hg rise over baseline
      (2) Edema: 1+ or 2+ edema of face/hands after 12 hours of bed rest or weight gain of 5 pounds or more in 1 week.
      (3) Urine: proteinuria of +1 or greater
    b. Preeclampsia regarded as severe if one or more of the following are present
      (1) Blood pressure readings of a patient on bed rest of at least 160 mm Hg systolic pressure or 110 mm Hg diastolic pressure
      (2) Urine: proteinuria of +3 or greater
      (3) Oliguria; epigastric pain
      (4) Cerebral or visual disturbances (e.g., headache, dizziness, or blurred vision)
      (5) Pulmonary edema or cyanosis
    c. Eclampsia: occurrence of convulsions not caused by neurologic condition
    d. Chronic hypertension with superimposed preeclampsia: development of preeclampsia in a woman with chronic hypertensive vascular or renal disease prior to 20th week of gestation
  2. Physical examination

　　　　a. Monitor vital signs and perform physical assessment; assess for clonus and edema.
　　　　b. Assess deep tendon reflexes.
　　　　c. Check urine for protein.
　　　　d. Monitor fetal heart tones and measure fundal height.
　　　　e. Assess nutrition and weight gain pattern.
　　　　f. Assess compliance with activity restrictions.
　　　　g. Assess home environment to identify stress-producing factors.
　　　　h. Assess for rupture of membranes, vaginal bleeding, or abdominal pain.
　　　　i. Assess for headache, dizziness, visual changes, or epigastric pain.
　　3. Treatment
　　　　a. Advise bed rest in left lateral position.
　　　　b. Give patient instruction on disease.
　　　　c. Physician may order nonstress testing once or twice a week: monitor patient's uterine activity and fetal heart rate; assess for fetal heart rate accelerations with fetal activity; should only be done in home by specially trained nurses.
　　4. Patient instruction
　　　　a. Instruct in signs/symptoms of increasing severity of disease.
　　　　　(1) Headache; dizziness
　　　　　(2) Blurred vision or any vision changes
　　　　　(3) Epigastric or right-sided pain
　　　　　(4) Unexplained weight gain or edema in face, hands, feet, or lower back
　　　　b. Stress importance of bed rest in left lateral position.
　　　　c. Offer nutritional counseling for well-balanced diet.
　　　　d. Teach blood pressure self-measurement with automatic blood pressure machine and urine protein test (if available).
　　　　e. Teach patient to weigh self daily.
　　　　f. Call physician immediately for any symptoms.
G. Gestational diabetes
　　1. Abnormal glucose tolerance test during pregnancy
　　　　a. Diagnosed by glucose tolerance test.
　　　　b. Results from hormonal changes during pregnancy.
　　　　c. Patients at higher risk for hypertension in pregnancy.
　　　　d. Patients tend to have large babies.
　　2. Physical examination

        a. Monitor vital signs; perform physical assessment.
        b. Monitor fetal heart tones and fundal height.
        c. Assess for signs/symptoms of hypo- or hyperglycemia.
        d. Assess for signs/symptoms of hypertension in pregnancy.
        e. Assess urine for glucose, ketones, and protein.
        f. Evaluate nutritional value of diet and assess weight.
    3. Treatment
        a. American Diabetes Association diet; average 2,200 to 2,500 calories per day
        b. May need to administer insulin
        c. Home monitoring of glucose levels
        d. May order nonstress testing
    4. Patient instruction
        a. Explain physician-ordered diet.
        b. Instruct in aspects of insulin administration if ordered.
        c. Monitor glucose levels: glucometer; blood glucose sticks (not as accurate). Testing glucose in urine is no longer done because of its inaccuracy.
        d. Instruct patient to call physician for
            (1) Hypo/hyperglycemic episodes
            (2) Abnormal glucose levels
            (3) Signs/symptoms of hypertension
            (4) Decreased fetal movement after quickening
            (5) Vaginal bleeding or rupture of membranes
H. Hyperemesis gravidarum
    1. Severe vomiting in pregnancy
        a. Usually starts during first trimester.
        b. Results in dehydration and electrolyte imbalance.
        c. Exact cause not well understood, but condition could be due to hormone changes or stress factors.
    2. Physical examination
        a. Monitor vital signs; perform physical assessment; take diet and weight history.
        b. Assess for stress factors in patient's environment; assess support system.
    3. Treatment
        a. Give intravenous fluids for dehydration; in severe cases, hyperalimentation may be used.
        b. Give small, frequent feedings as tolerated.
        c. Antiemetics or sedatives, as ordered

4. Patient instruction
   a. Eat small, frequent meals; avoid strong odors or spicy foods; review nutrition.
   b. Instruct on administration of intravenous fluids in the home; medication administration.
I. Postpartum
   1. Period of time from childbirth to 6 or 8 weeks after childbirth
   2. Physical assessment
      a. Vital signs: Particularly note fever over 100.6°F and elevated blood pressure.
      b. Fundus
         (1) Assess fundal height for level and firmness; fundus should be firm.
         (2) Fundus should decrease one fingerbreadth below umbilicus every day after delivery.
         (3) If fundus is elevated, patient may need to empty bladder or is constipated.
      c. Assess lochia for color, amount, and odor.
      d. Assess incision
         (1) Episiotomy: intact, edema, pain
         (2) Cesarean birth incision: intact, edema, induration, redness, pain, drainage, or other sign of infection
      e. Assess breasts/nipples for signs of mastitis (e.g., pain, fever, erythema, cracked nipples).
      f. Assess maternal/infant bonding.
   3. Patient instructions
      a. Take frequent rest periods and space activity with gradual increase as tolerated.
      b. Ensure proper nutrition.
      c. Increase fiber in diet and drink 8 to 12 glasses of fluid per day to promote bowel regularity.
      d. Shower daily; avoid tub baths, douches, tampons, and intercourse until first postpartum visit with physician.
      e. Follow medication regimen as prescribed by physician.
      f. Instruct in care of suture line, episiotomy, hemorrhoids.
         (1) Continue sitz bath as needed.
         (2) Apply Tucks or ointment.
         (3) Take pain medication as ordered.
         (4) Practice pelvic floor exercises.
         (5) Use peri bottle with every voiding.

g. Care of abdominal incision: keep incision line clean; teach signs/symptoms of infection.
h. Care of breast or nipples
   (1) If bottle feeding
      (a) Wear a bra and apply ice if breasts become hard, painful, or drip milk.
      (b) Take pain medication as ordered.
      (c) Avoid hot water on breasts when showering.
      (d) Do not express milk from breasts.
   (2) If breast-feeding
      (a) Wear a well-fitting, supportive nursing bra.
      (b) Avoid use of soap, alcohol, and other astringents on nipples.
      (c) Cleanse nipples before each feeding with plain water.
   (3) If engorgement occurs
      (a) Encourage baby to nurse more often.
      (b) Use warm compresses to breasts.
      (c) Express milk to provide relief and allow baby to nurse more easily.
i. Discuss family planning methods
   (1) Birth control pills
   (2) Diaphragm: needs to be fitted
   (3) Intrauterine device: needs to be placed by physician
   (4) Condoms/foam, contraceptive sponge
   (5) Breast-feeding: not a method of birth control
   (6) Can get pregnant without having menses return first
J. Newborn: period from birth to 4 to 6 weeks postpartum
   1. Physical examination
      a. Vital signs
         (1) Temperature: axillary range 97° to 99°F
         (2) Apical heart rate: 120 to 160 beats per minute (may increase while crying or decrease with deep sleep)
         (3) Respiratory rate: 30 to 60 breaths per minute
      b. Measurements
         (1) Head circumference: measured at widest diameter; average 33 to 35 cm
         (2) Chest circumference: measured around chest at nipple line; may be equal to circumference of head but should not exceed it

c. Integumentary
   (1) Color: should be pink; note any jaundice, cyanosis, or acrocyanosis.
   (2) Rashes: Note normal variations below:
      (a) Erythema toxicum (newborn rash): red pimples with yellow centers
      (b) Telangiectatic nevi (stork bite marks): reddened areas often seen on neck, eyelids, forehead, or nose
      (c) Milia: small white pimples frequently seen on nose, forehead, or face
      (d) Mongolian spots: areas of dark pigmentation frequently noted on buttocks area (common in blacks and Orientals)
   (3) Umbilicus: note any drainage or odor.
   (4) Assess for any visual forceps marks, anomalies, or deformities.
d. Cardiorespiratory
   (1) Auscultate for normal heart rate/rhythm.
   (2) Assess for signs of respiratory distress: nasal flaring, grunting, retractions, cyanosis, or poor color.
e. Bladder
   (1) Assess skin turgor and mucous membranes for hydration.
   (2) Assess number of wet diapers: normal is six to eight per day.
f. Bowel
   (1) Palpate abdomen; it should be soft.
   (2) Auscultate bowel sounds.
   (3) Note color, consistency, and number of stools per day.
g. Genitals: female
   (1) Discharge of clear to white or pink mucus from vagina is called pseudomenses, caused by maternal hormones.
   (2) Labia and clitoris are edematous.
   (3) May have smegma inside labia.
h. Genitals: male; see bathing, J.2.a.
i. Neurology
   (1) Assess for spontaneous movement of all extremities; check for symmetry of facial muscles.
   (2) Palpate sutures and fontanelles; sutures may override each other and fontanelles should be soft.

                (3) Assess ears and eyes; should be symmetrically placed.
                (4) Reflexes
                    (a) Check coordinated suck and swallow.
                    (b) Root: elicit by stroking corner of baby's mouth; baby should turn in that direction.
                    (c) Moro (startle reflex): sudden jarring or change in position will cause baby to extend, then abduct, legs and arms.
            j. Nutrition: formula
                (1) Assess type of formula, amount taken, how often fed, whether baby is tolerating feedings.
                (2) Determine whether mother is making formula correctly.
                (3) Assess weight gain/loss pattern; may lose up to 10% of birth weight.
            k. Nutrition: breast-feeding
                (1) Assess amount of time required for nursing and how often baby is fed; baby may nurse every 2 or 3 hours.
                (2) Assess whether baby is tolerating feeding.
                (3) Assess weight gain/loss pattern.
    2. Patient instruction
        a. Bathing
            (1) Give sponge baths until umbilical cord falls off; wash hair twice a week.
            (2) Give bath in warm area; work quickly, keeping area not being bathed covered.
            (3) Avoid giving bath when baby is overly hungry or has just been fed.
            (4) Observe head for signs of cradle cap; brushing hair or rubbing head with towel will help prevent baby's scalp from peeling.
            (5) Lotions and oils are not necessary and will not prevent peeling skin.
            (6) May notice newborn rash or milia.
            (7) Use a mild soap or baby soap.
            (8) Wash buttocks and genital area well after each diaper change.
            (9) Umbilical cord
                (a) Cord will dry/fall off within 7 to 10 days.
                (b) Apply alcohol-saturated cotton ball to cord when changing diaper.
                (c) Cord may bleed or ooze slightly when it falls off.

(10) Genitals: female
    (a) Wipe from front to back when cleaning.
    (b) May notice a mucous, blood-tinged vaginal discharge.
(11) Genitals: male
    (a) Uncircumcised: wash with soap and water; consult physician about whether to retract/clean under foreskin.
    (b) Circumcised
        1) Yellowish exudate will form at circumcision site as part of normal healing process.
        2) Wet diaper is irritating to penis; change as soon as possible; apply A&D ointment to head of penis with every diaper change until healed.
(12) Buttocks: diaper rash
    (a) Wash area well, dry, and expose to air.
    (b) Apply ointments ordered.
    (c) Change diapers more frequently.
(13) Stools
    (a) Meconium: first stool; dark, tarry
    (b) Transitional stool: brownish green
    (c) Normal stool: yellow, pasty (stools of breast-feeding infants are mushier)
    (d) Baby stools frequently in first 1 to 2 days of life
(14) Nail care
    (a) Use blunt-ended baby scissors or emery board to trim nails; best done when baby is asleep.
b. Diaper changing
    (1) Change diapers often, but not necessary to wake baby.
    (2) Disposable diapers may not feel wet like cloth diapers.
    (3) Long exposure of skin to urine is irritating.
c. Feeding: bottle
    (1) Formula should be room temperature; be careful if heating formula in microwave oven; it can heat unevenly and burn baby.
    (2) Test temperature of formula on wrist.
    (3) Burp newborns every ½ to 1 ounce; older babies can be burped middle and end of feeding.
    (4) Do not save unused formula.
    (5) Keep prepared formula refrigerated; wash bottles in hot, soapy water or dishwasher.

                (6) Feed baby every 3 or 4 hours, but do not allow more than 5 hours between feedings.
            d. Feeding: breast
                (1) Breast-fed babies may eat more frequently (every 2 or 3 hours) than bottle-fed babies.
                (2) Burp baby when moving to other breast.
            e. Burping
                (1) Hold baby upright against chest with head on shoulder; gently pat or rub back.
                (2) Also can hold baby upright in lap, supporting head and chest to burp.
            f. Holding and handling baby
                (1) Support baby's head and neck.
                (2) Hold baby firmly and close to body.
                (3) Demonstrate cradle, football, and lap positions.
                (4) Demonstrate wrapping baby in blanket.
            g. Safety
                (1) Never place baby on his or her back after feeding.
                (2) Never leave baby on bed, chair, or couch unattended.
                (3) Most states require babies to be secured in a car seat when riding in a car.
                (4) Keep medications/cleaners out of reach.
                (5) Use child safety plugs in outlets.
                (6) Keep small objects out of reach, to prevent choking.
                (7) Never leave baby unattended in a car or near water.
                (8) Keep regularly scheduled appointments with physician; receive immunizations as scheduled.
            h. Call physician for
                (1) Elevated or low temperature
                (2) Change in normal behavior
                (3) Excessive regurgitation or changes in stool; poor eating behavior
                (4) Abnormal or unusual skin lesions
K. Apnea of prematurity
    1. Cessation of breathing for more than 20 seconds; may be associated with cyanosis, hypotonia, or bradycardia
    2. Physical examination: see J.1.
    3. Treatment: cardiac/apnea monitor; medication
    4. Patient instruction
        a. Cardiac/apnea monitor

(1) Several types of home monitors are available; see directions specific for each type.
(2) Place monitor on firm, nonskid surface.
(3) Keep pets and other children away from monitor.
(4) Keep away from other appliances that may cause electrical interference (e.g., TV).
(5) Check periodically to make sure monitor is working.
(6) Inform local utility companies (e.g., telephone and electric companies) and rescue squad of emergency equipment in home.
(7) Post emergency numbers on all telephones.
(8) Never leave baby where caregiver cannot reach baby within 10 seconds or less.
(9) Disconnect monitor from baby during bathing only.
(10) Assess caregiver's knowledge of cardiopulmonary resuscitation (CPR); only a CPR-trained caregiver should care for baby.
b. Instruct caregiver on the appropriate response to alarms:
(1) Go immediately to the infant's side at the first sound of the intermittent alarm.
(2) Look at the infant and check the following:
(a) breathing
(b) color
(c) muscle tone
(3) If the infant is not breathing or the color is pale or blue, put a hand on the infant's back.
(4) If infant does not respond, gently stimulate infant with your hand.
(5) If the infant still does not respond, turn infant onto his back and vigorously stimulate. Flick the feet. (Never shake the infant as this could cause injury, especially to the brain.)
(6) If there is still no response, begin CPR.
c. Medication: central nervous system stimulants
(1) Theophylline and caffeine are commonly given in formula.
(2) Assess apical heart rate for toxicity.
(3) Physician may order blood test to determine drug level.
L. Hyperbilirubinemia
1. Excessive accumulation of bilirubin in the blood; causes yellowing of skin and sclerae.
a. Levels peak at about 3 days of age.

b. Common disorder in newborn period.
   c. Untreated, it can lead to brain damage.
2. Physical examination (see J.1): assess baby's color in natural light by blanching the skin; assess sclerae for yellowing.
3. Treatment
   a. Phototherapy: expose baby's skin to fluorescent light.
   b. Maintain good hydration.
   c. Expose baby to sunlight if phototherapy is not ordered.
4. Patient instruction
   a. Phototherapy (continuous therapy)
      (1) Halogen or fluorescent lights
         (a) Place baby naked under light.
         (b) Protect eyes with eye patches.
         (c) Diaper male infants for protection of genital area.
         (d) Make sure area where phototherapy is set up is warm.
         (e) Note and record temperature three times a day.
         (f) Note and record amount of fluids and time or length of nursing if breast-feeding.
         (g) Note and record number of wet diapers; color, consistency, and amount of stool.
         (h) Note times when baby is not under phototherapy (e.g., during feeding).
         (i) Remove eye patches when baby is not under phototherapy.
         (j) Check baby frequently to make sure eye patches do not slip, occlude nasal passages, or come off.
         (k) Check diaper frequently for wetness.
      (2) Fiberoptic "blanket"
         (a) Flexible 4-inch strip placed around baby's torso; it is attached to a machine, which is the light source; light travels from source to strip through fiberoptic cables.
         (b) There is no need for eye patches or genital protection.
         (c) Assess underarms and torso for skin breakdown; may use moleskin on edges of fiberoptic strip.
         (d) Baby can be dressed over top of fiberoptic blanket.
         (e) Can hold, feed, or cuddle baby while on this type of phototherapy.

  (f) Note and record temperature daily.
  (g) Note and record intake and output.
 b. Side effects of phototherapy: loose greenish stools; increased temperature; increased metabolic rate.
 c. Nursing note
  (1) Check intensity of light with an irradiance meter during every visit; range 7 to 10 μW.
  (2) Transcutaneous bilirubin meter is useful screening device, but phototherapy reduces its accuracy.
  (3) Physician may order a check of bilirubin blood levels on a regular basis; blood samples are drawn only by trained nurses.
5. Call physician for: increased lethargy; poor feeding; worsening jaundice.

STUDY QUESTIONS AND EXERCISES

1. Discuss the physical examination of a pregnant patient.
2. Define preterm labor and discuss the nursing care of a patient in preterm labor.
3. Define the different classifications of hypertension in pregnancy and discuss the nursing care.
4. Discuss the physical examination of a newborn.
5. Define hyperbilirubinemia and discuss the nursing care.

BIBLIOGRAPHY

American College of Obstetricians and Gynecologists. 1986. *Management of preeclampsia.* ACOG Technical Bulletin 91. Washington, D.C.

American College of Obstetricians and Gynecologists. 1986. *Management of diabetes mellitus.* ACOG Technical Bulletin 92. Washington, D.C: ACOG.

American College of Obstetricians and Gynecologists. 1989. *Preterm labor.* ACOG Technical Bulletin 133. Washington, D.C.: ACOG.

March of Dimes Birth Defects Foundation. 1989. *Recipe for healthy babies.* White Plains, N.Y.

Pritchard, J., et al. 1985. *Williams obstetrics.* Norwalk, Conn.: Appleton-Century-Crofts.

Savinetti-Rose, B., et al. 1990. Home phototherapy with the fiberoptic blanket. *Journal of Perinatology* 10, no. 4:435–438.

Sherwin, L., et al. 1991. *Nursing care of the childbearing family.* Norwalk, Conn.: Appleton & Lange.

Whaley, L., and D. Wong. 1991. *Nursing care of infants and children.* St. Louis: Mosby-Year Book, Inc.

Part VIII

Nursing Management of the Patient Requiring Nutritional Intervention and/or Enteral/Parenteral Therapy

47
Nutritional Problems
Joyce K. Keithley

A. Introduction
 1. Very young, pregnant women, recent immigrants, persons with low incomes, acute and chronically ill, and elderly are at greatest risk for malnutrition.
 2. Malnutrition encompasses undernutrition (inadequate nutrition intake/reserves) and overnutrition (excess consumption of nutrients).
 3. Malnourished persons experience greater dependency/disability, higher health care costs, and poorer quality of life.
 4. Early and appropriate interventions prevent many causes of malnutrition.
B. Age-related changes: physiologic, psychosocial, and medical factors affect nutritional status and contribute to malnutrition
 1. Physiologic factors: grouped according to changes in body composition, energy expenditure, organ systems, and the senses
    a. Body composition: Changes make it difficult to assess nutritional status accurately.
       (1) Lean body mass/skeletal muscle mass loss: most significant body composition change; 50% decrease between ages 25 and 70 years
       (2) Total body water: gradually declines, making elderly more susceptible to dehydration
       (3) Total body fat: increases slowly with age and shifts to truncal area and internal organs
       (4) Bone mass: decreases 5% to 8% per decade after age 45 years, contributing to osteoporosis and other skeletal disorders
    b. Energy expenditure or metabolic rate: Reduced; related to body composition and activity changes.

(1) Lean body mass: Loss is major reason for reduced energy expenditure (protein tissues most metabolically active).
(2) Activity level: less physically active, so lower energy needs.
c. Major organ systems: Variable functional declines in each system.
(1) Cardiopulmonary: decreased myocardial contractility, coronary blood flow, and oxygen transport to tissues
(2) Gastrointestinal: decreased esophageal motility, decreased production and activity of digestive enzymes, slowed gastric emptying and peristalsis, and decreased muscle tone
(3) Hepatic and renal: decreased liver size and protein and enzyme synthesis; decreased nephrons, filtration rates, and capillary blood flow
(4) Musculoskeletal: decreased bone mass, motor skills, and range of motion
d. Sensory factors: Sensory deficits are common in most elderly; contribute to difficulty in procuring, preparing, and consuming food.
(1) Vision/hearing: loss due to cataracts, glaucoma, and auditory changes
(2) Taste/smell: decline in number of taste buds and olfactory cells
(3) Tactile: decline in fine movement
2. Psychosocial factors: compromise ability to consume an adequate diet
a. Low socioeconomic status (e.g., 15% to 30% of elderly live below poverty level): limits ability to purchase desired quality/quantity of food
b. Social isolation (e.g., living alone, loss of support systems): affects appetite and limits intake
c. Depression/bereavement: decreases interest in eating and appetite
d. Lack of transportation/cooking facilities: limits food purchasing and preparation capabilities
e. Dependence/disability: interferes with ability to shop, prepare meals, feed self
f. Impaired cognition (e.g., Alzheimer's disease, dementia, chronic disorders, dehydration): interferes with appropriate food consumption

3. Other risk factors/conditions: affect appetite, digestion, absorption, utilization of nutrients, ability to chew, swallow, or feed self
   a. Acute and chronic conditions: oral health problems, arthritis, heart disease, obesity, surgery, osteoporosis, diabetes, dehydration, pressure ulcers, neurologic disorders, alcoholism, cancer, and infection
   b. Drug-nutrient interactions: chronic or concurrent medication use: prescription and over-the-counter (OTC)
C. Nutritional assessment: Three major components (used to identify individuals at risk for or experiencing malnutrition): use specific forms as appropriate (e.g., nutrition checklists and screens for elderly; minimum data sets and triggers for long-term care resident assessment)
   1. Clinical/dietary history: most important component; memory impairment or dementia makes it difficult to obtain an accurate history
      a. Change in appetite: increased/decreased? why?
      b. Recent weight change: how much? over what time period? due to? 20% below or above desirable weight?
      c. Recent major surgery or trauma: type of surgery or trauma? any effect on nutrient intake?
      d. Presence of acute or chronic diseases: effect on nutrient intake or metabolic needs?
      e. Presence of gastrointestinal alterations/symptoms: difficulty chewing or swallowing? problems with diarrhea or constipation?
      f. Relevant psychologic/social/cultural history: mental status? drug or alcohol abuse? income? education? ethnic background/religion?
      g. Typical nutrient intake/special diet/food allergies: adequacy of intake? fad diets? supplements? food intolerances?
      h. Use of medications that alter food intake/utilization: prescriptions? OTC? polypharmacy? drug-nutrient interactions?
      i. Level of independence: able to prepare meals/feed self? activity level?
   2. Physical examination: pinpoints physical changes representing poor nutritional status
      a. Anthropometric measures: difficult to measure because of body composition changes. Compare with measures in standard reference tables.
         (1) Height: declines after age 30; alternatives to standing

height include recumbent length, incremental length, and arm span.
            (2) Weight: compare usual, current, and ideal weights to determine gain or loss; weight typically declines after age 70 years.
            (3) Midarm muscle circumference: estimates skeletal muscle mass
            (4) Triceps skinfold measurement: estimates fat stores
            (5) Body mass index weight divided by height (inches) multiplied by 100: indicative of obesity if value is greater than 27; indicative of undernutrition if less than 22
        b. Clinical signs of malnutrition: check areas with rapid turnover of epithelial and mucosal tissue (e.g., skin, eyes, oral cavity) for early signs of vitamin and mineral deficiency.
    3. Laboratory studies: visceral protein status
        a. Albumin: maintains oncotic pressure; a carrier protein
            (1) Half-life of 20 days; reflects less acute changes in nutritional status
            (2) Values below 3.5 g/dL: indicative of poor nutritional status; affected by hydration status and changes in organ function
        b. Transferrin: carrier protein for iron
            (1) Half-life of 10 days; responds more quickly to deficiency and repletion
            (2) Increased levels with iron deficiency
        c. Other laboratory studies (e.g., folate, iron, ascorbic acid, zinc): indicative of specific nutrient deficits
    4. Malnutrition: four major types due to increased or decreased intake, increased or decreased need
        a. Obesity: current weight 20% or more than ideal body weight; excess caloric intake over time
        b. Protein-calorie malnutrition: prolonged starvation, anorexia, and acute or chronic illness; anthropometric measures (e.g., weight, body mass index) decreased; emaciated appearance
        c. Protein malnutrition:
            (1) Decreased protein intake (e.g., long-term use of dextrose intravenous fluids, diets low in protein)
            (2) Caloric intake adequate, so individuals appear well-nourished or obese because of edema; depressed visceral proteins and immune function

Nutritional Problems 361

    d. Mixed protein–calorie malnutrition; both protein-calorie and protein malnutrition:
       (1) Anthropometric measures and visceral proteins depressed
       (2) Cachectic appearance; high risk for morbidity and mortality

D. Criteria for adequate diet
  1. Recommended dietary allowances (RDAs)
    a. Levels of essential nutrients essential to meet nutritional needs of healthy persons
    b. Standards for determining nutrient intake and planning and evaluating diets
    c. Modify for acute or chronic illnesses
  2. Food groups/food pyramid
    a. Milk: 2 to 3 servings per day (e.g., milk, cheese, cottage cheese, ice cream, yogurt)
    b. Meat: 2 to 3 servings per day (e.g., eggs, fish, poultry, red meats, dry beans, nuts)
    c. Fruit: 2 to 4 servings per day, especially those high in vitamins and minerals
    d. Vegetable: 3 to 5 servings per day, especially those high in vitamins and minerals
    e. Grain: 6 to 11 servings per day (e.g., breads, pastas, rice, cereals)
    f. Other: use sparingly (e.g., fats, oils, sweets, alcohol)
  3. United States dietary goals/guidelines
    a. Eat a varied diet according to food pyramid recommended servings and following percentages:
       (1) Carbohydrate: 60% of total caloric intake
       (2) Protein: 10% of total caloric intake
       (3) Fat: 30% of total caloric intake
       (4) Cholesterol: 300 mg/day
       (5) Salt: 5 g/day
       (6) Fiber: 20 to 30 g/day
    b. Maintain desirable body weight
    c. Limit alcohol intake to 1 to 2 drinks/day

E. Normal energy and nutrient requirements
  1. Energy needs: can be estimated or calculated
    a. Estimated: 1,600 to 2,200 kcal/day for women; 2,200-2,800 kcal/day for men
    b. Calculated: Harris-Benedict equations determine basal energy expenditure based on age, height, and sex

2. Nutrient needs
   a. Protein: 1 g supplies 4 kcal
      (1) 0.8 to 1 g/kg body weight/day: higher amounts needed for surgery and fever (1.2 to 1.5 kg/day)
      (2) Important for growth and maintenance
      (3) Good sources: meat, eggs, cheese, grains, beans, peas
      (4) Meat relatively expensive; requires facilities/energy to prepare
   b. Carbohydrate: no specific RDAs
      (1) 1 g supplies 4 kcal
      (2) Protein-sparing and antiketogenic effect
      (3) Good sources: cereals, potatoes, beans, corn, rice, bread, sugar
      (4) Easy to prepare, eat, and digest; relatively inexpensive
   c. Fat: no specific RDAs
      (1) 1 g supplies 9 kcal (concentrated source of energy)
      (2) Protein-sparing effect; aids absorption and transport of fat-soluble vitamins
      (3) Good sources: butter, margarine, salad dressing, avocados, egg yolk
      (4) Distribute fat intake equally (33%) among three types: monounsaturated, polyunsaturated, saturated
   d. Fiber: 20 to 30 g/day
      (1) Recommended ratio of insoluble to soluble: 3:1
      (2) Excessive intakes (>40 g/day) cause gastrointestinal obstruction and interfere with nutrient absorption
      (3) Good sources: whole grains, fresh fruits, and vegetables
      (4) Difficult to eat with dentures or no teeth; chop, dice, or shred food
   e. Water
      (1) 4 to 6 cups or 32 to 48 ounces per day, or 30 mL/kg per day
      (2) Monitor fluid intake/output in persons with fever, diarrhea, confusion, or renal or cardiac failure, because of increased risk for dehydration or fluid overload.
   f. Vitamins: Acute or chronic illnesses alter requirements; drug-nutrient interactions are the major cause of vitamin/mineral deficiencies in elderly persons.

(1) Fat-soluble vitamins (A, D, E, K)
    (a) Mineral oil, neomycin, cholestyramine interfere with absorption; required for normal vision, absorption of calcium and phosphorus, antioxidant action, and blood clotting
    (b) RDAs variable
    (c) Good sources: yellow fruits and vegetables; liver; dairy products; eggs; and green, leafy vegetables
(2) Vitamin C: RDA = 60 mg/day
    (a) Anticonvulsants and antacids interfere with absorption; required for wound and fracture healing, iron absorption
    (b) Good sources: citrus fruit, tomatoes, cabbage, potatoes, melon, strawberries
(3) B-complex vitamins: RDAs = variable
    (a) Anticonvulsants, antacids, and alcohol interfere with absorption; function as coenzymes in carbohydrate, fat, and protein metabolism
    (b) Good sources: meats, enriched grains

g. Selected minerals: Similar to vitamins; acute and chronic illnesses and drug-nutrient interactions are major causes of deficiencies.
(1) Calcium: RDA = 800 mg/day
    (a) Barbiturates, diuretics, and corticosteroids interfere with absorption/excretion; required for bone formation, blood clotting, nerve transmission, muscle contraction/relaxation
    (b) Good sources: milk, cheese, green leafy vegetables, sardines, salmon
(2) Iron: RDA = 10 mg/day
    (a) Milk and eggs decrease absorption; requirements lowest in old age because of high stores; required for hemoglobin formation
    (b) Good sources: liver, meat, dark green vegetables, egg yolk, whole grains, enriched bread and cereal
(3) Zinc: RDA = 12 to 15 mg/day
    (a) Diuretics or high-fiber diets interfere with absorption;

deficiency associated with poor wound healing, poor vision, decreased immune function, and taste alterations
            (b) Good sources: shellfish, liver, muscle meats
F. Nutrition nursing diagnoses
    1. Altered nutrition: less than body requirements (common contributing factors are inadequate nutrient intake/absorption/utilization, increased nutrient losses, and increased nutrient requirements)
    2. Altered nutrition: more than body requirements or potential for more than body requirements (common contributing factors include excessive calorie/fat/salt intake, low intake of complex carbohydrates and fiber, lack of nutrition knowledge, lack of physical activity)
G. Nutrition interventions
    1. Identify causes for nutritional problems: base on nutritional assessment.
    2. Develop practical, creative, and individualized solutions; make minimal/gradual diet changes; incorporate nutrition education; refer for counseling (e.g., for depression, alcoholism), dental, or medical care; physical activity and exercise regimens as appropriate.
    3. Implement interventions for common problems and evaluate efficacy (Table 47-1).
    4. Initiate nutritional support techniques, if oral intake is inadequate or not feasible: enteral or parenteral nutrition.
    5. Community resources and federal programs
        a. Title III food program
            (1) Congregate meals at churches, community centers.
            (2) One hot meal per day during weekdays; each meal provides one third of RDAs
            (3) Home delivery and more frequent meal options are available.
        b. Food stamp program
            (1) Not particularly successful with elderly; 10% of elderly participate.
            (2) Food stamps can be used to pay for Meals on Wheels and congregate meals.
        c. Programs for mothers and children
            (1) School lunch program: children from low-income households eat breakfast and lunch for free or at reduced prices.
            (2) Women's, infants', and children's program (WIC): Pro-

Table 47–1 Interventions for Common Nutrition Problems

Problems	Causes	Interventions
1. Change in nutritional status/ development of protein-calorie malnutrition	Lack of assessment/ documentation of changes	Routinely assess for early signs of malnutrition, especially inadequate/inappropriate food intake, weight loss, fall in serum albumin, reduced midarm circumference and/or skinfold, and nutrition-related disorders (obesity, heart disease, osteoporosis, etc.)
2. Inappropriate use of restricted diets	Failure to evaluate continued need for restricted diet at regular intervals	Replace with appropriate therapeutic or ad lib diet
3. Use of multiple medications	Lack of periodic review of medications, including indications/adverse effects	Discontinue or replace offending medications; reduce number of medications; simplify dosing regimen
4. Inability to procure and prepare foods	Age-related physiologic and psychosocial risk factors	Provide food-shopping assistance, homemaker/home health aide services, home-delivered meals
5. Inability to feed self	Inadequate assessment/ observation of need for assistance	Provide feeding assistance or assistive devices; allow sufficient time to feed/eat
6. Suboptimal dining environment	Unattractive/uncomfortable facilities	Create an environment conducive to eating
7. Difficulty chewing	Poor dentition or ill-fitting dentures	Correct dental problems; cut food into bite-sized pieces; vary food choices; avoid tendency to resort to supplements or puréed foods
8. Difficulty swallowing	Age-related changes or acute or chronic illnesses	Order diagnostic evaluation if appropriate; implement techniques to strengthen muscles

continues

Table 47–1 Continued

Problems	Causes	Interventions
		and facilitate swallowing; modify food consistency (e.g., thickening agents; smooth, soft foods)
9. Inadequate nutritional support during acute illness	Failure to recognize increased nutrient needs	Provide oral supplements, tube feedings, or parenteral nutrition as appropriate
10. Unrecognized infection/febrile illness	Daily temperature not taken/no infection-control program	Identify and treat infection; institute infection-control program for high-risk patients
11. Social isolation	Lack of interaction due to living alone, loss of spouse, etc.	Arrange for congregate community meals, volunteers, other measures to reduce social isolation
12. Decreased taste	Diminished taste and smell	Use flavor enhancement of foods; avoid restricted diets such as 2 g sodium diet
13. Specific diseases that impair ability and desire to eat	Chronic obstructive pulmonary disease	Offer small, frequent meals
	Alzheimer's disease	Use foods that can be carried; remove all non-edible items from plates; simply meals
	Depression	Treat cause; give antidepressants
14. Anorexia	Psychosocial, pharmacologic, and physical factors	Identify and treat specific causative factor(s); determine food preferences; provide nutrient-dense foods
15. Lack of nutrition knowledge	Psychosocial and physical factors; difficult to change lifelong habits	Gear teaching plan to older learner
16. Failure to thrive	Organic (e.g., gastrointestinal disorders, cardiopul-	Conduct a detailed patient/family, nutritional history and

continues

Table 47–1 Continued

Problems	Causes	Interventions
	monary diseases, central nervous system disturbances), or nonorganic (e.g., accidental, neglectful, deliberate behaviors)	physical exam; observe food intake directly
17. Malabsorption	Conditions that alter structure and function of small bowel (e.g., Crohn's disease, extensive small bowel resection, radiation enteritis)	Modify fat, protein, carbohydrate, vitamin, mineral, fluid intake according to specific condition

Source: Adapted from Adil Abbasi, MD, Veterans Administration, Clement J. Zablocki Medical Center, Milwaukee, Wisconsin; personal communication, 1991.

vides nutritious food, nutrition counseling, and medical checkups for eligible women who are pregnant or breastfeeding and their infants and children under age 5.

STUDY QUESTIONS AND EXERCISES

1. What are the major risk factors associated with poor nutritional status?
2. How does poor nutritional status affect health care costs and quality of life?
3. What are the three components of a nutritional assessment?
4. What criteria are used to plan adequate diets?
5. What interventions can be used to prevent or minimize common nutrition problems?

BIBLIOGRAPHY

American Society for Parenteral and Enteral Nutrition. 1988. Standards for home nutrition support. *Nutrition in Clinical Practice* 3, no. 5:202–205.

Chernoff, R. 1990. Physiologic aging and nutritional status. *Nutrition in Clinical Practice* 5:8–13.

Dwyer, J.T. 1991. *Screening older Americans' nutritional health: Current practices and future possibilities.* Washington, D.C., Nutrition Screening Initiative.

Elliot, J. 1988. Swallowing disorders in the elderly: A guide to diagnosis and treatment. *Geriatrics* 43, no. 1:95–100, 104, 113.

Folds, C.C. 1983. Practical aspects of nutritional management of the elderly. *Clinical Nutrition* 2, no. 6:15–18.

Frisancho, A.R. 1984. New standards of weight and body composition by frame size and height for assessment of nutritional status of adults and the elderly. *American Journal of Clinical Nutrition* 40:808–819.

Goodwin, J.S. 1989. Social, psychological and physical factors affecting the nutritional status of elderly subjects: Separating cause and effect. *American Journal of Clinical Nutrition* 50:1201–1209.

Goodwin, J.S., et al. 1983. Association between nutritional status and cognitive functioning in a healthy elderly population. *Journal of the American Medical Association* 249, no. 21:2917–2921.

Hale, G., ed. 1979. *The source book for the disabled.* Philadelphia: W.B. Saunders Co.

Horwath, C. 1991. Nutrition goals for older adults: A review. *Gerontologist* 31, no. 6:811–821.

Kurfees, J.F., and R.L. Dotson. 1987. Drug interactions in the elderly. *Journal of Family Practice* 25:477–488.

Mitchell, C.O., and D.A. Lipschitz. 1982. Arm length measurement as alternative to height in the nutritional assessment of the elderly. *Journal of Parenteral and Enteral Nutrition* 6, no. 3:226–229.

Morley, J.E. 1990. Anorexia in older patients: Its meaning and management. *Geriatrics* 45, no. 12:59–66.

National Research Council. 1989. *Recommended dietary allowances.* Washington, D.C.: National Academy Press.

Natow, A.B., and J. Heslin. 1986. *Nutritional care of the older adult.* New York: Macmillan Publishing Co.

Norberg, A., et al. 1987. A model for the assessment of eating problems in patients with Parkinson's disease. *Journal of Advanced Nursing* 12:473–481.

Nutrition Screening Initiative. 1992. *Nutrition intervention manual for professionals caring for older Americans.* Washington, D.C.

Rudman, D., and A.G. Feller. 1989. Protein-calorie undernutrition in the nursing home. *Journal of the American Geriatric Society* 37:173–183.

Schiffman, S.S., and Z.S. Warwick. 1988. Flavor enhancement of foods for the elderly can reverse anorexia. *Neurobiology of Aging* 9:24–26.

Sullivan, D.H., et al. 1991. Protein-energy undernutrition and the risk for mortality within 1 y of hospital discharge in a select population of geriatric rehabilitation patients. *American Journal of Clinical Nutrition* 53:599–605.

48

Enteral/Parenteral Therapy

Fran Free and Kathryn Hennessy

A. Advantages of home infusion therapy
   1. Lower cost; convenient
   2. Safer environment
   3. Conducive to family dynamics
   4. Continued employment possible
B. Disadvantages of home infusion therapy
   1. Lack of on-site medical personnel
   2. Noncompliance with prescribed therapy
C. Patient admission criteria
   1. Willing/able to administer therapy
   2. Significant other support system
   3. Ability to complete a training program specific to therapy
   4. Available access specific to therapy
   5. Safe environment: phone availability, electricity, refrigerator, emergency medical services available
   6. Reimbursement: Medicare, Medicaid, commercial, case-managed, self-pay
D. Traditional home infusion therapies
   1. Enteral nutrition
   2. Hydration
   3. Antibiotic (antibacterial)
   4. Pain management
E. Specialized home infusion therapies
   1. Parenteral nutrition (TPN)
   2. Chemotherapy: vesicants; nonvesicants
   3. Blood components: packed cells, platelets, immunoglobulins, factor 8, cryoprecipitate

4. Antibiotics: antiviral; antifungal
5. Tocolytics
6. Heparin
7. Investigational/clinical trials
F. Access selection
1. Patient's diagnosis
2. Type of therapy
3. Expected length of treatment and dosing schedule
4. Condition of anatomy
5. Prior surgeries or illnesses
6. Patient preference
G. Peripheral venous access
1. Placed by RN trained in intravenous (IV) insertion techniques; radiopaque
2. Appropriate for short-term therapy (generally less than 4 weeks)
   a. Material: e.g., silicone, Teflon, Aquavein
   b. Hypertonic infusion contraindicated
   c. Extreme caution during vesicant administration
3. Types
   a. Angiocath™ (length ¾ to 1½ inches)
   b. Midline (6 to 7 inches)
   c. Long line (>6 inches, but remains outside central vasculature); single- or double-lumen
4. Nursing care
   a. Sterile dressing; Luer-lock connections
   b. Site rotation every 48 hours or as ordered
   c. Site assessment
      (1) Infiltration: inadvertent administration of nonvesicant solutions/medications into surrounding tissue
      (2) Phlebitis: redness at the site >1 cm, possible edema, and palpable cord
      (3) Infection: localized redness; may or may not be accompanied by drainage
      (4) Extravasation: inadvertent administration of vesicant solutions/medications into surrounding tissue
      (5) Pain: may or may not accompany any of the above
   d. Flushing
      (1) Every 12 hours or postinfusion with 1 to 2 mL of 10 to 100 U/mL of heparin solution

                (2) Use of only NaCl to flush Angiocath™ is controversial
                (3) Saline-antibiotic/saline-heparin (SASH): required if drug given incompatible with heparin
                (4) Flush with saline between administration of multiple incompatible drugs
            e. Troubleshooting/nursing interventions
                (1) Infiltration: pull line
                (2) Phlebitis: chemicals further dilute infusate; warm, moist compresses; reassess in 24 hours; may require line removal
                (3) Infection
                    (a) Re-evaluate dressing technique
                    (b) Pull line and culture site
                    (c) Physician order for topical/systemic antibiotics
                (4) Extravasation: depends on type of drug and physician order
    H. Central venous access
        1. Appropriate for long-term therapy (generally more than 4 weeks); radiopaque silicone material
        2. Placed by a physician during a minor surgical procedure; single-, double-, or triple-lumen
        3. Peripherally inserted central catheter (PICC): individual states may allow specially trained RN to insert
        4. Suitable for all types of solution/medication administration
        5. Placement verified by X-ray prior to infusion with tip of catheter in superior vena cava
        6. Blood draws
            a. Discard initial 6 mL drawn from catheter
            b. Draw required amount for tests ordered
            c. Do not draw blood for aminoglycoside levels from central line unless ordered
        7. Types
            a. Tunneled
                (1) Dacron cuff secures catheter and helps prevent infection
                (2) Examples: Hickman™; Broviac™; Groshong™
                (3) Nursing care
                    (a) Sterile, occlusive dressing: if gauze, change every 48 hours and as needed if nonocclusive; if transparent, change every 7 days and as needed if nonocclusive
                    (b) Luer-lock or locking connections

(c) Site assessment for redness, tenderness, or drainage
(d) Flushing (check manufacturer's guidelines)
   1) Broviac™ and Hickman™: 3 mL flush of heparin, 100 U/mL, utilizing a 10-mL syringe every 24 hours or postinfusion
   2) Groshong™: 10-mL flush of NaCl utilizing a 10-mL syringe every 7 days or postinfusion
   3) Antibiotic lock per order
(4) Troubleshooting/nursing interventions
   (a) Inability to infuse or obtain blood sample: attempt aspiration; reposition patient; wait 24 hours and try again; verify placement by X-ray if indicated; treat occulsion as follows: if suspect
      1) Lipid occlusion—use ethyl alcohol
      2) $CaPO_4$ precipitate—use HCl
      3) Medication precipitate—treat depending on drug: use $NaHCO_3$ (increase pH); use HCl (decrease pH)
      4) Blood occlusion—use urokinase
   (b) External catheter breakage: clamp catheter proximal to break (follow manufacturer's guidelines)
   (c) Internal catheter breakage: catheter tip severs, chest pain palpitations, arrhythmias; retrieval with fluoroscopy required
   (d) Internal catheter migration: symptoms depend on tip location; X-ray verification
   (e) External catheter migration: MD reposition required; X-ray verification
   (f) Air embolism: shortness of breath and chest pain; clamp catheter; place patient in prone position on left side; call for emergency medical assistance
   (g) Infection localized: culture positive at site, with negative peripheral blood cultures; topical/systemic antibiotics as ordered; re-evaluate catheter care technique
   (h) Sepsis: cultures from catheter and peripheral site are positive for same organism
      1) Systemic antibiotics per order
      2) Re-evaluate catheter care technique
      3) Line removal/replacement may be required
   (i) Fibrin sheath formation; infusions of fibrinolytics and heparin; sodium warfarin (Coumadin) controversial

b. Nontunneled
    (1) Sutured in place (e.g., Arrow[R]; Centrasil[R]; V-Cath[R]; PICC) (PICC lines may be anchored by dressing only)
    (2) Nursing care: same as for tunneled catheter
    (3) Troubleshooting: same as for tunneled; in addition
        (a) Sutures dissolve; RN may suture per order if state practice act allows; anchor with Steri-strips until physician sutures
        (b) Line falls out: occlusive dressing; new line insertion
c. Implanted
    (1) Subcutaneous placement of port (e.g., Port-a-Cath[R]; Med-a-Port[R]; Harbour Port[R])
    (2) Nursing care
        (a) Sterile, occlusive dressing if accessed; otherwise not required
        (b) Luer-lock or locking connections
        (c) Accessed with Huber needle
        (d) Site assessment: same as for tunneled and verification of Huber needle placement in septum of port
        (e) Flushing: 5 mL of heparin, 100 U/mL, monthly or postinfusion (refer to manufacturer's guidelines)
    (3) Troubleshooting/nursing interventions same as for tunneled; in addition
        (a) Huber needle rocking
            1) Support Huber needle with gauze pad or port support device.
            2) Crisscross Huber needle with sterile tape or Steri-strips.
        (b) Port flipping: contact physician.
        (c) Catheter disconnect or breakage: discontinue infusion; notify physician.
        (d) Inability to withdraw blood: do not infuse a vesicant; notify physician.

I. Arterial access
  1. Appropriate for long-term therapy
  2. Placement by physician
  3. Subcutaneous abdominal placement
  4. Silicone catheter attached to an implanted pump mechanism
  5. Types: programmable (Syncromed[R]); nonprogrammable (Infusaid[R])

6. Nursing care
   a. Site assessment for redness or edema
   b. Refill pump chamber utilizing manufacturers' guidelines
   c. Programming pump
7. Troubleshooting/nursing interventions
   a. Pump malfunction; lack of drug efficacy
   b. Catheter disconnects from pump; lack of drug efficacy and possible redness and edema at site: notify physician
   c. Inability to access pump septum: use manufacturer's template and reposition patient

J. Spinal access
   1. Appropriate for long-term therapy if the catheter is tunneled and short-term therapy if not tunneled; placement by physician
   2. Preservative-free infusions
   3. Routine flushing not required: filter required
   4. Types: epidural (placement into the epidural space); intrathecal (placement into the spinal canal); e.g., Sky™, DuPenn™
   5. Nursing care
      a. Sterile, occlusive, transparent dressing
      b. Luer-lock or locking connections
      c. Site assessment for redness and edema
      d. Assess length of catheter in nontunneled catheter
   6. Troubleshooting/nursing interventions
      a. Misplacement of catheter, changes in drug efficacy: notify physician; insufficient pain control or drowsiness with lack of response can lead to decreased respirations and death
      b. Non-tunneled catheter falls out: apply sterile, occlusive dressing and notify physician

K. Intraperitoneal access
   1. Appropriate for short- or long-term therapy; placement by physician
   2. Types: temporary percutaneous placement; permanent surgical placement
   3. Examples: Tenckhoff™; intraperitoneal Port-a-Cath®
   4. Nursing care
      a. Sterile occlusive dressing three times per week or as needed if nonocclusive; securely tape catheter to patient's abdomen to prevent accidental dislodgment; Luer-lock/locking connections

Enteral/Parenteral Therapy 375

    b. Organize catheter care to minimize entry into the system
    c. Site assessment for redness, edema, or drainage; maintain sterile technique
    d. Flushing: per manufacturer's guidelines
  5. Troubleshooting/nursing interventions
    a. Catheter occlusion: resistance met while instilling solution or will not infuse
      (1) Check catheter for kinking.
      (2) Notify physician; follow manufacturer's guidelines to declot.
    b. Infection/pain: notify physician

L. Intrapleural access
  1. Appropriate for short- or long-term pain management; intermittent or continuous
  2. Placement: by an experienced physician
  3. Types: polyurethane catheters; 0.2-μm antibacterial filter (e.g., Arrow Blue Flextip™ interpleural catheter)
  4. Nursing care
    a. Adhere to sterile technique
    b. Sterile transparent occlusive dressing, change weekly or as needed if nonocclusive
    c. Change the 0.2-μm filter every 72 hours or when clogged; change injection cap at time of filter change; Luer-lock/locking connections
    d. Tape off all ports of IV tubing to prevent inadvertent injection of other medications.
    e. Site assessment for signs of infection daily
    f. Correct positioning of patient critical in determining extent of block/pain relief
  5. Troubleshooting/nursing interventions
    a. Inability to infuse
      (1) Verify catheter placement; visualize for external kinking
      (2) Check for clogged filter; change as needed
    b. Pleural fibrosis in long-term catheters: catheter removal
    c. Inadvertent removal of catheter
      (1) Inspect distal tip of catheter to ensure that entire catheter has been removed from pleural space; assess breath sounds.
      (2) Contact physician.

M. Enteral access
   1. Appropriate for short- or long-term therapy
   2. Placement into stomach or small intestine by physician or RN; radiopaque
   3. Suitable for all types of enteral solutions
   4. Placement verified by X-ray, aspiration of stomach contents, or auscultation
   5. Feedings: bolus, intermittent, or continuous; may be given by gravity or pump
   6. Feeding containers must be kept clean and free from contamination. Once container is removed from patient, rinse with warm water and store in clean, dry area. Controversy exists regarding frequency of feeding container change.
   7. Solution must not hang for more than 24 hours and, depending on environmental conditions, may have to be replaced more frequently.
   8. Initiate feeding with full-strength formulas at low drip rates; increase as tolerated.
   9. Nursing care
      a. Nasogastric/nasojejunal
         (1) Securely tape to avoid dislodgment
         (2) Verification of feeding tube tip prior to feeding; daily oral/nares care
         (3) Troubleshooting/nursing interventions
            (a) Clogged tube
                1) Flush feeding tube with 50 mL of water before and after feeding; flush with at least 50 mL of water before and after medication administration. If administering multiple medications, give each medication separately and flush between each administration with at least 50 mL of water.
                2) Use of diet cola, meat tenderizer, or tea has been shown to help declot feeding tubes.
            (b) Aspiration of feeding: head of bed elevated during feeding; if gastric distention, decrease flow rate
            (c) Diarrhea/dumping syndrome
                1) Constant flow rate via pump
                2) Decrease rate
                3) Formula changes as necessary

4) Antidiarrheals
5) Medicare reimbursement for delivery via pump
(d) Constipation
1) Constant flow rate via pump
2) Increase water unless contraindicated
3) Formula change as necessary
4) Cathartics
5) Medicare reimbursement for delivery via pump
b. Gastrostomy/percutaneous gastrostomy (PEG)
(1) Daily oral care
(2) Post-tube insertion: cleanse with half-strength hydrogen peroxide daily; antimicrobial ointment as needed; secure tube with tape or tube anchor, split sterile gauze dressing
(3) Healed insertion site: secure tube with tape or tube anchor; cleanse site with soap and water as needed
(4) Verify placement of tube by auscultation or aspiration of stomach contents
(5) Appropriate for long-term feeding
c. Jejunostomy
(1) Follow steps b.(1). and b.(2)
(2) Verification of placement: not necessary
(3) Small-bore jejunostomies may prohibit instillation of fiber-containing enteral formulas
N. Equipment: infusion pumps
1. Patient safety, comfort, and ease of use are prime considerations.
2. Choose pump depending on patient diagnosis, duration of therapy, medication/solution to be administered, and available access. Rural areas may warrant use of backup pump.
3. Reimbursement may have an impact on selection of device.
4. Utilize portable pumps if patient is ambulatory.
5. Battery backup is required.
6. Follow manufacturer's guidelines.
7. Types
a. Roller clamps/flow rate regulators: gravity infusions; accuracy varies; appropriate for short-term, intermittent infusions
b. Controllers
(1) More accurate than gravity infusions
(2) Calibrated to infuse a specific volume or fluid at a specific rate (milliliters per hour)

(3) Sensitive to alterations in position and pressure.
(4) Appropriate for peripheral infusions via an Angiocath™; generally not appropriate for central line infusions
c. Elastomeric devices
  (1) Accuracy: generally ±15% of set rate; rate preset by manufacturer based on design of device
  (2) Disposable/easy to use; does not depend on height of container to infuse; can be kept in patient's pocket during infusion
  (3) Appropriate for intermittent, short-term infusions
d. Positive-pressure pumps
  (1) Accuracy: generally ±5% of set rate
  (2) Will continue to infuse despite changes in access site condition; pressure settings referred to as pounds per square inch (psi); should not exceed 20 psi.
  (3) Pump specifications vary with manufacturer: continuous, bolus, and circadian rates, and remote programmability are available
  (4) Appropriate for all types of infusions
e. Patient-controlled analgesia (PCA)
  (1) Accuracy: generally ±5% of set rate
  (2) Generally consists of a basal rate with demand capabilities
  (3) Patient has control over analgesic dose for breakthrough pain
  (4) Appropriate for short- and long-term analgesic administration
f. Syringe-type: works on piston principle
  (1) Administers minute amounts of medication
  (2) Accuracy varies greatly
  (3) Generally requires a small-bore administration set
  (4) Appropriate for neonatal, pediatric, and oncology settings
g. Implanted
  (1) Refer to section I.
  (2) Appropriate for continuous, small-volume administration of chemotherapy or analgesic
h. Enteral
  (1) Accuracy: generally ±5% to 15%
  (2) Technology not as advanced as that for infusion pumps; appropriate for intermittent or continuous feeding in patients requiring an accurate, consistent flow rate

O. Supplies
   1. Tubing
      a. Pump-specific, micro- and macro-bore
      b. If intermittent infusion, change every 24 hours
      c. If continuous infusion, non-TPN/lipid, change every 48 hours
      d. Valve check generally required
      e. In-line or add-on filters available
      f. Y-sites for dual, compatible infusions
      g. Luer-lock connection locking device
      h. Needle-less system recommended
   2. Dressing supplies
      a. Transparent dressing preferred
      b. Gauze and tape, if drainage present
      c. If combination gauze and transparent dressing used, dressing is treated like a gauze dressing and changed every 48 hours
      d. Routine use of antimicrobial ointment is controversial
   3. Ancillary
      a. Biohazardous/sharps container
      b. Chemo container if chemotherapy administered
      c. Gloves and apron/gown
      d. Mask and eye shield for insertion of PICC lines or when splashing of blood is expected
      e. Central line repair kits that are specific to manufacturer's guidelines.
P. Therapies/guidelines
   1. Patient/significant other should be given written as well as verbal instruction in the therapy and be able to return demonstrate without assistance before being allowed independence
   2. Patient/significant other must be able to troubleshoot and access emergency medical services as needed
   3. Patient/significant other should have 24-hour availability to the home infusion company
   4. Written policies and procedures must be available to the clinician; follow all state, federal, and professional laws/guidelines
   5. Infusion therapy requires specialized education of the clinician and ongoing verification of competency
   6. Obtain informed consent
   7. Universal precautions to be used
Q. Enteral nutrition
   1. Assessment

    a. Patient unable to maintain nutritional status via oral intake
    b. Gastrointestinal tract able to absorb nutrients
    c. Determine most appropriate type of feeding tube and mode of administration (e.g., bolus, continuous, pump, etc.)
    d. Assess patient's nutritional status, including protein and calorie needs; select most appropriate enteral feeding formula
  2. Plan/intervention
    a. Instruct patient/significant other
    b. Refer to section M.
  3. Evaluation/monitoring
    a. Clinical laboratory testing to monitor metabolic status and improvements in nutritional parameters (e.g., chemistry profile, albumin, and transferrin level)
    b. Blood glucose monitoring every 6 hours during initiation of enteral feeding and as indicated thereafter
    c. Evaluate gastrointestinal function (e.g., diarrhea, constipation, etc.)
    d. Evaluate competency of patient/significant other
    e. Monitor oral intake if indicated, and discontinue enteral feeding when oral intake meets nutritional needs; weekly weights
R. Hydration
  1. Assessment
    a. Patient unable to maintain adequate fluid intake or output exceeds intake
    b. Physical assessment: dry lips and mucous membranes, poor skin turgor, hemoconcentration, decreased urine output, and increased thirst
  2. Plan/intervention
    a. Administer solution as ordered; generally 2 to 3 L of IV fluid with electrolytes per day
    b. Consideration must be given to patient's cardiac and renal status
    c. Instruct patient/significant other
  3. Evaluation/monitoring
    a. Monitor fluid status and reversal of physical findings
    b. Clinical laboratory testing to include electrolytes
    c. If patient continues to require fluid replacement for more than 1 week, assess for nutritional deficits and implement nutritional support as ordered
    d. Evaluate competency of patient/significant other

S. Antibiotic (antibacterial)
 1. Assessment: documented source of infection; sensitive to drug prescribed; allergies reviewed
 2. Plan/intervention
    a. Identify drug prescribed; duration of therapy
    b. Assess adequacy of venous status
    c. Select appropriate mode of administration (e.g., elastomeric device, IV push, or minibag)
    d. Instruct regarding
       (1) Refrigeration of solution and removal from refrigerator 1 hour before administration
       (2) Signs/symptoms of reactions
       (3) Observe solution for particulate matter and clarity
    e. Consult manufacturer's drug information guide (e.g., some antibiotics are light sensitive and must be protected)
 3. Evaluation/monitoring
    a. Evening temperatures daily
    b. Observe for adverse reactions/side effects specific to drug
    c. Aminoglycosides: peak and trough levels
T. Pain management
 1. Assessment: patient has failed to obtain pain relief via oral, subcutaneous, and rectal routes; utilize pain rating scale
 2. Plan/intervention
    a. Instruct in side effects and activity restrictions as indicated
    b. Verify drug and dosage; morphine sulfate is generally drug of choice
    c. Develop titration schedule and breakthrough dosing regimen (PCA may be ordered)
    d. Get order for appropriate narcotic antagonist; instruct on usage
 3. Evaluation/monitoring
    a. Evaluate pain per pain scale
    b. Monitor breakthrough pain and adjust basal rate as necessary
    c. Evaluate patient/significant other competency
U. TPN
 1. Assessment
    a. Patient unable to maintain nutritional status via the oral or enteral route
    b. Gastrointestinal dysfunction/malabsorption

c. Nutritional assessment to determine degree of malnutrition and recommended daily intake of calories and protein (>10% weight loss, depletion of visceral/somatic proteins)
2. Plan/intervention
   a. TPN formula should generally provide 25 to 35 cal/kg of body weight with 1.2 to 1.6 g of protein per kilogram of body weight; hypermetabolic patients may require additional calories and protein; electrolytes, vitamins, and trace elements are added to the solution.
   b. Calories are derived from dextrose and lipid (fat) sources; protein is derived from amino acids.
      (1) 1 g of dextrose = 4 cal
      (2) 1 g of lipids = 9 cal
      (3) 2 L of 50% dextrose/8.5 amino acids provide 2,050 cal with 85 g of protein
      (4) Lipids 10% 500 mL = 550 cal
      (5) Lipids 20% 500 mL = 1,000 cal
   c. TPN/lipids may be given together as a 3-in-1 solution or using a dual-chamber bag, using a 1.2-µm filter. Lipids may also be piggybacked into the TPN Y-site past the filter.
   d. TPN can be given continuously or on a cyclic schedule; 12-hour cyclic preferred.
   e. Instruct in injecting additives such as vitamins and/or insulin into the TPN as ordered.
   f. Instruct to keep refrigerated and remove at least 2 hours before administering; do not allow TPN to hang for more than 24 hours.
3. Evaluating/monitoring
   a. Daily weights
   b. Glucose monitoring every 6 hours at initiation of TPN and daily as needed thereafter
   c. Laboratory testing: chemistry profile, complete blood count, prothrombin/partial thromboplastin time, transferrin, magnesium, and albumin levels; suggested frequency is twice weekly for 1st week, weekly for next 2 weeks, and as needed thereafter.
   d. Long-term TPN patient may have blood sample for vitamin and trace element levels drawn every 6 months with periodic monitoring of liver function tests.

Enteral/Parenteral Therapy 383

      e. Monitor for metabolic bone disease (bone pain, decrease in bone density)
      f. Monitor oral intake if allowed
   4. Special considerations
      a. Initiation of TPN in home should be done only with patients metabolically stable and with close nursing support
      b. Nurse must be present for initial hookup, first hours of infusion, and disconnection.
      c. Monitoring: high blood glucose levels and fluid tolerance (hyperglycemia or blood levels >250 mg/dL are most common complications of TPN)
      d. Begin TPN with low concentrations of dextrose; increase gradually as tolerated over several days
V. Chemotherapy
   1. Assessment
      a. Confirmed cancer diagnosis and/or chemotherapy indicated for cure, remission, or palliation of disease
      b. Review drug regimen. Many chemotherapy agents are given according to patient's body surface area (square meters) and have lifetime maximal doses.
      c. Side effects of chemotherapy depend on type of chemotherapeutic agent given; most common side effects involve gastrointestinal tract and bone marrow.
      d. Chemotherapy is classified by cell cycle activity and chemical derivation: alkylating agents, nitrosoureas, antibiotics, mitotic inhibitors, antimetabolites, hormones, antihormones, and miscellaneous.
      e. They are further defined as vesicant and nonvesicant agents. Vesicant agents have potential for causing severe tissue damage if there is an inadvertent administration of the agent into the surrounding tissue.
      f. Review clinical laboratory values prior to chemotherapy administration (e.g., complete blood count).
   2. Plan/intervention
      a. Explain possible side effects; premedicate for symptom control as indicated (e.g., nausea/vomiting).
      b. Prior to administration of a vesicant, access used must be confirmed; a blood return must be present before drug is given. Instruct to report burning or pain during infusion.

        c. Antidote for chemotherapeutic agent ordered should be readily available for use; vary depending on drug.
        d. Gown/apron, latex gloves, and mask with face shield must be worn during administration.
        e. Reconfirm dosage and nadir of drug prior to administration.
        f. Reconfirm peripheral access frequently during administration; new peripheral site is always used for a vesicant; consideration should be given to size of the vein before venipuncture.
        g. Dispose of all chemotherapy waste in chemotherapy container; home infusion company is responsible for proper disposal.
        h. Instruct to use care when handling vomitus or excreta for 48 hours after treatment and good hand-washing technique.
        i. Chemotherapy spill kits must be available.
        j. For accidental exposure: remove gloves and wash hands with soap and water; flood an exposed eye with water or isotonic eyewash for at least 5 minutes; medical evaluation as soon as possible; complete incident report.
    3. Evaluation/monitoring
        a. Clinical laboratory testing as ordered; complete blood count and differential are usually ordered to evaluate bone marrow status.
        b. Each chemotherapeutic agent has a specific nadir, which usually occurs 10 to 14 days after administration; susceptibility to infection is greatest during this time.
        c. Monitor side effects and implement appropriate interventions.
        d. Provide dietary consulting/interventions as needed.
        e. Do follow-up within 24 to 48 hours after administration.
W. Blood components
    1. Assessment
        a. Patients with myelosuppression or chronic blood loss are candidates for home transfusion
        b. Initial transfusions to be given in an acute care setting; if history of transfusion reaction, do not transfuse at home
        c. Assess medical history and current status (e.g., hydration, cardiac and renal status)
        d. Peripheral site vein must be large enough to support an 18-gauge or 20-gauge Angiocath™
        e. Laboratory testing: complete blood count, platelets, and coagulation studies; type and crossmatch to be made and patient identification process completed prior to administration; obtain blood consent

f. Family member or significant other must be present with RN during transfusion and should be available for 24 hours after transfusion
  g. Blood components appropriate for home transfusion: packed cells; platelets; immunoglobulins; coagulation factors
  h. Blood bank must be certified by American Association of Blood Banks or Joint Commission on Accreditation of Healthcare Organizations
2. Plan/intervention
  a. Follow blood bank procedures for identification and transport of ordered blood component
  b. Instruct in signs/symptoms of reaction; blood transfusion reaction kit to be available
  c. Obtain baseline vital signs
  d. Obtain venous access; use indicated filters
  e. Packed cells: initiate NaCl infusion; begin transfusion slowly for the first 15 minutes; if no reaction, increase to ordered rate
  f. Immunoglobulin IV is initiated slowly and titrated to ordered rate of infusion; side effects rate-related
  g. Take vital signs frequently
  h. Dispose of blood containers, tubing, etc. appropriately
3. Evaluation/monitoring: review written signs/symptoms of blood reaction; leave in home; follow-up laboratory testing 24 to 48 hours after transfusion

X. Tocolytics
  1. Assessment
    a. Appropriate for pregnant patients who are predisposed to preterm labor
    b. Uterine monitoring must accompany therapy
    c. Assess for willingness to monitor and administer drug orally or subcutaneously via a microinfusor
  2. Plan/intervention
    a. Instruct on home uterine monitoring and on oral or subcutaneous administration
    b. Verify tocolytic drug regimen and instruct patient; uterine monitoring done twice daily and transmitted to monitoring center; instruct to call monitoring center if experiencing symptoms of labor
    c. Instruct on-demand dosing if symptoms of labor occur; instruct on activity limitations
  3. Evaluation/monitoring: patient must have 24-hour availability to

monitoring center; arrange schedule for patient to call in and transmit uterine data as well as report demand tocolytic usage and any symptoms of labor
Y. Heparin
  1. Assessment
     a. Appropriate for patients with thrombolytic conditions
     b. Verify dosage and route of administration
     c. Review laboratory data (prothrombin/partial thromboplastin time)
  2. Plan/intervention
     a. Instruct in overt/covert signs of bleeding and prevention of injuries (e.g., use of knives, hard-bristle toothbrushes, razors, etc.)
     b. Dietary consulting on avoiding foods with high concentrations of vitamin K
     c. Initiate infusion utilizing a pump to regulate flow
  3. Evaluation/monitoring
     a. Follow-up laboratory testing to evaluate efficacy of heparin therapy (e.g., prothrombin/partial thromboplastin time); adjust flow rate as indicated.
     b. Monitor for reversal of signs/symptoms of thrombolytic disease and place on anticoagulant maintenance therapy
Z. Investigation/clinical trials
  1. Assessment
     a. Evaluate trial drug protocol and suitability for home care; obtain patient consent.
     b. Verify availability of sufficient patient population to support clinical trial.
     c. Investigational drug therapy usually is not reimbursed; address payment issues with patient/significant other.
     d. Review study protocol and establish visit and reporting schedule.
  2. Plan/interventions
     a. Administer therapy per protocol
     b. Data collection and reporting of adverse effects per protocol
  3. Evaluation/monitoring: effects of therapy; adverse effects of therapy

STUDY QUESTIONS AND EXERCISES

1. For which group of drugs should blood samples for testing levels not be drawn from a central line?
2. List two symptoms of air emboli.
3. Which type of access mandates preservative-free infusions?
4. What is the most common side effect of TPN?
5. How much water is used to flush an enteral feeding tube before and after feeding and/or medications?
6. When should IV pain management be considered?

BIBLIOGRAPHY

American Association of Blood Banks. 1990. *Technical manual.* Washington, D.C. Library of Congress.

American Association of Blood Banks. 1989. *Out of hospital transfusions.* Washington, D.C. Library of Congress.

American Society for Parenteral and Enteral Nutrition. 1992. Standards of practice: Standards for home nutrition support. *Nutrition in Clinical Practice* 7:65–69.

Baggerley, J. 1986. Epidural catheters for pain management: The nurse's role. *Journal of Neuroscience Nursing* 18, no. 5:290–295.

Bennett, K., and G. Rosen. 1990. Cyclic total parenteral nutrition. *Nutrition in Clinical Practice* 5:163–165.

Bjeletich, J. 1987. Declotting central venous catheters with urokinase in the home by nurse clinicians. *NITA* (National Intravenous Therapy Association) November/December:428–430.

Brown, J. 1990. Peripherally inserted central catheters: Use in home care. *Journal of Intravenous Nursing* 3:144–150.

Camp-Sorrell, D. 1991. Controlling adverse effects of chemotherapy. *Nursing '91* (April): 34–41.

Camp-Sorrell, D. 1992. Implantable ports: Everything you always wanted to know. *Journal of Intravenous Nursing* 15, no. 5:262–273.

Carney-Gersten, P., et al. 1991. Factors related to amphotericin-B-induced rigors. *Oncology Nursing Forum* 18, no. 4:745–750.

Cowan, C. 1992. Antibiotic lock technique. *Journal of Intravenous Nursing* 15, no. 5:283–287.

Hill, W., et al. 1990. Home uterine activity monitoring is associated with a reduction in preterm birth. *Obstetrics and Gynecology* 76, no. 1:135–185.

Hoff, S.T. 1991. Nursing perspectives on intraperitoneal chemotherapy. *Journal of Intravenous Nursing* 14, no. 5:309–314.

Holcombe, B.J., et al. 1992. Restoring patency of long-term central venous access devices. *Journal of Intravenous Nursing* 15, no. 1:36-41.

Hurley, D., and M. McMahon. 1990. Long-term parenteral nutrition and metabolic bone disease. *Endocrinology and Metabolism Clinics of North America* 19, no. 1:113–129.

Kennedy-Caldwell, C., and P. Guenter. 1988. *Nutrition support nursing care curriculum.* Silver Spring, Md.: American Society for Parenteral and Enteral Nutrition.

Larkin, M. 1990. *Intravenous nursing standards of practice.* Cambridge, Mass.: Intravenous Nurses Society.

Lehmann, S., and J. Barker. 1991. Giving medications by feeding tube. *Nursing '91* (November):58–61.

Littrell, R. 1991. Epidural analgesia. *American Journal of Home Practitioners* 48 :2460–2474.

Maki, D. 1991. *Improving catheter site care.* London/New York: Royal Society of Medicine Services.

McClave, S., et al. 1990. Total parenteral nutrition: Conquering the complexities. *Postgraduate Medicine* 88, no. 1:235–248.

Meares, C. 1992. P.I.C.C. and M.L.C. lines options worth exploring. *Nursing '92* (October): 52–55.

Miaskowski, C. 1988. *Cancer chemotherapy guidelines: Modules I-V.* Pittsburgh: Oncology Nursing Society.

Miaskowski, C. 1989. *Access device guidelines: Modules I-III.* Pittsburgh: Oncology Nursing Society.

Millam, D. 1992. Starting IV's: How to develop your venipuncture expertise. *Nursing '92* (September):33–46.

Richardson, D., and P. Bruso. 1993. Devices management of common complications. *Journal of Intravenous Nursing* 16, no. 1:44-49.

Rodvien, R. 1993. Antithrombotic therapies associated with VADS, *Journal of Venous Access Nursing* 3, no. 2:8.

Samaripa, J. 1991. Obstetrical home care: Outgrowing its infancy. *Homecare* October:50D–58.

ter Borg, F.B., et al. 1992. Use of sodium hydroxide solution to clear partially occluded vascular access ports. *Journal of Enteral and Parenteral Nutrition* 17:289-291.

Update: Universal precautions for prevention of transmission of human immunodeficiency virus, hepatitis B virus, and other bloodborne pathogens in health care settings. 1988. *Morbidity and Mortality Weekly Report* 37, no. 2:377–388.

Weber, T. 1991. Is heparin really necessary in the lock, and, if so, how much? *Directions in Chemical Pharmacy, The Annals of Pharmacotherapy* 25:399–407.

Part IX
Professional Considerations

49

Ethical Considerations for the Home Health Nurse

Ann H. Cary

A. Definitions relevant for understanding nursing ethics
   1. Ethics: a field of study that examines what ought to be
   2. Ethical problems: situations in home health care practice that raise the question of: what is morally justified and what ought to be done in a given situation
   3. Ethical dilemma: a situation in which alternatives for resolution present multiple consequences and imperfect answers
   4. Ethical dimensions of nursing practice: moral obligations of the nurse to self, patient, caregivers, colleagues, agency, community, and the profession of nursing
   5. Moral accountability: a moral obligation directing the home health nurse to act in a certain way according to moral norms; this requires the nurse to be answerable for the actions taken
   6. Bioethics or ethics committees: a group of individuals tasked with considering the ethical aspects, including legal and societal facets, of health care decisions
   7. Moral judgments: evaluations of good or bad, and right or wrong, which may differ from the nonmoral evaluations of personal preferences or beliefs
   8. Ethical theories: collection of principles and rules; provide basis for deciding what to do when principles and rules conflict
   9. Ethical principles: guides and statements that serve as foundations for moral rules
   10. Ethical rules: statements of actions that should (should not) be performed because they are right (wrong)
B. Sources of guidance on ethical consideration for the home health nurse

1. American Nurses' Association: *Code for Nurses with Interpretive Statements* (1985); statements of professional nurse ethics
2. American Public Health Association, Public Health Nursing Section: *The Definition and Role of Public Health Nursing Practice . . .* (1980); statements of public health ethics reflecting the provision of health services to maximize the total health of a population group
3. National Association for Home Care: *Code of Ethics*
4. American Nurses' Association publications: *A Statement on the Scope of Home Health Nursing Practice,* 1992; *Standards of Home Health Nursing Practice,* 1986; *Standards of Community Health Nursing Practice,* 1986; and Position Statements: *Nursing Care and Do Not Resuscitate Decisions,* 1992; and *Foregoing Artificial Nutrition and Hydration,* 1992

C. Ethical principles: accountability for assurance by the home health nurse
   1. Autonomy: respecting patients as individuals capable of determining their own choices
      a. Nursing actions include
         (1) Showing respect for an individual's thoughts and actions, and acknowledging the capacity of the patient in an unconditional manner
         (2) Providing adequate information for an informed consent so that the patient can make a correct choice on what shall and shall not happen to him or her; information must be current and include risks, benefits, and alternatives; patient must know the degree of confidentiality available; patient must be informed of rights of appeal and clarification, and how to initiate changes in treatment and/or termination of services; three essential components of assuring informed consent:
            (a) Providing complete information
            (b) Providing information in a manner that is understandable to the patient and allows time for the patient to consider the choices and have questions answered
            (c) Providing a climate of voluntariness, free of undue coercion
         (3) Providing privacy and confidentiality through: obtaining authorization for release of information; protecting patient records in accordance with policy; providing patient information to colleagues and caregivers on a need-to-know basis only

(4) Providing for a patient's self-determination to accept or refuse treatment; implementing actions in accordance with the Patient Self-Determination Act and acknowledging the patient's responsibility for determining his or her living will
(5) Protecting a patient's diminished autonomy by careful assessment and validation through a preponderance of evidence-gathering actions
2. Beneficence: a nurse's obligation to secure the benefits of service for the patient while preventing harm in the process
   a. Nursing actions include
      (1) Assessing the benefits and risks of admitting or discharging home health patient when the needs of the patient may not be able to be met or greater harm may come to the patient
      (2) Examining the risks and benefits of options in the treatment plan with the patient in order to achieve the goal
3. Justice: the nurse ensures that there is a fair allocation of burdens and benefits in health care goods and services to home health patients
   a. Consider Perelman's six aspects of the principle of distributive justice:
      (1) To each the same thing.
      (2) To each according to his merits.
      (3) To each according to his works.
      (4) To each according to his needs.
      (5) To each according to his rank.
      (6) To each according to his legal entitlement.
   b. Theories of justice
      (1) Entitlement theory: all persons are entitled to what they get in life as long as they do not cheat to get it; inequities among individuals in receiving health care are tolerated; there is no responsibility for a community or organization to provide more for those less fortunate.
      (2) Utilitarian theory: resources are to be distributed so that the greatest good can be achieved for the maximal number of people.
      (3) Maximum theory: providing health care benefits first to the least advantaged members of the community without regard for the greatest aggregate benefit; goal is to improve and benefit the underserved.

c. Nursing actions include
   (1) Setting priorities in caseload visits
   (2) Providing services that may (or may not) be compensated
   (3) Making choices about which patient/diseases will be accepted for services
   (4) Deciding on allocating time to prevention activities rather than acute care delivery
D. Ethical problems: systematic approach for identification and intervention
   1. Identify problem: How do you know it when you see it?
      a. Conflict of values, needs, demands, wants, obligations, loyalties, or interests in a health care situation
      b. Choices are required
      c. Ethical principles are at stake
      d. Situation requires a reflective thinking process
      e. Values and feelings of the parties affect the decision makers, patient, and caregivers
   2. Gather as much data as possible from as many participants as possible.
   3. Determine available options/choices in a brainstorming process.
   4. Determine what ethical values and principles are reinforced and negated with each option/choice.
   5. Allow time for processing, reflection, and digestion of competing values.
   6. Decide on recommendations/actions and implementation strategies.
   7. Evaluate and reaffirm the intent in line with the actions.
   8. Evaluate the process by which decisions were made; incorporate useful processes into subsequent situations that raise difficult ethical problems and questions.
E. Ethics committees in home health care agencies
   1. Ethics committees: provide a voluntary, non–federally mandated structure and forum for communication among home health providers and participants as well as an effective process for decision making
   2. Composition: typically composed of interdisciplinary professionals; nurses, social workers, physician, attorney, clergy, administra-

tor, consumer, ethicist, allied health professional; may include intra- and extra-agency representatives
3. Size: large enough to have a variety of views, small enough to allow for manageable and effective decision making
4. Characteristics of group members: assertiveness, able to tolerate ambiguity and diversity of opinion, respectful of confidentiality, goal-oriented, knowledgeable about conflict management, compassionate
5. Functions
    a. Use group reasoning to anticipate, process, and resolve dilemmas.
    b. Detect and apply ethical theories, principles, and rules to guide actions and judgments.
    c. Educate group members through the study of ethical principles and techniques; teaching can expand to others through efforts ranging from casual lunch group sessions and ethics rounds to formal ethics workshops.
    d. Policy and procedural development: members can construct/adopt policies and agency position statements related to the detection and resolution of ethical problems; written guidelines become the agency standard against which standards of care and practice are measured and refined.
    e. Counseling and support: anticipated, current, and retrospective problems and dilemmas can be discussed openly with the goal of defining the resolution process; health care providers will benefit from a support structure that can assist in the recognition, processing, and successful intervention options for ethical problems.
    f. Continuous quality improvement: structure and process provide a vehicle for supporting ethical principles in the delivery of home health services, and reduce the likelihood of isolated decision making and superficial and hastily constructed solutions to complex choices; evaluation of structure and process of this committee can be incorporated into periodic refinements in the organization.
6. Ethics committee can serve one agency or be constructed from representatives of multiple agencies in a community to meet the needs of more than one agency.

STUDY QUESTIONS AND EXERCISES

1. Identify three practice situations that presented ethical problems in your practice. For each, identify
   a. Ethical principles in conflict
   b. The value, obligations, and needs of each party involved
   c. The process you used to resolve the problem
   d. The decisions that were implemented
   e. Gauge the satisfaction with the decisions of the parties involved.
2. Compare the American Nurses' Association code of ethics with the National Association for Home Care code of ethics. What do you believe are the strengths and weaknesses in each as they relate to guiding your day-to-day practice? What statements would you add to each to improve both documents?
3. Write a policy and develop procedures for the creation and implementation of an ethics committee in your agency. Include names of people, size, professions represented, mission, functions, how the committee would be evaluated within the agency, budget, library resources, and continuing education needs. If you have a committee in place, read about the committee, read the minutes, and interview committee members about their participation and their opinions about its effectiveness. Volunteer to serve on it for at least a year.

BIBLIOGRAPHY

Abel, E.P. 1990. Ethics committees in home health agencies. *Public Health Nursing* 7, no. 4:256–259.

American Nurses' Association. 1985. *Code for nurses with interpretive statements*. Washington, D.C.

American Nurses' Association. 1986. *Standards of community health nursing practice*. Washington, D.C.

American Nurses' Association. 1986. *Standards of home health nursing practice*. Washington, D.C.

American Nurses' Association. 1991. *Standards of clinical nursing practice*. Washington, D.C.

American Nurses' Association. 1992. *Position statement: Foregoing artificial nutrition and hydration*. Washington, D.C.

American Nurses' Association. 1992. *Position statement: Nursing care and do not resuscitate decisions*. Washington, D.C.

American Nurses' Association. 1992. *Statement on the scope of home health nursing practice.* Washington, D.C.

American Public Health Association, Public Health Nursing Section. 1980. *The definition and role of public health nursing practice in the delivery of health care: A statement of the Public Health Nursing Section.* Washington, D.C.

Aroskar, M.A. 1989. *Home care: The ethical challenges.* In *Home healthcare nursing,* eds. I.M. Martinson and A. Widmer, 381–389. Philadelphia: W.B. Saunders Co.

Beauchamp, T.L., and J.F. Childress. 1989. *Principles of biomedical ethics.* New York: Oxford University Press.

Blumefield, S., and J.I. Lowe. 1987. A template for analyzing ethical dilemmas in discharge planning. *Health and Social Work* 12, no. 1:47–56.

Cary, A.H. 1987. Institutional review boards and ethics committees: Their role in ensuring ethical home care research. *Home Care Economics* 1, no. 4:113–121.

Cary, A.H. 1989. Promoting research endeavors in home health. In *Home healthcare nursing,* eds. I.M. Martinson and A. Widmer, 401–417. Philadelphia: W.B. Saunders Co.

Collopy, B., et al. 1990. The ethics of home care: Autonomy and accommodation. *Hastings Center Report* 20, no. 2.

Curtin, L., and M.J. Flaherty. 1982. *Nursing ethics.* Bowie, Md.: Brady Publishing.

Dowd, T.T. 1989. Ethical reasoning: A basis for nursing care in the home. *Journal of Community Health Nursing* 6, no. 1:45–51.

Erlen, J.A., et al. 1990. Making an ethical decision in the home setting: The case of Stan. *Home Healthcare Nurse* 8, no. 6:30–34.

Fowler, M.D.M., and J. Levine-Ariff. 1987. *Ethics at the bedside.* Philadelphia: J.B. Lippincott Co.

Fry, S.T. 1992. Ethics in community health nursing practice. In *Community Health Nursing,* eds. M. Stanhope and J. Lancaster. St. Louis: Mosby-Year Book, Inc.

Grundner, T.M. 1986. *Informed consent.* Owings Mills, Md.: National Health Publishing.

Haddad, A.M. 1992. Ethical problems in home care. *Journal of Nursing Administration* 22, no. 3:46–51.

Harris, M.D. 1990. The ethical dilemmas. *Home Healthcare Nurse* 8, no. 6:47–48.

Hosford, B. 1986. *Bioethics committees.* Gaithersburg, Md.: Aspen Publishers, Inc.

Murphy, C.P. 1978. The moral situation in nursing. In *Bioethics and human rights,* eds. E.L. Bandman and B. Bandman. Boston: Little, Brown and Co.

National Association for Home Care. 1982. *Code of ethics.* Washington, D.C.

National League for Nursing. 1990. *Ethics in nursing: An anthology.* New York.

Perelman, C. 1963. *The idea of justice and the problem of argument.* London: Routledge and Kegan Paul.

President's Commission for the Study of Ethical Problems in Medicine and Biochemical and Behavioral Research. 1982. *Making health care decisions: A report on the ethical and legal implications of informed consent in the patient-practitioner relationship 1.* Washington, D.C.: U.S. Government Printing Office.

Reckling, J.B. 1989. Abandonment of patients by home health nursing agencies: An ethical analysis of the dilemma. *Advances in Nursing Science* 11, no. 3:70–81.

Sherry, D. 1990. Autonomy versus beneficence: The dilemma and its implications in home care. *Home Healthcare Nurse* 8, no. 6 :13–15.

Veach, R.M. 1981. *A theory of medical ethics*. New York: Basic Books, Inc.

Watts, D.T., et al. 1989. Dangerous behavior in a demented patient. *Journal of the American Geriatric Society* 37, no. 7:658–662.

50

Legal Principles and Home Care Nursing

Carol L. Schaffer

A. Law defined
   1. Law: a set of rules and principles derived from several sources; enforceable by legal processes
   2. Laws: provide a means of settling disputes, compensating for injuries caused by another, and disciplining and isolating individuals for wrongdoing. Laws are important for nursing practice.
B. Origins of laws: four sources of law form legal basis of nursing practice
   1. Constitution: sets forth how an organization governs itself; e.g., federal government and each state have written constitutions
   2. Judicial opinion: court's official position on a legal dispute, written by the judge who presides over a case
      a. Usually emanates from appeals or higher courts in the state or federal court system; also referred to as case law or case decisions
      b. Form precedent: a body of law that is often the basis for future decisions
      c. Address nursing practice in such areas as employment, licensure, malpractice, negligence, and crimes
   3. Legislation: set of rules created by legislative branch of government at the federal, state, or local (city or county) level
      a. Also called statutes or statutory law; published and made available to the public
      b. Nursing practice: shaped by many pieces of legislation, particularly state nurse practice act and state and federal public health laws

c. Occurs from a process that involves the study of issues, drafting of a bill, redrafting, and voting for or against the bill's passage
  4. Regulations: the rules created by the executive branch of government
     a. Created through the regulatory process, which involves the study of issues, publication of the proposed rule, a period of public input (through written opinions or testimony at hearings), possible redrafting, and publication of the final regulation
     b. The government agency created by the state nurse practice act, usually called the state board of nursing, writes rules that govern and control nursing practice
C. Types of law
  1. Civil law: legal issues unrelated to criminal acts
     a. Civil disputes related to safe nursing practice may involve an employment contract, a tort, or a violation of a patient's rights
  2. Administrative law: concerned with government agencies' rules and regulations
     a. Licensure and state's power to discipline nurses involve administrative law and process.
     b. States have power to make nursing rules and regulations based on its "police" that protect public health, safety, and welfare; e.g., barring a nurse from practice is authority that a state can exercise to protect public health, safety, and welfare.
  3. Criminal law: a set of laws that define offenses against society
D. Contracts
  1. Federal and state statutes and judicial opinions, employer personnel handbooks, civil service rules, employer practice, collective bargaining agreements, and employment contracts all govern the nurse's employment setting
  2. Contract: written or oral agreement between two or more individuals that has several elements to its formation, interpretation, and enforcement
     a. Include offer, acceptance, and consideration (usually, monetary compensation)
E. Civil disputes: Torts (home health nurse generally signs a contract that outlines terms of employment, e.g., the fee per visit, term of agreement, responsibilities of each party, insurance requirements, etc.)
  1. Tort: a breach of a legal duty to the rights and interests of others

2. An injured litigant can receive remedy for a tort, commonly in the form of damages, if the litigant presents adequate evidence to prove that an injury occurred
3. Courts recognize three types of torts
   a. Unintentional tort: act that fails to meet a duty owed to another person; results in money to a person; two most common types of unintentional tort: negligence and malpractice
      (1) Negligence involves four elements
         (a) Duty: the nurse's legal duty to provide nursing care to a patient
            1) Duty to meet a reasonable and prudent standard of care
            2) Deliver care as any other reasonable and prudent nurse would do under similar circumstances
            3) Standards of care are found in policy and procedure manuals, nursing education, experience, publications, standards manuals of professional associations, and accreditation groups
         (b) Breach of duty: failure to provide the expected reasonable standard of care
            1) Omission: nurse may fail to provide care
            2) Commission: nurse may provide care in an unreasonable manner
         (c) Proximate cause: causal relationship between breach of duty and resulting injury
            1) Does not necessarily involve a direct cause-and-effect relationship; plaintiff must show evidence that nurse's action or inaction led to plaintiff's injury
            2) State laws have different definitions of proximate cause
            3) If definition uses the term *but for,* plaintiff must prove that injury would not have occurred but for the nurse's breach of duty
            4) If definition uses the term *substantial factor,* plaintiff must prove that nurse's breach of duty was a substantial factor in injury
            5) If definition uses the term *foreseeability,* plaintiff must prove that nurse's breach of duty foreseeably led to plaintiff's injury

(d) Damages: physical or psychologic injury and monetary compensation awarded to plaintiff for incurring injury
   1) Plaintiff must prove that an injury occurred and present evidence showing its monetary value
   2) Plaintiff can request compensatory, nominal, or punitive damages
   3) Compensatory damages: awarded to reimburse plaintiff for expenses, rehabilitation, and pain and suffering related to injury
   4) Nominal damages: awarded to indicate a defendant's wrongdoing when little if any injury occurred
   5) Punitive damages: awarded to plaintiff in special circumstances, usually to punish defendant for an especially egregious or outrageous act
   6) Negligence in home care nursing can involve omissions, e.g., failure to administer medications as ordered, failure to administer ordered treatments, failure to detect signs and symptoms of illnesses, or failure to report adverse effects or symptoms to physicians; negligence can involve commissions, e.g., home care nurse might administer wrong drug to a patient, administer a treatment incorrectly, report inaccurate information to physician
(2) Malpractice: negligence by a member of a profession, e.g., nursing, differing from negligence only in that standard or duty owed is a professional one, based on special knowledge and skills
   (a) Plaintiff in a malpractice action must prove all the elements of negligence.
   (b) Not all states automatically apply a professional standard to nurses; some still apply a nonprofessional one, and others apply a professional standard only when nurse's act required special knowledge and skill.
(3) Negligence and malpractice lawsuits: legal principles about who bears liability (responsibility) for resulting injuries
   (a) Personal liability: responsibility for one's acts, e.g., if a patient is injured by a home care nurse who administers the wrong drug

- (b) Vicarious liability: responsibility for another person's acts; such liability can take one of two forms
  1) Principle of respondeat superior: an employer's responsibility for injuries caused by an employee's negligent acts, if those acts were performed within the scope of employment and when an employment relationship existed; e.g., if a home health nurse fails to detect an elevated blood pressure because he or she failed to take vital signs during a visit, both nurse and home care agency are liable
  2) Corporate liability: an employer's responsibility for injury caused by an employee who acted according to the employer's decision; e.g., if home care agency is inadequately staffed by nurses and a patient is injured due to the home care agency's scheduling practice that left out a required patient visit, the agency may be responsible for failing to assign a nurse to go to the home
- (4) Nurses can avoid or defend negligence and malpractice lawsuits by
  - (a) Knowing standard of care: the duty owed the patient before delivering care
  - (b) Providing care that is consistent with the standards
  - (c) Documenting care accurately and concisely, following the agency's policies and procedures
- (5) Best defense against an allegation that the home care nurse failed to meet the standard of care: documentation that ensures care delivered is consistent with the standard; e.g., documentation regarding the management of a wound involving a full description of the wound and treatment used is best defense against negligence

b. Intentional tort: a willful act that injures another person or person's property.
  - (1) Assault: the threat of imminent harmful or offensive bodily contact
  - (2) Battery: bodily contact with another person without the person's permission or consent. A home health nurse who delivers a treatment without a patient's consent would be liable for battery if the patient refused the treatment. In

general, physicians are responsible for obtaining an informed consent and order the home care nurse to act accordingly; the home care nurse will not be liable if there was no informed consent unless the patient protests and the nurse proceeds.
- (3) False imprisonment: unlawful restraint of a person against the person's will
- (4) Intentional infliction of emotional distress: extreme, outrageous, or intolerable conduct toward another, causing emotional harm

c. Quasi-intentional tort: an act that interferes with a person's intangible interests, e.g., privacy or reputation
- (1) Nurse may be charged with invasion of privacy and breach of confidentiality for revealing personal information about a patient to an unauthorized person; home health nurses have access to information that, if exposed publicly, can constitute an invasion of privacy and breach of confidentiality.
- (2) Nurse may be charged with defamation for injuring plaintiff's reputation in the community as result of a false statement that is spoken (slander) or written (libel).

F. Civil disputes and nursing practice: patient rights
1. Medicare requires a list of patient rights. Although not law, this code lists many recognized patient rights.
2. Generally include informed consent, freedom of unreasonable restraint, right to refuse treatment, and right to privacy and confidentiality.
   a. Informed consent: patient's involvement in and agreement with treatment decisions based on adequate knowledge; legally recognized and has several key requirements:
      (1) The consent must be voluntary.
      (2) The physician's professional judgment may dictate that fully informing a patient would act as a substantial detriment to the patient and cause harm, known as the physician's therapeutic privilege.
   b. Freedom from unreasonable restraint: patient's autonomy and freedom of movement
      (1) Patient must receive care in a safe manner.
      (2) Health care providers can legally restrain a patient under certain conditions, e.g., a home care nurse can restrain a

patient to protect the patient from harming others or himself or herself.
- (a) Restraints must be necessary to meet patient's therapeutic needs or to ensure safety of patient or others.
- (b) The least-restrictive type of restraint must be used.
- (c) Use of restraints must be accompanied by the physician's orders (except in an emergency).
- (d) Home care nurses must closely monitor patient, release restraints periodically, and remove them when condition no longer warrants.
- (e) Accurate and thorough documentation must reveal pertinent details of care given to patient, including how and why restraints were applied/removed.

c. The right to refuse treatment: provides that every competent adult may refuse treatment
  (1) All requirements of informed consent apply to a patient's decision to refuse treatment.
  (2) Right to refuse treatment: not absolute; must be considered by the court in relation to interests of society; court may override a patient's request if outweighed by court's responsibility to preserve human life, protect innocent third parties, prevent suicide, or maintain ethical integrity of medical profession.
  (3) Many states have enacted legislation that permits a patient to make health care decisions in advance, known as advance directives; agencies are required to ask patients upon admission if they have advance directives.
     (a) Living will: document in which patient instructs family and health care professionals about medical care that should or should not be provided if patient becomes incapacitated; copy of living will should become part of medical record; requirements of living wills are outlined in state law. Living wills are applicable to patients in terminal illness or persistent vegetative states.
     (b) Durable power of attorney: legal document in which a patient identifies a proxy, or surrogate, decision maker in case patient becomes incapacitated; copy of this document should be included in medical record.
  (4) Substituted consents: covered in state laws if patient lacks

capacity to make informed decisions; health care professionals usually turn to patient's family members or close friends; court may or may not formally appoint these surrogate decision makers.
    d. Right to privacy and confidentiality: recognizes a patient's autonomy and right to be left alone
       (1) Patient may reveal private information that will enhance treatment; in return, the health care provider must keep the information confidential.
       (2) Patient has right to access personal health records and to obtain a copy of records.
       (3) Health care providers have responsibility to maintain health records in a secure, controlled manner.
       (4) Information can be revealed only with patient's permission or when required by law; e.g., a home care agency must obtain consent prior to releasing diagnostic or other information to insurance companies to avoid a break of confidentiality.
G. Administrative matters and nursing practice
  1. State governments regulate nursing practice through an executive branch office, usually called a state board of nursing.
  2. Legislation known as the state nurse practice act creates the state board.
  3. Each state typically regulates several areas of nursing practice:
    a. Nursing profession's licensure examination: determines rules and requirements for admission or entry into nursing practice
    b. Nurse practice act: defines legal scope of nursing practice. The state can discipline, fine, censure, or take other appropriate steps against one who practices nursing without meeting state requirements.
    c. Professional conduct of licensed nurses: defining unprofessional conduct.
       (1) State has power to initiate investigations, bring charges of misconduct, and levy disciplinary measures.
       (2) Chemical impairment (drug or alcohol abuse) is the most common reason for disciplinary action against a nurse.
       (3) A nurse charged with unprofessional conduct has the right to due process, including notice of specific charges, an opportunity to present evidence to counter the charges, and representation by an attorney hired by the nurse.

  d. Nursing education: establishing requirements of and approving educational programs for nurse preparation.
H. Criminal matters and nursing practice
 1. Most states recognize two types of crime: felonies and misdemeanors.
 2. Degree of severity of crime is the difference.
  a. Felonies involve more serious offenses and result in lengthy prison sentences.
  b. Misdemeanors (less serious offenses) generally result in a short prison sentence, a fine, or both.
 3. Criminal codes or statutes define elements of each crime; prosecutor must prove the existence of elements beyond a reasonable doubt.
 4. Defendant in a criminal case has constitutionally provided rights, e.g., right to legal counsel.
I. Home care considerations: key legal considerations
 1. Admission criteria to home care: nurses should be careful to assess patient's needs and match these with ability of agency to meet patient's needs.
  a. If care that agency can provide is inadequate, and patient is injured, plaintiff may argue that the agency and nurse are liable for providing negligent care.
 2. Environmental assessment for suitability and adaptability of environment for home care.
  a. Home care nurse has legal duty to examine environment for suitability/adaptability for home care; nurse is charged with evaluating if the environment can be made safe; e.g., a situation in which care would not be safe is a situation in which patient refuses to remove throw rugs and wants nurse to walk him or her on the rugs; if nurse proceeds and patient falls and is injured, nurse can expect to be held for negligence.
 3. Transfer criteria
  a. Home care nurse should have explicit policies and procedures regarding how to manage patient emergencies; nurse should know that he or she has the right to send a patient in an emergency to the hospital without prior approval by physician; nurse certainly must inform physician that patient has been transferred, but nurse must transfer patient to the hospital or other appropriate environment in which the patient can be safely cared for if home care is inadequate.

4. Discharge criteria
    a. Home care agency must ensure that patients are discharged from home care only if their needs have been met, they have been transferred, they refuse further care, etc.; if a nurse fails to provide necessary care and patient is injured, the nurse may be held liable for negligence along with the agency, which may be held liable for corporate negligence.
    b. Specific concerns arise regarding insurance company-directed care that is capped.
    c. Agencies need to assess carefully whether they are willing to run the risk of providing potentially not reimbursed care, or being held liable for negligence if they discharge a case.
5. Assignment of appropriate care providers
    a. Agency has responsibility for assignment of appropriately prepared personnel to manage care of patients.
    b. If agency assigns an ill-prepared home care nurse to manage cases and patient is injured, home care nurse and agency may be held liable for negligence.

STUDY QUESTIONS AND EXERCISES

1. Discuss the origins of laws.
2. List the three broad types of laws.
3. List those persons who can create contracts.
4. Discuss the three types of torts.
5. The tort of negligence includes what four elements?

BIBLIOGRAPHY

Better documentation, clinical skillbuilders. 1992. Springhouse, Pa.: Springhouse Corporation.
Cournoyer, C.P. 1989. *The nurse manager and the law.* Gaithersburg, Md.: Aspen Publishers, Inc.
Creighton, H. 1986. *Law every nurse should know.* Philadelphia: W.B. Saunders Co.
Nurse's handbook of law and ethics. 1992. Springhouse, Pa.: Springhouse Corporation.

51

Continuous Quality Improvement in Home Care

Nancy L. Bohnet

A. Concepts/key points
   1. Quality improvement (QI) in an organization is driven by managers: top-down process
   2. Emphasis on customer
   3. Knowledge of who customers are: internal and external
   4. Planned, systematic process that examines organizational key functions
   5. People who do the work create the method of process improvement
   6. Need to use QI tools and statistical tools
B. Initiation
   1. Leaders learn the fundamental principles of QI.
   2. Leaders educate the next level, on down the line.
   3. Leaders identify the organization's key functions.
   4. Leaders create a resource group made up of organizational leaders from all departments.
   5. Resource group develops quality vision to help everyone understand the commitment to quality.
C. Implementation
   1. Resource group establishes priorities for process/function improvement.
   2. Resource group selects one or two functions and chooses task force members from across the organization who understand and work with the process.
   3. Resource group educates task force members to
      a. Set goal for process improvement
      b. Set guidelines for meetings

        c. Establish ground rules for group work/outcome
    4. At the task force meeting members
        a. Assign task force leader
        b. Assign group facilitator
        c. Set agenda for all meetings
        d. Assign minute taker
        e. Limit meeting time to 1½ hours
    5. Use of continuous quality improvement (CQI) tools
        a. Brainstorming: free flow of ideas regarding problem/improvement from task force members that are written on flip charts
        b. Multivoting: Each member chooses two or three of the ideas listed on flip chart sheets; ideas with most total votes receive priority attention.
        c. Cause-and-effect diagram (fishbone): schematic representation of all things (cause) that have an impact on outcome (effect)
        d. Flow chart: step-by-step pictorial presentation of the flow of a process/function
        e. Run chart: depicts data that represent time and performance trends on an X and a Y axis
        f. Control chart: run chart that is statistically controlled for upper and lower limits of normal variation set by determining the average and controlled with 2 to 3 standard deviations above and below the mean
        g. Histogram: vertical bar graph depicting variation of data by time and frequency
        h. Pareto chart: histogram arranged in descending order from left to right to depict the areas in need of priority for process improvement
D. Understanding variation
    1. The performance of all processes involves variation.
    2. Control charts depict variation.
    3. Common-cause variation is normal and is the result of fluctuations that occur in everything from nature to organizational processes.
    4. Common-cause variation needs no "fixing."
    5. Special-cause variation is out of the ordinary and requires investigation.
    6. Variation is essential to understand so time and money are not spent on "fixing" common cause variation.

E. Benchmarking
   1. Internal: departments of same organization compare their performance with each other for the same process
   2. External:
      a. Compare organization's performance with the best in the field in an effort to emulate their performance
      b. Compare organization's performance with the reference data bases available
F. Process improvement systems
   1. PDCA: plan, do, check, act
   2. FOCUS: find, organize, clarify, understand, and select
   3. Ten-step model:
      a. assign responsibility;
      b. delineate scope of care;
      c. identify important aspect of care;
      d. determine indicators;
      e. establish a means to trigger evaluation;
      f. collect data;
      g. evaluate;
      h. take action to improve;
      i. assess effectiveness of action;
      j. communicate results
   4. FADE: focus, analyze, develop, execute
G. Barriers to successful QI activities
   1. Leadership not committed
   2. Lack of support from management information services
   3. Organizational unreadiness; too many competing factors at once; QI not a priority
H. Successful QI
   1. Leadership sets the tone and believes in the value of QI.
   2. Successful QI has been introduced appropriately to all staff.
   3. Staff from the entire organization is involved.
   4. Successful QI results in a cultural change that focuses on:
      a. Doing the right thing well
      b. Meeting customers' needs
      c. Constantly striving for improvement in processes
      d. Confirming that improvements hold up over time
      e. Changing the role of the supervisor to the role of a mentor and coach

STUDY QUESTIONS AND EXERCISES

1. List four concepts/key points of quality improvement.
2. Identify two QI tools and two statistical tools.
3. Define benchmarking and how to approach it.

BIBLIOGRAPHY

Bohnet, N. 1994. Continuous quality improvement. In *Handbook of home health care administration,* ed. M. Harris. Gaithersburg, Md.: Aspen Publishers, Inc.

Bohnet, N., et al. 1993. Continuous quality improvement: improving quality in your home care organization. *Journal of Nursing Administration* 23:42-48.

Joint Commission on Accreditation of Healthcare Organizations. 1991. *An introduction to quality improvement in health care.* Oakbrook Terrace, Illinois.

Joint Commission on Accreditation of Healthcare Organizations. 1994. *Framework for improving performance.* Oakbrook Terrace, Ill.

Joint Commission on Accreditation of Healthcare Organizations. 1993. *Quality improvement in home care.* Oakbrook Terrace, Ill.

Juran, J. 1988. *Juran on planning for quality.* New York: McGraw-Hill Publishing Co.

Scholtes, P. 1988. *The team handbook.* Madison, Wisc.: Joiner Associates.

Walton, M. 1986. *The Deming management method.* New York: Putnam Publishing Group.

52

Home Care Standards: Joint Commission on Accreditation of Healthcare Organizations

Maryanne L. Popovich

A. History of the Joint Commission on Accreditation of Healthcare Organizations (Joint Commission)
   1. Founded in 1951 as the Joint Commission on Accreditation of Hospitals.
   2. Original members
      a. American College of Physicians
      b. American Medical Association
      c. Canadian Medical Association
      d. American Hospital Association
      e. American College of Surgeons
   3. Changes
      a. 1959: Canadian Medical Association withdrew
      b. 1979: American Dental Association added as corporate member
      c. 1987: name changed to Joint Commission on Accreditation of Healthcare Organizations
   4. Governed by Board of Commissioners
      a. Some appointed by member organizations
      b. Public members also appointed
   5. Mission: enhances quality of health care provided to the public by
      a. Establishing contemporary standards
      b. Evaluating health care organizations
      c. Rendering accreditation decisions
      d. Providing educational and consultative support to health care organizations
   6. Nation's largest voluntary, private, not-for-profit, independent accrediting organization with approximately 10,000 health care organizations currently accredited

7. Accreditation services/programs
    a. Hospitals
    b. Ambulatory care
    c. Long-term care facilities
    d. Mental health
    e. Home care organizations
    f. Networks
    g. Laboratories
B. Standards
    1. Ongoing, dynamic process incorporates experience and perspective of health care professionals, other individuals, and organizations throughout the country
    2. Focus on essential elements of providing quality health care; nationally recognized as contributing to improving care delivered to patients in the United States
    3. Development process
        a. Need identified to address a particular issue or dimension of care in the delivery of services
        b. Brought to the Joint Commission by multiple and varied sources, e.g., lay groups, government agencies, accredited organizations, Joint Commission surveyors
        c. Task force and experts may be convened
        d. Professional and Technical Advisory Committee (PTAC) specific to program involved: reviews
        e. Standards and Survey Procedure Committee (S-SP) of Board of Commissioners: reviews
        f. Draft standards extensively reviewed by thousands of individuals and organizations: "field review"
        g. Based on field review and sometimes pilot tests, draft standards again reviewed by PTAC and S-SP.
C. Home care program
    1. Initiated in 1988
    2. Developed in response to:
        a. Rapidly growing segment of health care delivery system
        b. Public policy concerns regarding potential for poor quality and high risk in delivery of home care services
        c. Four standards manuals published in 1988, 1991, 1993, and 1995
D. Eligibility for accreditation for home care
    1. One or more of the following services provided either directly or through contractual agreement

a. Home health services: provided by health professionals, e.g., nursing, physical therapy, speech-language pathology, social work, dental, medical, nutrition counseling
b. Personal care: assistance in personal care, e.g., activities of daily living: bathing, feeding, or administration of treatments
c. Support services: maintenance and management of household routines
d. Pharmaceutical services
   (1) Procure, prepare, preserve, compound, dispense, and/or distribute pharmaceutical products
   (2) Monitor patient's clinical status
e. Equipment management
   (1) Select, deliver, set up, and maintain equipment used for health care purposes
   (2) Educate patient and/or caretaker on proper usage
f. Clinical respiratory services: ongoing clinical services by health care professionals, e.g., chest assessment, monitoring of vital signs, pulmonary function testing, chest physical therapy
g. Hospice services
   (1) Provided/coordinated through an interdisciplinary team at a frequency appropriate to meet the needs of patients who have a limited life span and are diagnosed with a terminal illness
   (2) Continuum of interdisciplinary team services across all settings
   (3) Availability of 24-hour access to care
   (4) Utilization of volunteers and bereavement care
   (5) Palliative management of pain/other symptoms
   (6) Meeting psychosocial/spiritual needs of patient/family/caregivers
2. Eligible services provided in an individual's place of residence
3. Eligible services provided on an intermittent or hourly basis
4. Organization applying for accreditation is formally organized, has legal entity, and has been servicing patients for at least 4 months
5. At least one active patient at time of survey
E. Survey process
   1. Purpose
      a. Assess the extent of an organization's compliance with applicable standards
      b. Evaluate processes and systems that contribute to patient care
   2. Methods used to achieve purpose

a. Home visits
b. Direct observation of staff performing care/service or techniques/procedures applicable to care/service delivery, e.g., cleaning of equipment, drug compounding by pharmacist, bathing by home health aide
c. Interviews (direct or by telephone)
   (1) Patients and/or caregivers
   (2) Staff: administrative as well as direct service
   (3) Members of governing body/leadership
   (4) Referral sources (including physicians)
d. Documentation review
   (1) Administrative and clinical policies and procedures
   (2) Patient records
   (3) Personnel records (including verification of orientation, training, ongoing education)
   (4) Equipment maintenance logs, recalls, etc., when applicable
e. Review of system for improving organizational performance
f. Inspections of appropriate physical facilities when applicable
   (1) Equipment warehouse or storage facility
   (2) Pharmacy
g. Vehicle inspections, when applicable (when used for delivery of products, equipment)

F. Surveyors
  1. Conduct on-site survey review
  2. Qualifications
     a. Registered nurse, registered pharmacist, respiratory care practitioner
     b. Minimum educational requirements
     c. Knowledgeable and experienced home care professionals

G. Awarding of accreditation decision
  1. On-site survey review evaluates compliance with each applicable standard using a 5-point scoring scale
  2. Verbal summation of findings presented to organization at conclusion of on-site survey by surveyor
  3. Surveyor forwards written report of findings to Joint Commission's central office
  4. Surveyor's findings analyzed by central office staff for consistency with published interpretations of intent and accuracy
  5. Analyzed report reviewed by central office program staff
  6. Accreditation committee of the Board of Commissioners awards decision based on published decision rules

H. Categories of accreditation
   1. Accreditation with commendation
   2. Accreditation
   3. Conditional accreditation
   4. Not accredited
   5. Provisional accreditation
I. Benefits of accreditation
   1. Recognition by external organization, e.g., third-party payers, case managers, government
   2. Satisfaction of state licensure requirements, in some states
   3. Visible demonstration of the organization's commitment to excellence
   4. Enhancement of community confidence in home care
   5. Enhancement of employee morale and retention through achievement of an organizationwide goal of excellence
   6. Evaluation of organization's processes and systems
   7. Consultation and education

STUDY QUESTIONS AND EXERCISES

1. Discuss the process for standard development at the Joint Commission.
2. Detail at least five methods utilized by home care surveyors to evaluate a home care organization's compliance with standards during on-site survey process.
3. Explain categories of accreditation provided by the Joint Commission.

BIBLIOGRAPHY

Joint Commission on Accreditation of Healthcare Organizations. 1990. *Committed to quality: An introduction to the Joint Commission on Accreditation of Healthcare Organizations.* Oakbrook Terrace, Ill.

Joint Commission on Accreditation of Healthcare Organizations. 1994. *The 1995 Joint Commission Accreditation Manual for Home Care.* Oakbrook Terrace, Ill.

Index

A

Abuse, 8, 16
  of child, 8
  of elderly, 8
  factors contributing to, 8
  signs and symptoms of, 8
  types of, 8
Acebutolol, for angina pectoris, 92
Acetohexamide, for diabetes mellitus, 266
Acetylcysteine, 159
Acquired immunodeficiency syndrome (AIDS), 318–329
  AIDS dementia complex, 324–325
    communicating with patient with, 324–325
    definition of, 324
    home management of, 324
    prevalence of, 324
  case definition for, 318, 319, 321
  CD4+ lymphocyte count and, 319–320
  classification for infection in children, 320
  clinical management of patient with, 325–329
  common symptoms and their etiologies in, 323–324
  continuum of disability in, 321–323
    acutely ill, 322
    apparently well, 322
    chronically ill, 322–323
    terminally ill, 323
  establishment of home and hospice care for, 319
  experimental therapies for, 325
  first reported cases of, 318
  goals of therapy for, 325
  hepatitis C and, 319
  history of, 318–321
  incidence of, 319, 320
  incubation period for, 319
  indicator conditions for, 321
  modes of transmission of, 318
  Pneumocystis carinii pneumonia and, 162, 321, 328
  tuberculosis and, 178, 321, 328
  viral cause of, 319
Activity intolerance, 157–158
Acyclovir, for herpes simplex virus, 327
Administrative law, 400, 406–407
Admission criteria, 407
Adolescents, cystic fibrosis in, 197
Advance medical directives, 13, 405
Advocacy, 13–17
  conflicts related to, 15–16

for consumer protection, 16
definitions related to, 13
models for, 13–14
nurse actions for, 15
process of, 14–15
situations for, 16–17
Affective blunting, 253
Affective disorders, 253–255
   bipolar disorder, 253–254
   depression, 254–255
Age effects. *See also* Elderly persons
   on amyotrophic lateral sclerosis, 243
   on cerebrovascular accident, 209
   on coronary artery disease, 88
   on hypertension, 106
   on malnutrition, 357–359
   on multiple sclerosis, 221
   on Parkinson's disease, 234
   on pneumonia, 161
β-Agonists
   for chronic obstructive pulmonary disease, 150, 158
   side effects of, 158
Air pollution, 155
Albumin, 360
Albuterol, 158
   for cystic fibrosis, 195
Alcohol use and abuse
   hypertension and, 106, 107
   pneumonia and, 161
   during pregnancy, 340
   recommended limit on intake, 361
   symptoms of, 255
   treatment of, 255
Alcoholics Anonymous, 255
Aldactone. *See* Spironolactone
Aldomet. *See* Methyldopa
Aldosterone, 105
Alzheimer's disease, 247–250
   aging and, 247
   brain pathology in, 247
   diagnosis of, 247
   family education to maximize ability to care for patient with, 249–250
   goals of treatment for, 248–249
   interventions for, 249
   pathophysiology of, 247
   prevalence of, 247
   symptoms of, 248
   tacrine for, 249
   theories on cause of, 248
Ambulation, progressive, 69
Ambulation aids, 33, 70–71
   care planning for patients with, 71
   features and uses of, 70
   safety and troubleshooting for, 71
American Cancer Society, 317, 335
American Heart Association, 144
American Hospital Association's *Patient's Bill of Rights*, 20
American Journal of Public Health, 4
American Lung Association, 153
American Medical Association
   Committee on Allied Health Education and Accreditation, 31, 39
   Council on Medical Education, 31
American Nurses' Association, 20
   Code for Nurses with Interpretive Statements, 392
   Do Not Resuscitate Decisions, 392
   Foregoing Artificial Nutrition and Hydration, 392
   Nursing's Agenda for Health Care Reform, 5
   Standards of Community Health Nursing Practice, 5, 392
   Standards of Home Health Nursing Practice, 5, 392
   Statement on the Scope of Home Health Nursing Practice, 5–6, 20
American Occupational Therapy Association, 39
American Physical Therapy Association, 31, 32

American Public Health Association, 392
American Red Cross, 4
American Speech, Language and Hearing Association, 45
Amikacin
  adverse effects of, 183
  for *Pseudomonas* infection, 194
  for tuberculosis, 183
Amiloride, aerosolized, for cystic fibrosis, 195
Aminoglycosides, for *Pseudomonas* infection, 194
Aminosalicylic acid
  adverse effects of, 182
  for tuberculosis, 182
Amitriptyline hydrochloride
  for amyotrophic lateral sclerosis, 246
  for depression, 254
Amphotericin-B
  for candidiasis, 326
  for cryptococcosis, 326
Amyotrophic lateral sclerosis, 243–246
  cause of, 243
  causes of death in, 244
  clinical features of, 243–244
  definition of, 243
  demographics of, 243
  diagnostic studies in, 244
  drug therapy for, 245–246
  incidence of, 243
  nursing interventions for, 244–245
    physical mobility, 244
    skin integrity, 245
    swallowing, 245
    verbal communication, 245
  occupational therapy for, 245
  pathophysiology of, 243
  physical therapy for, 245
  social work services for, 245
  speech-language pathology services for, 245
  treatment of, 244

Angina pectoris, 89–93
  assessment of, 90
  diagnosis of, 90
  diet and, 93
  drug therapy for, 91–93
    antiplatelet agents, 92–93
    β-blockers, 92
    calcium-channel blockers, 91–92
    nitrates, 91
  intractable, 89
  nonpharmacologic treatment of, 90–91
  pathophysiology of, 89
  patient teaching about, 93
  precipitants of, 89
  Prinzmetal's, 89
  procedures for relief of, 93
  signs and symptoms of, 89
  stable, 89
  unstable, 89
Angiocath, 370–371
Angioplasty. *See* Percutaneous transluminal coronary angioplasty
Angiotensin, 105
Angiotensin-converting enzyme inhibitors
  for congestive heart failure, 102, 103
  for hypertension, 108
  side effects of, 108
Anistreplase, 97
Anorexia, 367
Anoxia, 209
Anthropometric measurements, 359–360
Antiarrhythmic drugs, 119
  affecting pacemaker function, 124
Antibiotics
  antipseudomonal, 193–194
  antistaphylococcal, 192–193
  for bacterial pneumonia, 163–164

for Duchenne muscular dystrophy, 231
parenteral, 381
Anticholinergic agents, 150
for amyotrophic lateral sclerosis, 246
for Parkinson's disease, 238
side effects of, 238
Anticoagulation
for cerebrovascular accident, 210
for pulmonary embolus, 171
for valvular heart disease, 119
Anticonvulsants, 215–216
blood levels of, 217
drug interactions with, 217
patient teaching about, 216–217
side effects of, 217
Antidepressants, 254
Antihistamines
for Parkinson's disease, 237
side effects of, 237
Antiplatelet agents
for angina pectoris, 92–93
for cerebrovascular accident, 211
Antipsychotic drugs, 253
Aortic regurgitation, 118
Aortic stenosis, 118
Apathy, 253
Aphasia, 49–50, 210
Apnea monitors, 76–79, 350–351. *See also* Respiratory care equipment
Apnea of prematurity, 350–351
definition of, 350
drug therapy for, 351
patient teaching about, 350–351
response to alarms, 351
Appetite stimulants, 329
Apraxia, 49
Apresoline. *See* Hydralazine
Arrhythmias
drug therapy for, 119

pacemakers for, 122
valvular heart disease and, 119
Arrow Blue Flextip catheter, 375
Artane. *See* Anticholinergic agents
Arterial access, 373–374
Arthritis, 284–288
crystal-induced, 284
definition of, 284
demographics of, 285
diagnosis of, 285
drug therapy for, 286
goals of, 286
patient teaching about, 286
side effects of, 286
etiology of, 285
home management of patient with, 287–288
goals, 287
nursing documentation, 287–288
psychosocial issues, 287
record keeping, 287
safety issues, 287
incidence of, 285
infectious, 284
osteoarthritis, 284
pathophysiology of, 284–285
rheumatoid, 284
treatment of, 285–286
Articulation
definition of, 48
disorders of, 49
Artificial larynx, 45, 51
Ascites, 112
Aspiration pneumonia, 162
pulmonary edema and, 166
Aspirin
for angina pectoris, 92–93
for anticoagulation, 119
for arthritis, 286
for cerebrovascular accident, 211
after percutaneous transluminal coronary angioplasty, 131

to prevent myocardial infarction, 98
Assault, 403
Asthma, 149–153, 155. *See also* Chronic obstructive pulmonary disease
  assessment of patient with, 150
  diagnostic tests for, 150
  etiology of, 149
  management of, 150–152
    breathing exercises and physical conditioning, 151–152
    coping measures, 152
    home oxygen therapy, 151
    improving gas exchange, 150–151
    nutritional intake, 151
    preventing bronchopulmonary infections, 151
    removing bronchial secretions, 151
    self-care activities, 152
  pathogenesis of, 149
  patient education about, 152–153
  signs and symptoms of, 149
  structural changes in, 149
Atenolol
  for angina pectoris, 92
  for hypertension, 107
Atherectomy, 132
Atherosclerosis, 87
  hypertension and, 106
Atovaquone, for *Pneumocystis carinii* pneumonia, 328
Atrial fibrillation
  pacemaker for, 122
  valvular heart disease and, 119
Atropine, for cryptosporidiosis, 326
Auditory training, 46
Aural rehabilitation, 45
Autonomy of patient, 16, 392–393, 404, 406
Azathioprine, after cardiac transplantation, 135
Azithromycin, for *Mycobacterium avium* complex, 327

Azlocillin (Azlin), for *Pseudomonas* infection, 193
AZT. *See* Zidovudine

B

Baccalaureate programs, 6
Bacille Calmette-Guérin (BCG) vaccine, 186
Baclofen, for amyotrophic lateral sclerosis, 246
Bactrim. *See* Trimethoprim-sulfamethoxazole
Barrel chest, 155
Basal energy expenditure, 361
Bathing, 63
  of newborn, 348–349
Bathroom aids, 74–75
  care planning for patients with, 74
  features and uses of, 74
  infection control and, 74
  reimbursement for, 74–75
  safety and troubleshooting for, 74
Battery, 403–404
Becker's muscular dystrophy, 228
Beclomethasone, for chronic obstructive pulmonary disease, 159
Bed boards, 72
Bed rest, pneumonia and, 162
Bedrails, 72, 73
Beds
  hospital, 71–74
  rocking, 203
Behavior
  after cerebrovascular accident, 210
  measuring changes in, 25
Benadryl. *See* Diphenhydramine hydrochloride
Benchmarking, 411
  external, 411
  internal, 411

Beneficence, 16, 393
Beta-mimetics
　for preterm labor, 341–342
　side effects of, 341
Betaxolol, for angina pectoris, 92
Biaxin. *See* Clarithromycin
Biliary disease, in cystic fibrosis, 191
Biotherapy for cancer, 308–309
　agents used for, 308
　classifications of, 308
　nursing care for patient receiving, 309
　patient education about, 309
　side effects of, 308–309
Bipolar disorder, 253–254
　age at onset of, 253
　definition of, 253
　incidence of, 253
　symptoms of, 253
　treatment of, 253–254
Birth control pills, 106
α-Blockers, for hypertension, 107
β-Blockers
　affecting pacemaker function, 124
　for angina pectoris, 92
　for arrhythmias, 119
　contraindications to, 92
　for hypertension, 107
　indications for, 92
　mechanism of action of, 92
　after myocardial infarction, 98
　side effects of, 92, 107
　withdrawal of, 92
Blood component therapy, 369, 384–385
　administration of, 312–313, 385
　advantages of, 311
　for cancer patient, 311–313
　disadvantages of, 311
　evaluation and monitoring of, 385
　guidelines for, 385
　nursing responsibilities for, 312–313
　patient assessment for, 312, 384–385

　patient selection for, 311–312
　treating reactions to, 313, 385
Blood glucose monitoring, 265–267
　advantages of, 265–266
　disadvantages of, 266
　recommendations for, 265
Blood glucose monitoring machines, 79–80
　care planning for patients with, 79
　documenting use of, 80
　features and uses of, 79
　infection control and, 79
　reimbursement for, 80
　safety considerations for, 79
"Blue bloater," 150
Bluestone, E.M., 4
Body composition, 357
Body mass index, 360
Bone marrow suppression, 307
Bone marrow transplantation, 309–311
　complications of, 310
　indications for, 309
　patient preparation for, 310
　patient selection for, 309
　patient/family education about, 311
　postdischarge care after, 310–311
　treatment process for, 309–310
　types of, 309
　　allogeneic, 309
　　autologous, 309
　　syngeneic, 309
Bone mass, 357
Borg perceived exertion scale, 141
Boston Dispensary home care program, 3
Bottle feeding, 346, 348–350
Bowel elimination
　of newborn, 347, 349
　of Parkinson's disease patient, 239
　during pregnancy, 340
Bradycardia-tachycardia syndrome, 122

Bradykinesia, 233, 235
Brainstorming, 410
Breach of duty, 401
  proximate cause and, 401
Breast cancer screening, 303–304
Breast-feeding, 346, 348, 350
Breasts
  engorgement of, 346
  postpartum care of, 346
  self-examination of, 303
Breathing
  exercises for, 151–152
  teaching energy-conserving pattern of, 157
Brethine. *See* Terbutaline
Bronchitis, chronic, 149–153, 155. *See also* Chronic obstructive pulmonary disease
  assessment of patient with, 150
  diagnostic tests for, 150
  etiology of, 149
  management of, 150–152
    breathing exercises and physical conditioning, 151–152
    coping measures, 152
    home oxygen therapy, 151
    improving gas exchange, 150–151
    nutritional intake, 151
    preventing bronchopulmonary infections, 151
    removing bronchial secretions, 151
    self-care activities, 152
  pathogenesis of, 149–150
  patient education about, 152–153
  signs and symptoms of, 149–150
  structural changes in, 149
Bronchodilators
  for chronic obstructive pulmonary disease, 150, 158
  for cystic fibrosis, 195
Broviac catheter, 371–372
Bumetanide (Bumex), for pulmonary edema, 169

C

Caffeine
  for apnea of prematurity, 351
  intake during pregnancy, 340
Calan. *See* Verapamil
Calcium, 363
Calcium-channel blockers
  affecting pacemaker function, 124
  for angina pectoris, 91–92
  contraindications to, 92
  for hypertension, 107
  after percutaneous transluminal coronary angioplasty, 131
  side effects of, 92, 107
Calorie intake, 361
Cancer, 302–317
  age distribution of, 302
  biotherapy for, 308–309
    agents used for, 308
    classifications of, 308
    nursing care for patient receiving, 309
    side effects of, 308–309
  bone marrow transplantation for, 309–311
    complications of, 310
    indications for, 309
    patient preparation for, 310
    patient selection for, 309
    patient/family education about, 311
    postdischarge care after, 310–311
    treatment process for, 309–310
    types of, 309
  causes of, 302
  chemotherapy for, 307–308
    nursing care for patient undergoing, 308
    routes of administration for, 307
    side effects of, 307–308
  definition of, 302
  factors affecting mortality from, 302

gender differences in types of, 302
goals of treatment for, 304
home care and personal needs of
    patient with, 315
incidence of, 302
nursing role in home care of patient
    with, 316–317
  goals, 316
  interventions, 316
  resources, 317
patient education and support for,
    315–316
prevention of, 302–304
  primary, 302–303
  secondary, 303–304
psychologic issues and, 315–316
radiation therapy for, 305–307
  nursing care for patient
    undergoing, 306–307
  prevalence of use of, 305
  side effects of, 306
  types of radiation for, 305–306
resource management for patient
    with, 315
risk factors for, 302
  diet and obesity, 303
  estrogen, 303
  occupational hazards, 303
  smoking, 303
  sun exposure, 303
screening for, 303–304
  breast cancer, 303–304
  cervical cancer, 304
  colorectal cancer, 304
  prostate cancer, 304
supportive therapies for, 311–315
  blood product home transfusion,
    311–313
  pain management, 313–314
  physical rehabilitation, 314–315
  total peripheral nutrition, 314
surgical treatment of, 304–305
  nursing care for patient
    undergoing, 305

side effects/complications of, 305
survival from, 302
Candidiasis
  in AIDS, 321, 325–326
  oral, 159
  treatment of, 326
Canes, 70–71
  care planning for patients with, 71
  documentation of use of, 71
  features and uses of, 70
  infection control and, 71
  reimbursement for, 71
  safety and troubleshooting for, 71
Capreomycin
  adverse effects of, 182
  for tuberculosis, 182
Captopril (Capoten)
  for hypertension, 108
  for pulmonary edema, 168
Carbamazepine, for seizures, 216
Carbidopa/levodopa. *See*
    Dopaminergic drugs
Carbohydrate intake, 361, 362
Cardene. *See* Nicardipine
Cardiac output, of patient with
    hypothyroidism, 282
Cardiac rehabilitation, 138–144
  benefits of, 138
  candidates for, 139
  contraindications to, 139
  exercise prescription for, 141–143
  goals of, 138
  indications for, 138–139
  phases of, 139–141
    community-based, 140
    home-based, 140–141
    immediate postdischarge, 140
    inpatient, 139–140
Cardiac support groups, 144
Cardiac transplantation, 133–136
  assessment and interventions after,
    134–135
  chest pain after, 134
  complications of, 133–134

Index   427

contraindications to, 133
heterotopic, 133
immunosuppression after, 135
indications for, 133
infection after, 134, 136
orthotopic, 133
patient teaching about, 135–136
procedures for, 133
rejection of, 134–135
Cardiac trauma, 116
Cardiac workload reduction, 168–169
Cardiomyopathy, 109–114
  congestive or dilated
    pathophysiology of, 109
    signs and symptoms of, 110
    treatment of, 111
  diagnosis of, 110
  home care assessment and monitoring of, 111–113
  hypertrophic
    pathophysiology of, 109
    signs and symptoms of, 110
    treatment of, 111
  patient teaching about, 113–114
  restrictive
    pathophysiology of, 109–110
    signs and symptoms of, 110
    treatment of, 111
  valvular heart disease and, 116
Cardiovascular disease, 85–144
  cardiac rehabilitation and support, 138–144
  cardiac transplantation, 133–136
  cardiomyopathy, 109–114
  cerebrovascular accident and, 209
  congestive heart failure, 101–103
  coronary artery disease/angina pectoris, 87–93
  hypertension, 105–108
  invasive interventions, 127–132
    coronary artery bypass grafting, 127–130
    new procedures, 132

percutaneous transluminal coronary angioplasty, 130–131
myocardial infarction, 95–99
pacemakers, 122–126
pulmonary edema and, 166
valvular heart disease, 116–120
Cardizem. *See* Diltiazem hydrochloride
Cardura. *See* Doxazosin mesylate
Carotid endarterectomy, 211
Carotid sinus syndrome, 122
Case management, 7–9
Catapres. *See* Clonidine hydrochloride
Cause-and-effect diagram, 410
CD4+ cell count, 319–320
Cefaclor (Ceclor), for staphylococcal infection, 193
Cefpodoxime proxetil, for staphylococcal infection, 193
Cefprozil (Cefzil), for staphylococcal infection, 193
Ceftazidime, for *Pseudomonas* infection, 194
Centers for Disease Control, 10
Cephalexin, for staphylococcal infection, 193
Cerebral palsy, 40
Cerebrovascular accident, 209–212
  clinical manifestations of, 209–210
  definition of, 209
  diagnostic tests for, 210
  etiology of, 209
  hypertension and, 105, 106
  medical management of, 210–211
  nursing management of, 211
    altered family processes, 211
    altered thought processes, 211
    impaired communication, 211
    impaired mobility/self-care deficit, 211
    sensory perceptual alteration, 211
  pathophysiology of, 209
  risk factors for, 209
Certification, 5–6

Cervical cancer screening, 304
Cervix
  examining during pregnancy, 340
  incompetent, 342
Chatterton's model, 22
Chemotherapy, 307–308
  accidental exposure to, 384
  classification of agents for, 383
  for Kaposi's sarcoma, 327
  nadir for, 384
  nursing care for patient
    undergoing, 308
  parenteral, 369, 383–384
    assessment for, 383
    evaluation and monitoring of, 384
    plan/intervention for, 383–384
  patient education about, 308
  routes of administration for, 307
  side effects of, 307–308, 383
  vesicant and nonvesicant agents
    for, 383
Chest circumference of newborn, 346
Chest pain
  of angina pectoris, 89–93
  after cardiac transplantation, 134
  of myocardial infarction, 96
  pleuritic, 175
Chest physical therapy, 157, 204
Children
  abuse of, 8
  classification of HIV infection in, 320
  home health aide services for, 64
  language delay in, 50
  learning in, 23–24
  newborn care, 346–353. *See also* Newborn
  occupational therapy services for, 40
  school lunch program for, 364
  seizures in, 214
Chlorpropamide
  for diabetes mellitus, 266
  hypoglycemia induced by, 265
Cholesterol intake, 88, 93, 361

Chronic illness, 20
Chronic obstructive pulmonary
  disease, 155–159. *See also*
  Asthma; Bronchitis;
  Emphysema
  complications of, 156
    acute respiratory failure, 156
    cor pulmonale, 156
    hypercapnia, 156
    hypoxemia, 156
    peptic ulcer disease, 156
    pneumonia, 156
  definition of, 155
  drug therapy for, 158–159
    anti-inflammatory agents, 158–159
    bronchodilators, 158
    cromolyn sodium, 159
    mucolytics, 159
  goals of care for patient with, 156
  incidence of, 155
  mechanical ventilation at home for, 200
  nursing assessment of patient with, 156–157
  nursing interventions for patient with, 157–158
    activity intolerance, 157–158
    airway clearance, 157
    breathing pattern, 157
    gas exchange, 150–151, 157
    health maintenance, 158
  risk factors for, 155
Ciprofloxacin (Cipro)
  adverse effects of, 183
  for *Pseudomonas* infection, 194
  for tuberculosis, 183
Circumcision, 349
Clarithromycin, for *Mycobacterium avium* complex, 327
Clindamycin
  for *Pneumocystis carinii* pneumonia, 328
  for toxoplasmosis, 328

Clofazimine
  adverse effects of, 183
  for *Mycobacterium avium* complex, 327
  for tuberculosis, 183
Clonazepam
  for HIV encephalopathy, 327
  for seizures, 216
Clonidine hydrochloride
  for amyotrophic lateral sclerosis, 246
  for hypertension, 107
Clotrimazole, for candidiasis, 326
Cloxacillin (Cloxapen), for staphylococcal infection, 192
Cluttering, 51
Coccidioidomycosis, in AIDS, 321
Codeine, 313
Codes of ethics, 392. *See also* Ethical issues
Cogentin. *See* Anticholinergic agents
Cognex. *See* Tacrine
Cognitive disorganization, 51–52
Cognitive impairment
  in AIDS, 324
  Alzheimer's disease, 247–250
  malnutrition and, 358
  occupational therapy for, 42
  in Parkinson's disease, 236–237
Cognitive language functions, 48
Cognitive retraining, 211
Colon conduit, 297
Colony-stimulating factors, 308
  for Kaposi's sarcoma, 327
Colorectal cancer screening, 304
Colostomy. *See also* Fecal diversion
  constipation in patient with, 291
  definition of, 289
  irrigating stoma for, 290–291
    contraindications to, 290
    good candidates for, 290
    problems with, 290–291
    procedure for, 290
    purpose of, 290
  reasons for, 289

  stoma sites for, 289
  types of stomas for, 289–290
    double-barrel colostomy stoma, 289
    end colostomy stoma, 289
    loop colostomy stoma, 290
Commodes, 74–75
  care planning for patients with, 74
  features and uses of, 74
  infection control and, 74
  reimbursement for, 74–75
  safety and troubleshooting for, 74
Communication
  after cerebrovascular accident, 211
  with mechanically ventilated patient, 205
  with patient with AIDS dementia complex, 324–325
  with patient with amyotrophic lateral sclerosis, 245
  with patient with Parkinson's disease, 240
  with terminally ill patient, 332–333
Communication devices, 45
  for aphasia, 50
  for apraxia, 49
  for dysarthria, 49
Community Health Services Facility Grant, 5
Compassionate Friends, 335
Confidentiality, 392, 406
  breach of, 404, 406
Congestive heart failure, 101–103
  definition of, 101
  diagnosis of, 102
  etiology of, 101
  left-sided, 101–102
  medical management of, 102
  nursing management of, 102–103
  pathophysiology of, 101
  patient teaching about, 103
  right-sided, 102
  signs and symptoms of, 101–102
  valvular heart disease and, 118

Constipation
  narcotic-induced, 314
  in patient on enteral nutrition, 377
  in patient with colostomy, 291
  during pregnancy, 340
Constitutional law, 399
Consumer philosophy, 20–21
Consumer protection, 16
Continuity of care, 9
Contraception, 346
Contracts, 400
Control chart, 410
Cool-down period, 143
Coordination of care, 9
  assignment of appropriate care
    providers, 408
  durable medical equipment, 66–83
  role of homemaker/home health
    aide, 57–64
  role of occupational therapy, 39–43
  role of physical therapy, 31–38
  role of social work, 54–55
  role of speech-language pathology
    services, 45–53
Cor pulmonale, 156
  definition of, 156
  pulmonary embolus and, 171
  symptoms of, 156
Corgard. *See* Nadolol
Coronary artery bypass grafting, 93,
    98, 127–130
  exercise after, 129–130
  home assessment and intervention
    after, 127–129
  pain management after, 128
  patient teaching about, 129–130
  postpericardiotomy syndrome
    after, 130
  procedure for, 127
  purpose of, 127
Coronary artery disease, 87–93
  angina pectoris and, 89–93

complications of, 87
incidence of, 87
myocardial infarction and, 95
New York Heart Association
  functional classification of, 88
pathophysiology of, 87
pulmonary edema and, 166
risk factors for, 87–88
Coronary stents, 132
Corticosteroids, 106
  affecting pacemaker function, 124
  avoiding abrupt withdrawal of, 159
  for cerebrovascular accident, 210
  for chronic obstructive pulmonary
    disease, 158–159
  for hyperthyroidism, 275
  inhaled, 159
  oral, 159
  for *Pneumocystis carinii* pneumonia,
    328
  side effects of, 159
Cost containment, 20
Cough reflex, 161
Coughing technique, 157, 164
Coumadin. *See* Sodium warfarin
Cradle cap, 348
Cretinism, 278
Criminal law, 400, 407
Cromolyn sodium, for asthma, 159
Crutches, 70–71
  care planning for patients with, 71
  documentation of use of, 71
  features and uses of, 70
  infection control and, 71
  reimbursement for, 71
  safety and troubleshooting for, 71
Cryptococcosis
  in AIDS, 321, 326
  treatment of, 326
Cryptosporidiosis
  in AIDS, 321, 326
  treatment of, 326

Crystal-induced arthritis. *See also*
  Arthritis
  definition of, 284
  etiology of, 285
  pathophysiology of, 285
Cushing's syndrome, 106
Cyanosis, 112
Cycloserine
  adverse effects of, 182
  for tuberculosis, 182–183
Cyclosporine, after cardiac
    transplantation, 135
Cystic fibrosis, 188–198
  in adolescents, 197
  carriers of, 188, 189
  clinical manifestations of,
      190–191
    gastrointestinal tract, 191
    liver, 191
    pancreas, 190
    reproductive system, 191
    respiratory system, 190–191
  clinical presentation of, 190
  complications of, 188
  definition of, 188
  demographics of, 189
  diagnosis of, 189–190
  drug therapy for, 191–195
    antibiotics, 192–194
    bronchodilators, 195
    inhalation therapy, 194–195
    pancreatic enzymes, 191–192
    prednisone, 195
    vitamins, 192
  gene therapy for, 188
  incidence of, 189
  life expectancy and, 188, 189
  nutrition for patient with, 195–196
  pathophysiology of, 188–189
  patient education about, 197–198
  psychosocial interventions for, 188,
      196–197
  pulmonary therapy for, 196
  sweat test for, 190
Cytomegalovirus
  in AIDS, 321, 326
  treatment of, 326

D

Damages, 402. *See also* Legal issues
  compensatory, 402
  nominal, 402
  punitive, 402
Dapsone, for *Pneumocystis carinii*
    pneumonia, 328
Death and dying, 331–335. *See also*
    Terminally ill patient
Decubitus ulcer prevention, 80–81
Defamation, 404
Deinstitutionalization, 20
  of patients with mental illness, 252
Delusions, 253
Dementia, 51
  AIDS dementia complex, 324–325
  Alzheimer's disease, 247–250
  in Parkinson's disease, 236–237
deMusset's sign, 118
Depakene. *See* Valproate
Depression, 254–255
  in bipolar disorder, 253
  causes of, 254
  duration of, 254
  malnutrition and, 358
  medical conditions associated with,
      253
  in Parkinson's disease, 236
  suicide and, 253–254
  symptoms of, 253
  treatment of, 253
Developmental theory, 23–24
Dexamethasone, for cerebrovascular
    accident, 210

Diabeta. *See* Glyburide
Diabetes Control and Complications Trial, 265
Diabetes mellitus, 259–268
  cerebrovascular accident and, 209
  classification of, 259
  coronary artery disease and, 88
  definition of, 259
  drug therapy for, 263–266
    insulin, 263–264
    oral hypoglycemic agents, 263–266
  exercise for patients with, 262–263
  gestational, 260, 343–344
  hypertension and, 106
  incidence of, 260
  insulin-dependent (type I), 259
    age distribution of, 259
    pathophysiology of, 259
    symptoms of, 259
  non-insulin-dependent (type II), 259
    age distribution of, 259
    pathophysiology of, 261
    underdiagnosis of, 260
  nursing assessment of patient with, 265–268
    blood glucose monitoring, 265–267
    glycosylated hemoglobin, 267
    patient education, 267–268
    urine testing, 267
  nutritional management for, 261–262
    food exchange system, 262
  occupational therapy for patient with, 43
  secondary to other medical conditions, 260
  self-monitoring of blood glucose by patients with, 265–267
    advantages of, 265–266
    blood glucose monitoring machines for, 79–80
    disadvantages of, 266
    recommendations for, 265
Diabinese. *See* Chlorpropamide
Diagnosis-related groups (DRGs), 5, 20
Dialects, 47
Diaper changing, 349
Diaper rash, 349
Diarrhea
  in AIDS, 323
  in patient on enteral nutrition, 376–377
Diazepam, for amyotrophic lateral sclerosis, 245
Dicloxacillin, for staphylococcal infection, 192
Diet. *See also* Nutrition
  cancer and, 303
  carbohydrates in, 361, 362
  cholesterol in, 88, 93, 361
  criteria for adequate diet, 361
    food groups/food pyramid, 361
    recommended dietary allowances, 361
    United States dietary goals/guidelines, 361
  of cystic fibrosis patient, 195–196
  fat in, 88, 93, 361, 362
  fiber in, 361, 362
  foods causing ileostomy obstruction, 292
  hypertension and, 106, 107
  for patient with asthma/bronchitis, 151
  for patient with diabetes mellitus, 261–262, 344
  during pregnancy, 340
  protein in, 361, 362
  salt in, 361
  sodium-restricted, 102, 103, 168
  sources of minerals in, 363–364
  sources of vitamins in, 363
  vitamin K in, 172

Dietary history, 359
Dietary supplements, 196
Digoxin
　for arrhythmias, 119
　for congestive heart failure, 102
　toxicity of, 102
Dilantin. *See* Phenytoin
Dilaudid. *See* Hydromorphone
　　hydrochloride
Diltiazem hydrochloride
　for angina pectoris, 91–92
　for hypertension, 107
Diphenhydramine hydrochloride
　for Parkinson's disease, 237
　for transfusion reaction, 313
Dipyridamole
　for angina pectoris, 92–93
　for cerebrovascular accident, 211
Discharge criteria, 408
Discharge planning, 8, 46
Disclosure of patient information, 392,
　　404, 406
Disinfection. *See* Infection control
Disopyramide, 124
Diuretics
　for cerebrovascular accident, 210
　for congestive heart failure, 102–103
　for hypertension, 107
　for pulmonary edema, 169
　side effects of, 107
Do Not Resuscitate Decisions, 392
Dobutamine, for congestive heart
　　failure, 102, 103
Dopamine agonists
　for Parkinson's disease, 238
　side effects of, 238
Dopamine deficiency, 233. *See also*
　　Parkinson's disease
Dopaminergic drugs
　for Parkinson's disease, 238
　side effects of, 238
Doxazosin mesylate, for hypertension,
　　107

Doxil, for Kaposi's sarcoma, 327
Dressing, 63
Dressing changes, 63
Dressing supplies, 379
Dressler's syndrome, 97
Driving performance, of Parkinson's
　　disease patient, 237
Drop attack, 215
Drug therapy
　absorption in patient with
　　ileostomy, 292
　for amyotrophic lateral sclerosis,
　　245–246
　for angina pectoris, 91–93
　for apnea of prematurity, 351
　for arrhythmias, 119
　for arthritis, 286
　for asthma/bronchitis, 150
　for bacterial pneumonia, 163–164
　for bipolar disorder, 254
　for cancer, 307–308, 383–384
　for candidiasis, 326
　for chronic obstructive pulmonary
　　disease, 158–159
　for congestive heart failure, 102–103
　for cryptococcosis, 326
　for cryptosporidiosis, 326
　for cystic fibrosis, 191–195
　for cytomegalovirus, 326
　for depression, 254
　for diabetes mellitus, 263–265
　for herpes simplex virus, 327
　for herpes zoster virus, 327
　for HIV encephalopathy, 327
　for hypertension, 107–108
　for hyperthyroidism, 275
　for hypothyroidism, 281–282
　immunosuppressants, 135
　interaction with minerals, 363
　interaction with vitamins, 363
　for Kaposi's sarcoma, 327
　for *Mycobacterium avium* complex,
　　327

for myocardial infarction, 97–98
for Parkinson's disease, 237–238
after percutaneous transluminal coronary angioplasty, 131
pharmaceutical services for, 415
for *Pneumocystis carinii* pneumonia, 328
during pregnancy, 340
for pulmonary edema, 169
for pulmonary embolus, 171–172
for schizophrenia, 253
for seizure disorder, 215–216
tocolytics, 385–386
for toxoplasmosis, 328
for tuberculosis, 181–183, 328
for wasting syndrome, 329
Duchenne muscular dystrophy, 228–231. *See also* Muscular dystrophy
Dumping syndrome, 376–377
DuPenn catheter, 374
Durable medical equipment, 66–83
  definition of, 66
  documenting use of, 66–67
  instructions for use of, 67
  management of, 415
  reimbursement for, 66, 67
  types of, 67–83
    blood glucose monitoring devices, 79–80
    commodes and bathroom aids, 74–75
    hospital beds, 71–74
    pressure aids, 80–81
    respiratory care equipment, 76–79
    specialized equipment, 81–83
    trapeze and patient lifters, 75–76
    walkers, crutches, and canes, 70–71
    wheelchairs, 67–70
Durable power of attorney, 13, 405
Duty, 401

breach of, 401
definition of, 401
standards of care and, 401
Dycill. *See* Dicloxacillin
Dying patient, 331–335. *See also* Terminally ill patient
Dymelor. *See* Acetohexamide
Dysarthria, 49
  in amyotrophic lateral sclerosis, 244
  due to cerebrovascular accident, 210
  in Parkinson's disease, 236
Dysphagia, 50–51
  in AIDS, 323
  in amyotrophic lateral sclerosis, 244
  in Parkinson's disease, 236
Dyspnea
  in AIDS, 323
  in amyotrophic lateral sclerosis, 244
  in chronic obstructive pulmonary disease, 155
  due to pleural effusion, 175
  due to pulmonary edema, 167
  in pneumonia, 163, 165
Dysrhythmia, 51

E

Eating, 48
Ebstein's anomaly, 116
Eclampsia, 106, 342
Edema
  in AIDS, 323
  peripheral, 112
  pulmonary, 166–169
Education and training. *See also* Patient education
  of home health aide, 62
  of nurse, 407
  of occupational therapist, 39
  of occupational therapy assistant, 40
  of physical therapist, 31

of physical therapy assistant, 31
of social work assistant, 54
of social worker, 54
of speech-language pathologist, 45
Elavil. *See* Amitriptyline hydrochloride
Elbow protectors, 80, 81
Elderly persons. *See also* Age effects
  abuse of, 8
  Alzheimer's disease in, 247
  cancer in, 302
  hypothyroidism in, 279
  learning in, 24
  malnutrition in, 357–359
  pneumonia in, 161, 163
  sensory deficits in, 358
Electrocardiogram
  after cardiac transplantation, 134
  during exercise, 143–144
  myocardial infarction on, 96
  pulmonary embolus on, 171
Electroconvulsive therapy, 254
Embolization, 119
  anticoagulants for, 119
  pulmonary, 170–173. *See also* Pulmonary embolus
  symptoms of, 119
Emotional distress, intentional infliction of, 404
Emphysema, 155
  clinical course of, 155
  definition of, 155
  pathophysiology of, 155
  signs and symptoms of, 155
Enalapril maleate, for hypertension, 108
Encephalopathy, HIV-related, 319, 321, 327
Endometrial cancer, 303
Energy requirements, 361
Enteral access, 376–377
  gastrostomy/percutaneous gastrostomy, 377

guidelines for, 376
jejunostomy, 377
nasogastric/nasojejunal, 376–377
verifying placement of, 376
Enteral nutrition, 364, 369, 379–380
  access for, 376–377
  aspiration of feeding, 376
  constipation and, 377
  diarrhea/dumping syndrome and, 376–377
  evaluation and monitoring of, 380
  feeding containers for, 376
  initiation of, 376
  patient assessment for, 379–380
  plan for, 380
  replacing solution for, 376
Enteral/parenteral therapy, 369–386
  access for, 370–377
    arterial, 373–374
    central venous, 371–373
    enteral, 376–377
    factors affecting selection of, 370
    intraperitoneal, 374–375
    intrapleural, 375
    peripheral venous, 370–371
    spinal, 374
  advantages of home infusion therapy, 369
  applications of, 379–386
    antibiotics, 381
    blood component therapy, 384–385
    chemotherapy, 383–384
    enteral nutrition, 379–380
    heparin, 386
    hydration, 380
    investigation/clinical trials, 386
    pain management, 381
    tocolytics, 385–386
    total parenteral nutrition, 381–383
  disadvantages of home infusion therapy, 369
  guidelines for, 379

infusion pumps for, 377–378
patient admission criteria for, 369
patient teaching about, 379
specialized types of, 369–370
supplies for, 379
  ancillary supplies, 379
  dressing supplies, 379
  tubing, 379
traditional types of, 369
Entitlement theory, 393
Epidural access, 374
Epilepsy, 213. *See also* Seizure disorder
Episiotomy, 345
Equipment. *See* Durable medical equipment
Erb's dystrophy, 228
Erythema toxicum, 347
Erythrityl tetranitrate, for angina pectoris, 91
Estimated date of confinement, 339
Estrogen replacement therapy, 303
Ethambutol
  adverse effects of, 181
  for *Mycobacterium avium* complex, 327
  for tuberculosis, 181–182, 328
  use in children, 182
Ethical issues, 391–395
  codes of ethics, 392
  definitions related to, 391
  ethical principles, 392–394
    autonomy, 16, 392–393
    beneficence, 16, 393
    justice, 16, 393
  ethical problems, 394
    definition of, 394
    identification of, 394
    interventions for, 394
  ethics committees, 394–395
    characteristics of members of, 395
    composition of, 394–395
    functions of, 395

purpose of, 394
size of, 395
related to dying patient, 335
sources of guidance on, 391–392
Ethionamide
  adverse effects of, 182
  for tuberculosis, 182
Ethosuximide, for seizures, 216
"Exchange Lists for Meal Planning," 262
Exercise
  breathing, 151–152
  for cardiac rehabilitation, 138–144
  cool-down, 143
  after coronary artery bypass grafting, 129–130
  duration of, 141–143
  frequency of, 143
  home guidelines for, 143–144
  for hypertension, 106
  intensity of, 141
  interval training, 143
  isometric, 141
  isotonic, 141
  metabolic equivalents for, 141, 142
  monitoring for abnormal response to, 143
  for patients with diabetes mellitus, 262–263
  range of motion, 34
  supervision by physical therapist, 33
  target heart rate for, 141
  warm-up, 141–142
Eye care, for patient with hyperthyroidism, 277

F

Facioscapulohumeral muscular dystrophy, 228
Failure to thrive, 366–367
  due to cystic fibrosis, 189, 190

False imprisonment, 404
Family
  of dying patient, 333
  involvement of speech-language pathologist with, 47
  of patient with Alzheimer's disease, 249–250
  of patient with cerebrovascular accident, 211
Family planning methods, 346
Family theory, 21–22
Fat, dietary, 88, 93, 361, 362
Fecal diversion, 289–296. *See also* Colostomy; Ileostomy
  characteristics of healthy stoma, 293
  characteristics of stool from, 293–294
  colostomy, 289–291
  hints for increasing pouch's seal, 295
  ileostomy, 291–293
  pouch change procedure for, 294–295
  teaching goals for patients with, 294
    pouch changing, 294
    pouch emptying, 294
  types of pouches for, 295–296
    one-piece, 295–296
    two-piece, 296
Feeding, 63
Felonies, 407
Fetal heart tones, 339
Fetal movements, 340
Fever, in AIDS, 323
Fiber, dietary, 361, 362
Flow chart, 410
Fluconazole
  for candidiasis, 326
  for cryptococcosis, 326
Flucytosine, for cryptococcosis, 326
Fluid replacement therapy, 380
  assessment for, 380
  evaluation and monitoring of, 380
  plan/intervention for, 380
Fluid restriction
  for cardiomyopathy, 114
  for pulmonary edema, 168
Fluoxetine hydrochloride, for depression, 254
Fluphenazine dihydrochloride, 253
Fontanelles, 347
Food exchange system, 262
Food groups/food pyramid, 361
Food stamps, 364
Foot cradle, 80
Footboards, 80
Fortaz. *See* Ceftazidime
Foscarnet (Foscavir)
  for cytomegalovirus, 326
  for herpes simplex virus, 327
Frank-Starling mechanism, 101
Freedom from unreasonable restraint, 404–405
Frontier nursing services, 4
Functional assessment, 7
Furosemide
  for hypertension, 107
  for pulmonary edema, 169
  for transfusion reaction, 313

G

Gait abnormalities, in Parkinson's disease, 233, 235
Gait training, 33–34
Ganciclovir, for cytomegalovirus, 326
Gas exchange
  in chronic obstructive pulmonary disease, 150–151, 157
  after coronary artery bypass grafting, 128
Gastrostomy, 377
Gender differences
  in amyotrophic lateral sclerosis, 243
  in arthritis, 285
  in cerebrovascular accident, 209

in coronary artery disease, 88
in hypertension, 106
in hyperthyroidism, 270
in multiple sclerosis, 221
in Parkinson's disease, 233
in types of cancer, 302
Genitals, of newborn, 347, 349
Gentamicin, for *Pseudomonas* infection, 194
Gestational age, 339
Gestational diabetes, 260, 343–344
Glipizide (Glucotrol), for diabetes mellitus, 266
Glucose intolerance, 260
Glyburide, for diabetes mellitus, 266
Glycosylated hemoglobin, 267
Goiter. *See* Hyperthyroidism
Gold compounds
 for arthritis, 286
 contraindications to, 286
 side effects of, 286
Gout. *See also* Arthritis
 definition of, 284
 etiology of, 285
 pathophysiology of, 285
Graduate education programs, 6
Graft-versus-host disease, 310
Graves' disease, 270. *See also* Hyperthyroidism
Gravida, 339
Grief, 333–334. *See also* Terminally ill patient
 malnutrition and, 358
Grooming, 63
Groshong catheter, 371–372

H

Haemophilus influenzae infection, 191
Haemophilus influenzae vaccine, 151
Hallucinations, 253
Haloperidol (Haldol), 253

Handwriting difficulty, 236
Harbour Port, 373
Harris-Benedict equations, 361
Hashimoto's thyroiditis, 279. *See also* Hypothyroidism
Head circumference of newborn, 346
Head trauma, 40–41
Health assessment, 7
Health belief model, 22
Health care delivery system, 21
"Healthy Food Choices," 262
Healthy People 2000: National Health Promotions and Disease Prevention Objectives, 5
Hearing impairment
 in elderly, 358
 screening for, 45
Heart block, 122
Heart rate
 fetal, 339
 neonatal, 346, 347
 target, 141
Heel protectors, 80, 81
Height measurement, 359–360
Hemoglobin, glycosylated, 267
Henry Street Settlement House, 3
Heparin, 386
 evaluation and monitoring of patient on, 386
 for flushing central venous catheter, 372
 for flushing implanted catheter, 373
 for flushing peripheral venous catheter, 370–371
 patient assessment for, 386
 plan/intervention for, 386
 for pulmonary embolus, 171
Hepatic disease, in cystic fibrosis, 191
Hepatitis C, 319
Herpes simplex virus, 326–327
 in AIDS, 321, 326–327
 treatment of, 327
Herpes zoster virus, 327

in AIDS, 327
    treatment of, 327
Hickman catheter, 371–372
Histogram, 410
Histoplasma capsulatum pneumonia, 162
    in AIDS, 321
History of home health care nursing, 3–5
History taking, 7
HIV encephalopathy, 319, 321, 327
Homans' sign, 171
Home environment assessment, 7, 33, 35–36
    for cancer patient, 316
    legal duty to perform, 407
    for mechanically ventilated patient, 205
Home health aide, 57–64
    conditions of participation for, 57
        Joint Commission on Accreditation of Healthcare Organizations, 57
        Medicare, 57
    helping occupational therapist, 40
    helping speech-language pathologist, 47
    in-service requirements for Medicare-certified agencies, 62
    orientation program for, 58–59
    qualifying criteria for services of, 62
    role differentiation and responsibilities of, 63–64
    services for multiple sclerosis patient, 226
    specialty areas of, 64
    supervision of, 57–58
    tasks of, 63
    training and competency regulations for, 59–62
        Joint Commission standards, 62
        Medicare-certified home care organization, 59–62

Home health care nursing
    certification for, 5–6
    history of, 3–5
    legal issues related to, 407–408
        admission criteria, 407
        assignment of appropriate care providers, 408
        discharge criteria, 408
        environmental assessment, 407
        transfer criteria, 407
    nursing process in, 10
    role of registered nurse in, 7–11
    standards for, 5, 413–417. *See also* Joint Commission on Accreditation of Healthcare Organizations
Homemaker. *See* Home health aide
Hospice services, 64, 319, 415
Hospital beds, 71–74
    accessories for, 72
    care planning for patients with, 72–73
    features and uses of, 72
    indications for, 71
    infection control and, 73
    patient transfers and, 72
    reimbursement for, 73–74
    repositioning patients in, 72
    restraints for patients in, 72
    safety considerations and troubleshooting for, 73
    specialty, 72
    therapeutic, 73
    types of, 71–72
Hot packs, 34
Housekeeping services, 63
Huber needle, 373
Human immunodeficiency virus, 319. *See also* Acquired immunodeficiency syndrome
Hydralazine
    for hypertension, 107
    for pulmonary edema, 168

Hydrochlorothiazide, for
    hypertension, 107
Hydrocortisone, for chronic
    obstructive pulmonary disease,
    159
Hydromorphone hydrochloride, 313
Hyperbilirubinemia, 351–353
  definition of, 351
  phototherapy for, 352–353
  physical examination for, 352
  reasons to call physician for baby
    with, 353
  treatment of, 352
Hypercapnia, 155–157
  definition of, 156
  due to chronic obstructive
    pulmonary disease, 155
  nursing interventions for, 157
  symptoms of, 156
Hypercholesterolemia
  coronary artery disease and, 88
  hypertension and, 106
Hyperemesis gravidarum, 344–345
Hypertension, 105–108
  cerebrovascular accidents and, 105,
    106
  complications of, 106
  coronary artery disease and, 88
  definition of, 105
  diagnosis of, 106
  diastolic, 105
  drug therapy for, 107–108
    angiotensin-converting enzyme
      inhibitors, 108
    α-blockers, 107
    β-blockers, 107
    calcium-channel blockers, 107
    diuretics, 107
    sympatholytics, 107
    vasodilators, 107
  nonpharmacologic therapy for,
    106–107
  pathophysiology of, 105–106

  patient education about, 108
  of pregnancy, 106, 342–343
  primary, 105
  pulmonary edema and, 166
  risk factors for, 106
  secondary, 105–106
  signs and symptoms of, 106
  systolic, 105
Hyperthyroidism, 270–277
  clinical course of, 273–274
  clinical features of, 272–273
    cardiovascular, 272
    gastrointestinal, 273
    integumentary, 273
    metabolic, 273
    neurologic, 272
    respiratory, 273
    sexual/reproductive, 273
  complications of, 272
  definition of, 270
  demographics of, 270
  diagnosis and evaluation of patient
    with, 271–272
  drug therapy for, 275
  etiology of, 271
  nursing interventions for, 275–277
    activities of daily living, 277
    anxiety relief, 277
    drug therapy, 275–276
    eye care, 277
    nutrition, 276
    skin care, 276–277
  pathophysiology of, 270
  remission of, 274
  surgery for, 275
  treatment of, 274–275
Hypnotherapy, for pain, 314, 332
Hypoalbuminemia, 166
Hypoglycemia, 265
  complications of, 265
  definition of, 265
  sulfonylurea-induced, 265
Hypothyroidism, 278–283

clinical features of, 279–281
  cardiovascular, 280
  central nervous system, 280
  gastrointestinal, 280
  integumentary, 280
  pulmonary, 280
  sexual/reproductive, 280
cretinism, 278
demographics of, 279
diagnosis and evaluation of patient with, 279
drug therapy for, 281–282
in elderly persons, 279
etiology of, 279
incidence of, 279
nursing interventions for, 281–282
  drug therapy, 281–282
  improving cardiac output, 282
  increasing activity tolerance, 282–283
  nutrition, 283
pathophysiology of, 278–279
primary, 278, 279
secondary, 278, 279
tertiary, 278, 279
treatment of, 281
Hypoxemia, 156–157
  definition of, 156
  nursing interventions for, 157
  symptoms of, 156

I

I Can Cope, 335
Ibuprofen, for arthritis, 286
Ictus, 213
Ileal conduit, 296
Ileostomy. *See also* Fecal diversion
  absorption of oral drugs in patients with, 292
  definition of, 291
  food obstructions of, 292

hydration needs of patients with, 292
reasons for, 291
types of stomas for, 291–292
  double-barrel ileostomy stoma, 291
  end ileostomy stoma, 291
  loop ileostomy stoma, 291–292
Immunizations
  Bacille Calmette-Guérin, 186
  Haemophilus influenzae, 151
  influenza, 165
  for persons with asthma/bronchitis, 151
  pneumococcal, 151, 165
Immunosuppressant drugs, 135
  studies for Duchenne muscular dystrophy, 230
Immunosuppression, pneumonia and, 161
Immunotherapy, 308–309
Imodium. *See* Loperamide
Imuran. *See* Azathioprine
Incompetent cervix, 342
Inderal. *See* Propranolol
Indomethacin, for arthritis, 286
Infection control, 7, 9–10
  blood glucose monitoring equipment, 79
  commodes and bathroom aids, 74
  hospital beds, 73
  pressure aids, 81
  respiratory care equipment, 78
  specialized equipment, 82
  trapeze and patient lifters, 75–76
  walkers, crutches, and canes, 71
  wheelchairs, 70
Infections
  after bone marrow transplantation, 310
  after cardiac transplantation, 134, 136
Infectious arthritis, 284. *See also* Arthritis

etiology of, 285
pathophysiology of, 285
Infective endocarditis, 116, 118
Infertility, in cystic fibrosis, 191
Influenza vaccine, 165
Informed consent, 392, 404
  definition of, 404
  information required for, 392
  nurse's role in obtaining, 392
  physician's therapeutic privilege and, 404
  refusal of treatment, 405–406
  substituted consent, 405–406
  voluntariness of, 392, 404
Infrared treatments, 34
Infusaid, 373
Infusion pumps, 377–378
  enteral, 378
  implanted, 378
  for patient-controlled analgesia, 378
  portable, 377
  positive-pressure, 378
  reimbursement for, 377
  selection of, 377
  syringe-type, 378
  types of, 377–378
    controllers, 377–378
    elastomeric devices, 378
    roller clamps/flow rate regulators, 377
INH. *See* Isoniazid
Inhalation injury, pulmonary edema and, 166
Institutional advocate model, 14
Insulin therapy, 259, 263–264. *See also* Diabetes mellitus
  absorption of, 263
  concentrations of, 264
  duration of action of, 264
  injection sites for, 263
  mixed insulin for, 264
  onset of action of, 264
  self-monitoring of blood glucose for patients on, 265–266
  sources of insulin, 263
  time to peak action of, 264
Interferon, 308
Interleukin-2, 308
Intermittent positive pressure ventilation, 202
  via nasal, nasal-mouth, or mouth mask, 202
  via tracheostomy, 202
Internal cardioverter defibrillator, 125–126
  assessment of patient with, 125
  indications for, 125
  patient teaching about, 125–126
  procedure for insertion of, 125
International Normalized Ratio, 172
Intraperitoneal access, 374–375
Intrapleural access, 375
Intrathecal access, 374
Iodinated glycerol, 159
Iodine deficiency, 279. *See also* Hypothyroidism
Iron, 363
Isoetharine, 158
Isoniazid
  adverse effects of, 181
  for tuberculosis, 181, 328
    prophylaxis, 184
    resistance to, 186
Isoproterenol, 158
Isoptin. *See* Verapamil
Isosorbide dinitrate
  for angina pectoris, 91
  for pulmonary edema, 168
Isosporiasis, in AIDS, 321
Isradipine, for angina pectoris, 91–92
Itraconazole, for candidiasis, 326

J

Jaundice, 112
Jejunostomy, 377
Joint Commission on Accreditation of Healthcare Organizations, 20, 413–417
  accreditation services/programs of, 414
  awarding of accreditation decision by, 416
  benefits of accreditation by, 417
  Board of Commissioners of, 413
  categories of accreditation by, 417
  conditions of participation for home health aides, 57, 58
  development of standards of, 414
  eligibility for accreditation for home care, 414–415
  founding of, 413
  history of, 413–414
  home care program of, 414
  mission of, 413
  number of organizations accredited by, 413
  survey process of, 415–416
  surveyors of, 416
Judicial opinion, 399
Jugular vein distention, 112, 117
Justice, 16, 393–394
  entitlement theory of, 393
  maximum theory of, 393
  nursing actions related to, 394
  principle of distributive justice, 393
  utilitarian theory of, 393

K

Kanamycin
  adverse effects of, 182
  for tuberculosis, 182

Kaposi's sarcoma
  in AIDS, 321, 327
  treatment of, 327
  viral cause of, 321
Keflex. *See* Cephalexin
Ketoconazole, for candidiasis, 326
Ketones, urinary, 267
Klonopin. *See* Clonazepam

L

Labetalol, for angina pectoris, 92
Labor, preterm, 340–342
Laboratory tests, 8
  for asthma/bronchitis, 150
  for bacterial pneumonia, 163
  for cardiomyopathy, 113
  for cerebrovascular accident, 210
  for hypertension, 106
  for malnutrition, 360
  for multiple sclerosis, 223
  for myocardial infarction, 96
  for pleural effusion, 175
  for pulmonary edema, 168
  for pulmonary embolus, 171
  for tuberculosis, 179–181
Landouzy-Dejerine dystrophy, 228
Language. *See also* Speech-language pathologist
  definition of, 48
  delay in children, 50
  disorders of, 49–50
Larynx, artificial, 45, 51
Laser surgery, cardiac, 132
Lasix. *See* Furosemide
Lean body mass, 357, 358
"Learning contract," 24
Learning theory, 23–24
Legal issues, 399–408
  administrative matters and nursing practice, 406–407

licensure, 406
    nurse practice acts, 406
    nursing education, 407
    state boards of nursing, 406
    unprofessional conduct, 406
contracts, 400
criminal matters and nursing
        practice, 407
    felonies, 407
    misdemeanors, 407
definition of law, 399
origins of laws, 399–400
    constitution, 399
    judicial opinion, 399
    legislation, 399–400
    regulations, 400
patients' rights, 404–406
    freedom from unreasonable
        restraint, 404–405
    informed consent, 404
    privacy and confidentiality, 406
    refusal of treatment, 405–406
related to home care, 407–408
    admission criteria, 407
    assignment of appropriate care
        providers, 408
    discharge criteria, 408
    environmental assessment, 407
    transfer criteria, 407
torts, 400–404
    damages awarded for, 401
    definition of, 400
    intentional, 403–404
    quasi-intentional, 404
    unintentional, 401–403
types of law, 400
    administrative, 400
    civil, 400
    criminal, 400
Legionella pneumonia, 162
Length of hospital stay, 20
Leopold's maneuvers, 339
Levothyroxine (Levothroid), for
        hypothyroidism, 281

Liability. *See also* Legal issues
    personal, 402
    vicarious, 403
        corporate liability, 403
        principle of respondeat superior,
            403
Licensure, 400, 406
Light therapy. *See* Phototherapy
Limb-girdle muscular dystrophy, 228
Lioresal. *See* Baclofen
Liotrix, for hypothyroidism, 281
Lisinopril, for hypertension, 108
Lithium carbonate
    for bipolar disorder, 254
    hypothyroidism induced by, 279
Living will, 13, 393, 405
Locus of control, 22
Lomotil. *See* Atropine
Loniten. *See* Minoxidil
Loperamide, for cryptosporidiosis,
        326
Lopressor. *See* Metoprolol
Lou Gehrig's disease. *See*
        Amyotrophic lateral sclerosis
Luer-lock, 371, 373–375
Lung cancer, 303
Lymphokine-activated killer cells, 308
Lymphomas, in AIDS, 321, 328

M

Make Today Count, 335
Malabsorption, 367
Malnutrition, 357–367. *See also* Diet;
        Nutrition
    age-related changes contributing to,
        357–359
    in AIDS, 324
    assessment for, 359–360
    community resources and federal
        programs for, 364, 367
    interventions for, 364–367
    nursing diagnoses for, 364

persons at risk for, 357
pneumonia and, 161
psychosocial factors and, 358–359
types of, 360–361
    mixed protein-calorie malnutrition, 361
    obesity, 360
    protein malnutrition, 360
    protein-calorie malnutrition, 360
Malpractice, 402–403. *See also* Legal issues
    definition of, 402
    lawsuits related to, 402–403
        avoiding/defending of, 403
Mammography, 304
Manic-depressive illness. *See* Bipolar disorder
Mantoux test, 179
Marfan's syndrome, 116, 118
Marinol, 329
Maslow's hierarchy of needs, 22
Mast-cell inhibitors, 151
Mattresses, 72
    cleaning of, 73
    pressure-relieving, 80, 81
    waterproof pads for, 81
Maximum theory of justice, 393
Meals on Wheels, 153, 364
Mechanical ventilation at home, 200–205
    assessment and reassessment for, 205
    communication techniques for patient on, 205
    criteria for, 201–202
    dependence on, 201
    diagnostic monitoring of patient on, 203–204
    disorders leading to dependence on, 200
    emergency measures for, 204–205
    goals of, 202
    nursing management for, 204–205
    patient selection for, 201

signs and symptoms of respiratory failure requiring, 200–201
    types of, 202–203
        intermittent positive pressure ventilation via nasal, nasal-mouth, or mouth mask, 202
        intermittent positive pressure ventilation via tracheostomy, 202
        negative pressure ventilators, 203
        Pneumobelt, 203
        rocking bed, 203
Meconium, 349
Meconium ileus, 189, 191
Med-a-Port, 373
Medicaid, 5, 315
Medicare, 315
    conditions of participation for
        home health aide, 57
        registered nurse, 10–11
    establishment of, 5
    prospective payment system of, 20
    reimbursement by, 5
Megace, 329
Memory loss
    in Alzheimer's disease, 248
    after cerebrovascular accident, 210
Mended Hearts, 144
Mental illness, 252–255
    Alzheimer's disease, 247–250
    bipolar disorder, 253–254
    deinstitutionalization of patients with, 252
    depression, 254–255
    role of home health nurse for patient with, 255
    schizophrenia, 253
    substance use and abuse, 255
Mental status assessment, 252
Mepron. *See* Atovaquone
Metabolic equivalents, 141, 142
Metabolic rate, 357
Metaproterenol sulfate, 158

Methimazole, for hyperthyroidism, 275
Methyldopa, for hypertension, 107
Methylxanthine derivatives
　for chronic obstructive pulmonary disease, 150, 158
　side effects of, 158
Metoprolol
　for angina pectoris, 92
　for hypertension, 107
　after myocardial infarction, 98
Metropolitan Life Insurance Company, 4
Micronase. *See* Glyburide
Microwave diathermy treatment, 34
Midarm muscle circumference, 360
Milia, 347
Minerals, 363–364
　calcium, 363
　iron, 363
　zinc, 363–364
Minipress. *See* Prazosin
Minoxidil, for hypertension, 107
Misdemeanors, 407
Mitral regurgitation, 117–118
Mitral stenosis, 117
Mitral valve prolapse, 116
Mitral valvulotomy (commissurotomy), 120
Mongolian spots, 347
Monoclonal antibodies, 308
Montefiore Hospital Home Care Program, 4
Mood disorders, 253–255
　bipolar disorder, 253–254
　depression, 254–255
Mood swings, 253
Moral judgments, 391
Moro reflex, 348
Morphine, 313
Mother's helper, 64
Motivation of patient, 22
Motor dysfunction, 41
　in amyotrophic lateral sclerosis, 244
　due to cerebrovascular accident, 210, 211
Mucolytics, 150, 159
Multiple sclerosis, 221–226
　definition of, 221
　demographics of, 221
　diagnosis of, 223
　forms of, 222–223
　　benign mild, 222
　　chronic/progressive, 223
　　relapsing/progressive, 222
　　relapsing/remitting, 222
　home management of patient with, 224–226
　　documentation, 226
　　goals, 224
　　home health aide services, 226
　　multidisciplinary team approach, 224
　　nursing interventions, 224
　　physical/occupational therapist interventions, 225
　　social worker interventions, 225
　　speech-language pathologist interventions, 225
　pathophysiology of, 221
　research on etiology of, 221–222
　　biology of glial cells, 222
　　genetics, 222
　　immunology, 221–222
　　virology, 222
　symptoms of, 223
　treatment of, 223–224
Muscular dystrophy, 228–231
　age at onset of, 229
　cause of death in, 231
　definition of, 228
　Duchenne, 228–231
　　characteristics of, 229
　　demographics of, 228–229
　　diagnosis of, 229
　　drug therapy for, 230–231

pathophysiology of, 229
treatment of, 229
nursing interventions for, 231
prognosis for, 231
types of, 228
Muscular Dystrophy Association, 228
Mycelex. *See* Clotrimazole
Mycobacterial infections
in AIDS, 321, 327, 328
M. avium complex, 321, 327
treatment of, 327
M. tuberculosis, 177–188. *See also* Tuberculosis
nontuberculous, 177
Mycoplasmal pneumonia, 162
Myelin, 221–222
Myocardial infarction, 95–99
complications of, 97
diagnosis of, 96–97
electrocardiographic findings with, 96
home care management after, 98
laboratory findings with, 96
location and size of, 95
nontransmural, 95
pain of, 96
pathophysiology of, 95–96
patient teaching about, 98–99
preventing recurrence of, 98
pulmonary edema and, 166
radionuclide imaging of, 96–97
signs and symptoms of, 96
transmural, 95
treatment of, 97–98
valvular heart disease and, 116
Myocardial ischemia
angina pectoris due to, 89
silent, 90
Myoclonia, 213, 214
Myotonic dystrophy, 228
Mysoline. *See* Primidone
Myxedema coma, 272

N

Nadolol
for angina pectoris, 92
for hypertension, 107
Nanny services, 64
Narcotic analgesics, 313–314
for cancer patient, 313–314
drug interactions with, 314
intermittent intramuscular or subcutaneous, 313
intrathecal, 313–314
intravenous, 313
oral, 313
for pain of bacterial pneumonia, 164
pneumonia and, 161
side effects of, 314
Nasogastric/nasojejunal tube, 376–377
National Association for Home Care *Code of Ethics*, 392
National Cancer Institute, 317
National Multiple Sclerosis Society, 224
National Organization of Public Health Nursing, 4
Nausea and vomiting
in AIDS, 324
hyperemesis gravidarum, 344–345
Negative pressure ventilation, 203
Neglect, 8, 16
Negligence, 401–402. *See also* Legal issues
due to commissions, 401, 402
due to omissions, 401, 402
elements of, 401–402
breach of duty, 401
damages, 402
duty, 401
proximate cause, 401
lawsuits due to, 402–403
avoiding/defending of, 403
Nephrostomy, 296

Nerve blocks, 314
Neurologic disorders, 207–250
  Alzheimer's disease, 247–250
  amyotrophic lateral sclerosis, 243–246
  cerebrovascular accident, 209–212
  mechanical ventilation at home due to, 200
  multiple sclerosis, 221–226
  muscular dystrophy, 228–231
  Parkinson's disease, 233–241
  seizure disorder, 213–219
New York City Mission, 3
New York Heart Association functional classification, 88
Newborn, 346–353
  apnea of prematurity in, 350–351
  bathing of, 348–349
  bladder function of, 347
  bowel elimination of, 347, 349
  burping of, 350
  cardiorespiratory system of, 347
  central nervous system of, 347–348
  diaper changing for, 349
  feeding of, 346, 348–350
  genitals of, 347, 349
  holding and handling of, 350
  hyperbilirubinemia of, 351–353
  integumentary system of, 347
  measurements of, 346
  reasons to call physician, 350
  reflexes of, 348
  safety of, 350
  umbilical cord of, 347, 349
  vital signs of, 346
Nicardipine
  for angina pectoris, 91–92
  for hypertension, 107
Nifedipine
  for angina pectoris, 91–92
  for hypertension, 107
Nitrates, 91
  for angina pectoris, 91
  contraindications to, 91
  after percutaneous transluminal coronary angioplasty, 131
  for pulmonary edema, 168
  side effects of, 91
  sublingual, 91
  tolerance to, 91
Nitrofurantoin hypersensitivity, 175
Nitroglycerin, for angina pectoris, 91
Nonmaleficence, 16
Nonsteroidal anti-inflammatory drugs
  for arthritis, 286
  for cancer patient, 314
  side effects of, 286
Nurse practice acts, 406
Nursing process, 10, 22
Nursing's Agenda for Health Care Reform, 5
Nutrition. *See also* Diet
  criteria for adequate diet, 361
    food groups/food pyramid, 361
    recommended dietary allowances, 361
    United States dietary goals/guidelines, 361
  enteral, 376–377, 379–380
  for newborn, 346, 348–350
  normal energy needs, 361
  normal nutrient requirements, 362–364
    carbohydrates, 362
    fat, 362
    fiber, 362
    minerals, 363–364
    protein, 362
    vitamins, 362–363
    water, 362
  for Parkinson's disease patient, 239–240
  for patient with diabetes mellitus, 261–262
    food exchange system, 262
  for patient with hyperthyroidism, 276

for patient with hypothyroidism, 283
during pregnancy, 340
problems with. *See* Malnutrition
total parenteral, 381–383
Nutritional assessment, 7, 359–360
clinical/dietary history, 359
laboratory studies, 360
physical examination, 359–360
for total parenteral nutrition, 382
Nystatin, for candidiasis, 326

O

Obesity
cancer and, 303
definition of, 360
hypertension and, 106
pneumonia and, 161
Obstetric patient. *See* Perinatal home care
Occupational exposures, 303
Occupational Safety and Health Administration, 10
Occupational therapist, 39–43
for cerebral palsy patient, 40
education and training of, 39
guidelines for referral to, 41
for health trauma patient, 40–41
interventions for multiple sclerosis patient, 225
interventions for patient with amyotrophic lateral sclerosis, 245
as member of team, 42–43
for pediatric patient, 40
problem/deficit areas addressed by, 41–42
role in home care, 41
Occupational therapy assistant, certified, 40
Octreotide, for cryptosporidiosis, 326
Odynophagia, in AIDS, 323

Ofloxacin
adverse effects of, 183
for tuberculosis, 183
Omnibus Budget Reconciliation Act of 1980, 20
Omnibus Budget Reconciliation Act of 1987, 20
Omnibus Budget Reconciliation Act of 1990, 13
Oncology Nursing Society, 317
On/off phenomenon, 236
Open-heart surgery. *See* Coronary artery bypass grafting
Ophthalmoplegic muscular dystrophy, 228
Opium tincture, for cryptosporidiosis, 326
Oral hygiene, 63
Oral hypoglycemic agents, 263–266. *See also* Sulfonylureas
Orinase. *See* Tolbutamide
Osteoarthritis. *See also* Arthritis
definition of, 284
demographics of, 285
pathophysiology of, 284
Ostomies, 289–300. *See also* Fecal diversion; Urinary diversion
fecal diversion, 289–296
urinary diversion, 296–300
Oxycodone-acetaminophen, 313
Oxygen delivery systems, 76–79. *See also* Respiratory care equipment
Oxygen therapy
for asthma/bronchitis, 151
for cardiomyopathy, 114
for pulmonary edema, 168
teaching appropriate use of, 157, 164

P

Pacemakers, 122–126
assessment of patient with, 123–124

components of, 123
definition of, 122
drugs affecting function of, 124
external sources affecting function of, 124–125
indications for, 122
internal cardioverter defibrillator, 125–126
modes of, 123
  demand, 123
  fixed rate, 123
  synchronous, 123
patient teaching about, 124–125
symptoms of failure of, 124
types of, 122–123
  epicardial, 123
  permanent, 122
  temporary, 122
  transthoracic, 123
  transvenous, 123
Pain
  angina pectoris, 89–93
  assessment in terminally ill patient, 331–332
  of myocardial infarction, 96
Pain management
  for bacterial pneumonia, 164
  for cancer patient, 313–314
    Agency for Health Care Policy and Research guidelines, 314
    narcotics, 313–314
    nerve blocks, 314
    non-narcotics, 314
    nonpharmacologic interventions, 314
    nursing responsibilities, 314
  after coronary artery bypass grafting, 128
  parenteral, 381
  patient-controlled analgesia, 378, 381
  for terminally ill patient, 331–332
Palatal lift, 45, 51

Pallor, 112
Pancreatic disease, in cystic fibrosis, 190
Pancreatic enzyme therapy (pancreatin, pancrelipase), 191–192
Papanicolaou test, 304
Paraffin baths, 34
Pareto chart, 410
Parkinson's disease, 233–241
  definitions related to, 233
  demographics of, 233–234
  diagnosis and evaluation of, 234
  drug therapy for, 237–238
  etiology of, 234
  incidence of, 233
  motor features of, 234–236
    bradykinesia, 235
    dysarthria, 236
    handwriting difficulty, 236
    on/off phenomenon, 236
    postural instability and gait disorders, 235
    rigidity, 235
    swallowing and speech disorders, 236
    tremor, 235
  non-motor features of, 236–237
    dementia, 236–237
    depression, 236
    driving performance, 237
    sexual dysfunction, 237
    sleep disturbances, 237
  nursing interventions for, 239–241
    bowel elimination, 239
    communication, 240
    drug therapy, 238
    injury prevention, 240
    mobility and functioning, 239
    nutritional status, 239–240
    positive, achievable goals, 240
    self-care, 239
  pathophysiology of, 233

psychosocial interventions for, 240
surgery for, 239
treatment of, 237
Parlodel. *See* Dopamine agonists
Paternalism, 13
Patient advocacy. *See* Advocacy
Patient advocate model, 14
Patient assessment, 7, 10
Patient education, 10, 20–26
　about angina pectoris, 93
　about asthma/bronchitis, 152–153
　benefits of, 25
　about cancer, 315–316
　　biotherapy, 309
　　bone marrow transplantation, 311
　　chemotherapy, 308
　　radiation therapy, 306–307
　about cardiac transplantation, 135–136
　about cardiomyopathy, 113–114
　compared with patient teaching, 21
　about congestive heart failure, 103
　after coronary artery bypass grafting, 129–130
　about cystic fibrosis, 197–198
　definition of, 21
　about diabetes mellitus, 267–268
　domains affected by, 21
　about effective coughing technique, 157
　about enteral/parenteral therapy, 379
　evaluation of, 25
　factors affecting prominence of, 20–21
　family theory and, 21–22
　about fecal diversion, 294–295
　goals and objectives of, 21, 23
　about hypertension, 108
　　during pregnancy, 343
　about internal cardioverter defibrillator, 125–126
　major health care goals of, 21
　models for, 22
　about newborn care, 348–350
　about oxygen therapy, 157, 164
　about pacemakers, 124–125
　after percutaneous transluminal coronary angioplasty, 131
　by physical therapist, 35
　about pneumonia, 164–165
　post-myocardial infarction, 98–99
　postpartum, 345–346
　about preterm labor, 341
　about pulmonary embolus, 172
　steps in, 22–25
　　assessment, 22–23
　　evaluation, 25
　　learning goals/objectives, 23
　　teaching plan and intervention, 23–25
　trends in, 25–26
　about tuberculosis, 184–185
　about urinary diversion, 299–300
　about valvular heart disease, 119–120
Patient lifters, 75–76
　care planning for patient with, 75
　documenting use of, 76
　features and uses of, 75
　infection control and, 75–76
　reimbursement for, 76
　safety and troubleshooting for, 75
Patient Self-Determination Act, 13, 393
Patient transfer, 34
　trapeze and patient lifters for, 75–76
　for wheelchair-bound patient, 69
Patient-controlled analgesia, 381
　infusion pump for, 378
Patients' rights and responsibilities, 7, 404–406. *See also* Ethical issues; Legal issues
　advance medical directives, 13, 405
　autonomy, 16, 392–393
　beneficence, 16, 393

freedom from unreasonable
restraint, 404–405
informed consent, 404
justice, 16, 393–394
nonmaleficence, 16
Patient's Bill of Rights, 20
privacy and confidentiality, 406
refusal of treatment, 405–406
Pentaerythritol tetranitrate, for angina pectoris, 91
Pentamidine isethionate, for *Pneumocystis carinii* pneumonia, 328
Perceptual dysfunction, 42
due to cerebrovascular accident, 210, 211
Percutaneous balloon catheter dilatation, 120
Percutaneous gastrostomy, 377
Percutaneous transluminal coronary angioplasty, 93, 97, 130–131
assessment and interventions after, 131
contraindications to, 131
definition of, 131
drug therapy after, 131
patient selection for, 131
patient teaching about, 131
Pericarditis, 97
Perinatal home care, 339–353
definition of, 339
gestational diabetes, 260, 343–344
abnormal glucose tolerance test, 343
patient education about, 344
physical examination for, 344
treatment of, 344
hyperemesis gravidarum, 344–345
definition of, 344
patient teaching about, 345
physical examination for, 344
treatment of, 344

hypertension of pregnancy, 342–343
classification of, 342
patient teaching about, 343
physical examination for, 342–343
treatment of, 343
incompetent cervix, 342
newborn, 346–353. *See also* Newborn
apnea of prematurity in, 350–351
hyperbilirubinemia of, 351–353
patient teaching about, 348–350
physical examination of, 346–348
physical examination of pregnant patient, 339–340
bowel function, 340
cardiovascular system, 340
cervix, 340
nutrition, 340
respiratory system, 340
urinary system, 340
uterus, 339–340
postpartum care, 345–346
breast care, 346
contraception, 346
definition, 345
patient education, 345–346
physical assessment, 345
preterm labor, 340–342
vocabulary related to, 339
Peripheral edema, 112
Permax. *See* Dopamine agonists
Perphenazine, for HIV encephalopathy, 327
Personal care services, 63, 415
Pharmaceutical services, 415
Phenobarbital, for seizures, 216
Phenytoin, for seizures, 215–216
Pheochromocytoma, 106
Phlebitis, 370, 371
Phototherapy, 352–353
nursing care for baby receiving, 353
side effects of, 353

using fiberoptic "blanket," 352–353
using halogen or fluorescent lights, 352
Physical therapist
  activities of, 33–35
  education and training of, 31
  interventions for multiple sclerosis patient, 225
  interventions for patient with amyotrophic lateral sclerosis, 245
  interventions with Parkinson's disease patient, 239
  as member of home health team, 32–33
  supervision of physical therapy assistant by, 37
Physical therapy assistant
  activities of, 37
  definition of, 31
  education and training of, 31
  supervision of, 37
Physical therapy services, 31–38
  cardiopulmonary, 34
  definition of, 31
  documentation of, 35–36
  eligibility for admission to, 32
  types of, 33–35
Physician advocate model, 14
Physician's therapeutic privilege, 404
Picture boards, 45
Pillows, 72
Pilocarpine iontophoresis, 190
Pindolol, for angina pectoris, 92
"Pink puffer," 155
Piperacillin (Pipracil), for *Pseudomonas* infection, 193
Plan of care, 8
Pleural effusion, 174–176
  definition of, 174
  diagnostic tests for, 175
  etiology of, 174
  exudate, 174
  management of, 175–176
  nursing interventions for, 176
  signs and symptoms of, 175
  transudate, 174
  types of, 174–175
Pleural fluid analysis, 175
Pleurectomy, 175
Pleurodesis, 175–176
Pneumobelt, 203
Pneumococcal vaccine, 151, 165
Pneumonia, 161–165
  aspiration, 162
    pulmonary edema and, 166
  bacterial, 162–165
    assessment of, 162–163
    complications of, 163
    diagnostic tests for, 163
    drug therapy for, 163–164
    patient/family teaching about, 164–165
    prevention of, 165
    signs and symptoms of, 163
  chronic obstructive pulmonary disease, 156
  in elderly persons, 161, 163
  Histoplasma capsulatum, 162
  hospital- vs. community-acquired, 161
  Legionella, 162
  mortality from, 161
  mycoplasmal, 162
  pneumococcal, 151, 162
    in cystic fibrosis, 191
    immunization against, 151, 165
    pathophysiology of, 162
  Pneumocystis carinii, 162
    in AIDS, 321, 328
    treatment of, 328
  risk factors for, 161–162
  viral, 162
Port-a-Cath, 373
  intraperitoneal, 374

Postpartum home care, 345–346
Postpericardiotomy syndrome, 130
  definition of, 130
  diagnosis of, 130
  duration of, 130
  incidence of, 130
  signs and symptoms of, 130
  treatment of, 130
Postural instability, 233, 235
Poverty, 358
PPD test, 179
Prazosin, for hypertension, 107
PRECEDE model, 22
Prednisone
  after cardiac transplantation, 135
  for chronic obstructive pulmonary disease, 159
  for cystic fibrosis, 195
  for muscular dystrophy, 230
Preeclampsia, 106, 342
Pregnancy. *See also* Perinatal home care
  gestational diabetes, 260, 343–344
  hyperemesis gravidarum, 344–345
  hypertension of, 106, 342–343
  preterm labor, 340–342. *See also* Preterm labor
  physical examination during, 339–340
  valvular heart disease and, 120
  weight gain during, 340
Pressure aids, 80–81
  care planning for patients with, 80–81
  documenting use of, 81
  features and uses of, 80
  infection control and, 81
  reimbursement for, 81
  safety considerations for, 81
  types of, 80
Preterm labor, 340–342
  assessing uterine contractions in, 341
  definition of, 340
  drug therapy for, 341–342
  nutrition and, 341
  patient education about, 341
  physical examination for, 341
  signs and symptoms of, 341
  tocolytics for, 385–386
  treatment of, 341
Primaquine, for *Pneumocystis carinii* pneumonia, 328
Primidone, for seizures, 216
Prinivil. *See* Lisinopril
Privacy, 392, 406
  invasion of, 404
Procainamide hydrochloride
  affecting pacemaker function, 124
  for arrhythmias, 119
  pleural effusion due to hypersensitivity to, 175
Procardia. *See* Nifedipine
Proctosigmoidoscopy, 304
Professional conduct, 406
Progressive multifocal leukoencephalopathy, in AIDS, 321, 328
Prolixin. *See* Fluphenazine dihydrochloride
Proloid. *See* Thyroglobulin
Pronestyl. *See* Procainamide
Propranolol
  for angina pectoris, 92
  for hyperthyroidism, 275
Propylthiouracil, for hyperthyroidism, 275
Prospective payment system, 20
Prostate cancer screening, 304
Prostatic specific antigen, 304
Prosthetic devices
  for communication, 45, 51
  training in use of, 35
Protein
  dietary, 361, 362
  malnutrition and, 360–361

visceral protein status
    determination, 360
Proventil. *See* Albuterol
Proximate cause, 401
Prozac. *See* Fluoxetine hydrochloride
Pseudomonas infection
    antibiotics for, 193–194
    in cystic fibrosis, 191
Psychosocial issues
    arthritis and, 287
    cancer and, 315–316
    cystic fibrosis and, 188, 196–197
    malnutrition and, 358–359
    Parkinson's disease and, 241
    seizure disorders and, 218–219
Psychotherapy, 254
Pulmonary atresia, 116
Pulmonary edema, 166–169
    assessment of patient with, 167–168
        cardiovascular, 167–168
        laboratory tests, 168
        respiratory, 168
        signs of fluid retention, 168
    cardiogenic, 166–167
    management of, 168–169
        enhance myocardial contractility, 169
        reduce cardiac workload, 168–169
    noncardiogenic, 166, 167
    pathogenesis of, 166–167
    symptomatology of, 167
Pulmonary embolus, 170–173
    complications of, 171
    definition of, 170
    diagnostic tests for, 171
    drug therapy for, 171–172
    mortality from, 170
    pathophysiology of, 170–171
    patient/family education about, 172
    prevention of, 172
    risk factors for, 170
    signs and symptoms of, 171
    vena cava filters for, 172–173

Pulmonary stenosis, 116
Pulmozyme, 194–195
Purified protein derivative test, 179
Pyelostomy, 296
Pyrazinamide
    adverse effects of, 181
    for *Mycobacterium avium* complex, 327
    for tuberculosis, 181, 328
Pyrimethamine, for toxoplasmosis, 328

Q

Quality improvement, 10, 47, 409–411
    barriers to successful activities for, 411
    benchmarking for, 411
    characteristics of successful program for, 411
    implementation of, 409–410
    initiation of, 409
    key concepts of, 409
    process improvement systems, 411
    role of ethics committee in, 395
    understanding variation and, 410
    use of tools for, 410
Quickening, 339
Quinidine
    affecting pacemaker function, 124
    for arrhythmias, 119

R

Racial differences
    in cerebrovascular accident, 209
    in coronary artery disease, 88
    in cystic fibrosis, 189
    in hypertension, 106
    in multiple sclerosis, 221
    in Parkinson's disease, 233

Radial pulse, 114, 143
Radiation therapy, 305–307
  nursing care for patient undergoing, 306–307
  patient education about, 306–307
  prevalence of use of, 305
  side effects of, 306
  types of radiation for, 305–306
    external beam therapy, 305–306
    internal therapy, 306
Radioiodine therapy, 274, 275
Radionuclide imaging, for myocardial infarction, 96–97
Range of motion, 34
Rashes, neonatal, 347
Recombinant tissue plasminogen activator, 97
Recommended dietary allowances, 361
Rectal examination, 304
Refusal of treatment, 405–406
Registered nurse home care services, 7–11
Regulations, 400
Rehabilitation
  of cancer patient, 314–315
  cardiac, 138–144. See also Cardiac rehabilitation
Reimbursement
  for durable medical equipment, 66, 67
    blood glucose monitoring machines, 80
    commodes and bathroom aids, 74–75
    hospital beds, 73–74
    pressure aids, 81
    respiratory care equipment, 78–79
    specialized equipment, 82–83
    trapeze and patient lifters, 76
    walkers, crutches, and canes, 71
    wheelchairs, 70
  by Medicare, 5
  of speech-language pathologist, 48
Release of patient information, 392, 404, 406
Renin-angiotensin-aldosterone system, 105
Research, 10, 26
Respect for persons model, 14
Respiratory care equipment, 76–79
  care planning for patient with, 77
  documenting need for, 78
  features and uses of, 76–77
  infection control and, 78
  reimbursement for, 78–79
  safety considerations for, 77–78
  types of, 76
Respiratory disease, 147–205
  asthma/bronchitis, 149–153
  chronic obstructive pulmonary disease, 155–159
  cystic fibrosis, 188–198
  mechanical ventilation at home, 200–205
  pleural effusion, 174–176
  pneumonia, 161–165
  pulmonary edema, 166–169
  pulmonary embolus, 170–173
  tuberculosis, 177–186
Respiratory failure, 156
  causes of, 156
  definition of, 156
  signs and symptoms of, 156, 200–201
Respiratory rate of newborn, 346
Respondeat superior principle, 403
Restraint of patient, 404–405
Rheumatic fever, 116–118
Rheumatoid arthritis. See also Arthritis
  definition of, 284
  demographics of, 285
  pathophysiology of, 284–285
Rifabutin, for *Mycobacterium avium* complex, 327

Rifampin
  adverse effects of, 181
  drug interactions with, 181
  for *Mycobacterium avium* complex, 327
  for tuberculosis, 181, 328
  resistance to, 186
Rights protection model, 13
Rigidity, 233, 235
Risk management, 10
Rocking bed, 203
Roles of nurse, 7–11
  patient advocate, 13–17
  patient educator, 20–26
Rooting reflex, 348
Run chart, 410

S

Safety issues, 48
  home environment assessment, 7, 33, 35–36, 205
  for newborn, 350
  for Parkinson's disease patient, 240
  for patient with arthritis, 287
  for patient with seizure disorder, 218
  for patients using durable medical equipment
    blood glucose monitoring machines, 79
    commodes and bathroom aids, 74
    hospital beds, 73
    pressure aids, 81
    respiratory care equipment, 77–78
    specialized equipment, 82
    trapeze and patient lifters, 75
    ventilators, 204–205
    walkers, crutches, and canes, 71
    wheelchairs, 69
Salmonellosis, in AIDS, 321
Salt, dietary, 102, 103, 168, 361

Schizophrenia, 253
  age at onset of, 253
  cause of, 253
  definition of, 253
  incidence of, 253
  symptoms of, 253
  treatment of, 253
Sedation, narcotic-induced, 314
Sedentary lifestyle, 139
Seizure disorder, 213–219
  definitions related to, 213
  demographics of, 213–214
  diagnostic work-up for, 214
  drug therapy for, 215–216
    drug interactions with, 217
    patient teaching about, 216–217
    side effects of, 217
  etiology of, 214
  home management of patient with, 217–218
    caregiver record keeping, 219
    goals, 217
    nursing documentation, 219
    psychosocial issues, 218–219
    safety issues, 218
    seizure management, 217–218
  pathophysiology of, 213
  types of seizures, 214–215
    complex partial, 215
    generalized, 215
    simple partial, 214–215
    tonic/clonic, 213
    unclassified, 215
Self-care, 21, 26, 239
Sensory deficits, 42
  after cerebrovascular accident, 210
  in elderly, 358
Septra. *See* Trimethoprim-sulfamethoxazole
Sexuality
  hyperthyroidism and, 273
  hypothyroidism and, 280
  Parkinson's disease and, 237

resuming sexual activity after
coronary artery bypass graft,
130
Sharps container, 79, 379
Shingles, 327
in AIDS, 327
treatment of, 327
Shortwave treatment, 34
Shower chair, 66
Sick sinus syndrome, 122
Sinemet. *See* Dopaminergic drugs
Skin assessment, 112
Skin cancer, 303
Skin care, 81
for patient with amyotrophic lateral
sclerosis, 245
for patient with hyperthyroidism,
276–277
for peristomal skin irritation, 299
for radiation therapy patient, 306
for wheelchair patient, 69
Skin disorders
in AIDS, 324
of newborn, 347, 349
Skinfold measurements, 360
Sky catheter, 374
Sleep disturbances
congestive heart failure and, 103
in Parkinson's disease, 237
Smokeless tobacco, 303
Smoking
cancer and, 303
cerebrovascular accident and, 209
chronic obstructive pulmonary
disease and, 149, 155
coronary artery disease and, 87–88
hypertension and, 106
pneumonia and, 161
Smoking cessation
for patient with chronic obstructive
pulmonary disease, 157
to prevent pulmonary embolus, 172
Social isolation, 358, 366

Social work assistant, 54
Social worker, 54–55
education and training of, 54
home care services of, 54
interventions for multiple sclerosis
patient, 225
interventions for patient with
amyotrophic lateral sclerosis,
245
interventions of, 55
patients needing services of, 54–55
Sodium restriction, 102, 103, 168
Sodium warfarin
for cerebrovascular accident, 210
for pulmonary embolus, 171–172
for valvular heart disease, 119
Somastatin. *See* Octreotide
Specialized equipment, 81–83
Speech reading, 46
Speech-language pathologist, 45–53
assessment by, 46–47
care planning by, 52
coordination of care by, 52–53
cultural/linguistic distinctions and,
47
documentation by, 46, 47
education and training of, 45
home health aide and, 47
interdisciplinary management by,
47
interventions for multiple sclerosis
patient, 225
interventions for patient with
amyotrophic lateral sclerosis,
245
involvement with family, 47
patient disorders treated by, 49–52
prevention services of, 46
quality improvement by, 47
referral to, 46
reimbursement of, 48
role in home care, 45–46
terminology related to, 48

treatment by, 47
working with occupational therapist, 43
Spinal access, 374
Spiritual issues, 334
Spironolactone, for hypertension, 107
Sporanox. *See* Itraconazole
Sputum culture
  for pneumonia, 163
  for tuberculosis, 180–181
Standards of care, 5, 401
Standards of Home Health Nursing Practice, 5
Staphylococcus aureus infection, 191–193
  antibiotics for, 192–193
  in cystic fibrosis, 191
Startle reflex, 348
State boards of nursing, 406
Statement on the Scope of Home Health Nursing Practice, 5–6, 20
Status epilepticus, 213, 218. *See also* Seizure disorder
Statutory law, 399–400
Steinert's disease, 228
Stool blood testing, 304
Stork bite marks, 347
Streptococcus pneumoniae pneumonia, 151, 162
  in cystic fibrosis, 191
  immunization against, 151, 165
  pathophysiology of, 162
Streptokinase, 97
Streptomycin, 182
  adverse effects of, 182
  for tuberculosis, 182
  use in elderly persons, 182
Stroke. *See* Cerebrovascular accident
Study questions and exercises
  AIDS, 329
  Alzheimer's disease, 250–251
  amyotrophic lateral sclerosis, 246
  arthritis, 288

asthma/bronchitis, 153
cancer, 317
cardiac rehabilitation and support, 144
cardiac transplantation, 137
cardiomyopathy, 114
cerebrovascular accident, 212
chronic obstructive pulmonary disease, 159–160
congestive heart failure, 104
coronary artery disease/angina pectoris, 94
cystic fibrosis, 198
diabetes mellitus, 268–269
durable medical equipment, 83
enteral/parenteral therapy, 387
ethical issues, 396
history of home health care nursing, 6
home health aide, 64–65
hypertension, 108
hyperthyroidism, 277
hypothyroidism, 283
invasive cardiac interventions, 127–132
Joint Commission on Accreditation of Healthcare Organizations, 417
legal issues, 408
malnutrition, 367
mechanical ventilation at home, 205
mental illness, 255–256
multiple sclerosis, 226–227
muscular dystrophy, 231
myocardial infarction, 99
occupational therapy, 43
ostomies, 301
pacemakers, 126
Parkinson's disease, 241
perinatal home care, 353
physical therapy, 38
pleural effusion, 176
pneumonia, 165

pulmonary edema, 169
pulmonary embolus, 173
quality improvement, 412
role of nurse as patient advocate, 17
role of nurse as patient educator, 26–27
role of registered nurse, 11
seizure disorder, 219
social work, 55
speech-language pathology services, 53
terminally ill patient, 335–336
tuberculosis, 187
valvular heart disease, 120–121
Stuttering, 51
Substance use and abuse, 255
 symptoms of, 255
 treatment of, 255
Substituted consent, 405–406
Suck and swallow reflex, 348
Suction machines, 76–79. *See also* Respiratory care equipment
Suicide, 253–254
Sulfadiazine, for toxoplasmosis, 328
Sulfonylureas, 263–266
 characteristics of, 266
 complications of, 265
 contraindications to, 265
 first- and second-generation, 264
 self-monitoring of blood glucose for patients on, 265
Sun exposure, cancer and, 303
Sunscreens, 303
Support groups
 for asthma/bronchitis patients, 153
 for cardiac patients, 144
 for dying patients and their families, 335
Swallowing, 48
 definition of, 48
 in newborn, 348
 stages of, 48
Swallowing disorders, 50–51, 365–366
 in AIDS, 323
 in amyotrophic lateral sclerosis, 244, 245
 in Parkinson's disease, 236
Sweat test for cystic fibrosis, 190
Symmetrel. *See* Dopaminergic drugs
Sympatholytics
 for hypertension, 107
 side effects of, 107
Sympathomimetics, 150
Syncromed, 373
Synthroid. *See* Levothyroxine

T

Tachycardia, pacemakers for, 122
Tacrine, for Alzheimer's disease, 249
Tegretol. *See* Carbamazepine
Telangiectatic nevi, 347
Tenckhoff catheter, 374
Tenormin. *See* Atenolol
Terbutaline, 158
 for cystic fibrosis, 195
Terminally ill patient, 64, 331–335
 with AIDS, 323
 assessment of family and, 331
 communication with, 332–333
 community resources for, 334
 concepts of death, dying, grief, and loss, 333–334
 ethical issues related to, 334
 family dynamics and, 333
 pain assessment in, 331–332
 pain management for, 332
 planned death at home, 334
 process of dying and death event, 334
 spiritual issues related to, 334
 symptoms requiring interventions in, 332
The Definition and Role of Public Health Nursing Practice, 392
Theophylline
 for apnea of prematurity, 351
 for cystic fibrosis, 195

Theos, 335
Therapeutic privilege, 404
Thionamides, for hyperthyroidism, 275
Thoracentesis, 175
Thorazine, for HIV encephalopathy, 327
Thought disorder, 253
Thrombolytic therapy
 for cerebrovascular accident, 211
 for myocardial infarction, 97
Thrombophlebitis, 172
Thrombus formation, 95
Thyroglobulin, for hypothyroidism, 281
Thyroid storm. *See also* Hyperthyroidism
 clinical features of, 272–274
  cardiovascular, 272–273
  gastrointestinal, 273
  integumentary, 273
  metabolic, 273
  neurologic, 272
  respiratory, 273
  sexual/reproductive, 273
Thyroid-releasing hormone, 278
Thyroid-stimulating antibody, 271
Thyroid-stimulating hormone, 270, 271, 278
Ticarcillin (Ticar), for *Pseudomonas* infection, 193
Timolol, for angina pectoris, 92
Title III food program, 364
Tobramycin, for *Pseudomonas* infection, 194
Tocolysis, 385–386
Tolazamide (Tolinase), for diabetes mellitus, 266
Tolbutamide, for diabetes mellitus, 266
Torts, 400–404
 damages awarded for, 401
 definition of, 400
 intentional, 403–404
  assault, 403
  battery, 403–404
  false imprisonment, 404
  infliction of emotional distress, 404
 quasi-intentional, 404
  defamation, 404
  invasion of privacy and breach of confidentiality, 404
 unintentional, 401–403
  defense against, 403
  lawsuits due to, 402–403
  malpractice, 402
  negligence, 401–402
Total parenteral nutrition, 364, 369, 381–383
 assessment for, 381–382
 for cancer patient, 314
 evaluation and monitoring of, 382–383
 formula for, 382
 initiation at home, 383
 plan/intervention for, 382
Toxoplasmosis
 in AIDS, 321, 328
 treatment of, 328
Tracheostomy
 care of, 204
 intermittent positive pressure ventilation via, 202
Transcutaneous electrical nerve stimulation, 314, 332
Transfer criteria, 407
Transferrin, 360
Transfusion. *See* Blood component therapy
Transfusion reaction, 313, 385
Transient ischemic attack, 106
Transplantation
 bone marrow, 309–311
 cardiac, 133–136
Trapeze, 75–76
 care planning for patient with, 75
 documenting use of, 76
 features and uses of, 75
 infection control and, 75–76

reimbursement for, 76
safety and troubleshooting for, 75
Tremor, 233, 235
Triamcinolone, for chronic obstructive pulmonary disease, 159
Triceps skinfold measurement, 360
Tricuspid atresia, 116
Trilafon. *See* Perphenazine
Trimethoprim-sulfamethoxazole, for *Pneumocystis carinii* pneumonia, 328
Trimetrexate, for *Pneumocystis carinii* pneumonia, 328
Tuberculosis, 177–186
   in AIDS, 178, 321, 328
   Bacille Calmette-Guérin (BCG) vaccine against, 186
   cause of, 177
   definition of, 177
   diagnosis of, 180–181
   drug therapy for, 181–183, 328
      adherence to, 184
      duration of, 181
      first-line drugs, 181–182
      multiple drugs, 181
      patient education about, 184–185
      second-line drugs, 182–183
   home care nursing management of, 184–186
   incidence of, 178
   infection control measures for, 185
   medical conditions associated with, 178
   multidrug-resistant, 186
   as national health problem, 178
   nursing diagnoses associated with, 186
   pathogenesis of, 177
   prevention of, 183–184
   risk factors for, 178
   screening for, 178–180
      anergy, 179–180
      high-risk populations, 179
      Mantoux skin test, 179
      two-step testing, 180
   signs and symptoms of, 178
   sites of, 178
   transmission of, 177
Tumor necrosis factor, 329
Tylox. *See* Oxycodone-acetaminophen

U

Ultrasound treatment, 34
Umbilical cord, 347, 349
United States Public Health Service, 32
   Chronic Disease Program, 4
Unprofessional conduct, 406
Ureterostomy, 296
Urinary diversion, 296–300
   catheterizing urinary stoma in patient with, 297–298
   characteristics of healthy stoma, 298
   characteristics of urine from, 298–299
   definition of, 296
   hints for increasing pouch seal, 300
   hydration needs of patient with, 297
   obtaining urine specimens from, 297
   pouch change procedure for patient with, 300
   reasons for, 296
   teaching goals for patient with, 299–300
      attaching pouch to bedside drainage at night, 299
      peristomal skin irritation, 299
      pouch changing, 299
      pouch emptying, 299
   types of pouches for, 300
   types of stomas for, 296–297
      colon conduit, 297
      continent urinary diversion, 297

ileal conduit, 296
nephrostomy, 296
pyelostomy, 296
ureterostomy, 296
vesicostomy, 296
urinary tract infection in patient with, 297
Urine testing, for diabetic patients, 267
Urokinase, 97
Uterus
assessing contractions during preterm labor, 341
examination during pregnancy, 339–340
postpartum assessment of, 345
Utilitarian theory, 393

V

Valium. *See* Diazepam
Valproate, for seizures, 216
Value-based decision model, 14
Values of patient, 15–16
Valve replacement surgery, 120
Valvular annuloplasty, 120
Valvular heart disease, 116–120
acquired, 116
aortic regurgitation, 118
aortic stenosis, 118
arrhythmias and, 119
classification of, 116
congenital, 116
congestive heart failure and, 118
definition of, 116
diagnosis of, 117
embolization and, 119
incidence of, 116
mitral regurgitation, 117–118
mitral stenosis, 117
myocardial infarction and, 116
nursing management of, 120

pathophysiology of, 116–117
regurgitation, 117
stenosis, 116–117
patient teaching about, 119–120
procedures to improve blood flow in, 120
pulmonary edema and, 166
treatment of, 118–119
Vantin. *See* Cefpodoxime proxetil
Variation, 410
Vasodilators
for congestive heart failure, 102, 103
for hypertension, 107
for pulmonary edema, 168
side effects of, 107
Vasotec. *See* Enalapril maleate
Vena cava filters, 172–173
Venous access, 370–373
central, 371–373
blood draws from, 371
implanted, 373
indications for, 371
nontunneled, 373
peripherally inserted central catheter for, 371
tunneled, 371–372
verifying placement of, 371
factors affecting access selection, 370
peripheral, 370–371
flushing of, 370–371
guidelines for, 370
materials for, 370
site assessment for, 370
troubleshooting for, 371
types of catheters for, 370
Venous stasis, 172
Ventilators, 76–79. *See also* Respiratory care equipment
Ventricular failure, 101. *See also* Congestive heart failure
Ventricular hypertrophy, 101

Verapamil
  for angina pectoris, 91–92
  for arrhythmias, 119
  for hypertension, 107
Vesicostomy, 296
Viscaid. *See* Amiloride, aerosolized
Vision impairment, 42, 358
Visiting nurse associations, 3, 4
Vitamin supplementation
  for asthma/bronchitis, 151
  for cystic fibrosis, 192
Vitamins
  B-complex vitamins, 363
  dietary sources of, 363
  fat-soluble, 363
  requirements for, 362–363
  vitamin C, 363
Voice disorders, 48, 51
Vomiting. *See* Nausea and vomiting

W

Wald, Lillian, 3
Walkers, 70–71
  care planning for patients with, 71
  documentation of use of, 71
  features and uses of, 70
  infection control and, 71
  reimbursement for, 71
  safety and troubleshooting for, 71
Warm-up period, 141–142
Wasting syndrome, 319, 321, 328–329

Water intake, 362
Weight gain
  cardiomyopathy and, 112
  during pregnancy, 340
Weight measurement, 360
Weight reduction, for hypertension, 106
Wheelchairs, 67–70
  accessories for, 68
  care planning for use of, 69
  infection control and, 70
  models of, 68
  obtaining for home use, 67
  pressure-relieving cushions for, 80
  progressive ambulation and, 69
  reimbursement for, 70
  safety and troubleshooting for, 69
  size of, 67–68
  skin care for patient using, 69
  transfer technique for patient with, 69
Whirlpool baths, 34
Women's, infants', and children's (WIC) program, 364, 367

Z

Zarontin. *See* Ethosuximide
Zestril. *See* Lisinopril
Zidovudine, 327
Zinc, 363–364
Zovirax. *See* Acyclovir